The JOY of EATING NATURAL FOODS

THE COMPLETE ORGANIC COOKBOOK

Formerly Titled "EAT, DRINK and be HEALTHY"

by Agnes Toms

Chairman of Homemaking Department in the Monrovia, California, City Schools

Foreword by W. CODA MARTIN, M.D.

The Devin-Adair Company, Conn.

DEDICATED TO MY DAUGHTER, SANDRA

Without whose help this book

could not have been written.

Reprinted November 1971

Foreword

THIS is not just another cookbook. It is one that fulfills a specific need for all—a way to better health through good nutrition. It represents a combination of two essential factors. First, it is an excellent "natural" cookbook, well organized and departmentalized so that any type of food or recipe may easily be found. The recipes are unique because all of the ingredients are natural, unrefined foods. Second, Agnes Toms fulfills the prerequisites for an author of such a cookbook. She has a Master's Degree in Home Economics and, for many years, she has taught nutrition and prepared menus of quality foods at Clifton Junior High School in Monrovia, California.

Those who are familiar with the concept of total nutrition will find her book a delightful addition to their present menus, and to those of you who are searching for better health through better nutrition, this book will be a great comfort and guide in the transition from the usual, ordinary food formulas to the more sophisticated and nutritious approach to menu planning.

Good nutrition is not just a "fad," but a way of life, and Agnes Toms' natural foods cookbook will introduce you to new adventures in pleasurable eating. It will be a real source of enjoyment to the young wives and mothers who are now becoming aware of the value of high quality, unrefined foods.

This book is not for the empty-calory and can-opener-cuisine type homemaker but rather an avant-garde approach to better living through recipes that are enhanced by unrefined foods, properly prepared and appetizingly served—a cookbook that should be in the kitchen of every home in which the desire to activate a program of good nutrition exists.

W. CODA MARTIN, M.D.

Hollywood, California

Endorsement

Agnes Toms has a wonderful flair for writing about food, and in this cook book she has incorporated all the joy and excitement with which she herself approaches the planning and preparation of meals.

Her recipes are mouthwatering and delicious—just to read. They make me want to go straight into the kitchen, put on my apron and cook and eat them right away. I'm one of the people who read cook books the way other people read whodunnits. With many of these books, I keep making mental notes to some day try this or that. But with Agnes Toms, I find that her recipes and menus call for immediate action.

Her chapter on nutrition is one of the simplest and best I have encountered. I believe that reading it carefully will help turn the greenest amateur into an expert.

The long experience Agnes Toms has had in serving appetizing, colorful and nutritious food to large groups makes her chapter on Food for Special Occasions an invaluable one. Any housewife who is in a rut about what to serve at such times will find fresh ideas that will add to her success as a hostess as well as to the health of her guests.

Some of my favorite Agnes Toms recipes are: Swordfish With Mushrooms, Suki-Yaki, Baked Eggplant With Brown Rice, Orange Juice Salad and . . . well, you will be choosing for yourself, and having a splendid adventure in good cooking, good eating and good health.

Linda Clark

Carmel, California

A Book to Cook by

I hope this book will give you exciting new ideas about food. I've collected all my favorite recipes . . . dishes I've made in my own kitchen and many I've invented for hungry children at our school in Monrovia. I've tried to make them easy to find and fun to follow.

Everywhere in the United States, starting at the White House, people are talking about good nutrition. It is a subject that can sound awfully dull and complicated, but in this book I believe you will learn it easily and happily. There are a number of excellent books available for those of you who wish to go into all aspects of natural foods and nutrition.*

I have not divided this book into vegetarian and non-vegetarian sections, but there are hundreds of recipes to delight the vegetarian under all chapter headings except those self-evident ones such as Milk, Eggs, Cheese, Meat, Poultry and Fish.

Now for a preview of some of the things you will find out as you get acquainted with this book:

Salads are a delightfully versatile combination of foods, and in that chapter you will discover ways to serve them as hors d'oeuvres, as an accompaniment to a meal, as a main course or as a dessert.

Foods for Special Occasions is a separate section because sooner or later most of us have to face up to the problem of what to do about a children's party, how to manage that assignment to help with the PTA supper, what to serve when both male and female members of a committee are going to be hungry after meeting at your house, and . . . well, any other such predicament you may and probably will find yourself up against.

* Linda Clark's STAY YOUNG LONGER and Cathryn Elwood's FEEL LIKE A MILLION are two books I highly recommend.

Left-overs are dealt with, certainly. But mostly they are left-over meats to be popped into soups, casseroles and salads. I have not included many left-over vegetables since they do tend to lose their food value and it's so much better to try to cook the amount you need for each meal.

Flour in this book ought always to be unbleached white flour or whole-wheat flour, although ordinary flour may be used when only a small quantity is required for such uses as thickening a sauce. Your own flour mill is the very best way of assuring good flour and cereals. It may be a hand mill or a power mill, and you really should grind the amount you need each day, since the fresh whole product spoils quickly. These flours and cereals should be kept under refrigeration or in a cool, dry place where they will not absorb or be exposed to light.

Fresh-ground flours and cereals are available in most localities if you do not find it possible to own a home mill. These commercial mills usually produce an unbleached white flour, for breads, cakes and other dishes where you prefer a white flour. In general, the whole seed, finely ground, is most nutritious for your all-around use. But the so-called whole-wheat flour on the general market is even less desirable than the white flour from which the nutrients have been removed, because the whole-wheat product has had so many chemicals added to keep it from spoiling.

Milk and whole-grain flour complement each other beautifully, since the calcium in the milk is made more useable by the addition of the phosphorus found in whole-wheat. That is why I have used milk as often as possible in the whole-grain recipes. Raw, certified milk is, of course, the best.

Sweetenings in these recipes are as unprocessed and unrefined as you can obtain. Honey, sorghum, molasses and raw or brown sugar are just fine, and when any recipe calls for sugar, do remember that raw sugar is meant. Honey has a high nutritive value; a little goes a long way.

You will not find a chapter on *jams and jellies,* although a few nutritionally sound ones are included in the section on Sandwich Spreads. Most jams and jellies are made with white sugar and are neither nutritious nor needed in your daily meals. If you raise your own fruits and vegetables and find yourself with a surplus and no freezer to deal with them, then by all means can them. Your State Department of Agriculture or the U.S. Department of Agriculture will supply you, on request, with excellent instructions for canning fruits, vegetables and meats.

Freezing of foods can be done without sugar, as you will discover in the chapter on that subject.

Pressure-cookers are not dealt with under a separate heading, since excellent instructions come with these appliances. However, for you who live at high altitudes, you may find it useful to consult the adapted cooking times for such altitudes in the P.S. of this book. I always try to remember the warning that the "worst difficulty about pressure-cooking is that too often the cook forgets to take the food out when the time is up and the result is over-cooking and loss of important nutrients."

I know it is a real problem for many people to find the food products mentioned in this book. To them, may I suggest some ways to deal with this problem:

1. Look in the Classified pages of your telephone book for health food stores in your area; or consult the advertisements in health magazines.

2. Search the shelves of your local market for unsulphured molasses, spray-dried milk, unflavored gelatin, honey, herbs, spices, nuts, vegetable oils.

3. Look for milling companies in your area and ask them about wheat germ, whole-grain flour, buckwheat, peanut, rice, and other flours. See if they have brown rice and whole soybeans.

4. Look for a hatchery near you for fertile eggs, or scour the neighborhood for some one who has a flock of chickens on the ground, with a rooster.

5. Get the health-minded women in your neighborhood together and demand that the local dairy produce raw certified milk; and be sure to ask your dairy where you can procure natural cheeses.

I have tried to meet the needs of everyone who may use this book; if there are omissions, or if you have suggestions about other things you might like to see in the next edition, please write to me in care of my publishers.

Good Health and Good Eating!
AGNES TOMS

P.S.

Abbreviations Used in These Recipes

Teaspoon—tsp.	Quart—qt.
Tablespoon—tbsp.	Pint—pt.
Cup—c.	Pound—lb.
	Ounce—oz.

Acknowledgments

THE author wishes first to thank those loyal friends in the American Academy of Applied Nutrition and the American Nutrition Society who encouraged her to write this book.

She is also very grateful to Dwight M. Lydell, former Superintendent of Monrovia City Schools, and to his office staff for making possible the first draft of this book.

The author wishes to acknowledge the women who in their kitchens have discovered ways to prepare food that is delicious, as well as nutritious, and have sent their recipes to her.

She also wishes to thank Francis M. Pottenger, Jr., M.D., H. E. Kirschner, M.D., Royal Lee, D.D.S., and Michael Walsh, M.S., for quotations or suggestions from their books or reports.

The author is also indebted and wishes to express her thanks to the following:

Alta-Dena Dairy, Monrovia, California · American Honey Institute, Madison, Wisconsin · American Meat Institute, Chicago, Illinois · American Molasses Company, New York, New York · Marie Antran, San Fernando, California · Armour and Company, Chicago, Illinois · Marguerite Barton, Porterville, California · California Honey Advisory Board, San Marino, California · Covalda Date Company, Coachella, California · El Molino Mills, Alhambra, California · Catharyn Elwood, Logan, Utah · R.T. French Company, Rochester, New York · H.J. Heinz Company, Pittsburgh, Pennsylvania · International Yogurt Company, Los Angeles, California · Kraft Foods Company, Consumer Service Department, Chicago, Ill. · Knox Gelatine, New York, New York · Lindberg Nutrition Service, Los Angeles, California · Mathews Nutrition Service, Pasadena, California · National Dairy Council, Chicago, Illinois · National Biscuit Company, New York, New York · National Live Stock and Meat Board, Chicago, Illinois · National Food Supplements, Inc., Sherman Oaks, California · Maple N. Robertson, Monrovia, California · Alfreda F. Rooke, Escondido, California · Shields Date Gardens, Indio, California · U.S. Department of Agriculture, Washington, D.C. · Western Growers Association, Los Angeles, California, and especially Adelle Davis.

A. T.

Table of Contents

CHAPTER 1

Nutrition

YOU start life as an embryo, receiving your food from the blood stream of your mother; then as you feed yourself, your blood distributes what you eat to make bone, muscle cells, and all the other component parts of the body. What you eat affects your size, rate of growth, how you feel, your appearance, and, indirectly, your behavior pattern and happiness. How well food is changed into vital substances depends upon whether the food was grown on fertile soil, harvested at the peak of development and brought into your kitchen immediately, prepared and served to retain vitamins and minerals, and eaten in a happy atmosphere.

Foods are divided into 5 groups: proteins, fats, carbohydrates, vitamins and minerals, and have 3 main uses in the body:

1. To provide materials for building and repair
2. To regulate body processes
3. To provide heat and energy

Protein is the main substance of all living tissue and is used not only in the building, but also in the repair of the vital parts of all tissue. Necessary for the proper functioning of the organs, it is a part of glandular secretion and blood, as well as a part of the many chemical changes that take place in the body. All proteins are broken down by digestion into amino acids before being absorbed. High protein foods are lean meat, liver, fish, eggs, poultry, cheese, milk and soybeans. Other foods supplying appreciable amounts of protein are nuts, sprouts, legumes, whole grains and seeds.

Vitamins regulate or are helpers in all body processes. Even though our knowledge of them is comparatively new, it has been known for centuries that certain foods could prevent or even cure certain diseases. The vitamins now known are believed to be essential nutriments. They are quite widely distributed and in eating a variety of unprocessed, unrefined foods, especially raw foods, you should get a good assortment of them.

Vitamin A is important for growth and repair. It protects the body against infection, keeps the skin healthy and is important for vision. Vitamin A is fat-soluble and is stored in the liver. Some important sources are:

Green Leafy Vegetables	Yellow Vegetables and Fruits	Animal Sources
Turnip greens	Carrots	Liver
Spinach	Sweet Potatoes	Egg yolk
Kale	Apricots	Yellow cheese
Broccoli	Cantaloupe	Butter
Beet greens	Pumpkin	Cream
Mustard greens	Yellow peaches	Cod liver and other
Alfalfa	Tomatoes	fish oils
Asparagus		
Dandelion greens		

Vitamin B is made up of a large number of separate vitamins. The B vitamins dissolve in water and are not easily stored, so they should be obtained each day. When these vitamins are lacking in the diet the nerves, the heart, digestion, tissues, skin, and general morale are adversely affected. Vitamin B is easily destroyed by heat, air, and light. It should not be overcooked, or cooked in a large amount of water and the water then discarded. Eat as many foods high in this vitamin as you can in their natural state, such as:

Lean pork	Fish	Peanuts
Liver (beef or	Chicken	Green leafy vegetables
pork)	Green peas and beans	Molasses
Lamb	Whole-grain products	Food yeast
Milk	Soybeans, soybean meal,	Sunflower seeds
Eggs	flour, grits	

Vitamin C is necessary for the tissues of the body. It is also water-soluble and some is needed each day, as the body stores little of it. Bleeding gums may be a sign of Vitamin C deficiency. It assists in the healing of wounds and keeps up the body's resistance. The important sources of this vitamin are: citrus fruits, wild rose hips, strawberries, cantaloupe, raw green foods, potatoes (both white and sweet) and tomatoes.

Vitamin D is needed to make use of calcium and phosphorus in building strong bones and teeth. It is called the "sunshine vitamin" because the sun's rays can change some of the oils in your skin into Vitamin D. Nursing mothers especially need Vitamin D to protect their teeth and bone structure. It is found in a few foods such as egg yolk, butter, oily fish and fish-liver oils.

Vitamin E is important for the heart, blood vessels, and the reproductive system. It is found in wheat germ, unprocessed, as well as in the germ of other seeds.

Vitamin K appears to be important for blood coagulation and a good source is gelatin.

Minerals are a necessary part of all body cells and fluids, and are essential to life itself. Calcium and phosphorus are the most important. The greatest part of the calcium in your body is found in the bones and teeth. Calcium is best used when phosphorus and Vitamin D are present. Important sources of calcium are milk and milk products, greens, dried peas and beans. Calcium is also very important to the body fluids, regulation of the beat of the heart, and in soothing the nervous system. Phosphorus is more widely distributed among foods so that one is not apt to get too little of it. Iron is required in smaller amounts. With the help of copper, iron combines to form hemoglobin, the red cells in your blood. Liver is the best source, but leafy green vegetables also have iron, as do molasses, dried peas, beans and soybeans, prunes, eggs and oysters. Iodine is especially needed by the thyroid gland to make thyroxin, a hormone needed to regulate many of the body's functions. Sea foods and foods grown on iodine-rich soil are the best sources.

The so-called "trace minerals" (because only traces of them are present), are extremely important. Liver, whole grains, seeds and leafy vegetables are good sources.

Refining and processing of food destroys most of the vitamins and minerals in food. Overcooking of food is so detrimental to vitamins, that one cannot afford to chance eating the largest part of one's food cooked.

Carbohydrates are divided into two main kinds, sugar and starch. All starch is changed into sugar in the body. Sugar may be refined as white sugar and glucose, or be unrefined in the natural forms found in honey, maple sugar, milk sugar, fruit sugars, molasses, and sorghum. Carbohydrate foods are the principal source of fuel food for all peoples, but the large consumption of refined sugars in this country is leading to a downgrading of our national health.

Fats are another fuel food and produce more energy than the same amount of carbohydrates. Fats that have been hydrogenated or saturated are not as beneficial as unsaturated fats. Fats are more slowly digested than other foods, and cooking at high temperature makes them even less digestable. There are satisfactory unsaturated oils available, made from seeds, in addition to butter and cream. Fats are also a source of fat-soluble vitamins from natural sources.

The calorie needs of adults are not as great as those for growing young people. However, the need for proteins, vitamins, and minerals in adults does not diminish.

OUR CHILDREN'S FOOD

All human beings are composed of what they eat, and defects that show up in children, and later when adults, are largely due to the kind and quality of food eaten, especially during the growing period.

The injurious effects of a poor diet are manifested in the bone structure, general health, and the nervous system. The body structure often shows curvature of the spine, flat chest, narrow pelvis and faulty occlusion resulting in poor mastication. There is increased susceptibility to fatigue and an excitability of a nervous character. The regulators of growth and of bodily appearance, the endocrine glands such as pituitary, thyroid, suprarenal and reproductive, are disturbed.

One of the most noticeable signs of injury is the condition of children's teeth. The cause of dental caries does not lie entirely in defective cleaning but from within, through the blood that reaches the pulp of the tooth. The condition of the teeth is a reliable indication of the condition of the bony structure, organs and tissues of our body.

The badly nourished child will show a weakness of immunity against infections such as the common cold. All this adds up to the fact that many children may be starving on a full stomach. How are we to correct this problem? Very simply: the food we eat, particularly in the growing period, must contain the greatest possible number of food factors, known and unknown, in their natural condition. Food that is *whole,* food that has suffered the least amount of tampering, is a key to good health. This rules out refined and processed foods. Nature provides the proper balance of food factors. When we remove one factor, the effectiveness of that food will be quite different from that in its natural state.

Milk is an excellent example of a whole food, vitally important for growing children. Certified milk is preferable. Since it has not been heated, none of its value has been destroyed.

Raw vegetables and fruits are next in importance. Vegetables, if cooked at all, should be done lightly, in the Chinese style, preserving crispness, color and flavor. Raw vegetables and fruits should be finely chopped for small children. Whole fruits are better than just the juices. Unless the fruit has been grown without poison sprays, it ought to be peeled. Two or more servings of fruit daily are a must in every child's diet.

Whole-grain foods, such as whole-wheat bread, brown rice and oats are nourishing and important, but should not represent the largest part of the diet.

Fresh, fertile eggs from chickens raised on the ground, should be eaten once a day whenever possible.

Meat, especially liver, beef, lamb and poultry, may be included in one meal a day, although pork and veal, which are not as readily digested, should be served less often. Ham and bacon are better for children than fresh pork.

Fish is most desirable, especially ocean fish because of their generous supply of minerals. Serve as often as possible.

Sweets should be confined to the natural sugar-containing foods, such as fruits, honey, root vegetables, or those little-processed, such as unsulphured molasses, brown or raw sugar. Carbonated drinks, coffee and tea have no place at all in a child's diet.

Fats are good in moderation, with butter from properly fed, healthy cows heading the list, then fish-liver oil, soybean, peanut or other seed oils.

An endless variety of special foods is available; whole-grain flour cookies, dried fruits, nuts, fruit candy, popcorn, olives, pickles, hard-cooked eggs, seeds of sunflower, pignolia, pumpkin and soy nuts, pieces of fresh coconut and parched corn.

Breakfast for the child should always start with fruit, preferably fresh; or dried fruit soaked and served in its own juice. If canned fruit is served, be sure it is unsweetened or in a very light honey syrup. Next comes whole-grain cereal, cooked only enough to make it palatable. Rolled oats need only 5-10 minutes over direct heat, or 30 minutes in a double boiler. Steel-cut oats or cracked wheat will require 1 hour in a double boiler, while whole grains take a little longer. For cereal topping, try honey, dates, sliced fresh fruit, raisins, currants and other dried fruits, chopped nuts, toasted seeds or coconut. An egg should be served daily, or at least three days a week; scrambled, poached, soft-cooked, coddled or cooked in any way that keeps the white from becoming tough.

Meats may be served occasionally at breakfast. Ham, bacon, sausage and liver are all important for growing children.

Hot cakes, waffles, muffins, biscuits, coffee cake and other quick breads should not be served too often.

And milk is a must for every meal!

Lunch at home for the child of 2-5 years should consist of a glass of milk and any of the following: chopped liver, lean beef, halibut, lamb, soft-cooked eggs, whole-grain bread, raw vegetables, cooked vegetables and fruit. Whole-grain cookies may be an occasional dessert, but junket, custard, tapioca, rice pudding and fruit-gelatin combinations are more desirable.

A child's school lunch ought to include some fruit, a whole-wheat bread sandwich with a protein-rich filling such as meat, fish, eggs, cheese, avocado, chopped nuts or nut butter, or fillings of raw foods such as carrots, celery, radishes, green pepper, tomato, cucumber or cherry-tomatoes. If the lunch box can be stored in a cool place, it is a good idea to add a plastic or cardboard container of salad or pudding.

A child who eats in the school cafeteria often selects poor foods. And too often the lunch brought from home is totally inadequate. After years of noon cafeteria duty I no longer wonder at the distressing number of colds, or the child's inability to work well in the afternoon. I have frequently watched a boy take double portions of mashed potatoes and gravy, with ice cream for dessert! And home lunches often consist solely of white-bread sandwiches. Some of the nutrition-minded girls in my classes have tried to hide their sandwiches as I walked by, knowing perfectly well what they *should* be eating, but unable to convince their parents to break with old, established eating habits.

If the school cafeteria serves health-giving food, there is no problem there at lunchtime. But this can only come about through an enlightened P.T.A. or Mothers' Club which insists upon good, body-building food. An intelligent group of mothers can also get together and plan box lunches which live up to good nutritional standards.

LUNCH BOX SUGGESTIONS

Sandwich combinations. Breads used must be whole-grain as rye, wheat, oat, or soy bread, or a combination of grains in bread. Corn bread, or other quick breads, may be used on occasion.

Grated carrot, salad dressing, raisins, and cream cheese.

Chopped olives stuffed or plain, moistened with cream or mayonnaise.

Baked beans, mashed, with chili sauce; chopped pickle if desired.

Chopped egg, relish, salad dressing.

Chopped ham, hard-cooked egg, pickle, cream or salad dressing.

Chopped bacon and hard-cooked egg.

Canned tuna or salmon, pickle relish, finely cut celery, salad dressing.

Peanut butter, bits of bacon or sliced bananas.

Chopped left-over meats, relish or olives, salad dressing.

Left-over liver, ground with a little onion, seasoned with thyme, salt and pepper.

Chopped peanuts, finely grated cabbage, salad dressing.

Cottage cheese, chopped celery, grated carrots, nuts, or dried fruit.

Minced ham, chopped deviled egg.

Grated Cheddar cheese, salad dressing, dried beef.

Cucumber and tomato slices.

Fried egg and lettuce.

Smoked beef or fish and horseradish.

Chili beans and chopped beef.

Nut butters.

Salami or other cold meats and sliced dill pickle.

All sandwiches should include lettuce or some sort of salad.

Accompanying foods

Dill pickles, bread and butter.

Ripe green olives.

Raw vegetables such as celery and celery root, carrot, cucumber sticks, sweet red or green pepper rings, radishes, cauliflower bits, tiny tomatoes or quartered tomatoes, crisp lettuce leaves, water cress, wedge of cabbage, sauerkraut, scallions.

Hard-cooked eggs, plain or deviled.

Pieces of sliced meat.

Cheese chunks, or celery or endive stuffed with cheese.

Cooked vegetables, such as pickled beets, marinated string beans, or cauliflower.

LUNCH BOX SUGGESTIONS

Baked beans, or whole-grain macaroni and cheese.
Salads (in plastic cups); potato, grated carrot, cabbage and raw
   apple, cottage cheese and grated pineapple.
Fruits; bananas, oranges or other fresh chopped fruits; dried fruits
   and raisins, dates, figs, prunes.
Cookies; whole-grain, made with honey or molasses.
Gingerbread, made with whole-grain flour.
Seeds; sunflower, pumpkin, pignolia, soy or squash.
Soups (especially milk soups) in thermos bottle.
Fruit juice, plain or made into gelatin desserts.
Fresh coconut.
Milk (at least a pint).
Milk puddings such as rice, custard, tapioca (in plastic cups).
Nuts; walnuts, almonds, pecans, cashews.

Desserts made of canned fruits or creamed puddings may be
frozen in small containers, and packed in the lunch box straight
from the freezer; they will thaw out by lunchtime but will still be
cold.

Supper for the child of 2-5 years should include any of
the following foods: cream soups, cooked whole-grain cereal,
creamed eggs on toast, cooked vegetables, soft-cooked eggs, cottage
cheese, chopped raw vegetables, whole-grain bread, non-homogenized peanut butter, milk pudding, stewed fruit or a small dish of
fresh fruit, and a glass of milk.

The child over five may eat dinner with the family. This
evening meal where the family gets together is terrifically important from a psychological as well as a nutritional standpoint.
Nowadays it is probably the only time when the family is together,
and therefore it should be the most pleasant hour of the day. Delicious, nutritious food served in a congenial atmosphere makes
for happy memories . . . and no indigestion! The food pattern
should include fresh raw vegetables, some cooked vegetables, some
type of protein as a main course, with whole-grain bread, butter,
raw fruit and cheese, or cooked fruit such as baked apples, or fruit
sauce, with or without whole-grain cookies . . . and milk for
everyone unless the adults prefer some other beverage.

The very small child's meals should never be whisked out of
a convenient can or bottle. He needs raw food combined with freshly
cooked food. Opening cans or bottles may be easy, but isn't it far
more important to consider what is best for the child's health? The

few minutes it takes to purée a small amount of meat, vegetables or fruit is certainly worth the added nutrients your child will be getting.

Eating habits are not inherited. The small child soon begins to imitate the grownups and older children, and his dislike for a certain food can often be traced directly to his mother's or father's dislike for it. If the whole family follows the nutritional eating patterns recommended in this book, then the child will grow up liking those things which are so good for him . . . whole-grain breads, certified milk, raw fruits and vegetables. When such a child comes into one of my classes, I never have to be told that he is eating correctly. His appearance and actions tell the whole story!

Remember that a child will learn to like new foods if you offer them to him for the first time when he is hungry, and if he sees others eating them with pleasure. A new food will always go over better if you don't coax, argue and scold, and if the family seems to be having a pleasant time together.

EVERYDAY EATING

Breakfast. If you want to feel your best and look your best, you can't afford to go without breakfast. An ideal breakfast to send you forth feeling fine and with the ability to think clearly, is one in which the largest part of the meal is protein foods and the rest vitamins, minerals and carbohydrates.

To assure yourself enough energy to last all morning, be sure to start breakfast with fruit, fruit juice or vegetable juice, followed by whole-grain cereal, eggs or meat, whole-wheat toast and milk. Sweeten the cereal with honey or fruit juice instead of sugar. Sweet rolls, coffee cake or doughnuts should be eaten rarely, if at all.

Because breakfast is usually prepared and eaten in a hurry, it is important to plan it ahead of time. The table can be set the night before, the cereal measured ready to pop into boiling water. But only stewed, canned or frozen fruits should be fixed the night before. Orange juice should never be squeezed and allowed to stand all night.

Lunch. Lunch must supply enough protein, and some carbohydrates, to maintain a feeling of well-being throughout the afternoon. It may be a light meal, with any combinations of the following: eggs, cheese, meat or fish, a big raw salad, nuts or a sandwich. Milk

EVERYDAY EATING

or herb tea should be served, and fruit with whole-grain flour cookies as dessert. For special occasions, a hot or cold soup (depending on the weather) might be added, or a vegetable casserole to replace the meat or fish. The cheese might be Cheddar, Swiss, or cottage; the meat, leftover cold meat, or luncheon meat, or meat ground and made into a sandwich spread. The bread should be whole-grain, rye or pumpernickle. Vegetables may be served as a finger salad or raw. Salads should be raw; or a meat and raw vegetable salad; or a fruit salad with cottage cheese or yogurt; or a fruit gelatin salad to serve as dessert.

Dinner. Dinner time should be family time, and the food should be planned and prepared so as to contribute to the happiness of all the members. You also must take into consideration the various foods the family has eaten at other meals during the day, so a balanced diet will be the result, complete in all the important nutrients.

The main course is usually meat or other protein foods such as eggs, fish, poultry, legumes, seed or nut dishes. There should be two vegetables, one of them green or yellow, a raw vegetable, whole-grain bread, butter and a light dessert, or none at all.

A more elaborate evening meal might start with a cocktail of seafood, avocado or fruit, or a clear soup.

Lunch and dinner menus may be interchangeable, depending upon personal preference or the habits of the family.

SOME RULES FOR MEAL PLANNING

Map out a general schedule for the entire week. Do this near the end of the week because of the market specials.

In planning your family's meals, keep in mind, age, sex, activity, and the occasion. Each member of the family should have 3 substantial meals each day, with particular emphasis upon the needs of a growing child for a high-protein diet.

In considering cost, it is more economical to grow your own vegetables and fruits and, if possible, to keep chickens and a cow or a goat. Buy the basic foods first, then the extras. Herbs, seasonings, dried fruits, olives, coconut and special cheeses add variety to a meal.

FAMILY FOOD GUIDE

What to Eat Each Day	How Much	Why
Milk, yogurt or non-fat dried milk, dried whey.	1 qt. milk for children; 1 pt. for adults. 1 c. yogurt; ⅓ c. non-fat milk or whey.	Milk contributes to good nutrition; rich in calcium needed for sound teeth and bones; also supplies protein, phosphorus, Vitamins A and B.
Meat, fish, or poultry, or cheese.	1 serving; 1 oz. Cheddar, or 1 c. cottage cheese.	Eat for Vitamins B_1 and B_2 and A, as well as proteins, minerals and Vitamin D. Eat liver once weekly.
Eggs.	1 or 2.	Rich in Vitamins D, A and iron. To preserve these vitamins, cook slowly over low heat.
Leafy green or yellow vegetables or sprouts.	1 serving of each or 2 servings of 1.	Leafy green (spinach, cabbage, beet tops, etc.) and yellow (carrots, sweet potatoes, yams, squash, corn, etc.) provide much-needed Vitamin A and riboflavin—Vitamin B_2. Serve some raw.
Other vegetables.	1 serving.	String beans, peas, beets, etc. Potatoes—cook with peel on (unless they have been sprayed) to preserve vitamins.
Fruits or juices, berries, melons, tomatoes.	1 orange, ½ grapefruit, 1 lemon, or 2 tomatoes.	Citrus fruits and tomatoes provide vital Vitamin C, good for keeping blood vessels and cells in condition. Daily requirement important since body does not store up Vitamin C.
Bread, whole-grain or whole-grain cereals, seeds or nuts.	1 serving at each meal.	Rich in Vitamins B_1 and B_2 and a cheap source of calories.

What to Eat Each Day	How Much	Why
Butter, cream, or nut and seed oils. Include bacon and pork as "fats" unless very lean. Nut and seed oils also count as fats.	2 to 3 tbsp.	These provide energy and body heat. Butter is rich in Vitamin A.
Water.	6 glasses each day.	Helps to assure good elimination of body waste and poison.

MENU PATTERNS FOR SPRING

Meat

BREAKFAST

A. Fresh fruit
Whole-grain cereal
Sausage, scrambled eggs
Milk, health drink, or other beverage

LUNCH

B. Raw vegetable salad, cottage cheese dressing
Whole-grain bread
Butter
Milk or substitute
C. Fruit

DINNER

D. Baked ham
Sweet potatoes or yam, baked
New peas, buttered
E. Waldorf salad, yogurt dressing
Whole-grain bread
F. Strawberries

Meatless

BREAKFAST

A. Sliced oranges
B. Scrambled eggs
Whole-grain toast
Milk, health drink, or herb tea

LUNCH

C. Grilled cheese sandwich
Carrot strips or raw vegetable salad with yogurt
Blueberries (frozen or canned) or fresh fruit

DINNER

D. Cheese soufflé or cheese fondue
E. Baked potatoes
Cole slaw
Whole-grain bread and butter
F. Baked apples, stuffed with currants, or dates, and cream

ALTERNATES

A. Stewed rhubarb or ½ grapefruit
B. Creamed chipped beef on whole-wheat toast, carrot strips
C. Custard
D. Swiss steak, lamb chops, fish
E. Tossed green salad
F. Gingerbread, lemon sauce, or wheat germ cookies

A. Strawberries or banana
B. Orange French toast
C. Creamed eggs on toast
D. Vegetable or nut loaf
E. Buttered asparagus or scalloped eggplant
F. Apple Betty with honey lemon sauce

MENU PATTERNS FOR SUMMER

Meat	*Meatless*
BREAKFAST	BREAKFAST

Meat

BREAKFAST

A. Cold melon
B. Orange French whole-grain toast with bacon
Milk, health drink or other beverage

LUNCH

C. Fruit salad with cheese slices or yogurt
Whole-grain rolls or muffins
Milk, tea or other beverage

LUNCH BOX

Cold sliced meat on rye bread
Cottage cheese and cucumber on whole-grain bread
Deviled eggs
Tomato sections
Cookies
Milk or herb tea, iced

DINNER

D. Baked stuffed green peppers or tomatoes with left over meat, or hamburgers
E. Spinach with bacon
F. Cottage cheese and pineapple salad
G. Fresh fruit cup
Cookies
Milk, or other beverage

Meatless

BREAKFAST

A. Berries
Whole-grain cereal with dates
Soy or wheat germ muffins
Milk or health drink

LUNCH

B. Raw vegetable sandwiches
Hard-cooked egg salad
Fresh fruit
Milk, herb tea, carrot juice

LUNCH BOX

Cheese, tomato, lettuce on any whole-grain bread
C. Green pea soup or vegetable juice
Fresh fruit
Herb tea, iced

DINNER

D. Carrot loaf with mushroom soup sauce
Buttered lima beans
Tossed green salad
Whole-wheat biscuits
E. Easy lemon sherbet or fresh fruit cup
Milk, or other beverage

ALTERNATES

A. Strawberries or peaches
B. Poached eggs on toast
C. Tomato and cucumber salad
D. Meat loaf or liver Creole
E. Buttered cauliflower
F. Pickled beets
G. Apple Betty or berry pie

A. Melon, or any fresh fruit
B. Raw vegetable salad with hard-cooked eggs
C. Milk drink such as molasses milk
D. Olive tacos, Spanish rice
E. Strawberry shortcake

MENU PATTERNS FOR FALL

Meat   ### *Meatless*

BREAKFAST   BREAKFAST

A. Melon or fruit   *A.* Grapes
B. Scrambled eggs with ham   Whole-grain cereal with sunflower
Whole-grain bread   seeds
Milk, health drink or other beverage   *B.* Poached egg on whole-grain
                                                       toast
                                                   Milk, or health drink

LUNCH   LUNCH

C. Clam chowder with croutons   Vegetable broth or molded vegeta-
D. Finger salad   ble salad
Whole-grain bread and butter   *C.* Soy wheat germ muffins
E. Baked pears   Baked potatoes with yogurt and
High protein cookies   chive dressing
                                                   Dates
                                                   Milk, or health drink

LUNCH BOX   LUNCH BOX

F. Tomatoes and cheese on whole-   *D.* Raw vegetable sandwich filling
grain bread   on buttered whole-grain bread
Bread and butter   *E.* Cream of tomato or bean soup
Finger salad   Dates and nuts
Fruit   Milk
Carrot
Oatmeal cookies
Milk

DINNER   DINNER

G. Meat stew with vegetables   *F.* Nut loaf with sour cream
H. Baked squash   Baked banana squash and Swiss
Cabbage and peanut salad   chard
Whole-grain biscuits and butter   Whole-grain bread and butter
I. Apple dumplings or baked ap-   *G.* Grated carrot, apple and raisin
ples   salad
                                                   H. Apricot gelatin
                                                   Fruit and cheese

ALTERNATES

A. Fruit juice   *A.* Pears or apple sauce
B. Liver and bacon   *B.* Omelet
C. Vegetable salad, stuffed eggs   *C.* Whole-wheat bread with nut
D. Corn bread   butter
E. Custard   *D.* Sunflower seed and date filling
F. Ground meat, chopped pickles   *E.* Baked yams with butter
G. Meat loaf, grated carrots, corn   *F.* Eggplant casserole
H. String beans   *G.* Tomato, cottage cheese salad
I. Peach tapioca or stewed fruit   *H.* Brown rice pudding

MENU PATTERNS FOR WINTER

Meat	*Meatless*
BREAKFAST	BREAKFAST
A. Baked apples	*A*. Baked apples
B. Fried scrapple with bacon	*B*. Fried cornmeal mush with maple syrup
Milk, health drink, or other beverage	Milk, or health drink

LUNCH	LUNCH
C. Beef vegetable soup	*C*. Baked beans
Whole-wheat crackers	Brown bread and cream cheese
Frozen fruit or berries	Carrots, celery, radishes
Molasses cookies	Herb tea or vegetable juice
Milk	

LUNCH BOX	LUNCH BOX
D. Ground liver on whole-wheat bread and butter	*D*. Peanut butter and carrot filling on whole-wheat bread or egg salad filling
Left over meat as sandwich filling	Pickled eggs
Stuffed celery	
E. Apple-molasses cookies	*E*. Apple-molasses cookies
Milk or herb tea	Milk or herb tea

DINNER	DINNER
F. Baked fish or fish fillets	*F*. Peppers stuffed with Spanish rice
Baked potato with sour cream and chive dressing	*G*. Raw vegetable salad with yogurt dressing
G. Steamed acorn squash	*H*. Steamed carrot pudding
Head lettuce with Thousand Island dressing	Coffee or herb tea
Oatmeal bread	
H. Pineapple upsidedown cake	
Milk or herb tea	

ALTERNATES

A. Orange juice or stewed dried fruit with honey	*A*. Dried fruit stewed with honey
B. Fried cornmeal mush or waffles with bacon	*B*. Waffles with dates
	C. Baked yams with butter
C. Oyster stew or fish chowder	*D*. Swiss cheese on rye bread or nut butter on whole-wheat
D. Dried beef and catsup on rye bread or Swiss cheese on rye	*E*. Unfired fruit cake
E. Baked cup custard	*F*. Lima bean loaf with mushroom sauce or whole-wheat noodles with cheese sauce
F. Rabbit casserole or roast pork or pot roast, or lamb	*G*. Cheddar cheese and tomato salad or apple salad
G. Mashed carrots or tomatoes	*H*. Baked Indian pudding or whole-wheat grain pudding or prune whip or lemon snow
H. Lemon pie, fruit jello or pears and cheese	

CHAPTER 2

Beverages

■ **HERB TEAS**

The subtle flavor of herb teas is enhanced by brewing them in pottery teapots and always using water brought to a rolling boil. Herb teas should not be steeped more than 5 minutes. If you like a stronger tea, use more herbs rather than lengthen the brewing time. Iced herb teas are more piquant with the addition of sprigs of fresh mint.

It is fun to try different herb combinations until you find the ones you and your family like best. Here are some ideas:

1. Mix 1 tsp. each of dried papaya, mint and alfalfa.
2. Mix 1 tsp. each of camomile, mint and oat straw.
3. Mix 1 tsp. each of oat straw, strawberry leaf and rose hips.
4. For mint teas, use 10-12 leaves per cup of fresh spearmint, apple mint or peppermint.
5. Mix 1 tsp. linden blossoms and papaya.
6. 1½ tsp. fenugreek; the tea strained and served hot; contains choline, a vitamin of the B-complex.
7. 1½ tsp. yerba mate, a stimulant and restorative tea used since ancient times in South America; strain and serve hot.
8. 2 tsp. dried comfrey steeped overnight in 1 qt. boiling water; reheat and serve hot. Also delicious served cold.

As a pleasant change, serve spiced herb teas. Spices should be left in the tea at least 10 minutes to give off flavors. Try some of these:

1. Alfalfa tea heated with 6 cloves and 1 piece of cinnamon stick.
2. Linden blossom tea with a pinch of cardamon.
3. Camomile tea with a dash of cinnamon and ground cloves.

4. Oat straw tea with a pinch of fenugreek and a sliver of dried lemon rind.
5. Strawberry leaf tea with a piece of cinnamon stick and a slice of orange peel.
6. Desert herb tea with a dash of ginger, cinnamon and ground cloves.

■ **SUNSHINE TEA**

In a 1-qt. glass jar of boiled water, put 4 tsp. of your favorite dried herbs. Place in full sunlight until the tea is the strength you desire. Strain, return to jar and refrigerate. It will keep several days refrigerated, and will be clear and delicious.

■ **PARTY PUNCH**

1 can apricot nectar	1½ c. orange juice
1 c. strong hot tea, comfrey, or alfalfa	1 medium can unsweetened crushed pineapple
1 c. honey	1 pt. sparkling water (soda)
¾ c. lemon juice	1 qt. ginger ale

Freeze apricot nectar in ice cube trays. Makes 2-3 doz. cubes.
Pour hot tea over honey; stir until honey is dissolved. Add orange and lemon juice. Chill. Just before serving, add crushed pineapple, sparkling water and ginger ale. Place fruit juice cubes in punch bowl and add punch, topping with sprigs of mint if desired. Serves 25 in 4-oz. cups.

■ **GRAPE FLOAT**

1 c. grape juice	1 c. loganberry juice
1 c. frozen orange juice	2 oranges, thinly sliced
1 c. frozen lemon juice	1 c. raw sugar or honey
4 c. warm water	

Freeze grape juice in ice-cube trays.
Mix sugar or honey with water; add frozen fruit juices. Chill several hours. Pour over grape juice ice cubes and add orange slices. Serves 8.

■ **FRUIT MILK DRINKS**

Buttermilk Orange Drink: Combine 2 c. cold buttermilk, 2 c. orange juice and a little honey to sweeten to taste. Chill. Serves 6.
Pineapple Milk Drink: Blend 1 6-oz. can frozen pineapple juice and 2 c. cold milk. Add dash of salt and 2 c. milk. Blend until smooth. Serves 6.

■ **FRUIT PUNCH**

Frozen or canned fruit juices can be combined in imaginative ways. If a concentrated fruit juice is used, be sure to dilute as specified on can. Some combinations might be:

1. **Orange, apricot and pineapple.**
2. **Pineapple and grapefruit.**
3. **Cranberry, pineapple and apple.**
4. **Pomegranate, orange and pineapple.**
5. **Loganberry, lemon and orange.**
6. **Grape, lemon and pineapple.**

Frozen fruit-juice cubes may be removed from ice tray and kept in a plastic bag for quick use.

■ **LEMON EGG NOG**

> 4 tbsp. lemon juice   3 c. milk
> 2 eggs, separated   ⅛ tsp. salt
> 4 tbsp. raw sugar or 3 tbsp.
>   honey

Beat egg whites until stiff enough to stand in peaks. Add ½ the sugar or honey to egg whites and beat again; add remaining sugar or honey to egg yolks and fold mixture into whites. Add milk and salt. Stir well and serve cold. Serves 4.

■ **ORANGE PICK-UP**

> 2 eggs   ½ c. orange juice
> 1 c. milk   Honey to taste
> ¼ c. powdered milk

Beat eggs until thick and foamy; add milk and powdered milk; mix well. Beat in orange juice and add honey if mixture needs sweetening. Pour into tall glasses with ice cubes. Serves 2.

■ **HONEY PICK-UP**

For each glass of chilled milk or non-fat milk, stir in 1 tsp. honey.

■ **DATE HEALTH DRINK**

> 5 chopped sun-dried dates   1 egg
> 2 c. orange juice

Mix in blender until smooth. Serve chilled. Serves 2.

■ **MILK SHAKE**

Shake, beat or put in blender 1 c. fresh cold milk. Add ¼ c. powdered milk, 1 tsp. vanilla and any of the following:

1. **Crushed pineapple, berries or other fruit.**
2. **Mashed banana, persimmon or dates.**
3. **Coconut powder, malted nuts, or nut butter.**
4. **Ice cream or sherbet.**
5. **1 egg.**

■ **HOT OR COLD CAROB MILK SHAKE**

Combine in blender 3 tbsp. carob powder, 3 tbsp. powdered milk, 2 tbsp. raw sugar or honey, 2 c. milk, ½ tsp. vanilla. Blend until smooth. Pinch of salt may be added if desired. Heat if desired. Serves 2.

■ **ALMOND MILK SHAKE**

1 tall glass milk	1 tsp. unsulphured molasses
1 tsp. finely ground whole-wheat	2 tsp. ground almonds

Mix together thoroughly and serve chilled. A perfectly balanced food drink.

■ **BANANA MILK SHAKE**

2 c. milk	1 banana, cut in chunks
½ c. powdered milk	⅛ tsp. salt

Mix in blender for only a few seconds, or in large bowl with an egg beater. If using an egg beater, mash the banana chunks first. Serves 2.

■ **TAFFY MILK**

Use 1 tbsp. unsulphured molasses for each cup of milk. Add molasses to milk; stir or shake well. Serve immediately or refrigerate until ready to use.

■ **HOT MOLASSES DRINK**

1 tbsp. unsulphured molasses	1 c. hot milk

Stir molasses into milk. Pour into mug or cup. Use stick cinnamon as stirrer, or top with whipped cream. Serves 1.

■ **MOLASSES EGG NOG**

2 eggs, separated   2 c. hot or cold milk
2 tbsp. unsulphured molasses   Nutmeg

Beat egg yolks and unsulphured molasses; gradually stir in milk. Beat egg white until stiff but not dry; stir in molasses-milk mixture. Top with whipped cream, if desired, and sprinkle with nutmeg. Serves 2.

■ **MOLASSES MILK**

½ c. nonfat dry milk   1 qt. milk (whole or skim)
3 tbsp. unsulphured molasses   Pinch of salt (if desired)

Add the dry milk and molasses to fresh milk. Shake or beat until light and frothy, or until the dry milk has been completely dissolved. Keep in refrigerator and use cold during the day between meals, and hot as a delicious nightcap. Skim milk is particularly recommended for low-calorie dieters. Serves 4.

■ **GOLDEN BLEND MILK SHAKE**

1 tall glass milk   1 banana, cut in chunks
1 diced carrot   6 chopped dates
3 green lettuce leaves

Mix in blender until smooth. Serve chilled. Serves 1.

■ **LUNCHEON COCKTAIL**

1 c. whole or skim milk   For added calcium and flavor,
2 tbsp. rice polishings   add 1 tbsp. powdered milk
1 tbsp. brown sugar   1 tsp. carob powder
¼ tsp. vanilla

Mix ½ c. milk with all other ingredients. Mix in blender; add remaining milk and mix a few seconds longer. Serves 1.

■ **AMBROSIA SHAKE**

½ c. honey   1 c. milk
½ c. pineapple juice   Flaked coconut
½ c. orange or apricot juice

Mix honey and fruit juices, add milk and shake to desired thickness. Serve in chilled glasses. Top with whipped cream and flaked coconut. Serves 2.

■ DR. KIRSCHNER'S GREEN DRINK

Soak overnight in 1 c. water

4-5 large almonds (with skins on)	1 tsp. rye
	1 tsp. barley
1 tsp. sunflower seeds	1 tsp. millet
1 tsp. hard spring wheat	1 tsp. sesame seeds
1 tsp. oats	1 tsp. flax seeds

Liquefy 3 minutes, add 1 c. unsweetened pineapple, orange, apple or other fruit juice. While liquefier is running add 1 tsp. raisins, or 6 pitted dates, 10 sprigs of parsley, 1 c. tightly packed alfalfa leaves, or other greens, juice of ½ lemon. Liquefy 3 seconds. This drink may be part of a meal, or served before a meal. Serves 4.

■ FAVORITE DRIED WHEY LUNCH DRINK

This drink I make frequently at school for my lunch. It is delicious and satisfying, giving me sufficient energy for the entire afternoon's work.

Place ¼ c. sunflower seeds (shelled) in a blender. Add 6-8 shelled almonds (with skin on), ½ c. powdered whey and 1 c. liquid certified milk. Add 1 tsp. granular honey (cream-type honey). Blend and pour in a tall glass. You may pulverize the seeds and nuts before adding the other ingredients. If you blend them together let the blender run until the seeds and nuts are finely ground. With this, I usually eat an apple, or other fruit in season.

■ ORANGE-APPLE DRINK OR PURÉE FOR BREAKFAST

This is another blended mix that I enjoy and have found helps keep me from taking the students' colds.

Peel the orange-colored skin from a medium-sized orange, leave all the white on. Cut up in pieces and place in a blender. Add 1 chopped apple including skin and seeds. If you do not know whether the apple was sprayed, you had better peel it. Add ½ c. grated pineapple and ½ c. powdered milk, or powdered whey. Blend until completely mixed and if too stiff to drink, spoon it out of your glass as you would sherbet; sprinkle ground nuts over the top.

Many other foods may be used, such as any of the following: yogurt, ground seeds or nuts, unsulphured molasses, brewer's yeast, small amount of wheat germ (as it has such a raw taste), few dates, raisins or other dried fruit.

■   **"FEEL LIKE A MILLION" BREAKFAST DRINK**

1 c. water	3 tbsp. brewer's yeast
1 tbsp. unsulphured molasses	½ tsp. sunflower seeds, raisins
1 tbsp. wheat germ	or almonds
1 tsp. powdered veal bone	
1 c. milk or 3 tbsp. powdered milk	

Pour into liquefier and blend. Raisins, nuts or seeds should be finely chopped if an egg beater is used to mix this drink. Add 1 tbsp. safflower oil for important unsaturated fat.

This drink may be part of your regular breakfast, or it may substitute for breakfast when you are in a hurry.

■   **HOT CHOCOLATE**

¼ c. raw sugar	¼ c. cocoa or carob powder
⅛ tsp. salt	1 c. water
3 c. milk	¼ tsp. vanilla

Cook sugar, salt, cocoa or carob powder, and water slowly, 5 minutes. Add milk and place in double boiler or over low heat and simmer until hot, never allowing to come to a boil. Add vanilla. Beat with egg beater. Serves 4.

■   **FLAXSEED TEA**

8 c. water	8 tbsp. flaxseed

Simmer flaxseed and water 15-20 minutes. Dip out seeds. Store in refrigerator. Mixture should be rather thick so that you "bite" each mouthful rather than drink it. Flaxseed tea is a laxative. Take 1-3 glasses daily, as needed. Lemon juice may be added to taste. Serve at room temperature. Makes 8 glasses.

■   **HONEYED SOY DRINK**

1 c. soy powder	1 tsp. honey
4 c. water	¼ tsp. salt

Mix powder with small amount of water until smooth; blend into remaining water, making certain lumps are removed. Let stand 2 hours. Cook 20 minutes in double boiler. Strain. Flavor with honey or salt. Keep refrigerated. Serves 4.

■ **TROPICAL COCKTAIL**

1 peeled grapefruit   ½ c. papaya pulp (optional)
1 peeled orange   1 c. water or unsweetened
4 tbsp. honey   pineapple juice
1 peeled lemon

Liquefy in blender. Chill. May be kept frozen or well refrigerated for future use. Serves 4.

■ **SUNSHINE COCKTAIL**

1 c. orange juice   3 sliced carrots
3 fresh or softened dried apri-
   cots

Mix in blender about 1 minute. Chill. Serves 1.

■ **JADE COCKTAIL**

1 c. grapefruit juice or un-   3 green lettuce leaves
   sweetened pineapple juice   1 tbsp. water cress leaves
1 tbsp. parsley   1 tbsp. celery leaves

Pour juices and greens in blender and liquefy. Chill and serve fresh. Serves 1.

■ **CRANBERRY COCKTAIL**

1 qt. cranberry juice   1 qt. apricot juice
1 qt. grapefruit juice   1 qt. pineapple juice

Mix together and chill. Pour over ice cubes in punch bowl. Garnish with mint or orange slices. Makes 4 qts.

■ **APPLE COCKTAIL**

1 qt. apple juice   1 tbsp. lemon juice
1 qt. ginger ale   ½ tsp. cinnamon

Mix apple juice, ginger ale and lemon. Add cinnamon. Chill. Makes 2 qts.

■ **YOGURT COCKTAIL**

1 c. yogurt   ¼ tsp. caraway seed
2 c. tomato juice   1 tsp. finely chopped onion and
½ tsp. salt   green tops

Liquefy in blender. Add 2 ice cubes, liquefy again. Serves 4.

■   **ROSY YOGURT DRINK**

    2 raw beets   **1 tbsp. yogurt**
    1 c. tomato juice   **1 tsp. grated parsley**
    1 tbsp. vegetable salt

Liquefy beets; add tomato juice and vegetable salt. Heat and serve garnished with yogurt and parsley. Serves 2.

■   **GELATIN DRINK**

Dissolve 1 pkg. unflavored gelatin in ½ c. cold liquid, such as consommé or bouillon, fruit or vegetable juice; add ½ c. same liquid, very hot.

For cold gelatin drink, soften gelatin as above in ½ c. liquid, then mix in ½ c. same liquid, very cold. Gelatin beverages should be drunk as soon as mixed. The protein and other substances are good for low-calorie diets and are often recommended by physicians to help harden brittle nails.

■   **"STAY YOUNG" COCKTAIL**

Linda Clark says this drink is by way of becoming a national favorite, and she adds that in her own family, no two members agree on what makes the perfect drink. However, here is the basic combination and also some of Linda's suggested variations:

    1 qt. milk   **½ c. brewer's yeast**
    ½ c. dried milk   **Small can frozen orange juice**

Mix in blender and keep refrigerated.

Variations

Liquids	*Flavorings*	*Solids*
Milk	Pulp of apricot, pineapple,	Brewer's yeast
Orange juice	or use frozen fruit juice,	Powdered skim milk or
Apple juice plus a	undiluted	powdered bone meal
little cider vinegar	Blackstrap molasses	Lecithin granules
½ tsp. vegetable oil	Lemon, put through blender,	Desiccated liver
Tomato juice	seeds, pulp and all	Yolks of egg

CHAPTER 3

Breads and Quick Breads

■ BREAD

The whole-wheat bread you bake at home will surpass in flavor, fragrance and nutritive value any bread you can buy. The old excuse that it takes too long to bake your own bread is refuted in the recipes you will find here. And your own satisfaction in knowing that you are giving your family the best bread that can be made is more than worth the little time it takes.

You will discover that it's fun to knead and shape the dough, and that it somehow satisfies the elemental desire of woman to prepare fine food for her family. True, bread-making is an art and you may have to experiment to find the exact technique suited to you. But it's worth it, just as it is to take any basic recipe and, by imagination and experiment, make it your own.

The best bread is that made with wheat you grind yourself. However, there are sources of excellent freshly stone-ground flour in most neighborhoods or from reputable mail-order firms.

It is best to heat milk gently rather than scald it, in order to promote enzymatic action and prevent the destruction of phosphatese in both the grain and the milk. Allow the sponge or first mixture to rise slowly so that the bran may soften and more gluten may develop. For the rising, cover with a clean linen cloth.

■ BASIC WHOLE-WHEAT BREAD

Dissolve 2 yeast cakes or 2 pkgs. dry yeast in ⅓ c. lukewarm water. In a 4-qt. kettle bring to blood heat 2 c. milk. Add 3 tbsp. oil or other fat, 3 tbsp. honey or unsulphured molasses or a mixture of both. Stir in dissolved yeast. Add 3 c. whole-wheat flour and beat well for 5 minutes.

Cover tightly and set in warm place, away from draught, until it rises to twice its bulk. Turn out on floured board, add 2 tsp. salt and knead about 10 minutes, until satiny, adding more flour if necessary. Dough should be soft and pliable but not stiff. Divide in half and shape into 2 loaves. Place in greased bread pans and put in warm place until loaves double in size.

Bake in hot oven, 400°, for 15 minutes. Reduce heat to 350° and continue baking for 40 minutes. Brush loaves with soft butter and turn out on rack to cool.

Variations

1. Wheat germ may be substituted for 1 c. flour.
2. Soy flour may be substituted for 2 c. flour.
3. Unbleached white flour may be substituted for 3 c. flour.
4. Cracked wheat may be substituted for 1 c. flour.
5. Sesame seeds may be used to cover the dough when shaping for pans. Brush loaves with egg white so seeds will stick.
6. Raisins and nuts may be added if a sweet bread is desired.

■ FRUIT-NUT BREAD

Into the basic whole-wheat bread recipe, work 1 c. chopped dates, ¼ c. raisins, ¼ c. chopped dried figs, 1 c. chopped walnuts, 2 tbsp. honey. These should be added when mixing the dough *after* its first rise.

■ CINNAMON ROLLS

Use half the whole-wheat dough for these rolls, saving the other half for bread. Pat out dough about ¼-inch thick. Brush with soft butter, sprinkle with dark brown sugar or cover lightly with honey and dust with cinnamon. Add raisins and nuts if desired. Roll up like jelly roll, cut in 1-inch pieces and set together in greased pans.

■ "NO EXCUSE" BREAD

Do you spend half an hour a week going to some special store or bakery for your favorite loaf of bread? Do you spend a couple of hours on odds and ends around the house? Well—then you can actually save 10 or 15 minutes each week by baking your own bread! So "it takes too long to bake bread at home" is no excuse. And the results will soon make all store bread tasteless. Here is your "no excuse" recipe:

3 lbs. freshly ground whole-wheat flour

1 qt. warm water, whey or potato water or milk

1 tsp. salt

1 tsp. honey, raw sugar or un-sulphured molasses

1 pkg. dry powdered yeast

Have all ingredients at room temperature. Soften yeast in a little warm water, add honey, sugar or molasses and set aside about 15 minutes, while you eat breakfast or wash the dishes. Mix flour and salt with a wooden spoon. Gradually stir in yeast mixture. Add water or milk until dough is consistency of thick porridge (more moist than the usual bread dough). Spoon dough into 3 greased pans, set in warm place until dough rises nearly to top of pans. This will allow you another 20-30 minutes to do more of those odds and ends about the house. Bake at 375°, 45-60 minutes, until crusty. Turn out on rack to cool.

■ **LOW CALORIE BREAD**

2 yeast cakes

3 tbsp. honey

1¾ c. water

2 tbsp. bacon fat or oil

2 c. whole-wheat flour

1 c. soy flour

1 c. rice flour

2 tsp. salt

Dissolve yeast in water; add 1 tbsp. of the honey. Heat water to blood temperature. Add fat or oil, remaining honey; stir in all flour. Cover and allow to rise in warm place until double its bulk. Add salt and enough more soy flour to make a stiff dough. Knead well for 3-4 minutes. Pour into greased bread pan and let rise again. Bake at 400°, 15 minutes. Reduce heat to 350° and bake 40 minutes. Brush with softened butter and turn out on rack to cool.

■ **OAT BREAD**

6 c. whole-wheat flour

½ c. soy flour

2 c. milk

¼ c. oil

½ c. molasses

2 c. water

1½ tbsp. salt

2 yeast cakes

1 c. steel-cut oats

Have all ingredients at room temperature. Sift flours. Heat milk to lukewarm and add oil. Add molasses, water and salt. Crumble yeast into mixture and stir until dissolved. Add flour and oats; knead 3 minutes. Allow to rise in warm place for 2 hours. Shape. into 3 or 4 loaves, place in greased pans, cover with damp cloth and allow to stand 1 hour. Bake at 375°, 45-60 minutes.

■ PUMPERNICKEL

1 cake yeast	2 tsp. salt
¼ c. water, luke-warm	1½ c. buttermilk
3 tbsp. molasses	2 c. whole-wheat flour
3 tbsp. oil	2 c. rye flour

Mix and proceed as for basic whole-wheat bread. More rye flour may be added if necessary. The dough should be a little stiffer than for whole-wheat bread. Shape into 2 loaves; bake in greased pans at 425°, 10 minutes; and at 300°, 50 minutes.

■ CORNMEAL BREAD

½ c. yellow cornmeal	1 cake yeast
2 c. boiling water	½ c. water, luke-warm
2 tbsp. oil	4¾ c. unbleached white flour
½ c. molasses	or whole-wheat pastry flour
2 tsp. salt	

Stir cornmeal very slowly into boiling water. Cook 5 minutes, stirring constantly. Add oil, molasses and salt. Cool to lukewarm and add yeast which has been softened in warm water. Add flour to make a stiff dough. Knead well and allow to rise until double in bulk. Shape into 2 loaves and place in greased bread pans. Let rise again until bulk is doubled. Bake 1 hour at 350°.

■ MOLASSES RYE BREAD

1 c. milk	1 pkg. yeast dissolved in ¼ c.
1 c. water	water
2 tbsp. butter	3½ c. rye flour
⅓ c. unsulphured molasses	3 c. whole-wheat flour
1½ tsp. salt	¼ c. luke-warm water

Heat milk to blood temperature. Add water, fat, molasses and salt; cool to lukewarm. Add softened yeast. Stir in whole-wheat flour and beat until smooth. Cover and let rise until light. Add rye flour to make a fairly stiff dough. Knead until smooth. Place in bowl and allow to rise until double in bulk. Punch down and let rest 15 minutes. Shape into 2 loaves and place in greased bread pans. Cover and let rise until again double in bulk. Make 4 diagonal slits in crust with sharp knife. Bake at 375°, 40-50 minutes.

■ SOURDOUGH BREAD

Starter

Dissolve 1 yeast cake in 2½ c. warm water and 1 tsp. honey. Add 2 c. flour, or enough to make a stiff batter. Beat well. Store in bean crock or enamel pitcher large enough to allow mixture to bubble to 4 times its volume. Do not use a tin or aluminum container. Cover loosely and let stand at least 3-4 days in a warm place. Stir down daily. When any of the starter is used, it must be replaced with equal amounts of flour and water. Keep starter at 70° when using daily. It is best when about a month old.

Bread

2 c. starter	½ tsp. soda
2 c. unbleached white flour	1 tsp. honey
1 tsp. salt	1 tbsp. butter

Sift together flour, salt and soda. Add to starter. Mix and add butter and honey. Dough should be thick. Turn out on floured board and work in enough additional flour to keep dough from sticking. Knead until smooth. Put in greased bowl, cover and allow to stand in warm place until nearly doubled in bulk. Shape into loaf and put in greased bread pan. Bake at 400°, 10 minutes, then reduce heat to 350° and bake 35 minutes until bread is nicely browned. Turn out on rack to cool.

■ CORNMEAL BUNS

½ cake yeast	1 tsp. sea salt or salt
¼ c. warm water	1 egg
1 c. milk	1 c. cornmeal
¼ c. butter or oil	3 c. whole-wheat flour
¼ c. raw sugar	½ c. oat flour

Dissolve yeast in warm water. Heat milk to blood temperature and add butter or oil, sugar and salt. Cool. Add beaten egg, cornmeal and flours. Mix well and knead 5 minutes. Let rise until double its bulk. Punch down; shape into small balls and place on greased baking sheet. Let rise again until double in size. Bake 15 minutes at 375°; raise heat to 400° and bake 10 more minutes.

■ POTATO WHEAT ROLLS

¼ c. milk	¼ c. unseasoned mashed white
2 tbsp. salad oil	potatoes
1 tsp. raw sugar	1 yeast cake
1 tsp. unsulphured molasses	1 c. whole-wheat flour
½ tsp. salt	¼ c. soy flour
1 egg, beaten	Unbleached flour for kneading

Bring milk to blood heat. Remove from fire and add oil, sugar, molasses, salt and mashed potatoes. Stir until well blended. Add egg and crumbled yeast cake. Stir until yeast disappears; add ½ c. flour. Stir or beat with electric beater until mixture becomes somewhat rubbery. Add remaining flour. Beat about 10 minutes. Knead lightly on floured board a few minutes and form into rolls. Place in oiled steel or Pyrex baking dish; cover with damp cloth and allow to rise until double in size. Bake at 400° for 10-15 minutes.

■ WHOLE-WHEAT EGG ROLLS

1 cake yeast	1 c. luke-warm milk
⅓ c. warm water	3 eggs, beaten
½ c. brown or raw sugar	3½ c. whole-wheat pastry flour
½ c. oil	1½ tsp. salt

Dissolve yeast in water. Add sugar and oil to milk. Stir in yeast and eggs. Add flour and salt to liquid mixture. Allow to rise to double its bulk. Beat down and add another ½ c. flour if necessary, to make dough stiff enough to handle. Shape into rolls, brush with melted butter. Let rise to double their size. Bake at 350° about 15 minutes.

■ QUICK HOT ROLLS

2 cakes yeast	2 tsp. salt
¼ c. luke-warm water	2 c. whole-wheat pastry flour
1 c. milk	3 c. unbleached white flour
¼ c. oil	2 eggs, beaten
1 tbsp. honey	

Dissolve yeast in water. Heat milk to lukewarm; add oil, honey, salt; stir. Add whole-wheat flour; add yeast and eggs. Beat well. Raise in warm place 15 minutes. Punch down, add remaining flour and knead for a few minutes. Pat out to 12-inch square and cut into 2-inch squares. Place on greased baking sheet. Cover and let rise in warm place 20 minutes. Bake at 425°, 12 minutes.

Variations

1. *Crescents*—Roll ball of dough into circular shape about ¼-inch thick. Cut in pie-shaped pieces. Brush with melted butter and roll up, beginning at wide end. Curve into crescents on greased baking sheet. Let rise until doubled.
2. *Bowknots*—Roll dough under hand to ½-inch thickness. Cut in pieces about 6-inches long. Tie in knots. Place on greased baking sheet. Let rise until doubled.
3. *Cloverleaf Rolls*—Form dough into small balls. Dip each in melted butter or oil and place 3 balls in each cup of greased muffin pan. Let rise until doubled.
4. *Fold 'N' Twist Rolls*—Fold ⅓ of dough into 12 x 18-inch rectangle. Brush with butter or oil. Fold over in thirds to form rectangle 12 x 6-inches. With sharp knife cut into strips ¾-inch wide and 6-inches long. Roll ends of each strip in opposite directions and bring together forming circle. Seal ends and place on greased baking sheet. Let rise until doubled.
5. *Parker House Rolls*—Roll out dough ¼-inch thick. Brush with melted butter. Cut with 3-inch biscuit cutter. Fold each round in half and seal edges. Place rolls 1-inch apart on greased baking sheet. Let rise until doubled.

■ **POPPY OR SESAME TOPPING FOR ROLLS**

Beat 1 egg yolk and 1 tbsp. water. Brush over rolls and sprinkle with sesame or poppy seeds before baking. Bake rolls with this seed topping at a slightly lower temperature, since seeds burn quickly, or dip rolls in canned milk and then in sesame or poppy seeds.

■ **HOT CROSS BUNS**

1 c. milk	3 c. unbleached flour or whole-wheat flour
¼ c. butter or oil	
2 tbsp. honey	1 tsp. salt
1 cake yeast	1 tsp. cinnamon
1 egg, beaten	½ c. dried fruit, cut up

Bring milk, butter or oil, and honey to blood temperature. Dissolve yeast in ¼ c. lukewarm water. When milk mixture has cooled, add yeast and 1½ c. flour. Let rise until doubled. Add fruit, which has been tossed in remaining flour, then salt, cinnamon, and egg. Let rise again until doubled. Knead and form into rolls. Place on greased baking sheet, brush tops with beaten egg yolk and bake about 20 minutes. Make cross on top of each roll with tip of spoon, using mixture of powdered milk and honey.

■ **WHEAT PUFFS**

1 c. milk	2 packages active dry or 2
⅓ c. honey	cakes compressed yeast
2 tsp. salt	½ c. wheat germ
¼ c. oil	2 c. whole-wheat flour

Bring milk to blood heat and then cool to lukewarm. Blend in honey, salt, and oil. Crumble yeast into mixture. When yeast is softened, add wheat germ and flour. Beat well. Fill greased muffin pans half full. Let rise until doubled. Bake at 375°, 20-25 minutes. Add flavor interest by folding in 1 c. finely grated Cheddar cheese. Bake at 350° to avoid burning.

■ **PIZZA**

Dough

1 pkg. yeast	½ tsp. salt
1 c. warm water	2 tbsp. oil
3 c. flour	

Soften yeast in a little warm water. Mix flour, salt, water, oil and yeast into stiff dough. Cover; set aside in warm place to rise.

Sauce

1 small onion, minced	1 can tomato sauce
1 clove garlic, minced	1 tsp. dried sweet basil

Brown onion and garlic in 1 tbsp. oil until golden; add tomato and basil. Simmer 5 minutes.

Topping

1 tbsp. oregano	¼ lb. sliced Mozerella or Jack
¼ c. grated Parmesan cheese	cheese
1 can anchovy fillets	

Pour 2 tbsp. oil into each of 2 large shallow baking pans. Divide dough, placing half in each pan and turning so that dough is well oiled over entire surface; spread with fingers over pan to about ¼-inch thickness. Pour over sauce and arrange anchovy fillets and sliced cheese on top. Sprinkle with grated Parmesan cheese and bake 15-20 minutes in 400° oven.

Variations—Black or green olives, mushrooms or Italian sausage pieces may be substituted for anchovy fillets in Pizza topping.

■ **GARLIC BREAD**

Use French bread or long loaf or sourdough bread. Do not cut clear through loaf, but make deep slices ¾-inch thick. Mince 1 clove garlic and mix with ¼-lb. softened butter. Spread liberally on both sides of slices. Wrap bread in foil and heat 10-15 minutes in 350° oven. Break slices and serve hot. Garlic bread served in a napkin-lined bread basket makes a handsome complement to an Italian dinner. It is wonderful with tossed green salads, as well as with main-course soups.

■ **PARKER HOUSE ROLLS**

1 c. warm milk	¼ c. honey
1 beaten egg	1 tsp. salt
1 yeast cake	2 c. whole-wheat flour
6 tbsp. soft butter	

Dissolve yeast cake in a little warm water. Combine flour and salt in large bowl and add other ingredients; beat well. Add more flour if necessary to make soft dough. Knead. Roll dough about 1-inch thick and cut with biscuit cutter on floured board. Spread melted butter over half of each round and fold over other half. Cover and let rise in warm place until double in bulk. Refrigerate until ready to bake. Bake 15 minutes at 400°. Makes 18 rolls.

■ **BOSTON BROWN BREAD**

1 c. whole-wheat flour	2 yeast cakes
1 c. whole kernel cornmeal	1¾ c. milk
1 c. rye flour	½ tsp. salt
¾ c. molasses	

Sift together dry ingredients. Crumble yeast cakes in milk. Add with molasses and salt to flour and beat thoroughly. Pour into well greased molds, filling only ⅔ full. Cover and steam 3 hours. Place in 375° oven just long enough to dry off bread. Baked beans and Boston brown bread is a classic Saturday night supper in New England.

Variations—Substitute 1 c. soy flour for rye flour. Substitute ½ c. wheat germ for ½ c. cornmeal. Substitute 2 c. sour milk for sweet milk and instead of yeast use ¾ tsp. soda dissolved in sour milk.

■ **WHEAT-SPROUT BREAD**

1 pt. clean wheat (from local   2 tbsp. salad oil
  health food store)   2 c. water from soaked wheat
2 tbsp. dry active yeast   2 c. whole-wheat or un-
2 tbsp. raw sugar or honey   bleached white flour
2 tsp. salt

Pick over wheat, wash well and soak about 18 hours in water. Do not worry if mixture has slight odor. Save water and grind the drained wheat with medium food-grinder blade. Wheat will form soft dough. Place in large bowl and add yeast, which has been softened in a little warm water. Add salt, oil, honey or sugar and 2 c. warmed water saved from wheat. Stir in flour to make stiff batter. Cover and set aside in warm place to rise until double in bulk. Knead on floured board until dough is smooth and heavy. Shape into 1 large or 2 medium loaves. For 1 loaf, use greased pan, 9½ x 5½ x 2½ inches. For 2 loaves, use greased pans, 7½ x 3½ x 2½ inches. Set aside in warm place to rise until pans are full. Slide bread gently into 350° oven. Bread may fall if jolted. Bake 1 hour, until brown. To toast, place slices in broiler under slow fire.

■ **GINA'S BASIC DRY MIX FOR BREAD AND ROLLS**

This dry mix should be refrigerated and used in amounts called for in the following recipes. If you wish, you may increase the amount of the dry mix to half again the quantity of the dry ingredients. You may wish to try the mix in the smaller quantity given on right.

1 qt. wheat germ	or	1 c. wheat germ
1 qt. soy flour	or	1 c. soy flour
1 qt. rice polish	or	1 c. rice polish
1 c. brewer's yeast	or	¼ c. brewer's yeast
1 c. bone meal	or	¼ c. bone meal

■ **WHOLE-WHEAT BISCUITS**

1½ c. whole-wheat pastry flour   ¼ c. powdered milk
½ c. basic dry mix   ⅓ c. butter or pure lard
3 tsp. baking powder   ¾ c. milk or water
½ tsp. salt

Sift dry ingredients. Cut in lard or butter with 2 knives until dough particles are size of rice grains. Make a well and add liquid all at once. Mix with dinner fork until dough is dampened. Add a little more milk if necessary to produce soft and tender dough. Roll out lightly on cloth-covered floured board. Cut with biscuit cutters and bake on greased cookie sheet or in shallow greased pan, 10-15 minutes at 450°. If desired, brush tops with butter or milk before baking to produce golden-brown glaze.

■ **CORN BREAD**

2½ tsp. baking powder	1½ c. milk
1 tsp. salt	2 eggs
½ c. basic dry mix	3 tbsp. honey
¾ c. whole-wheat flour	¼ c. soy oil
1 c. corn meal	

Mix dry ingredients in large bowl. Combine remaining ingredients in another bowl and add all at once to dry ingredients, mixing well. Bake in fairly shallow, well greased pan, 30 minutes at 400°, until well done and brown on top. Corn bread should be about 2-inches thick. Cut in squares and serve warm.

■ **MUFFINS**

1 pkg. dry yeast	2 tsp. salt
½ c. warm water	½ c. honey
3 c. whole-wheat flour	1½ c. water
½ c. powdered milk	⅓ c. soy oil
1 c. basic dry mix	

Dissolve yeast in warm water. Mix together dry ingredients. Stir honey into water and oil and add to dry ingredients, stirring gently to blend. Add softened yeast and stir again, gently. Let rise in warm place about 45 minutes. Stir down. Use oiled ice cream scoop or large oiled spoon to dip mixture into oiled muffin tins. Let rise again in warm place, about 30 minutes. Bake 20 minutes at 400°, until golden brown.

Variation—Along with softened yeast, add 1 c. chopped nuts or 1 c. sunflower seeds to muffin dough.

■ YEAST DOUGHNUTS-DROP BATTER

2 pkg. dry yeast	½ tsp. nutmeg
½ c. warm water	3½ c. sifted whole-wheat flour
¾ c. warm milk	2 eggs
4 tbsp. honey	⅓ c. soft butter
1 tsp. salt	

Add yeast to warm water and let stand. Pour milk in bowl, add honey and nutmeg. Add half the flour and beat until smooth. Beat in eggs and yeast. Add remaining flour, beat until smooth. Cover; let rise in warm place until doubled. Stir down; allow to rest. Test oil in deep-frying kettle, making sure it is not above 360°. Drop batter from tsp. into hot fat. Turn when brown. Takes about 1½ minutes per side. Drain doughnuts on absorbent paper.

■ CARROT CORN BREAD

1 c. stone-ground cornmeal	2 tbsp. oil
1 c. finely grated carrots	¾ c. boiling water
2 tbsp. honey	2 eggs, separated
1 tsp. salt	

Mix cornmeal, carrots, oil, honey and salt. Stir in boiling water.

To yolks of egg add 2 tbsp. water and beat until thick. Add to cornmeal mixture. Fold in stiffly beaten whites of egg. Pour into an oiled 8 x 6 x 2-inch pan. Bake at 400° for 30 minutes.

■ HONEY ORANGE TWIST

1 cake yeast	1 tsp. salt
½ c. luke-warm water	2 tbsp. oil
½ c. whole orange, ground	1 egg, beaten
¼ c. honey	2½ c. unbleached white flour

Soften yeast in water, add orange, honey, salt, egg, oil and mix well. Add flour to make a thick batter; mix again and add more flour to make soft dough. Turn out on board, knead for few minutes. Place in greased bowl, let rise in warm place until doubled. Punch down, let rest 10 minutes. Divide in half. Shape into 2 rolls, 14 inches long, then twist together loosely, sealing ends. Put in greased pan, let rise until doubled. Bake at 350°, 45-50 minutes. A delightful Sunday brunch feature.

■   **QUICK BREADS**

Breads which do not require raising and are usually made with baking powder are called Quick Breads. Soda is sometimes used, but since it causes destruction of Vitamin B, it is not as desirable as the tartrate baking powders. I have used it rarely, usually with sour milk and with baking powder added. Active dry yeast dissolved in a little warm water may be substituted for baking powder in many Quick Bread recipes. Experiment to find out which you prefer. It's half the fun of cooking to add your own frills to recipes which give you the correctly proportioned basic ingredients. That's why I often suggest variations which I hope will spark your own imagination.

Quick Breads include hot cakes, waffles, biscuits, scones, muffins, coffee cake, sweet breads and the like.

Flour for these breads should be sifted again after measuring, and then measured again. Also, it is a good idea to allow dough for sweet breads to stand about 20 minutes at room temperature.

■   **WHOLE-WHEAT HOT CAKES**

1¼ c. whole-wheat bread flour	1 egg
3 tsp. baking powder or 1 yeast cake dissolved in ¼ c. warm milk	2 tbsp. oil
	1 tsp. unsulphured molasses
	2 tbsp. honey
½ tsp. salt	¼ c. wheat germ
1 c. sweet milk	

Sift flour with baking powder and salt. Beat egg and mix well with milk, oil, molasses and honey. If yeast is used, add to liquid mixture. Add dry ingredients and wheat germ. Stir gently until smooth. Heat griddle lightly brushed with oil. Drop batter by spoonfuls to make cakes of desired size. Batter is thick, so it should be spread out on the griddle. Allow to cook until cakes are bubbly on top, then flip over with pancake turner and finish cooking. Stack and serve piping hot with butter and syrup.

■   **JOHNNYCAKES**

¾ c. milk	2 tbsp. oil
1 beaten egg	1 c. freshly ground cornmeal
1 tbsp. honey	1 tsp. salt

Mix egg and milk. Add honey and oil and stir in cornmeal and salt. Mix well and bake like pancakes on hot, greased griddle.

■ **WHOLE-GRAIN PANCAKES**

1 c. whole-grain wheat	3 eggs, separated
1 c. water	1 tsp. baking powder
½ c. milk	1 tbsp. honey

Soak wheat in water overnight. In the morning, grind wheat, using coarse-blade food grinder. Add milk, beaten egg yolks, baking powder and honey. Fold in stiffly beaten egg whites. Bake like pancakes on lightly greased griddle.

Variations—For whole-grain wheat, substitute soy flour or buckwheat grits.

■ **COTTAGE CHEESE HOT CAKES**

2 eggs	¼ tsp. salt
1 c. soft-curd cottage cheese	¼ c. milk
3 tbsp. whole-wheat pastry flour	2 tbsp. oil

Beat eggs and mix with cottage cheese. Sift dry ingredients. Add cheese and eggs, stir in milk and oil. Mix together lightly. Bake like pancakes on hot, lightly greased griddle.

■ **SUNFLOWER SEED PANCAKES**

2 pkgs. active, dry or compressed yeast	¼ c. finely chopped sunflower seeds or put seeds through a grinder to make a paste
1½ c. warm milk or yogurt	1½ c. sifted whole-wheat flour
1 tbsp. molasses	1 tsp. salt or substitute
2 tbsp. salad oil	

Soften yeast in lukewarm milk. Add remaining ingredients. Drop from tablespoon onto moderately hot griddle. Cook slowly. Turn when upper surface is full of bubbles and brown on other side.

■ **OATMEAL GRIDDLE CAKES**

½ c. whole-wheat pastry flour	1 tbsp. oil
4 tsp. baking powder	1 tsp. unsulphured molasses
1 tsp. salt	¾ c. water
1½ c. rolled oats	¾ c. milk
1 beaten egg	

Sift together dry ingredients; add rolled oats. Combine egg, oil, molasses, water and milk. Add to dry ingredients and beat until smooth. Bake like pancakes on hot, greased griddle, reducing heat after cakes begin to cook.

■ TRADITIONAL BUCKWHEAT CAKES

1 yeast cake	1 c. unbleached white flour
2 tbsp. brown sugar	1 c. milk
2 c. warm water	1½ tsp. salt
2 c. buckwheat flour	

Dissolve yeast and sugar in warm water, pour into large bowl and add flour and salt. Warm milk to blood temperature, cool and add gradually. Beat until smooth and set in warm place to rise, about 1 hour, or until light. Stir well and drop by spoonfuls on hot, greased griddle. Cook until cakes are bubbly, then turn and cook until done.

If you wish to set the batter overnight, use only ¼ cake yeast and add an extra ½ tsp. salt, then cover and keep in cool place.

■ QUICK BUCKWHEAT CAKES

1 c. buckwheat flour	2½ tsp. baking powder
1 c. milk	¾ tsp. salt

Sift together buckwheat flour, baking powder and salt; stir in milk and mix thoroughly. Drop by spoonsful on hot, greased griddle. Cook until bubbly, then turn and finish cooking.

Buckwheat cakes, pure maple syrup and country sausage are a good breakfast send-off for a brisk winter's day.

■ WAFFLES

1 c. whole-wheat pastry flour	2 eggs, separated
1 tsp. salt	1½ c. milk
¼ c. wheat germ	3 tbsp. melted butter or oil
1 yeast cake	2 tbsp. honey
¼ c. warm milk	

Sift flour and salt; in a large bowl, beat egg yolks and add milk, melted butter or oil, honey and yeast dissolved in warm milk. Add dry ingredients and wheat germ, stirring until smooth. Fold in stiffly beaten egg whites and pour enough to fill one side on hot, lightly oiled waffle iron. Bake until golden brown. Try serving with apple sauce instead of syrup.

Variations—Baking powder, about 3 tsp., may be substituted for yeast and warm milk. Chopped crisp bacon may be added to batter. ½ c. chopped dates may be substituted for honey. ½ c. sunflower seed meal may be substituted for ½ c. whole-wheat flour.

■   **BROWN RICE FLOUR WAFFLES**

2 eggs, separated	¼ tsp. soda
¾ c. milk	2 c. brown rice flour
½ c. sour cream	2½ tsp. baking powder
6 tbsp. butter, melted	½ tsp. salt

Combine beaten egg yolks, milk, cream and melted butter. Sift dry ingredients and add slowly to first mixture. Add stiffly beaten whites of egg and bake on hot waffle iron.

■   **SOY NUT WAFFLES**

2 eggs, separated	¼ tsp. salt
2 tbsp. melted butter	½ c. sour cream
½ c. soy flour	⅓ c. finely chopped walnuts or
½ tsp. baking powder	pecans

Beat yolks and melted butter. Sift flour, baking powder and salt, and add alternately with sour cream. Coat nut meats with a little soy flour; fold in stiffly beaten whites of egg. Bake on hot waffle iron.

To double this recipe, use 3 eggs and double rest of ingredients.

■   **HOMEMADE BISCUIT MIX**

4 c. whole-wheat pastry flour	4 tsp. salt
4 c. unbleached white flour	1½ c. shortening
¼ c. baking powder	

Sift flour, measure, sift again with baking powder and salt. Cut in shortening until mixture has a fine, even crumb. Keep in covered container in refrigerator. This amount will make 5 recipes, allowing 2 c. to each. Add only enough milk to make dough easy to handle. This mix may be used as a basis for biscuits, dumplings, shortcake, waffles and muffins.

■   **MUFFINS**

Muffins are made from a quick-bread mixture, which is richer, thinner and sweeter than biscuits.

Muffins should be moist, with a tender crust, rounded top and not shiny. They should be twice the original height of the dough, with no tunnels.

Muffin batters must be lightly stirred, never beaten.

■ WHEAT MUFFIN BASIC RECIPE

3 tbsp. oil	2 c. sifted whole-wheat flour
1 beaten egg	½ tsp. salt
1 c. milk	3 tsp. baking powder
3 tbsp. honey or brown sugar	

Combine oil, egg, milk and honey. Sift flour, measure again and sift with salt and baking powder. Add to first mixture, stirring only enough to mix. Fill 12 greased muffin wells. Bake 20-30 minutes at 400°.

Variations—Use unbleached white flour instead of whole-wheat. Omit ½ c. wheat flour and add ½ c. soy, peanut flour or coarse bran. Substitute ¼ c. wheat germ for flour.

■ BLUEBERRY MUFFINS

Use basic wheat muffin recipe, omitting ¼ c. milk and adding 1 c. fresh or well-drained cooked blueberries.

■ OATMEAL MUFFINS

Use basic wheat muffin recipe, omitting whole-wheat flour and substituting 1 c. cornmeal and 1 c. unbleached white flour.

■ SUNFLOWER MEAL MUFFINS

Use basic wheat muffin recipe, omitting ½ c. whole-wheat flour and substituting ½ c. sunflower meal.

■ FRUIT MUFFINS

Use basic wheat muffin recipe, adding ½ c. dried fruit, softened and cut in medium-size pieces.

■ APRICOT SCONES

2 c. whole-wheat flour	½ tsp. grated lemon rind
2 tsp. baking powder	1 egg, separated
½ tsp. salt	1 egg, whole
1 tbsp. brown or raw sugar	⅓ c. light cream
4 tbsp. butter	½ c. cooked apricots

Mix and sift flour, baking powder, salt and sugar. Cut in butter, lemon rind. Separate 1 egg and reserve about ½ of white for top. Beat rest of egg with another whole egg and add light cream. Mix dry and liquid ingredients and fold in cooked apricots. Turn onto board, roll into circle; brush top with egg white. Bake in hot oven 450° for 12 minutes.

■ **SPICED HONEY COFFEE CAKE**

1 c. whole-wheat pastry flour	1 tsp. cinnamon
3 tsp. baking powder	¼ c. butter or margarine
½ tsp. salt	1 beaten egg
¼ c. sorghum, honey or brown sugar	½ c. milk
¼ tsp. nutmeg	½ c. seedless raisins
	1 tbsp. melted butter

Sift together dry ingredients, including spices. Using 2 table knives, cut in butter or margarine. Mix egg with milk and add to dry ingredients. Dredge raisins with flour and stir into batter. Spread evenly in round, buttered cake pan. Brush top with melted butter and then with honey-nut topping. Bake at 400°, about 30 minutes, until brown and well done.

■ **HONEY-NUT TOPPING**

2 tbsp. butter	2 tbsp. honey
2 tbsp. brown sugar	4 tbsp. chopped nuts
2 tbsp. flour	

Cream butter, sugar and flour, add honey and stir in nuts. Spread on coffee cake batter and bake as instructed above.

■ **FRENCH TOAST**

2 eggs	Oil, to lightly grease griddle
1 c. milk	1 tbsp. grated orange rind (optional)
1 tbsp. brown sugar or honey	
⅛ tsp. salt	
4 slices day-old whole-wheat bread	

Beat eggs, add milk, sugar or honey, and salt. Pile bread in deep bowl. Pour liquid over. Turn slices to moisten completely. Place griddle over direct heat. Melt oil. Fry bread slices on both sides until golden brown. Serve hot with honey or maple syrup. Grated orange rind added to liquid makes pleasing variation. Moistened slices may be placed on well greased cookie sheet and browned in 500° oven, a few minutes on each side, until brown.

■ **BISCUITS**

2 c. whole-wheat flour or unbleached white flour	4 tsp. baking powder
½ tsp. salt	⅓ c. oil or other shortening
	¾ c. milk

Sift flour with salt and baking powder. Cut in shortening with pastry blender or 2 knives until mixture resembles coarse meal. Make a well in center and add milk. Mix with fork until dough leaves sides of the bowl. Turn onto floured board and knead lightly for 18 counts. Pat out 1-inch thick and cut with biscuit cutter. Bake at 450° for 12-15 minutes.

Variations

1. *Shortcake*—Add 2 tbsp. honey to flour mixture and use 5 tbsp. shortening.
2. *Sour Milk Biscuits*—Substitute sour milk or buttermilk for sweet milk. Add ½ tsp. soda and decrease baking powder to 1 tsp.
3. *Cheese Biscuits*—Add ½ c. grated Cheddar cheese with shortening.
4. *Cobblers*—Add 3 tbsp. honey to milk; place sliced peaches or berries in bottom of shallow pan, pour ¼ c. honey over fruit and dot with 2 tsp. butter, and sprinkle 2 tbsp. flour over all; cover with a dough rolled about ¼-inch thick and bake as in basic recipe.
5. *Cinnamon Rolls*—Shape mixture into rectangular sheet; flatten to about ⅓-inch; brush with butter, sprinkle with cinnamon, cover with honey and raisins and chopped nuts; roll like jelly roll and bake in greased pan as for biscuits.

■ DUMPLINGS—WITH MEAT STEW

1 egg	1 c. whole-wheat pastry flour
1 tbsp. melted shortening or oil	2½ tsp. baking powder
⅓ c. milk	1 tsp. salt

Beat egg, add shortening and milk. Mix dry ingredients and add liquid. Beat well. Should make a thick drop dough. Drop by spoonfuls on stew; cover tightly and cook about 15 minutes.

■ GINGERBREAD

2 c. whole-wheat flour	1 beaten egg
½ tsp. salt	1 c. blackstrap molasses
1 tbsp. ginger	7 tbsp. melted butter or oil
1 tsp. soda	9 tbsp. boiling water
2 tsp. baking powder	

To dry ingredients add beaten egg and molasses. Melt butter in pan in which gingerbread is to be baked. Add melted butter or oil and boiling water. Beat well; should be a thin mixture. Pour into well greased pan and bake in slow oven, 325°, for 40 minutes.

■ **ENTIRE CORNMEAL BREAD**

2 beaten eggs	2 tsp. salt
2 c. buttermilk, yogurt or sour milk	3 tsp. baking powder
	¼ c. wheat germ
2 c. yellow cornmeal	3 tbsp. melted butter or oil

Melt butter in 9 x 9 x 2-inch pan. Beat eggs in mixing bowl; add buttermilk. Add dry ingredients, then liquid fat. Stir only enough to blend. Pour into pan in which fat was melted. Bake at 400° about 30 minutes. Makes coarse, crunchy bread.

■ **NUT BREAD**

1 beaten egg	1 c. soy flour
2 c. sour milk, yogurt or buttermilk	½ tsp. soda
	3 tsp. baking powder
½ c. molasses	½ c. raw or brown sugar
3 tbsp. melted butter	1 tsp. salt
½ c. wheat germ	2 c. whole-wheat flour
1 c. chopped nuts	

Beat egg in large bowl, add all liquid ingredients. Add all dry ingredients, including nuts and butter. Beat just enough to combine. Pour into greased and floured loaf pan. Bake in moderate oven, 350°, 1 hour or until done. Dates may be used in place of nuts, or half and half.

■ **NUT-DATE BREAD**

½ tsp. salt	1 c. chopped nuts
½ tsp. soda	1½ c. sour milk
2 tsp. baking powder	1 c. raw or brown sugar
3 c. whole-wheat flour	1 egg, beaten
1 c. chopped, sun-dried dates	2 tbsp. melted butter

Sift dry ingredients and add dates and nuts. Stir in milk, sugar, egg and melted fat. Beat well. Let stand 1 hour and bake in greased loaf pan in moderate oven, 350°, 1 hour.

■ **APRICOT WHOLE-WHEAT BREAD**

1 c. dried or fresh apricots, cut up	4 tsp. baking powder
	¼ tsp. soda
1⅔ c. water (boiling hot for dried fruit)	1 tsp. salt
	1 c. raw sugar
3 c. whole-wheat pastry flour	3 tbsp. oil
5 tbsp. powdered milk	

If dried apricots are used, place in bowl with boiling water. If fresh fruit, use 1 c. hot water and ⅔ c. cold water. Sift flour with powdered milk, baking powder, soda and salt. Add sugar and oil to flour mixture. Blend in apricot mixture, pour into greased loaf pan and bake at 350°, 55 minutes.

■ TOASTED COCONUT BREAD

3 c. whole-wheat pastry flour	1 beaten egg
2 tsp. baking powder	1½ c. milk
½ tsp. salt	1 tsp. vanilla
1 c. raw sugar	1 c. shredded, toasted coconut

Sift flour, baking powder and salt; add sugar. Mix egg with milk; add vanilla. Stir into dry ingredients and fold in coconut. Pour into greased loaf pan and bake at 350°, about 1 hour.

■ APPLESAUCE COFFEE CAKE

¾ c. unsweetened applesauce or 1 c. ground raw apple	½ tsp. soda
	½ tsp. salt
1 beaten egg	1 tsp. vanilla
1 c. raw sugar or brown sugar	½ tsp. cinnamon
⅓ c. oil	¼ tsp. nutmeg
2½ c. unbleached white flour	¼ tsp. ground cloves
2 tsp. baking powder	

Mix applesauce or raw apple with beaten egg and sugar; add oil. Sift together dry ingredients. Add liquids and mix thoroughly. Spread batter thinly in shallow loaf pan. Top with sunflower seeds or chopped nuts if desired. Bake at 350°, about 20 minutes.

■ SUPERB CRUMB COFFEE CAKE

1 c. raw or brown sugar	1 beaten egg
2 c. whole-wheat flour	½ c. sour milk or buttermilk
½ tsp. ginger	2 tsp. baking powder
½ tsp. cinnamon	1 tsp. salt
½ tsp. nutmeg	½ c. nuts and ½ c. raisins
½ c. butter or ⅓ c. salad oil	

Sift together flour, sugar, spices, and work in fat. Take out 1 c. of mixture. Mix together beaten egg and sour milk, to which baking powder has been added, and stir into flour and fat mixture. Add raisins and nuts last. Grease deep cake pan and spread half of crumbs in bottom, pour in batter, and sprinkle remaining crumbs over top. Bake 40 minutes at 350°. Let cool in pan.

■ **CORN FRITTERS**

2 c. fresh or 2 pkgs. frozen corn	½ tsp. honey (if desired)
2 eggs	⅛ tsp. cream of tartar
½ tsp. salt	¾ tbsp. butter

Grate uncooked corn off cob with a medium size grater. With frozen corn, thaw according to package directions. Scrape every last bit of corn off cob. Separate eggs and mix yolks, salt and honey into corn. Mix thoroughly. Mix or fold corn mixture into egg whites, which have been beaten with cream of tartar until they hold a peak. Mix gently. Drop fritter batter from teaspoon into melted butter. Fry several minutes on each side over medium heat. Serve crisp and hot. Serves 4.

■ **SOUTHERN SPOON BREAD**

1 c. yellow whole-grain corn-meal	1 tsp. salt
	2 c. milk
2 c. boiling water	2 tsp. baking powder
1 tbsp. butter	2 eggs

Pour boiling water over meal. Boil 5 minutes, stirring constantly. Remove from heat, add butter, salt, milk. Mix thoroughly, add well beaten eggs. Sift in baking powder. Mix and pour in greased baking dish. Preheat oven to 350° and bake ½ hour. Serve from dish in which it was baked.

■ **QUICK WHOLE-WHEAT BREAD**

3 c. whole-wheat flour	½ c. honey
1 c. unbleached white flour	2 c. buttermilk
1 tsp. soda	½ c. raisins or chopped nuts, if
1 tsp. salt	desired

Sift together dry ingredients. Mix honey and buttermilk. Stir into dry ingredients. Batter should be thick, so you may need slightly less than 2 c. buttermilk. Add raisins or nuts. Bake in well-greased loaf pan at 325°, about 1 hour, until brown and well done.

■ **BANANA BREAD**

½ c. butter or other shortening	1 tsp. salt
1 c. brown sugar	4 tsp. baking powder
3 beaten eggs	⅔ c. milk
4 ripe bananas, mashed	1 tsp. vanilla
2 c. whole-wheat pastry flour	

Cream shortening and sugar; add eggs and bananas and mix well. Sift together dry ingredients and stir into banana mixture. Add milk and vanilla; beat well. Turn into greased loaf pan and bake at 350°, about 1 hour, until brown and well done. Cool before cutting.

■ BANANA-DATE BREAD

1 c. date crystals or finely chopped dates	1 c. brown sugar
	2 eggs
1 c. ripe bananas, finely chopped	2 c. unbleached white flour
	2 tsp. baking powder
½ c. butter or other shortening	½ tsp. salt

Mix chopped dates and bananas. Cream shortening and sugar; add well beaten eggs and mix thoroughly. Add sifted flour, baking powder and salt. Beat well. Turn into well greased loaf pan and bake at 350°, about 1 hour, until brown and well done.

■ STEAMED DATE BROWN BREAD

3 yeast cakes	¼ c. powdered milk
2 c. warm milk or yogurt	1 tsp. salt
¾ c. blackstrap molasses	½ c. raisins
1 c. whole-wheat pastry flour	1 c. chopped sun-dried dates
1 c. yellow cornmeal	1 c. chopped nuts
⅔ c. wheat germ	

Soak yeast in warm milk or yogurt and molasses. Sift together dry ingredients and add to yeast mixture. Mix thoroughly and stir in raisins, dates and nuts. Stir this mixture about 40 strokes. Pour into 2 oiled pint cans and cover tightly with lid or oiled paper held on with rubber bands. Let rise about ½ hour. Set on rack in pan in which water has been added to depth of 2 inches. Cover and steam slowly 2 hours.

■ WHOLE-WHEAT NOODLES

Beat until very light, 3 egg yolks and 1 whole egg. Beat in 4 tbsp. cold water, 1 tsp. salt. Work in with hands 2 c. whole-wheat pastry flour. Divide dough into 3 parts. Roll out each piece as thin as possible on lightly floured board. Place between 2 towels until partially dry; remove from towels, roll up like jelly roll, and with sharp knife cut into desired noodle widths. Shake out noodles and dry before storing.

■ **DOUBLE BOILER MILLET BREAD**

1 c. whole-wheat flour	2 tbsp. honey
¾ c. millet meal	½ lb. pitted sun-dried dates or
¼ c. yellow cornmeal	¾ c. raisins
2½ tsp. baking powder	1½ c. milk
1 tsp. salt	2 tbsp. melted butter

Mix and sift dry ingredients. Stir in honey and fruit. Add milk, then butter, stirring only enough to mix well. Turn into top of well oiled double boiler, cover and cook over boiling water, about 2 hours. Slice and serve hot with butter or honey. Makes about 8 large slices.

■ **WHOLE-WHEAT POPOVERS**

Popovers depend upon air for the leavening. This is achieved by beating eggs and beating air into the mixture and also baking at high heat.

1 c. plus 2 tbps. whole-wheat	1 tsp. oil
pastry flour	1 tsp. honey
½ tsp. salt	1¼ c. milk
3 eggs, beaten	

Sift flour and salt. Combine eggs, oil, honey and milk and stir into flour. Beat thoroughly. Have ready well oiled muffin pan, piping hot. Fill pans half full of batter and bake in hot oven, 450°, 20 minutes. Lower heat to 350° and bake 15-20 minutes longer.

■ **POPOVERS**

1 c. cold milk	½ tsp. salt
1 c. unbleached white flour	3 eggs
2 tbsp. oil	

Place all ingredients in bowl. Beat hard for 5 minutes, using electric mixer or egg beater. Pour into hot muffin pans which have been well oiled. Bake at 475° for first 15 minutes, then at 400° for 15 minutes.

■ **WHOLE-WHEAT CRACKERS**

When making bread, save out a lump of dough and mix in more flour so that it can be rolled out fairly thin. Mix in grated cheese if desired. Cut with cookie cutter and prick a couple of times with a fork to let out air bubbles. Bake on cookie sheet.

■ **TORTILLAS**

1 c. whole-kernel cornmeal	5 tbsp. cornstarch
1 c. unbleached white flour	1 tsp. salt
2 c. milk	2 eggs, beaten
2 tbsp. olive oil or salad oil	

Mix cornmeal, flour, cornstarch and salt. Add beaten egg, milk and oil. Mix well. Pour batter into pitcher and pour enough on hot griddle to make 4-inch pancake. Bake 3 minutes on each side. Stack on top of each other, wrap in oiled paper, then cloth or foil to keep moist until ready to use. Refrigerate if not to be used at once.

■ **SESAME COCKTAIL STRIPS**

2 c. unbleached white flour	½ c. salad oil
1 tsp. salt	¼ c. ice water
¼ tsp. cayenne pepper	1 c. toasted sesame seeds

Blend dry ingredients with shortening to make dough of pie crust consistency. Stir in sesame seeds; roll thin and cut into narrow strips about 2 inches long. Bake in slow oven, 300°, 15-20 minutes. While still warm, sprinkle with additional salt. Store in covered jar or tin, and before serving, put into oven for a few minutes to crisp.

■ **HONEY-CINNAMON TOAST**

Lightly toast slices of whole-wheat bread on one side. Spread untoasted side with honey-butter; (suggested quantity, ½ c. butter to 1 c. honey, well-blended at room temperature and stored in refrigerator). Top slices with cinnamon and place under broiler until golden-brown. Serve hot.

CHAPTER 4

Casseroles

*J*UST before dinner, you whisk it out of the oven, bring it to the table, bubbling hot and golden brown on top, and serve it forth while the guests look on admiringly and you as hostess are fresh-looking and relaxed. That's one of the joys of casserole cooking.

Another is the infinite number of ways in which you can use left-over meats; also the intriguing variety of fresh vegetables you can introduce. Add to a casserole a big wooden bowl of tossed green salad and your meal is complete. You've done the work that morning, or even the preceding day.

You can have a glorious time inventing your own versions of the tried and proven recipes I've collected in this chapter. Casseroles made with a basic cream sauce should not be kept overnight.

Since you will want to bring your casserole straight from the oven to the table, it should be an attractive dish of earthenware or glass. When you do top burner cooking in your casserole, it is a good idea to place an asbestos mat underneath. A covered casserole dish must have a tight-fitting lid to prevent the loss of the steam which is cooking the food inside.

So here are some casserole recipes to save your disposition, cut down on dish-washing and allow your imagination free rein.

■ CARROT CHEESE CASSEROLE

1 large onion, chopped	¼ tsp. pepper
1 tbsp. butter	⅓ c. grated Cheddar cheese
4 c. cooked sliced carrots	6 tbsp. dry bread crumbs
¼ tsp. powdered dill	2 eggs, slightly beaten
1 c. commercial sour cream	1 tbsp. mint flakes
½ tsp. salt	

Brown chopped onion in butter. Combine carrots with onion, salt, pepper and dill. Turn into 1½-qt. casserole. Combine egg with sour cream. Sprinkle onion-carrot mixture with grated cheese and crumbs. Dot with butter. Pour sour cream-egg mixture over top. Bake 30 minutes at 350°. Top with mint flakes. Serves 4-6.

■ CHILI BEANS

2 c. pinto or kidney beans (dry)	1 small can tomato sauce, or
1 medium onion, chopped	tomato paste, or 1 medium
½ green pepper, chopped	can tomato purée
2 cloves garlic, chopped	2 tsp. salt
1 tsp. cumin powder	1 tsp. chili powder

Wash and place beans in water to cover. Cook over low fire, 1 hour. Add other ingredients and enough water to cover. Cook slowly (covered) until beans are tender. Add just enough water to keep beans from sticking. May be served with grated Parmesan cheese. Serves 4-6.

■ TAMALE PIE IN CASSEROLE

1 c. yellow cornmeal dampened in a little cold water	2 c. chopped beef or 1 lb. hamburger
3 c. boiling water	½ tsp. cumin powder
1 tsp. salt	2 c. tomatoes
1 medium onion	1 tbsp. chili powder
1 tbsp. oil	Few ripe olives

Cook cornmeal, water and salt, as for mush, about 30 minutes. Chop onion and fry in oil until brown. Add meat and fry until red color disappears. Add cumin, tomatoes, chili powder and olives. Line oiled casserole with mush, put meat mixture in center, cover with mush and bake in moderate oven 350°, 2 hours. Serves 4.

■ GARBANZA PEAS WITH TOMATO SAUCE

1 c. garbanza peas	1 clove garlic minced
3 c. water	1 tsp. powdered cumin
2 c. tomatoes or purée	Salt to taste
1½ c. chopped onions	Grated Parmesan cheese

Soak garbanza peas in water overnight. Cook until tender in water in which they were soaked; ½ hour before done (you can tell by tasting when peas are soft), add tomatoes or purée, chopped onions, garlic, powdered cumin and salt to taste. Top with grated cheese. Serves 4.

■ **CARROT LOAF**

4 c. cooked mashed carrots   2 tbsp. chopped parsley
3 eggs, slightly beaten   1 tsp. salt
1 medium onion, chopped
1 c. dry whole-wheat bread
    crumbs

Combine carrots and bread crumbs. Stir in beaten eggs. Blend in parsley, onion and salt. Bake in 4½ x 8½-inch loaf pan, 30-40 minutes in 350° oven. Slice and serve with seafood sauce. Serves 6.

■ **SEAFOOD SAUCE**

4½ tsp. butter   3 tbsp. flour
1 c. milk   ¾ c. cooked peas
1 can shrimp or crabmeat,   ¼ tsp. nutmeg
    chopped

Melt butter in top of double boiler; blend in flour and add milk, stirring until sauce is smooth and thick. Add nutmeg, seafood and peas and continue cooking until all ingredients are heated.

■ **GOLDEN CARROT CASSEROLE**

4 eggs, beaten   1 tbsp. grated onion
2½ c. grated raw carrots   1 c. whole-wheat bread crumbs
2 tbsp. oil   1 c. grated Cheddar cheese
1½ tsp. salt   1 can mushroom soup, heated
½ tsp. pepper   1 tbsp. chopped parsley
1½ c. milk

Mix all ingredients thoroughly. Place in well greased casserole and set in shallow pan of hot water. Bake in 350° oven, about 30 minutes, until brown. Pour canned mushroom soup over top and sprinkle with chopped parsley. Serves 6.

■ **BAKED YAM CASSEROLE**

3 medium yams   3 tbsp. melted butter
⅓ c. chopped pecans   1 egg, lightly beaten
¼ c. whole-wheat bread crumbs   ½ c. milk
1 tsp. salt   4 unsweetened pineapple slices
½ c. chopped celery

Steam yams and mash. Stir in butter, salt, egg and milk. Add pecans, celery and bread crumbs. Place in well greased casserole and top with pineapple slices. Bake in 350° oven 1 hour. Serves 4.

■ TOMATO-BURGER CASSEROLE

1 medium onion, chopped	2 8-oz. cans tomato sauce
1 garlic clove, chopped	1 8-oz. pkg. noodles
1 medium green pepper, chopped	1 c. grated Cheddar cheese
2 tbsp. soy bean or other oil	⅓ c. milk
1 lb. ground beef	¾ c. slivered almonds, if desired

Cook onion, garlic and pepper in oil until onion is golden. Add meat and brown lightly. Add tomato sauce and cook 15 minutes over low heat. While meat mixture is simmering, cook noodles in large kettle of salted boiling water, 8 minutes. Drain noodles thoroughly. Mix with meat sauce, cheese and milk. Pour in 2-qt. greased casserole; bake in 350° oven, 30 minutes. Serves 6.

■ BOSTON BAKED BEANS

2 c. white Navy beans	1 medium onion and any one of the following: ¼ lb. salt pork; bone and meat from shank end of baked ham; ¼ lb. bacon; slice of ham
1 tbsp. dry mustard	
1 tsp. salt	
⅓ c. dark, unsulphured molasses	

Wash and soak beans several hours in water to cover, or put on to cook in water to cover, over low fire. Cook 1 hour. Then add mustard, salt, and molasses. If salt pork is used, scrape and score in ½-inch strips. Bury meat and onion in beans; add water to cover; cover pot or pan and bake in 350° oven, about 6 hours. Look at beans after 2 hours to see if more water is necessary. They should be tender, but separate, not mushy. Serves 6.

■ STEAK AND NOODLE CASSEROLE

1 lb. round steak, cut in ½-inch pieces	1½ c. water
¼ c. salad oil	1 can mushroom soup
1 large onion, chopped	1 small can mushrooms
1 garlic clove, chopped	1 tsp. salt
1 c. uncooked whole-wheat noodles	½ c. chopped celery
	½ c. chopped green pepper

Brown steak in oil; remove from pan and brown onion and garlic until golden. Add meat, mushroom soup and mushrooms, celery, green pepper, noodles and water. Mix together. Place in well greased 3-qt. casserole. Bake in 350° oven 1½ hours. Top with sour cream or yogurt. Serves 6.

■ BAKED LIMA BEANS AND HAM

3 c. large dry lima beans	2 tbsp. molasses
6 c. boiling water	1 tsp. whole cloves
1 large ham shank (3-4 lbs.)	1 bay leaf
1 tsp. whole allspice	2 medium-sized onions
1 tsp. peppercorns	1 tsp. salt

Rinse limas, add boiling water and cook 2 minutes. Cover and let stand 1 hour. Cut ham in large pieces, removing excess fat. Tie whole spices and bay leaf in small piece of cheesecloth. Combine limas, ham, spices, whole onions and salt and simmer 1 hour. Remove spice bag and ham bones. Turn into baking dish; add molasses. Bake at 350°, 1 hour. Taste beans before baking and add more molasses if necessary. Serves 6.

■ LENTIL LOAF

½ c. finely-cut green onion tops	1½ c. cooked lentils, seasoned
1 clove garlic, minced	with
1 c. finely shredded raw beet	1 tsp. salt
Rind of 1 small lemon,	¼ tsp. crushed thyme
shredded	2 eggs, well beaten
¼ c. chopped parsley	2 tbsp. melted butter

Combine in above order and mix. Pack in greased loaf pan, at 350°, 30 minutes. Loaf should be brown on bottom and can be turned out. Serve with lemon butter. Serves 4.

■ KIDNEY BEAN CASSEROLE

1 c. whole-wheat bread crumbs	2 small cans tomato sauce
½ c. milk	1 chopped green pepper, if de-
1 tsp. salt	sired
½ tsp. chili powder	3 No. 2 cans red kidney beans
1 lb. ground beef	½ lb. grated sharp Cheddar
5 tbsp. oil	cheese
2 c. chopped onion	

Combine bread crumbs, milk, salt, chili powder and ground beef. Form into 24 small balls. Heat oil in skillet and brown meat balls in hot fat. Remove and cook chopped onion in same skillet. Add tomato sauce and chopped green pepper (if desired). Place red kidney beans in casserole. Pour tomato sauce over beans. Place grated cheese on beans. Place meat balls around sides. Beans may be drained first if a thicker mixture is desired. Bake at 350°, 45 minutes to 1 hour. Serves 8.

■ **GREEN BEAN CASSEROLE**

2 pkg. French-cut green beans	1 c. water chestnuts, sliced
1 pkg. or 1 c. bean sprouts	1 7-oz. can mushrooms
1 can or 1 c. mushroom soup	1 can French-fried onion rings
½ c. grated Cheddar cheese	

Arrange all ingredients except onion rings, in layers in well greased casserole, adding cheese and mushroom soup to each layer. Bake in 400° oven 30 minutes. About 10 minutes before completing cooking, place onion rings over top. Serves 6.

■ **EGG, STRING BEAN CASSEROLE**

1 pkg. frozen green beans or 2 c. fresh green beans	1 can undiluted mushroom soup
1 medium onion, chopped fine	½ c. grated Cheddar cheese
2 tsp. butter	¼ c. buttered crumbs
6 hard-cooked eggs	

Cook green beans until tender. Brown onion lightly in butter. Cut hard-cooked eggs in slices and mix with cooked green beans. There should not be any liquid left on beans if cooked properly. Place beans, eggs and onion in a 1½-qt. casserole. Pour mushroom soup over all. Sprinkle cheese and crumbs over top. Bake 40 minutes at 350°. Serves 4.

■ **EGGPLANT RICE CASSEROLE**

2 tbsp. oil	¼ tsp. pepper
1½ lbs. ground beef	1 tsp. salt
1 large onion, chopped	2 tsp. chili powder
2 cloves garlic, chopped	1 tsp. oregano
½ c. sliced ripe olives	1 sliced eggplant
1 c. beef consommé	3 medium tomatoes, sliced
½ c. cooked wild rice or ½ c. cooked long-grain brown rice	1 c. grated Cheddar cheese
1½ c. sliced fresh mushrooms or 1 large can sliced mushrooms	

Mix together all ingredients except eggplant, tomatoes and cheese; cook in frying pan about 5 minutes. Remove. Dip eggplant slices in flour and sauté in frying pan. Arrange layers of meat mixture, eggplant, tomato and cheese in well greased casserole. Bake in 300° oven about 2 hours. Serves 4.

■ **CORN AND ZUCCHINI CASSEROLE**

2 c. sliced unpeeled zucchini	¾ c. grated Parmesan cheese
2 c. whole kernel corn	½ c. whole-wheat bread crumbs
2 c. diced celery	1 can undiluted celery soup
½ c. chopped onion	4 eggs, beaten
1 clove garlic minced	2 c. milk
½ c. chopped parsley	Salt and pepper to taste
¼ c. chopped green pepper	Pinch of thyme and marjoram

Combine zucchini with corn, celery, onion, garlic. Add parsley and green pepper. Add cheese and crumbs. Add celery soup and beaten eggs mixed with milk. Season with salt and pepper to taste. Add pinch of thyme and marjoram. Pour into greased 1½-qt. casserole and bake in a moderate oven, 350°, 45 minutes. Serves 8.

■ **RICE-TOMATO CASSEROLE**

2 tbsp. butter or oil	1½ tsp. salt
½ onion	⅛ tsp. paprika
1 c. brown rice	½ c. grated Cheddar cheese
1 c. tomato juice	
2½ c. chicken consommé or beef bouillon	

Melt fat in frying pan; add chopped onion, cook 1 minute, stirring constantly. Add rice and brown. Add tomato juice, consommé and seasonings. Cook covered until rice is tender, about 50 minutes. Stir in grated cheese. Serves 4.

■ **PARSLEY RICE**

2 eggs, beaten	1 medium minced onion
2 c. milk	1 clove minced garlic
2 c. cooked brown rice	¼ c. soy bean oil
1 c. grated American cheese	½ tsp. salt
½ c. chopped parsley	⅛ tsp. pepper

Beat eggs, add milk and remaining ingredients, saving some cheese for top. Pour in greased baking dish and bake at 350°, 40 minutes.

May be baked in greased ring mold and when served, turn out on large platter and fill center with creamed chicken, tuna, crab, lobster or shrimp. Serves 4.

■ RICE ORIENTAL

1 large onion, chopped	2 eggs
3 tbsp. oil	4 tbsp. milk
1 medium green pepper, chopped	2 c. cooked brown rice
½ c. chopped cooked ham or shrimp	Soy sauce or ½ tsp. paprika

Chop onion and sauté in 1 tbsp. oil until golden. Remove from pan. Chop green pepper and sauté in added oil until tender. Remove from pan. Sauté chopped cooked ham or shrimp. Remove from pan. Scramble eggs with milk, add ham, onions, green pepper and rice. Mix and heat. Add Soy sauce or paprika. Serves 4.

■ CHINESE FRIED RICE

2 tbsp. oil	**Use any of the following:**
2 c. chopped onions	1 c. chopped roasted peanuts
2 c. cold cooked rice	1 c. chopped green pepper
2 eggs, lightly stirred	2 c. chopped left-over meat, such as ham or chicken
1 tbsp. soy sauce	
½ tsp. salt	1 c. chopped cooked bacon or shrimp

Fry onions in oil until golden brown. Add rice and sauté. Mix eggs, soy sauce and salt with rice and cook until done, stirring lightly. Combine rice mixture with whatever you have selected. Heat thoroughly. Serves 4-6.

■ WILD RICE CASSEROLE

⅔ c. wild rice, or ½ c. wild rice and ½ c. brown rice	¾ tsp. celery salt
	½ tsp. garlic salt
2 c. water	½ lb. fresh mushrooms or 1 small can mushrooms
1 lb. ground round steak	
3 tbsp. oil	1 can chicken-rice or mushroom soup
1 clove garlic, minced	
¾ tsp. onion salt	

Wash rice several times and cook in water in covered pan until water is absorbed and rice is fluffy. Brown meat and garlic in oil. Add seasonings, cooked rice, mushrooms and soup. Bake in well greased casserole 1 hour. Serves 4.

■ **SAUSAGE RICE CASSEROLE**

1 lb. sausage meat	1 c. slivered almonds
2 c. finely chopped celery	1 chicken bouillon cube, dis-
1 c. chopped onion	solved in ⅓ c. water
1 c. uncooked brown rice	4½ c. water
1 pkg, dehydrated chicken-	1 can mushroom soup
noodle soup	

Sauté sausage, but do not allow it to brown. Remove to well greased casserole. Cook celery and onion in remaining sausage fat until light gold and tender. Add to sausage and stir in chicken-noodle soup, rice, bouillon and water. Bake, covered, in 350° oven 1 hour. Remove cover, pour over mushroom soup; cook until bubbly. Serves 6-8.

■ **RICE PILAFF**

1 c. raw long-grain rice	½ tsp. salt
⅓ c. oil	2½ c. chicken broth
½ c. slivered almonds	

Brown rice in oil, stirring constantly. When golden brown, place in greased casserole. Add almonds and salt; pour over chicken broth. Cover and bake at 325° about 1½ hours. Serves 4.

This Rice Pilaff may also be cooked, covered, over low heat on top of stove, until rice is tender and liquid absorbed.

■ **QUICK SPANISH RICE (MEATLESS)**

¼ c. olive or peanut oil	1 c. hot water
1 medium onion, thinly sliced	1 tsp. salt
½ medium green pepper, diced	Pepper to taste; cumin powder
1½ c. cooked rice	and chili powder to taste
2 cans tomato sauce	

Heat oil, add onion, green pepper and rice. Cook and stir over high heat until lightly browned. Add hot water, tomato sauce and seasonings; mix well; bring to a boil; cover and simmer 20 minutes; stir occasionally. Serves 4.

■ **MUSHROOM-BROWN RICE**

6 c. cooked brown rice	1 c. bread cubes
1½ c. melted butter or oil	2 c. fresh mushrooms, sliced
¼ c. minced parsley	Salt and pepper

Sauté bread cubes in ½ c. melted butter; remove, then sauté

mushrooms. Add remaining butter to cooked rice and toss lightly; add mushrooms and sautéed crumbs. Season with salt and pepper. Serve with parsley sprinkled over each serving. Serves 8-10.

■ RICE AND CHEESE WITH SUNFLOWER SEEDS

2 c. milk	⅔ c. grated American cheese
1 c. brown rice	¾ c. sunflower seeds, ground
2 tbsp. oil	1 tbsp. soy sauce
¼ tsp. crushed white pepper-corns (optional)	½ c. powdered milk
1 tsp. salt	

Heat 1½ c. milk to simmering in heat-resistant casserole. Add (so slowly that simmering does not stop) rice, oil and peppercorns. Cover and simmer until tender, about 45 minutes. Add salt, ½ of cheese, ½ of sunflower seeds, soy sauce, and ½ c. milk shaken with ½ c. powdered milk. Do not boil after milk or cheese is added. Sprinkle remaining sunflower seeds and grated cheese over top. Cover casserole until cheese is melted. Serves 4.

■ SUNFLOWER SEED-MILLET LOAF

1 c. cooked millet	½ tsp. soy sauce
¼ c. finely chopped green pepper	1 c. whole-wheat bread crumbs
3 tbsp. finely chopped onion	1 c. grated cheese
1½ tsp. salt (optional)	½ c. powdered milk or powdered whey
2 tsp. lemon juice	1 egg
¾ c. ground sunflower seeds	½ c. milk

Combine all ingredients. Bake in oiled loaf pan at 350°, about 1 hour.

Serve hot with mushroom or tomato sauce. Serves 6.

■ PORK SAUSAGE-CORN CASSEROLE

1 lb. pork sausage meat	1 tsp. minced onion
3 tbsp. flour	1 c. whole-wheat bread crumbs
1½ c. milk	1 No. 2 can cream-style corn

Form 4-5 small sausage patties. Brown remaining sausage with onion. Stir in flour (first mixed with little cold milk). Add rest of milk and cook until thickened. Add corn and all but ¼ c. of crumbs. Place in greased casserole. Cover with remaining crumbs, arrange patties on top. Bake 30 minutes at 350°. Serves 4.

■ CURRY APPLE RICE

½ c. soy oil or ¼ c. butter	1 large grated apple
2 c. brown rice	1 c. currants
1 c. celery diced	3 c. consommé
1 c. chopped green pepper	2 tsp. curry powder
½ c. grated onion	

Heat oil or butter and lightly brown rice; remove from oil. In remaining oil, brown celery, green pepper, onion and apple. Drain from oil and add to rice. Blend in currants, consommé, curry powder. Cover tightly and cook over medium to low fire, 45 minutes. Serves 4.

■ PORK CHOP OR HAM CASSEROLE

4 c. pared, sliced potatoes	2 tbsp. bacon fat or butter
1 tsp. salt	2 c. milk
⅛ tsp. pepper	4 shoulder or loin pork chops,
2 tbsp. unbleached white flour	or 1 slice of ham
1 medium onion, sliced	
¼ c. green pepper or parsley, chopped	

Place 2 c. potatoes in 2-qt. baking dish. Sprinkle with half the salt, pepper, flour, onion, green pepper, and bits of butter. Repeat. Add sufficient milk so that it can be seen between the top slices. Place pork chops or ham on top. Bake in moderate oven, 350°, 1-1½ hours. Serves 4.

■ SUKIYAKI

¾ lb. round steak	⅓ c. soy sauce
½ lb. mushrooms	2 tbsp. honey
1 mild onion	1 can chicken bouillon
3 stalks celery	½ lb. young spinach leaves
1 8-oz. can bamboo shoots	

Cut steak diagonally across the grain into very thin slices. Thinly slice mushrooms, onion and celery. Drain bamboo shoots. Brown meat quickly in greased, heavy frying pan. Add all ingredients except spinach. Simmer 10 minutes; add spinach; cook 5 minutes. Vegetables should be crisply tender. Serve with hot seasoned rice. Serves 4.

■ **ITALIAN EGGPLANT**

1 medium eggplant	¼ lb. Mozarella cheese
1 egg, beaten	¼ c. onions, minced
2 tbsp. water	1 c. tomato sauce
½ tsp. salt	¼ tsp. oregano
⅓ c. oil	

Peel and cut eggplant into ¼-inch crosswise slices. Combine egg, water and salt. Dip each slice of eggplant in egg mixture. Sauté slowly in oil until browned on both sides. Place slices of eggplant in casserole with a slice of cheese between and on top. Add onion and oregano to tomato sauce and heat; pour around eggplant. Bake at 375°, until cheese is melted and browned. Serves 4.

■ **SICILIAN SPAGHETTI AND MEAT BALLS**

1 lb. thin whole-wheat spaghetti	3 qts. salted boiling water

Cook spaghetti in rapidly boiling salted water about 8 minutes, or until just tender. Add 2 c. cold water to halt boiling. Drain and serve with sauce and meat balls.

■ **SICILIAN SAUCE**

1 garlic clove, minced	2 cans tomato sauce
1 medium onion, chopped	2 tsp. dried sweet basil
2 tbsp. olive oil or other oil	1 tsp. salt
1 can tomato paste, with 2 cans water added	½ tsp. pepper

Cook garlic and onion slowly in oil a few minutes. Add tomato paste, water and tomato sauce. Mix together and add seasonings. Simmer slowly while making meat balls.

■ **SICILIAN MEAT BALLS**

1 lb. ground beef	1 garlic clove, minced
½ c. dry bread crumbs	1 tsp. salt
2 tbsp. chopped parsley	¼ tsp. pepper
2 eggs	

Mix meat with other ingredients and form into small meat balls. Brown well in oil. Add to Sicilian sauce and cook slowly about 1 hour. Add water if sauce becomes too thick or dry. Serves 6.

■ **LASAGNA**

1 lb. Ricotta or cottage cheese, finely sieved	½ lb. Mozarella or Jack cheese, sliced thin
¾ c. grated Parmesan cheese	1½ lbs. wide Lasagna macaroni

Make Sicilian Spaghetti Sauce, adding 1 lb. ground beef which has been browned in oil.

Cook macaroni about 8 minutes, or until not quite tender. Pour on cold water and drain. Use large, deep square or oblong baking pan, well greased. Cover bottom with thin layer of sauce. Lay in macaroni, allowing ends to hang over edges so they may be folded later. Cover with sauce, add cheese slices, Riccota and sprinkle with grated Parmesan cheese. Repeat procedure until pan is filled. Fold over overhanging macaroni and top with sauce and Parmesan cheese. Bake in 350° oven 30 minutes. Let stand 15 minutes before serving. Serves 6.

■ **MACARONI CUSTARD**

1 heaping c. uncooked macaroni (whole-wheat or soy)	Salt, pepper and paprika
	3 eggs, beaten
1½ c. hot milk	½ c. finely chopped onion
1 c. soft bread crumbs	1½ c. grated Cheddar cheese
¼ c. butter	

Cook macaroni until tender in boiling salted water. Drain. Pour hot milk over bread crumbs, add butter, seasonings and beaten eggs. Add chopped onion and cheese. Put macaroni into buttered pan. Pour cheese mixture over it. Sprinkle parsley on top. Bake 1 hour at 325° in pan of water. Serve with following sauce:

Melt 2 tbsp. butter, add 1 tbsp. flour, 1 can beef bouillon and ½ can water. Add ½ c. mushrooms. Serves 6.

■ **VEGETABLE CASSEROLE AU GRATIN**

1 c. whole-wheat macaroni or soy macaroni	2 c. milk
	1 tsp. salt
2 qts. boiling salted water	¼ tsp. curry powder
1 pkg. frozen mixed vegetables or 2 c. mixed raw vegetables	¼ c. grated Cheddar cheese
	¼ c. buttered whole-wheat bread crumbs
2 tbsp. melted butter or oil	
2 tbsp. flour	

Cook macaroni in boiling salted water about 8 minutes, or until just tender. Pour cold water over and drain well. Cook frozen vegetables as directed, or cook raw vegetables until tender. Make sauce of butter or oil, flour and milk. Add salt, curry powder and cheese. Mix with vegetables and macaroni. Pour into greased 1½-qt. casserole. Sprinkle with more grated cheese and cover with bread crumbs. Bake in 350° oven about 1 hour. Serves 4-6.

■ **SPAGHETTI WITH MEAT SAUCE**

4 c. salted boiling water	½ pkg. whole-wheat spaghetti

Add spaghetti to rapidly boiling water, slowly so that boiling does not stop. Cook about 8 minutes, or until just tender. Pour on cold water to stop boiling and drain well. Serve with Tomato Meat Sauce and grated Parmesan cheese.

■ **TOMATO MEAT SAUCE**

1 tbsp. olive oil	1 tsp. salt
½ lb. ground beef	½ tsp. oregano
2 chopped onions	2 tbsp. finely chopped parsley
1 garlic clove, minced	¼ c. grated Parmesan cheese
1 chopped green pepper	
2 c. tomato purée or 1 c. tomato paste blended with 1 c. water	

Brown beef lightly in oil, with onions, garlic and green pepper. Add tomato purée or paste. Stir in seasonings and cook slowly 10 minutes, stirring occasionally. Before serving add parsley. Pour over spaghetti and top with grated Parmesan cheese. Serves 2-4.

■ **RUMANIAN MEAT AND PEPPERS**

1½ lb. lamb	½ c. boiling water
1½ lb. veal	6 green peppers
4 onions	4 tomatoes
3 tbsp. oil or butter	2 cloves garlic
2 tsp. salt	Few sprigs of parsley
½ tsp. herb seasoning	

Cut meat into cubes. Chop onions fine. Heat oil or butter in a Dutch oven or similar covered cooking vessel. Add meat and onions, brown and season. Add boiling water, cover and cook over low heat about 1½ hours. Cut peppers into thin slices; skin and cut tomatoes in pieces. Crush garlic and snip parsley. Heat oven to 375°. Combine vegetables and meat; bake 15 minutes, covered. Remove lid and cook 15 minutes longer. Serves 8.

■ **VEGETABLE NUT LOAF**

2 c. grated uncooked carrots	2 c. ground peanuts
2 c. chopped celery	2 tbsp. finely chopped parsley
½ c. finely shredded cabbage	1 tsp. minced onion
1 avocada, peeled and mashed	1 tsp. salt
or ½ c. nut butter	¼ tsp. pepper

Mix vegetables together thoroughly; stir in nuts; add parsley, onions and seasoning and press into well oiled loaf pan. Chill. Turn out on platter. Serves 6.

■ **VEGETABLE LOAF**

1½ c. chopped walnuts	4 tbsp. whole-wheat flour
1 small eggplant, peeled and chopped	3 tbsp. oil
2 raw carrots, grated	3 slices toasted whole-wheat bread, crumbed
2 c. finely chopped celery	3 eggs, beaten
3 large onions, minced fine	1 tsp. salt

Mix vegetables together; add flour and oil; mix in crumbs, nuts and beaten eggs. Bake in oiled casserole in 350° oven, 1 hour. Serves 4.

■ **MOCK SAUSAGES**

1 c. cooked long grain rice	1 egg, beaten
1 c. chopped walnuts	1 tsp. salt
▸ 1 c. whole-wheat bread crumbs	¼ tsp. sage
1 finely chopped onion	¼ tsp. pepper

Mix rice and nuts; add crumbs, onion, egg and seasonings. Blend well and form into small patties. Brown lightly in hot oil. Makes about 12 patties.

■ **PIGNOLIA NUT LOAF**

1 egg, beaten	1 small onion, minced
½ c. milk	1 tsp. dehydrated onion soup
1 c. ground pignolia nuts or peanuts	1 c. grated raw carrots
1 c. whole-wheat bread crumbs	½ tsp. salt

Mix together beaten egg and milk; stir in other ingredients and bake in oiled casserole at 350°, 1 hour. Serves 4.

■ **KASHA**

2 c. buckwheat grain, whole or split	1 egg
	½ tsp. salt
Water	2 tbsp. butter

Place buckwheat in ungreased frying pan. Add unbeaten egg and mix well. Place over low heat, stirring constantly until each grain is coated and separated, and mixture looks like a mass of tiny nuts. Place in baking dish, add salt and butter and cover with boiling water. Cover and bake in moderate oven, 350°, 1 hour. Every 20 minutes, add a little water if necessary, to prevent grains from scorching. Repeat until thoroughly cooked. Serve like rice.

■ **MEAT-VEGETABLE PLATTER**

2 pkgs. frozen broccoli or asparagus	1 can condensed cream of chicken soup
Sliced frozen, canned or fresh-cooked meat, or chicken	½ c. Parmesan cheese
	2 tbsp. butter

Arrange crisp-cooked broccoli or asparagus on heat-proof platter. Over the vegetable place thin slices of chicken, ham or lamb. Pour chicken soup over top and sprinkle with cheese. Dot with butter. Place in broiler compartment under low flame and broil until mixture is heated through and bubbly. Serves 6.

■ **VEGETABLE POTPOURRI**

1 c. sliced raw carrots	1 clove garlic, minced
1 c. sliced onions	1 tbsp. finely chopped parsley
1 c. sliced parsnips	2 tsp. salt
1 pkg. frozen peas or 2 c. fresh-cooked peas	½ tsp. celery seed
1 c. whole-wheat bread crumbs	¼ tsp. pepper
¼ c. grated Cheddar cheese	2 tbsp. melted butter
	2 eggs, beaten

Place carrots, onions and parsnips in saucepan and steam or cook in just enough water to cover bottom of pan. When tender, mash and add peas, garlic, seasonings and butter. Stir in beaten eggs and add enough of the bread crumbs to absorb moisture and produce a consistency like dough. Bake in well greased loaf pan at 350°, 30 minutes, or until firm. Sprinkle cheese over top and return to oven until cheese is melted. Serves 6.

■ **TUNA OR CHICKEN CASSEROLE**

2 7-oz. cans or 2 c. tuna or chicken	1 c. diced celery
1 7-oz. can sliced mushrooms	½ c. diced onions
2 cans mushroom soup	1 can cashew nuts
2 c. milk	1 bag potato chips or 2 c. but-
2 cans Chinese crisp noodles or	tered whole-wheat crumbs
2 c. fresh bean sprouts	

Mix together all ingredients except the potato chips or crumbs.
Line a 2-qt. oiled casserole with ½ the potato chips or crumbs.
Pour in mixture and top with remaining crumbs or chips. Bake at
350°, ½ hour covered and ½ hour uncovered. Serves 10.

■ **TOASTED CHEESE-GREEN BEAN CASSEROLE**

3 pkgs. frozen cut green beans	1 c. commercial sour cream
2 tbsp. butter	½ lb. Swiss cheese, grated
2 tbsp. flour	½ c. whole-wheat bread
1 tsp. salt	crumbs, buttered
½ medium onion, grated	

Melt butter in double boiler or over low heat. Stir in flour, salt
and onion. Add sour cream and green beans, which have been
cooked according to directions (about 10 minutes; little or no water
should be left if properly cooked). Pour bean mixture into buttered
casserole. Top with grated cheese and buttered crumbs. Bake in
400° oven, 20 minutes. Serves 6.

■ **CASSEROLE TROPICALE**

6 cooked medium sweet pota- toes	¼ tsp. nutmeg
¼ c. butter	½ c. orange juice
2 medium oranges	¼ c. whole-wheat bread
½ c. honey	crumbs, buttered

Peel and cut potatoes in thin slices. Place a layer in oiled
casserole and dot with butter. Cut oranges into thin slices (leaving
skin on if unsprayed). Top layer of potatoes with orange slices.
Repeat alternate layers until all are used. Mix honey, nutmeg and
orange juice, and pour over all. Top with crumbs and bake covered,
in 370° oven, 30 minutes. Remove cover and bake 10 more minutes
to brown crumbs. Serves 6-8.

■ SQUASH-PEANUT PIE

¼ c. dry bread crumbs	1 small onion, grated
2 lb. fresh, or 1 pkg. frozen yellow squash	1 c. cream
	1 c. chopped Spanish or salted
½ tsp. salt	peanuts
¼ tsp. pepper	8 strips crisp-cooked bacon,
2 tbsp. butter	crumbled

Start oven at 350°. Grease a 9-inch pie pan, or shallow baking dish, and dust lightly with bread crumbs. Cook squash in small amount of salted boiling water until tender and all water disappears. (Cook frozen squash according to package directions.) Mash squash in mixing bowl. Add salt, pepper, butter, grated onion and cream. Mix well. Spoon into crumbed pie pan or baking dish and bake 50 minutes. Before serving, sprinkle top with peanuts and crisp, crumbled bacon. Delicious served with fried chicken. Serves 6.

■ CORN PUDDING

2 tbsp. butter or oil	2 c. cream-style corn
2 tbsp. flour	1 egg
1½ c. milk	1 tbsp. Worcestershire sauce
1 tsp. salt	Buttered crumbs
¼ tsp. mustard	Paprika

Make cream sauce of fat, flour, milk and seasoning. Add corn, egg (slightly beaten), and Worcestershire sauce. Pour into buttered baking dish, cover with crumbs, sprinkle with paprika and bake in moderate oven 350°, 20-30 minutes. Serves 4.

■ BAKED SOYBEANS

1 c. new dried green soybeans	3 c. boiling water
Small ham hock or 1 tbsp. oil	1 small diced onion
⅓ c. molasses	1 tbsp. dry mustard
2 bay leaves	

Soak soybeans in boiling water overnight or several hours. Add other ingredients. If necessary add water to cover. Bring to a boil, lower heat and simmer 2 hours or until tender. Pour into bean pot or baking pan, taste to see if more salt is needed. Cover and bake 1 hour at 325°. Remove cover last 40 minutes if you wish them brown on top. Serves 4.

■ **HAMBURGER CHOP SUEY**

3 large stalks celery	2½ tbsp. cornstarch
1 medium onion	½ tsp. brown sugar
3 tbsp. oil	⅛ tsp. pepper
1 lb. ground beef	2 tbsp. soy sauce
1 beef bouillon cube	2 tbsp. cold water
⅓ c. boiling water	1 pkg. bean sprouts or chop
1 can water chestnuts	suey vegetables

Cut celery into thin slices; chop onion fine; cook in oil in heavy skillet, onions and beef over high heat until cooked through, stirring constantly so that meat does not brown. Add celery and bouillon cube, dissolve in boiling water. Cover tightly and cook 5 minutes longer. Celery will still be crisp, but it should be crisp. While meat cooks, mix cornstarch, brown sugar, pepper, soy sauce and cold water into a smooth paste; add to meat mixture and stir thoroughly. Mix in bean sprouts or vegetables and water chestnuts. Heat thoroughly and serve with steamed rice and more soy sauce, if desired. Serves 6.

■ **OKRA AND TOMATOES**

¼ c. chopped onion	¼ tsp. oregano
1 small garlic clove, minced	½ tsp. salt
2 c. sliced okra	¼ tsp. pepper
2 tbsp. oil	Parsley
2 c. cooked tomatoes	

Brown onion, garlic and okra in oil. Add tomatoes and seasonings. Cook over moderate heat until okra is tender and mixture thickens. Add a little chopped parsley before serving. Serves 4-6.

■ **BAKED CORN CREOLE**

2 c. corn	1 tsp. salt
2 c. tomatoes	Pepper
½ c. minced green pepper	3 tbsp. salad oil or melted but-
2 minced pimientos	ter
1 c. buttered crumbs	

Mix vegetables with half of the crumbs, salt and pepper. Pour into greased casserole, cover with remaining crumbs. Bake in moderate oven, 375°, 30 minutes. Serves 6.

■ CHOW MEIN

1 c. onions, sliced lengthwise	¾ c. mushrooms, canned or fresh
3 tbsp. oil	
1 lb. pork, shrimp or chicken, cut in fine strips	2½ c. celery, sliced thin crosswise
1 can bamboo shoots, drained and cut in fine strips	3 c. fresh bean sprouts

Sauté onions in 1 tbsp. oil until golden; remove. In same pan sauté meat in 1 tbsp. oil until done. In another pan sauté bamboo shoots and mushrooms in 1 tbsp. oil; remove and sauté celery slightly in small amount of oil. Combine above ingredients and add 3 c. fresh bean sprouts. Vegetables must be crisp. Make sauce of 3 tbsp. cornstarch, 6 tbsp. soy sauce, dash of ginger and ¾ c. beef bouillon. Add to meat mixture, stirring carefully so as not to break up bean sprouts. When sauce bubbles, remove from fire and serve with fried noodles, boiled noodles or rice. Serves 6-8.

CHAPTER 5

Cereals

CEREALS are valuable for active, growing children, but should be used sparingly by those who must watch their weight. The cereals to be selected for breakfast should be whole-grain, unprocessed and unrefined. Cereals need not be cooked several hours as was formerly believed. The starch in the grain is digested when heated to only 180°. Heating a long time or at high temperatures decreases the value of the protein and causes partial destruction of the B vitamins. Reheating causes further destruction. Cook only enough for a single meal unless, as in the case of cornmeal mush, you wish to fry it next morning. Brown rice, millet, oats, corn and wheat are the best cereals to serve. All of them are seeds and, for that reason, are very valuable for the E vitamin. Seeds such as nuts, sunflower seeds, sesame, celery seed and seeds of fruits should be eaten raw as frequently as possible, as there is little loss of important nutrients.

HOW TO COOK WHOLE GRAINS

Soak wheat in unprocessed milk when possible before cooking, as more minerals are made available. Add salt just before serving, as it is an enzyme inhibitor. Several methods may be used to cook grains: in double boiler, over direct heat, in deep-well cooker, in pressure cooker, in fireless cooker.

If you wish to use the double boiler, wash 1 c. grain in warm water and place in upper part of double boiler with 2 c. milk and 1 c. water. Have water boiling in lower part of boiler. Place upper part on and cover tightly. Put on simmer burner or lowest heat and cook about 3 hours or until tender. Salt may be added to taste before serving. The boiler may be placed over the pilot light overnight. The proportions are the same if you wish to cook the cereal in a deep-well cooker, but it must cook on low heat all night.

To cook over direct heat: Place 2 c. water or milk in a heavy kettle with a tight-fitting lid. Bring water to boil, or milk to blood temperature. Add 1 c. whole washed grain. Cover tightly, turn fire to simmer, and cook about 2 hours. This must be watched, as the cereal may cook dry and more water be needed. Add only enough water to keep cereal from sticking, and remember to keep flame as low as possible. An asbestos pad may be used if heat cannot be turned low enough.

To cook in pressure cooker, soak wheat in milk overnight; if all liquid is absorbed in the morning, add 1 c. water, cook at 15 lb. pressure 1 hour. For fireless cooker or similar arrangement overnight.

HOW TO COOK MILLET, CORNMEAL AND OATS

Bring to boil 2 c. water. Add 1 c. cereal, stir often until it begins to boil. Turn heat to simmer, cover tightly, cook 10 minutes. Water should be absorbed, cereal soft but not mushy. Salt to taste. Milk may be used instead of water but should not be boiled.

To cook stone-ground cornmeal, put 3 c. water and 2 tsp. salt in kettle, bring to boil. Mix 1 c. cornmeal with cold water to make thin paste. Pour into boiling water. Turn fire to lowest heat. Cover tightly and cook 10-15 minutes, stirring constantly.

Rolled oats should be cooked in only enough water to cover, with salt added to taste, for 3-5 minutes. Never cook to mushy consistency; flakes should retain shape. Do not buy "quick" oats, as additional mangling destroys much of the Vitamin B complex.

BREAKFAST CEREAL

⅔ c. wheat, ⅓ c. whole oats, 1 tbsp. sunflower seeds. Wash, add 2½ c. cold water; bring to rolling boil; steam overnight. Serve with polished rice powder or wheat germ, 1 tsp. to serving. Honey to sweeten.

HOW TO COOK GROUND GRAINS

Cracked Grains, Grits, Meal

Cracked Wheat	To 1 c. cereal add approximately 2 c. cold water and salt. Place in saucepan over fire and stir cereal frequently until it comes to a rolling boil. Cover with tight lid and turn off heat. After standing 20 minutes it will be ready to serve. However, if softer consistency is desired, cover and put over pilot light as soon as rolling boil has been reached. When this method is used for making cornmeal mush there is no lumping. Wheat germ or rice polish may be added to cooked cereal just before serving. (These essential foods have a higher nutritional value uncooked.) Natural grains are an excellent source of Vitamins B_1 and E. These important factors are destroyed by high temperatures: therefore, special attention should be given to the preparation of hot breakfast cereals.
Wheat Grits	
Seven-Grain Cereal	
Steel-Cut Oats	
Rolled Oats	
Cornmeal	
Millet Meal	
Brown Rice Grits	
Wheat Germ & Middlings	
Soy Grits	
Rye Grits	
Barley Grits	
Buckwheat Grits	

■ "SUNSHINE"- CEREAL

2½ c. high protein wheat
1 c. whole-grain barley
1 c. whole-grain rye
1 c. millet seed
1 c. yellow seed corn
1 c. soy flour, sifted

1 c. fresh wheat germ
1 c. shredded coconut
⅔ c. honey
1 c. oil
½ c. water

Grind together in your mill the wheat, barley, rye and millet. Grind corn separately, medium fine. Mix lightly with other ingredients, using fork or your fingers, until small granules are formed, as for pastry dough. Spread on shallow pan and bake until light brown, in 250° oven, tasting to make certain starchy flavor is gone, and avoiding over-cooking which produces scorched taste.

The wheat, barley, rye, millet and corn may be bought pulverized at a health food store if you do not have your own mill.

This cereal can be kept under refrigeration in tightly closed jar.

Chop 1½ c. sunflower seeds to use as a topping, if desired. Serve with milk or cream, or just as is.

FRIED MUSH WITH FRUIT

Cook cornmeal or whole-grain cereal by usual method. When cooked add any of the following:

½ c. dried apricots, softened   pitted and mashed
and mashed   ½ c. applesauce
1 c. prunes cooked or softened,   ½ c. banana, mashed

■ RAW FRUIT PORRIDGE

The night before you plan to use the porridge soak 1 tbsp. rolled oats or rolled wheat in 3 tbsp. milk. The next morning grate whole apple into milk mixture. Add 1 tsp. lemon juice and 1 tbsp. honey. Sprinkle over the top 1 tbsp. grated or chopped walnuts, almonds or other nuts. Other fruit may be used instead of apple.

■ OATMEAL WITH RAW APPLE

In saucepan place 1 c. rolled oats, add approximately 2 c. cold water and ½ tsp. salt. Place over medium fire until the mixture comes to a rolling boil. Cover with tight lid and turn heat to low. After cooking 10 minutes add 2 peeled grated apples and dash of nutmeg. Cover and cook about 5 more minutes. Serve with cream, or yogurt and honey.

NOTE: Apples need not be cooked, but added to the cooked cereal for a hot morning cereal.

CHAPTER 6

Desserts

---

*D*ESSERT can be the crown jewel of a meal. Perhaps it is a ripe melon filled with dewy-fresh blueberries. Or the cake that is your special pride, light and velvety of crumb, festive with frosting.

And is there anything better than homemade ice cream, rich with the eggs and cream, fruit and flavorings you've chosen yourself for their quality and freshness!

Thank goodness we've graduated from the sterile era when desserts were virtually taboo for people who valued natural foods and sound nutrition. We've learned how to adapt time-honored favorites to our way of eating, and in this chapter you will find feathery light cream puffs, custards of delicate texture, a whole parade of cakes, confections and cookies; desserts baked, boiled, frosted, frozen . . . yours is the choice.

CAKES

There are two types of cakes, those made with butter or shortening and those made without, such as sponge cake and Angel Food. Here are some of the abc's of cake-making.

Choose the Right Ingredients:

Fat: It may be butter or vegetable oil. Butter gives the best flavor, so when a recipe specifically calls for it, do not substitute any other shortening.

Sugar: For good nutrition use brown or raw sugar, or honey.

Flavoring: Use the best vanilla and other extracts that you can afford. Try *not* to use the synthetics.

Eggs: Use fertilized eggs when possible and have them a day or two old for cake-making.

Cake Flour: Soft wheat, which has a very high starch content, is most frequently used. The difference between bread and pastry flour is the higher quantity of gluten in bread flour. Gluten is tough and rubbery, and holds the carbon dioxide given off by yeast and baking powder. The more starchy pastry flour does not hold the carbon dioxide so readily and is preferred for cake. Good cake can also be made from freshly ground whole-wheat pastry flour.

Salt: Try to use iodized salt, or salt substitute for those on low salt diet.

Baking Powder: The tartrate type baking powders are best.

Spices: Spices will darken a cake batter as well as add piquant flavor.

Milk: Liquid milk, preferably raw certified milk, is used for most cakes, but evaporated or powdered milk, diluted as per the instructions on the package, may be substituted. When sour milk is called for, a little baking soda is added to neutralize the sourness of the milk.

Cornstarch: Cornstarch may be added to cake flour as follows: remove 2 tbsp. of the flour called for in the recipe and add 2 tbsp. cornstarch, sifting several times. Arrowroot may be substituted for cornstarch.

Have all ingredients at same temperature before mixing batter. Do not over-mix ingredients:

Pans. Bright shiny metal cake tins are best, as they warm quickly and reflect the heat, allowing the cake to brown delicately. Cup cakes and other small cakes should be baked in pans greased on bottom, but not on sides.

Size of pans. Choose cake pans by the amount and type of batter. Angel Food and sponge cakes rise higher than butter cakes. Fruit cake rises little. Pan sizes are given in some recipes, but you may always adapt to the pans you already have.

Never grease pans for Angel Food and sponge cakes.

Spread batter evenly in pans. Cut through with knife to break air bubbles.

Desired oven temperature should be reached before cake is put in to bake. Do not open oven for first half of baking time.

Bake cakes as near to the center of the oven as possible; cookies slightly above center. Do not place one pan directly above another in the oven, but stagger them on oven racks.

Cake is done when (a) top of cake, pressed with fingertips, springs back; (b) cake has separated from sides of pan; (c) cake tester, such as broom-straw, inserted into cake comes out clean.

Invert pans containing butterless cakes such as Angel Food and sponge cake, first running a knife blade around the edges.

Do not ice cake when oven-hot, but while still slightly warm.

■   CAKE PROBLEMS

1. **Cake falls in center:** Could be inaccurate measuring; insufficient baking; too much leavening; too little flour.
2. **Cake small and flat:** Too large a pan or too little leavening.
3. **Cake cracks on top:** Temperature too high, so sides baked quickly and batter rose in center, breaking hardened top.
4. **Heavy soggy layer** on bottom: Could be under-mixing or too hot an oven.
5. **Cake breaks** when removed from pans: Might be because cake was not cooled 10 to 15 minutes before removing from pan, or you waited too long.
6. **Cake runs over sides** of pan: Could be too much batter or too shallow a pan.
7. **Angel food cake** has custard-like layer at bottom: Egg whites were not mixed with ingredients carefully or they were beaten too dry.
8. **Angel food cake falls** out of pan when pan has slightest trace of grease on it: Baking at too high a temperature, or trying to remove it from pan before being sufficiently cooled. Angel food cakes should be baked at 375°; placed in center of oven.

■   WHOLE-WHEAT BUTTER CAKE

½ c. butter	¼ tsp. salt
1 c. raw or brown sugar	3 tsp. baking powder
2 eggs	⅔ c. milk
1 tsp. vanilla	
2 c. pastry whole-wheat flour (measure after sifting)	

Cream butter and sugar until well blended, add eggs and vanilla; mix well.

Sift flour, salt and baking powder together 2 or 3 times. Add dry ingredients alternately with milk to butter mixture. Beat well and pour into 2 greased 8-inch pans. Bake 20-25 minutes at 375°, or moderate oven.

■   SPICE CAKE

½ c. butter	½ c. chopped nuts
1½ c. raw sugar	1 c. seeded raisins
2 egg yolks	1 c. sour milk or buttermilk
2 c. whole-wheat pastry flour (sifted)	1 tsp. soda
1 tsp. baking powder	2 egg whites
½ tsp. each cloves, nutmeg and cinnamon	

Cream butter and sugar together. Add egg yolks and beat well. Mix and sift dry ingredients. Add nuts and raisins to dry ingredients. Add to first mixture alternating with buttermilk, mixed with soda. Mix well and fold in beaten egg whites. Pour into 2 well oiled 8-inch cake pans and bake in moderate oven, 350°, 20-30 minutes. Cool and spread with whipped cream sweetened with brown sugar and maple flavoring.

■ FRUIT CAKE—UNBLEACHED WHITE FLOUR

1½ c. shelled whole Brazil nuts	⅔ c. chopped candied orange
1½ c. walnut pieces	peel
2 c. pitted dates	¼ c. chopped candied lemon
½ c. seedless raisins	peel
¾ c. unbleached white flour	½ c. candied pineapple
1 tsp. baking powder	¾ c. raw sugar or ½ c. honey
1 tsp. vanilla	3 eggs
½ tsp. salt	

Grease bottom and sides of 10 x 5 x 3-inch loaf pan or 2 1-lb. coffee cans. Line with oiled paper. Place Brazil nuts, walnuts, dates, orange and lemon peel, raisins, and pineapple, in large bowl. Measure flour, sugar, baking powder and salt into sifter. Sift over nuts and fruit, mix well. Beat eggs until light, add vanilla, blend into nut mixture. (If honey is used, add to egg mixture.) Batter will be stiff. Spoon into loaf pan or coffee cans. Bake loaf in slow oven at 300°, 3½ hours (in coffee cans, 1¾ hours). Cool in pan for 10 minutes, then turn out.

■ INEXPENSIVE FRUIT CAKE

½ c. butter	½ tsp. cloves
1 c. raw or dark brown sugar	½ tsp. nutmeg
1½ c. unsweetened apple sauce	½ tsp. allspice
3 c. whole-wheat pastry flour	½ tsp. salt
1 c. raisins	½ tsp. vanilla
1 c. nuts	2 tsp. lemon juice
½ tsp. cinnamon	2 tsp. soda

Cream butter and sugar, add applesauce. Sift 1 c. flour over raisins and mix well. Stir into first mixture. Add nuts, spices, salt, vanilla and lemon juice. Mix and sift remaining flour with soda and add to batter. Line loaf pan with oiled paper. Spoon in batter. Bake in slow oven, 300°, 1½ hours.

■ **DEVIL'S FOOD CAKE**

6 tbsp. cocoa	1½ c. brown sugar
2 c. unbleached flour sifted	2 eggs, beaten
¼ tsp. salt	¾ c. butter or oil
1 tsp. soda	1 tsp. vanilla
½ tsp. baking powder	1 c. cold water

Mix cocoa, flour, salt, soda, baking powder, sugar. Add beaten eggs, melted fat, vanilla, and lastly the water. Beat well 2 minutes. Pour batter into greased pans. Bake in moderate oven, 350°, until done, 25-30 minutes. Makes 2 8-inch layers. Spread with any desired frosting.

■ **RICH CHOCOLATE CAKE**

½ c. butter	1 tsp. vanilla
1½ c. brown or raw sugar	2 c. sifted whole-wheat pastry
2 sq. chocolate melted in ½ c.	flour or unbleached white
water	2 tsp. baking powder
2 eggs	½ tsp. soda
1 c. sour milk or buttermilk	

Cream fat and sugar. Add melted chocolate and unbeaten eggs. Beat well. Add liquids and dry ingredients. Beat again until well blended. Turn into two 8-inch greased pans. Bake at 350° about 25 minutes.

Variation—substitute 5 tbsp. carob powder for chocolate. Sour milk may be changed to sweet and eliminate soda and increase baking powder to 3 tsp.

■ **HONEY CHOCOLATE CAKE**

2 c. sifted unbleached cake	¼ c. honey
flour	3 sq. chocolate melted in ¼ c.
1¼ tsp. soda	water
¼ tsp. baking powder	2 eggs, beaten
½ tsp. salt	⅔ c. water
½ c. butter	1 tsp. vanilla

Sift flour, measure and sift again with dry ingredients. Cream butter and honey, adding honey slowly. Add ½ c. flour, beat until smooth, add chocolate and eggs. Add remaining flour alternately with water and vanilla. Beat well. Pour into 2 greased 9-inch layer pans. Bake in moderate oven, 350°, 30-35 minutes.

■ APPLESAUCE CAKE

⅓ c. butter
¾ c. honey
1 beaten egg
2 c. flour
¼ tsp. cloves
½ tsp. nutmeg
¼ tsp. salt

1 tsp. soda and 1 tsp. baking powder
1 c. cold unsweetened apple-sauce
1 c. seedless raisins
½ tsp. cinnamon

Cream shortening, add honey gradually, creaming after each addition. Add egg. Mix and sift together dry ingredients and add alternately with applesauce to the creamed mixture. Fold in raisins. Pour batter into a well greased 8 x 8-inch pan. Bake in moderate oven, 350°, about 45 minutes.

■ CAROB BUTTER CAKE

½ c. butter or shortening
1 c. raw sugar
2 eggs
1 tsp. vanilla
1¾ c. sifted whole-wheat pas-

try flour mixed with ¼ c. carob powder
¼ tsp. salt
3½ tsp. tartrate baking powder
⅔ c. milk

Cream shortening and sugar until well blended. Add whole eggs, mix well. Add vanilla. Sift flour, salt and baking powder together twice. Add dry ingredients alternately with milk. Mix well, pour into 2 greased pans and bake 20 minutes at 375°.

■ SUNSHINE CAKE

6 egg yolks
½ c. brown sugar
¼ c. orange juice
1 tsp. grated orange rind
1 tsp. vanilla
1⅓ c. sifted whole-wheat pastry flour

7-8 egg whites or 1 c. of whites
½ tsp. salt
¾ tsp. cream of tartar
1 c. raw or brown sugar

Beat egg yolks until lemon colored. Gradually beat in sugar, orange juice and grated orange rind. Add vanilla and sifted flour all at once. Beat egg whites and when frothy add salt and cream of tartar. When whites stand up in peaks, gradually add sugar. Fold egg yolk mixture into beaten whites. Bake in an Angel Food pan at 325°, slow oven, 60-65 minutes. When done, invert pan. When cool, cut out.

■ UNCOOKED FRUIT CAKE

1 lb. raisins	1 lb. dates
2 c. walnuts	½ c. cream honey
1 lb. figs	1 tbsp. lemon rind
1 lb. prunes	1 c. ground sunflower seeds
½ c. coconut macaroon, crumbled	

Grind sunflower seeds and then grind dried fruits and walnuts. Mix all ingredients and press into an oiled bread pan. Allow to chill until firm, covered in refrigerator paper or aluminum foil. Slice thin to serve.

■ DATE NO-BAKE FRUIT CAKE

1 c. prunes	½ tsp. almond extract
1 c. date crunchies or chopped dates	3 tsp. vanilla
	1½ c. butter
1 c. dried apricots	1 c. honey
3 c. seedless raisins	1 tsp. cloves
2¼ c. cut citron	2 tsp. cinnamon
1½ c. chopped figs	¼ tsp. ground cardamon
1 c. chopped walnuts or pecans	9½ c. fine graham cracker crumbs
1 c. blanched almonds	
1 c. thick orange marmalade	

Cover prunes with cold water and boil 5 minutes. Drain. Cut into small pieces. Pit and chop dates, or use crystals or crunchies. Cover apricots with boiling water. Let stand 3 minutes. Drain and cut into strips. Cover raisins with boiling water. Let stand 5 minutes. Drain. Slice citron into thin slivers. Combine raisins, figs, dates, prunes, apricots, citron, walnuts, almonds, marmalade, and flavorings. Blend well. Cream butter and beat in honey and spices. Add about half the crumbs and mix well. Add fruit mixture and remaining crumbs. Blend well. Pack in tube pans or casseroles. Chill 4-5 days before cutting. Makes about 7½ pounds.

■ SOY CAKE (WITHOUT WHEAT FLOUR)

3 c. soy flour	4 eggs well beaten
3 tsp. baking powder	⅓ tsp. soda
½ c. brown or raw sugar	½ tsp. salt
1 tsp. almond extract	1 c. cream
⅓ c. orange juice	1 c. milk
½ tsp. vanilla extract	

Sift dry ingredients together, except sugar and soda which are to be blended smoothly with the eggs. Add to egg mixture the orange juice and extracts; then milk and cream. Add sifted ingredients. Bake at 350°, about 25 minutes. This makes a nice loaf cake, finely grained, rich and moist.

■ FRUIT CAKE—WHOLE-WHEAT FLOUR

¼ lb. mixed citron, orange and lemon peel	1 c. butter
½ lb. raisins	2 c. dark brown sugar
¼ lb. diced pineapple	4 eggs
¼ lb. dried apricots	3 c. whole-wheat pastry flour
¼ lb. prunes	1 tsp. salt
1 c. chopped walnuts	2 tsp. baking powder
½ c. hulled sunflower seeds, or chopped pecans or almonds	1 c. concentrated orange juice or other concentrated fruit juice

Be sure all fruits are properly prepared. Plump raisins by washing and placing in covered flat pan in 350° oven for several minutes. Steam apricots and prunes until soft; chop.

Cream together butter and sugar. Beat in eggs. Sift together flour, salt, baking powder and add to butter mixture alternately with fruit juice. Blend in fruits and nuts. Fill 2 or 3 loaf or round cake pans, lined with greased brown paper. Pans should be almost full. Bake in 300° oven 3 hours, or until a toothpick comes out clean. Cool. Brush with brandy if desired. Wrap in freezer paper and store in covered, air-tight container.

■ CAROB SUNSHINE CAKE

3 tsp. baking powder	1 c. raw sugar
1½ c. pastry whole-wheat flour mixed with ¼ c. carob powder sifted several times	3 tsp. vanilla
	Grated rind of large lemon
4 large eggs, separated	⅓ c. water

Have ingredients at room temperature. Sift baking powder with ½ c. flour. Beat egg yolks until light and thick. Add sugar gradually and continue beating. Add flavoring and lemon rind. Add water and 1 c. mixed, sifted flours alternately; then baking powder mixture; lastly, fold in stiffly beaten egg whites. Place in greased tube pan. Bake at 325°, 40-50 minutes. When done, invert pan. When cool, cut out. Frost with whipped cream, if desired; or Carob Frosting.

■   **CHEESE CAKE**

4 eggs, separated	⅔ c. whole-wheat pastry flour
½ tsp. salt or substitute	or unbleached white flour
2 tbsp. lemon juice	1½ tsp. grated lemon rind
1 tsp. vanilla	2 c. cottage cheese
1 tsp. almond extract	1 c. yogurt
1 c. honey	

Beat egg yolks until light and frothy. Add salt, lemon juice, extracts, honey, flour and lemon peel. Beat well, adding small amounts at a time of cottage cheese and yogurt. Pour into unbaked graham cracker shell or crumb-lined spring-form pan. Bake at 325°, 1 hour, or until set. Chill before serving.

■   **PINEAPPLE UPSIDE-DOWN CAKE**

½ c. raw sugar	1¼ c. unbleached white flour
¼ c. butter	¼ tsp. salt
1 beaten egg	2½ tsp. baking powder
1 tsp. vanilla	⅓ c. milk

Cream butter and sugar; add vanilla and egg. Add sifted dry ingredients alternately with milk. In 8 x 8-inch loaf pan, place the following mixture:

1 large can crushed pineapple	2 tbsp. butter
or 1 No. 2 can sliced pine-	½ c. brown sugar
apple, cut in pieces	

Pour cake batter over pineapple mixture and bake in moderate oven, 350°, about 35 minutes.

CAKE FILLINGS AND FROSTINGS

■ RICH CAROB FROSTING

Part 1

⅓ c. raw sugar	2 tbsp. honey
¼ c. cream or top milk	¼ tsp. salt
¼ c. butter	3 egg yolks

Part 2

½ c. carob powder	⅓ c. evaporated milk or cream
¾ c. dried milk	1½ tsp. vanilla

Cook first five ingredients over boiling water until hot, about 3 minutes. Gradually add hot mixture to well beaten egg yolks, blending about 3 minutes. Return mixture to heat and cook until rather thick, about 6 minutes.

Transfer hot mixture to warm mixing bowl. Combine ½ c. dried milk with the carob powder; add alternately with milk to hot mixture. Add remainder of dried milk and enough scalded milk to make good spreading consistency.

■ HONEY-NUT FILLING

½ c. ground walnuts	2 tbsp. orange juice
3 tbsp. honey	Nut butter, or cream cheese

Lightly blend honey and nuts; add orange juice and enough nut butter, or cream cheese to make a soft filling. More orange juice may be necessary in order to make the filling of a consistency to spread.

■ COCONUT FILLING

1 c. fine coconut	1 c. raw powdered sugar
3 tbsp. oil	½ c. non-fat dry milk
Milk, or top cream or soy milk	1 tsp. vanilla

Mix together. Add milk slowly so filling will spread.

■ CAROB FILLING

1 c. non-fat dry milk	½ c. carob powder
⅓ c. honey	½ tsp. vanilla
Light cream	

Mix dry milk and carob powder. Add honey, vanilla and enough cream to spread. Taste for sweetness.

■   **CHEESE NUT FILLING**

1 3-oz. pkg. cream cheese	Ground nuts or fine coconut
½ c. powdered milk	Chopped dates or chopped
⅓ c. honey	dried fruit
Cream	

Cream cheese, honey and powdered milk, add fruit, nuts, coconut or any combination and enough cream to enable filling to spread. Taste for sweetness.

■   **HURRY-UP CAKE FROSTING**

Bake your favorite cake in a square pan. Cut into serving pieces and top with Sweet 'n Tart Cake topping:
Whip 1 c. whipping cream until stiff. Fold in ½ c. commercial sour cream and ¼ c. honey. Delicious over orange or spice cake.

■   **POWDERED MILK FROSTING**

2 tbsp. butter	1 or 2 tbsp. cream or top milk
⅓ c. honey	1 tsp. vanilla
¾ c. powdered milk (spray method)	

Cream butter and honey; add cream and vanilla. Blend in powdered milk, adding more cream or powdered milk to make desired consistency.

■   **CAROB ICING**

2 tbsp. butter	⅓ c. carob powder
¼ c. honey	1 tsp. vanilla
4 tbsp. cream	
¾ c. spray method powdered milk	

Cream butter and honey; add cream and vanilla. Blend in powdered milk and carob powder until of desired consistency.

■   **COCONUT BROWN SUGAR FROSTING**

Mix 5 tbsp. dark brown sugar with 3 tbsp. melted butter and 2 tbsp. cream. Add ⅓ c. fine coconut. Spread on warm cake and place under broiler until bubbly and brown. Nuts may be used instead of coconut.

■ **HONEY-EGG WHITE FROSTING**

1 c. honey   ½ tsp. vanilla or other flavor-
2 egg whites   ing

Heat honey over low fire 8 minutes. Remove from fire, cool. Beat egg whites stiff. Pour honey slowly over whites, beating constantly until thick. Add flavoring. Finely chopped nuts or dried fruits or coconut may be added for different flavor and texture.

■ **CREAM CHEESE FROSTING**

Blend 1 or 2 pkg. (3-oz.) cream cheese with little honey or concentrated fruit juice to a consistency to spread.

CONFECTIONS

■ **FRUIT CONFECTIONS**

You can make a variety of wonderful candies with dried fruits. Put through your food chopper any combinations that you fancy, such as pitted prunes, pitted dates, figs, raisins, apricots, currants, peaches and apples.

Dried prunes, apricots, peaches and pears must stand in boiling water for 5 minutes before using in candy mixtures.

■ **COCONUT FRUIT BARS**

Mix thoroughly together any combination of the above ground dried fruits. Form into strips and roll in finely chopped plain or toasted coconut. Cut in 1-inch strips.

■ **NUT FRUIT ROLLS**

Mix thoroughly together any combination of ground dried fruits. Form into long rolls. Roll in finely ground nuts and cut in 1-inch pieces.

■ **NEOPOLITANS**

Form ground dried apricots into strip about ½-inch thick. Spread with mixture of coconut and honey. Top with ground pitted dates and cut in 1-inch slices.

Creamed or sugared honey is less sticky than the regular and should be used in all candy recipes calling for honey.

■ **STUFFED PRUNES**

Wash large prunes and steam 5 minutes in colander over boiling water. While warm, split open and pit. Stuff with blanched almonds or other nuts, or coconut mixed with honey.

■ **MIXED FRUIT CANDY**

1 lb. dates	½ c. sesame seeds (browned in
1 lb. apricots	soy oil)
½ c. raisins or figs	2 tsp. honey
½ c. almonds	½ c. grated coconut

Grind fruits, nuts and seeds. Mix well. Roll in coconut. Mold in pan and chill. Cut in desired amounts.

■ **SUNFLOWER DATES**

Make paste of ground sunflower seeds, sesame meal, honey, or raw sugar and a few chopped almonds. Pit dates and stuff with mixture.

■ **DATES WITH PEANUT BUTTER**

½ c. smooth or crunchy peanut butter	¾ to 1 c. powdered milk
½ c. strained or cream honey	1 pkg. dates

Combine ingredients and stir well. Pit and stuff dates with mixture.

■ **NUT HONEY CANDY**

Melt 3 tbsp. butter. Add ½ c. honey and mix in enough non-fat dry milk to make a thick mixture. Add ½ c. ground walnuts. Form into a roll, chill and slice.

■ **CANDIED ORANGE PEEL**

Use the peel of 3 large oranges after the juice has been removed from fruit. Cover peel with water to which has been added 1 tsp. salt. Simmer for 30 minutes. Drain and cover with water and simmer until tender. Cut into strips. Drain again and cover with about ¾-1 c. honey. Simmer very slowly until peel is clear (about 45 minutes). Lay on waxed paper and let stand 2-3 days before using. Roll in raw sugar, coconut, chopped nuts or coat with chocolate.

■ FRUIT NUT CANDY

Grind through food chopper 1 c. dates, ½ c. raisins, ¼ c. sunflower seeds, ½ c. nuts. Use fine knife. Shape into balls and roll in fine natural coconut (obtainable at health food stores). Other fruits may be used, or combined with the dates and raisins.

■ WHEAT GERM CANDY

3 c. wheat germ	1 c. blackstrap molasses or
1 c. powdered skim milk	honey
1 c. crunch style peanut butter	1 c. raisins

Add more honey or molasses as required to produce a mixture that will hold together when kneaded. Press in buttered loaf pan and score.

Wheat germ has a raw flavor, so you may want to start with much less, increasing gradually as your family learns to like it.

■ SESAME CANDY

1 c. Turkish sesame-seed cream	¼ c. chopped nuts or seeds
½ c. maple syrup, honey or molasses	4 tbsp. carob powder
	3 tbsp. rice polish
2 tbsp. coconut	2 tbsp. vanilla

Mix well; roll in toasted sesame seeds. Coat with fine coconut. Chill. To toast sesame seeds, stir and toast lightly in heavy skillet.

■ HEALTH CANDY

⅔ c. soy-milk powder	¼ c. honey
⅓ c. carob flour	½ tsp. vanilla
¼ c. butter	

Mix dry ingredients, blend with honey, butter and vanilla. Roll in little balls, place nuts on top or roll in coconut. Keep refrigerated.

■ COCONUT PEANUT BUTTER FUDGE

Mix peanut butter, date granules and powdered or macaroon coconut. Roll between 2 pieces of oiled paper. Slice and serve.

■ FIG PATTIES

Form ground figs into small patties. Place ½ walnut on each pattie.

■ **MOLASSES CRUNCH CANDY**

½ c. blackstrap molasses   1 c. powdered milk
1 c. date crunch or crystals   ½ c. raisins

Turn on oiled paper, sprinkled with powdered milk, and knead until consistency of pie dough. Pat ½-inch thick and cut into small squares.

■ **CAROB HONEY COCONUT CANDY**

Mix ¼ c. carob powder with ½ c. powdered milk and ⅓ c. coconut macaroon or powder. Add just enough liquid honey to form into a roll. Be careful not to add too much honey as it gets sticky. Form into balls the size of a walnut and roll in ground nuts or fine coconut.

■ **COCONUT HONEY MARSHMALLOWS**

Soak 1 tbsp. gelatin (or 1 pkg.) in ¼ c. water. Add 1 c. mild honey, warmed; dissolve gelatin in warm honey. Cool and beat to a light and fluffy consistency, much like whipped cream. Let stand in cool place 24-48 hours. Buy fine coconut from a health food store and toast it lightly in oven. Cut marshmallows into squares or rounds and roll in toasted coconut. Coconut may be colored and not toasted. Marshmallows may be rolled in finely chopped nuts.

■ **PANOCHA FUDGE**

Stir together in saucepan ⅓ c. milk and 1 c. brown sugar, 2 tbsp. butter. Boil 2 minutes; begin to count time when bubbles cover entire surface. Remove from heat, cool thoroughly and add 2 tsp. vanilla, ½-1 c. walnuts, ⅔ c. powdered milk. Stir until smooth and creamy. Turn into buttered pan.

■ **FRESH COCONUT-ALMOND BALLS**

¼ c. cream honey   2 c. fresh shredded coconut
2 tbsp. almond butter   Rice polish
1 tsp. vanilla   Fine-grated dry coconut
¾ c. finely-chopped almonds

Cream honey, almond butter and vanilla. Combine with chopped almonds and fresh coconut. Add enough rice polish to make mixture stiff enough to roll in balls. Roll in balls the size of walnuts, then roll in grated dry coconut. Keep refrigerated. Makes 2 doz.

■ PERFECT HEALTH CANDY

⅔ c. soy flour
¼ c. peanut butter
⅓ c. carob flour
¼ c. rice polish
2 tbsp. bone meal
2 tbsp. dulse (dried seaweed)

2 tbsp. wheat germ
2 tbsp. brewer's yeast
2 tbsp. vegetable oil
Enough cream honey to make
  of consistency to knead.

Knead well. Pack on oiled glass pie dish. Press chopped nuts over top. Chill and cut in squares.

COOKIES

Cookies should contribute as many nutrients as possible, and not be composed largely of sugar.

■ **KINDS OF COOKIES**

I. Butter Cookies

Rolled	Molded
Dropped	Bar
Pressed	Filled

II. Meringue Cookies

Kisses	Macaroons

III. Refrigerator Cookies

Plain	Checkerboard
Ribbon	Pinwheel

Cookies are mixed in the same way as cakes and contain approximately the same ingredients.

Over-mixing and handling of dough develops the gluten in the flour and causes toughness.

Nuts and fruits should be first sifted lightly with flour to keep particles separated.

1. *Rolled cookies*—are made from stiff dough, rolled thin. Before baking, they are cut into desired shapes. Cut as close together as possible to get all you can from the first rolling.
2. *Dropped cookies*—are made from soft dough, dropped from a teaspoon on a lightly greased cookie sheet and baked quickly in the oven. Leave about 2 inches between cookies.
3. *Molded cookies*—are made from stiff dough, rolled with the hands into balls or long, pencil-thick rolls; then flattened or shaped as directed. Chill before molding.
4. *Bar cookies*—are made from stiff batter put into a flat pan and cut into bars after baking.
5. *Pressed cookies*—are made of dough that is slightly stiffer than drop cookies. It should be soft enough to hold its shape. Chill first.
6. *Filled cookies*—are rolled cookies, put together with fruit or nut filling.
7. *Meringue cookies*—are made from flour and sugar carefully folded into stiffly beaten egg whites. Other ingredients may be used, such as coconut, almond paste or other ground nuts.
8. *Refrigerator cookies*—are made from stiff, rich dough. They are shaped into a long, thick roll, chilled and kept in refrigerator, then baked as needed. They are sliced thin with a sharp knife before baking.

It is best to grease cookie sheet very lightly.

Most people over-bake cookies, not realizing that they continue to bake after removal from oven.

Take cookies from oven while still soft.

■ BIG FOUR COOKIES

⅓ c. butter
⅓ c. sugar, brown or raw
½ c. unsulphured molasses
1 egg
¼ c. dry skim milk solids
1 c. sifted flour
¼ tsp. each nutmeg and cinnamon

½ tsp. salt
¼ tsp. soda
1 tsp. baking powder
1 c. grated carrots or grated raw sweet potatoes
¼ c. raisins
1¼ c. rolled oats

Cream together butter, sugar, molasses and egg. Sift together dry skim milk solids, flour, spices, salt, soda and baking powder; stir into creamed mixture. Add grated carrot or sweet potato, raisins, and rolled oats; mix well. Drop by level tablespoons on a lightly greased cookie sheet. Bake in a moderately hot oven, 400°, 10 minutes. Makes about 6 dozen.

■ CHOCOLATE-CHIP HONEY COOKIES

1¼ c. whole-wheat flour
¾ tsp. salt
½ tsp. soda
1 tsp. vanilla
⅓ c. butter or oil

½ c. honey
1 beaten egg
1 pkg. chocolate bits
1 c. chopped nuts, if desired

Sift flour, salt and soda together. Cream shortening and add vanilla, honey and egg. Add dry ingredients. Mix in chocolate chips and nuts. Beat well. Drop by teaspoon on ungreased cookie sheet. Bake in oven 375°, about 12 minutes. Makes about 50 cookies.

■ DELICIOUS CRUMB COOKIES

Sift together 1½ c. flour, 1 tsp. baking powder, ½ tsp. salt. Add 1 c. brown sugar. Mix well. Mix together 5 tbsp. butter and 2 egg yolks, slightly beaten. Add to dry ingredients and mix until crumbly. Pack into 8 x 12-inch baking pan.

Beat 2 egg whites, slowly add 1 c. brown sugar. Blend thoroughly. Add 1 c. chopped nuts and 1 tsp. vanilla. Spread on top of crumb mixture. Bake in oven 325°, 20 minutes. Cut in squares.

■ **MOLASSES NUT COOKIES**

1 c. butter	2 tsp. soda
1½ c. unsulphured molasses	2 tsp. cinnamon
¼ c. brown sugar	1½ tsp. ginger
4 c. sifted all-purpose flour	½ tsp. cloves
1½ tsp. salt	1 egg
⅔ c. finely chopped nuts	1 pkg. chocolate chips

Melt butter in saucepan large enough for mixing cookies. Stir in unsulphured molasses and sugar; cool. Sift together flour, salt, soda, and spices. Mix in small amount of flour; beat in egg. Blend in remaining flour, nuts, and chocolate chips. Chill dough about 2 hours. Shape into 1-inch balls. Place on ungreased cookie sheet about 2 inches apart. Bake in moderate oven, 350°, 15 minutes. Makes about 3 dozen

■ **SOFT MOLASSES DROP COOKIES**

1 c. butter or oil	½ tsp. soda
½ c. brown sugar	1½ tsp. ground ginger
1 egg beaten	¼ c. top milk and 1 tsp. vine-
¼ c. unsulphured molasses	gar
¼ tsp. salt	½ c. raisins or currants
2¼ c. whole-wheat pastry flour	

Combine butter and sugar; gradually mix in egg and molasses, mixing until fluffy. Sift together flour, soda, salt and ginger. Add vinegar to milk and mix all ingredients thoroughly. Add raisins and drop by teaspoonfuls on greased cookie sheet. Bake about 10 minutes at 350°. Makes 4 dozen.

■ **GINGER SNAPS**

1 c. dark brown or raw sugar	2 tsp. soda—1 tsp. in molasses,
¾ c. butter or oil	1 tsp. in flour
2 eggs	½ tsp. cloves
½ c. blackstrap molasses or	½ tsp. cinnamon
sorghum	1½ tsp. ginger
¼ tsp. salt	½ tsp. nutmeg
3 c. whole-wheat flour	

Mix in order given. Chill mixture in refrigerator. Roll in teaspoon-size balls. Roll balls in raw or white sugar. Place on greased cookie sheet (they flatten out as they bake). Bake 325°, 10-15 minutes. Makes about 80 cookies.

■ CARROT-OATMEAL COOKIES

2 c. sifted pastry whole-wheat flour	1 c. rolled oats
1 tsp. baking powder	1 c. raisins
¼ tsp. soda	½ c. butter or oil
½ tsp. salt	1 c. brown or raw sugar
¼ tsp. nutmeg	2 beaten eggs
¼ tsp. cinnamon	⅓ c. milk
	1½ c. grated raw carrot

Sift flour, measure and sift with baking powder, soda, salt and spices. Add rolled oats, raisins. Cream fat and sugar; add eggs, milk and carrots; then add to first mixture. Mix well. Drop by teaspoon onto a greased baking sheet. Bake 15 minutes at 350°. Makes about 5 dozen.

■ HONEY PEANUT BUTTER COOKIES

½ c. butter	½ tsp. salt
½ c. honey	1¾ c. pastry whole-wheat flour
½ c. dark brown or raw sugar	or white flour
1 egg, well beaten	¼ c. wheat germ or ¼ c. flour
½ c. chunky peanut butter, not homogenized	½ tsp. soda

Cream butter, honey, and sugar until fluffy. Add egg, peanut butter, and salt. Stir in flour sifted with soda and wheat germ. Form into small balls. Place on greased cookie sheet. Press with fork. Bake in moderate oven 350°, 8-10 minutes. Makes about 5 dozen.

■ ORANGE PECAN REFRIGERATOR COOKIES

1 c. butter or oil	2 tbsp. orange juice
½ c. brown sugar	2¾ c. flour (unbleached white)
½ c. raw sugar	¼ tsp. soda
1 beaten egg	¼ tsp. salt
1 tsp. grated orange peel	½ c. chopped pecans

Cream butter, add sugars until light and fluffy. To creamed mixture, add egg, orange peel and orange juice. Add sifted flour, soda, salt and pecans. Shape into a roll, store in refrigerator several hours. Remove; slice very thin. Bake on ungreased cookie sheet 400°, 10 minutes, or until lightly browned. Cool. Makes about 6 dozen.

■ **COCONUT CRISPIES**

1 c. butter or ¾ c. oil	¼ tsp. salt
1 c. dark brown sugar	½ tsp. soda
½ c. honey	½ tsp. baking powder
2 eggs	1 c. coconut
1 tsp. vanilla	2 c. rolled oats
2 c. pastry whole-wheat flour	1 c. bran flakes (optional)
½ c. wheat germ	

Mix in order given. Form in balls the size of a walnut, place on greased baking sheet. Bake at 350°, 10-12 minutes. Makes about 8 dozen.

■ **BREAD-DATE COOKIES WITH HONEY**

3 eggs	1 c. chopped dates (pack
1½ c. soft bread cubes (pack	tightly)
tightly)	1 tbsp. grated orange rind or 1
½ c. chopped nutmeats	tsp. vanilla extract
1 c. honey	

Beat eggs until thick and very light, about 5 minutes. Gradually dribble in ½ c. honey. Mix balance of honey with dates, nutmeats, bread cubes, and grated orange rind. Bake in shallow 10 x 7-inch greased pan. Bake in 350° oven, 30-35 minutes. Cool. Cut into squares as cookies or break into small pieces. Place in sherbet glasses and top with whipped cream. Makes 20 squares or 6 large desserts.

■ **CHINESE TEA COOKIES**

2 tbsp. butter	⅛ tsp. baking soda
2 tbsp. oil	2 tbsp. orange juice
1 c. brown sugar, packed	1 c. whole-wheat pastry flour
Finely snipped crystallized gin-	1 c. chopped sun-dried dates
ger	

Cream butter with oil until light and fluffy, gradually adding sugar. Combine baking soda, orange juice; add to creamed mixture. Stir in flour; beat well. Add dates. Drop by tablespoonfuls on greased cookie sheet. Top each cookie with a few pieces of ginger. Bake about 8 minutes or until delicately browned, in 400° oven. Makes about 3 dozen.

■ DATE BARS

Filling

1½ c. dates, chopped, or crystals·	⅔ c. water
¾ c. raw sugar or ½ c. honey	2 tbsp. lemon juice

Combine above and cook over low heat until thick. Cool.

Crust

1½ c. whole-wheat pastry flour	1 c. raw sugar or ⅔ c. honey
1¼ c. rolled oats	½ tsp. salt
¾ c. butter or oil	1 egg, well beaten

Sift flour, then measure again. Add sugar or honey, rolled oats and salt. Mix well. Cut in shortening with pastry blender or 2 knives, to consistency of coarse crumbs. Add egg. Spread half of mixture in 9 x 11 x 2-inch oblong pan. Cover with date filling and spread remaining half of mixture over filling. Bake in hot oven, 400°, 20-25 minutes. Cool and cut into bars. Makes 24. Very good.

■ DATE MACAROONS

2 egg whites	¾ c. raw sugar
¼ tsp. salt	1⅓ c. shredded coconut
½ tsp. vanilla	1 c. chopped sun-dried dates

Beat egg whites until stiff, add salt and beat in sugar ¼ c. at a time. Add vanilla and fold in coconut and dates. Drop by teaspoonfuls on baking pan which has been greased with unsalted fat. Bake at 275°, 20-30 minutes. Makes about 2 dozen.

■ DATE COOKIES

3 eggs, beaten	1 tsp. soda
2 c. brown sugar	2 c. whole-wheat pastry flour, sifted
¾ c. butter	
⅔ c. warm water	1 lb. sun-dried dates, cut fine
½ tsp. salt	1 c. pecan nut meats

Mix in order given. Drop by teaspoon on greased cookie sheet. Bake at about 425°. Makes about 36 cookies.

■ **SPICY PUMPKIN COOKIES**

¼ c. oil	½ tsp. salt
1 egg	1¼ tsp. cinnamon
½ c. pumpkin (cooked)	⅛ tsp. ginger
½ c. brown sugar	¼ tsp. nutmeg
1 c. sifted all-purpose flour	½ c. raisins or dates
2 tsp. baking powder	½ c. chopped nuts

Place first 3 ingredients in blender or mixer, mixing well. Sift all dry ingredients together. Add liquid mixture to dry ingredients, mixing well. Add raisins and nuts, mix in. Drop from teaspoon on greased baking sheet. Bake 15 minutes at 400°. Makes about 2 dozen.

■ **DELICIOUS FILLED COOKIES**

Filling

> 1 c. dates or chopped softened apricots. Cook 5 minutes with ¼ c. water and 2 tbsp. honey

Cookies

1 c. butter	3 c. whole-wheat pastry flour
1½ c. raw or brown sugar	3 tsp. baking powder
2 eggs, beaten	½ tsp. salt
3 tsp. vanilla	

Cream butter and sugar, add eggs and vanilla. Sift flour with baking powder and salt. Add to first mixture. Will make a stiff dough. Chill. Roll out small amount at a time so dough will not get warm. Cut with daisy-type cookie cutter. Half of cookies must have centers cut out with a thimble. Make date or apricot filling. Sweeten filling as desired. ¼ c. chopped walnuts may be added to filling. Place ½ tsp. filling on each cookie. Press on top of each a cookie with cut-out hole. Press just around edge. Bake 10-12 minutes, at 350°. Makes 4-5 dozen.

■ **CAROB NUT BROWNIES**

¾ c. sifted whole-wheat flour	½ c. honey
1 tsp. baking powder	½ c. carob powder
½ tsp. salt	2 tbsp. dry milk
2 eggs, beaten	1 tsp. vanilla
½ c. oil	1 c. chopped nuts

Sift flour with baking powder and salt. Beat eggs and blend with oil and honey. Stir into flour. Mix carob powder with dry milk, add to cookie mixture. Stir in vanilla and nuts. Batter will be stiff. Spread in 9-inch square baking pan which has been well oiled and floured. Bake at 350°, 30 minutes. Cool and cut in squares. Keep brownies in covered jar.

■ **WHOLE-WHEAT DOUGHNUTS**

2 eggs	⅔ c. sour cream or buttermilk
1 tsp. salt	1 tsp. soda
1 c. brown sugar	3 c. whole-wheat flour

Beat eggs until light; add salt and brown sugar; beat again until thick and smooth. Mix soda with buttermilk or sour cream. Add flour until dough is of consistency to handle. Roll on floured board, cut with doughnut cutter and fry in deep fat. Drain on brown paper.

■ **UNBAKED APPLE COOKIES**

½ c. butter	3 c. rolled oats
1½ c. honey	1 c. chopped nutmeats, or
4 tbsp. carob powder	grated coconut
1 c. peeled and grated apple	1 tsp. vanilla
¼ tsp. salt	

Melt butter, add honey, carob powder, grated apple and salt. Boil 1 minute. Remove from heat, add rolled oats, nuts and vanilla. Blend well. Drop by teaspoonfuls onto an oiled cookie sheet or paper. When cool, roll in powdered milk.

■ **NO-BAKE PEANUT BUTTER COOKIES**

3 c. rolled oats	¼ tsp. salt
½ c. milk	1 tsp. vanilla
½ c. peanut butter	Chopped peanuts, or grated
1½ c. honey	coconut

Lightly toast the rolled oats in a 350° oven. In a pan mix milk, peanut butter, honey and salt and bring to a boil. Pour over toasted oats. Add vanilla. Mix lightly until blended. Drop by teaspoonfuls on oiled paper. Roll in finely chopped peanuts.

OTHER DESSERTS

Fruits: Lucky you, indeed, who grow your own fruits and can pick them at their sun-ripe best, brim-full of the natural sugars, vitamins, minerals and cellulose that make fruit such a wonderful and essential food.

Next best, of course, is fruit from organic gardens and orchards. There are many reliable ones which will ship on order if you cannot locate one within driving distance of your community.

Good color usually means good flavor in fruits and berries, although a little green on an orange skin does not necessarily mean it isn't ripe. Citrus fruits should be weighty to the hand, indicating full juice and plump meats.

Most fresh fruits should be chilled before serving. Don't wash berries before storing them; spread them loosely on a plate or pie pan, or pack loosely into a covered jar. Other fruits should be washed quickly and lightly. Never allow them to stand in water as the sugar and vitamins C and B dissolve and are lost.

Frozen fruit, organically grown, is almost as good as fresh. Try serving it just before all the frost has melted.

Unsulphured dried fruits are excellent, too. Steam dried fruits to plump and soften. Last on the list come the canned fruits. Use those canned without sugar and try to avoid those in heavy syrups, since they contain undesirable glucose and sugar.

When you cook fruit, use a small amount of water and cook in the shortest possible time, avoiding contact with copper or iron.

Cheese, that ancient and honorable product, comes in a fascinating variety of kinds and flavors. Get to know the character of the fine Camemberts, Rocqueforts, Cheddars and all the rest, and then team them with the fruits for which they have an affinity. There's no better dessert to be had, as gourmets have known through the ages.

The recipes in this section should be your guide to all sorts of other combinations and adaptations. It's half the fun to take a recipe and with a touch of this and a dash of that, make it your own.

■ **FROZEN FRESH FRUIT**

Fruits suitable to freeze and serve frosted are: pears, peaches, plums, grapes, apricots, nectarines, berries, sections of oranges or grapefruit, wedges of pineapple, melon balls.

Wash fruit, removing any blemishes. Place fruit on serving dish and put in deep freeze or in ice cube part of your refrigerator for 24 hours. Bring to table at the beginning of the meal. Used as a centerpiece, or individual place arrangement, the frosted fruit is most attractive. Pass assorted cheese to eat with the "centerpiece" at dessert time.

■ **FRESH PEACH OR APRICOT PURÉE**

Wash, peel and purée in blender or food mill fully-ripened fresh peaches or apricots. Sweeten to taste with honey. The fruit must be blended and honey-sweetened quickly to prevent discoloration. Pour peach or apricot purée into ice cube trays, using dividers. Freeze for future use. Good as basis for refreshing salads or beverages.

■ **FRESH UNCOOKED APPLESAUCE**

3 red-skinned apples (un-sprayed)	**1 qt. water**
1 tbsp. lemon juice	**¼ tsp. cinnamon or nutmeg**
	¼ c. honey or more to taste

Thinly slice cored, peeled (or unpeeled) apples into water to which lemon juice has been added. Let stand 15 minutes to prevent discoloration. In blender combine spice and honey with half the apple slices. Run blender to mix, adding balance of apples until all have been blended to a smooth sauce. Chill before serving.

Uncooked applesauce may also be prepared by using a medium grater instead of blender.

■ **FRESH FRUIT DESSERTS**

Place strawberries, red raspberries or sliced peaches in sherbet glasses. Top with thick sour cream, yogurt or yogurt mixed with cottage cheese. Dribble honey over fruit if more sweetening is desired.

Fresh pineapple, mandarin orange slices, grapefruit slices and blue or red seeded grapes make another good combination.

■ **MIXED FRUIT COMPOTE**

Mix 2 c. each cherries, canned or fresh apricots, and pine-apple pieces with 1 medium sliced banana. Place in sherbet glasses. Sprinkle with powdered coconut or coconut macaroon. Serves 6.

■ **BAKED APPLES**

Select apples of uniform size; wash and core. Peel down ¼ way. Put in shallow pan. Fill cored center with any of the following: currants, chopped dates, raisins, nuts, mixture of honey and cinnamon, maple sugar, first-run molasses, nut butter or nut meal. Bake at 375°, 60 minutes or until apples are tender.

■ **BROILED APPLES**

Select smooth red apples, core and cut in half or in thick slices. Arrange on broiler pan, sprinkle with cinnamon, brush with butter or oil, and broil until tender.

■ **DRIED STEAMED FRUIT**

Wash dried fruit and soak ½ hour with very little water. Put in sauce pan with tight fitting lid. Add ½ as much water as fruit and cook over low fire 40-60 minutes. Sugar need not be added, but if fruit is too tart, some honey may be dribbled over.

■ **APPLE-CHEESE DESSERT**

Cut off a wedge of soft, creamy, robust Port du Salut. Add a quartered apple placed back in round shape. Add a few corn chips or soy crackers that have been broiler-toasted.

■ **CHEESE-PEAR-PUMPERNICKEL DESSERT**

Let a wedge of Brie stand until soft. Serve with chilled pear. Add thin slices of rye or pumpernickel bread or crackers.

■ **PRUNE WHIP**

1 c. sieved cooked prunes	**Honey to taste**
½ lemon, juiced	**2 stiffly beaten egg whites**

Mash or put through sieve enough cooked prunes to make 1 cup. Add to this juice of ½ lemon and dribble in enough honey to sweeten to taste. Fold in egg whites. Serve thoroughly chilled. Any fresh, or dried fruit pulp may be made this way. Serves 4.

■ PINEAPPLE BAVARIAN CREAM

1 pkg. unflavored gelatin	2 tbsp. honey
¼ c. cold water	¼ tsp. salt
1 can (1-lb. 4-oz.) crushed pine-apple	1½ c. whipped dry skim milk
	1 pt. strawberries

Soften gelatin in cold water; dissolve over boiling water. Drain syrup from pineapple; measure syrup; add water if needed, to make 1 cup. Combine honey and salt in medium sized bowl; stir in syrup mixture and dissolve gelatin. Chill until mixture thickens and begins to set; then beat with rotary beater until frothy. Fold whipped milk and drained pineapple into frothy gelatin mixture. Lightly oil 1-qt. mold. Pour dessert into mold. Chill until firm. Unmold; serve with sliced strawberries. Serves 4.

■ MELON MEDLEY

Peel a ripe honeydew or Persian melon, or cantaloupe and slice in rings 1-inch thick. Remove seeds from centers of rings and arrange on individual dessert plates. Fill with mixture of fresh pineapple, cut in chunks, and red or black raspberries. Sprinkle with flaked coconut.

Variations—Fill rings with pineapple or lime sherbet and top with chopped candied ginger; or fill with crushed pineapple or berries blended with yogurt; or combine ¼ c. powdered coconut with 1 c. whipped cream and ⅓ c. flaked almonds, filling rings and garnish with shredded pineapple. A large melon should serve 4 and is a delightful main course for a summer lunch.

■ APPLE DELIGHT

Shred 2 medium unpeeled apples, which you have carefully cored. Blend into apples 1 tsp. honey, 1 tsp. lemon juice and ¼ c. finely chopped dates or raisins. Serve in sherbet glasses, topped with grated coconut. Serves 2.

Custards, puddings and the like are infinitely adaptable to your own whim and taste. Serve them plain, adorn them with sauces and creams, garnish them with fruits and nuts; but first be sure of your basic recipe and procedure. You may substitute soy milk for regular milk.

■ **CLASSIC CUSTARD**

2 c. milk	**⅛ tsp. salt**
3 whole eggs or 4 egg yolks	**½ tsp. vanilla**
2 tbsp. honey	

Heat milk in upper part of double boiler, keeping water in lower part just below boiling point. Beat whole eggs or yolks with honey and salt; pour in hot milk, stirring until blended. Return to double boiler and cook gently, stirring constantly until mixture coats spoon. Add vanilla. Chill. Serves 4.

This soft custard is delicious poured over fresh fruits or gelatins. It is a rich basis for ice cream made in a regular freezer.

■ **FLOATING ISLAND**

Use Classic Custard recipe, but substitute 1 whole egg and 2 egg yolks. Chill in serving bowl. Beat remaining 2 egg whites with 2 tbsp. sugar, maple sugar or honey. Drop by spoonfuls on custard and chill thoroughly. Serves 4.

■ **BAKED CUSTARD**

1 qt. milk	**¼ tsp. salt**
¼ c. honey	**4 eggs**
¼ c. chopped pecans or pis-	
tachios, if desired	

Butter 8 individual custard cups. Spoon about 1 tbsp. honey into each cup; add chopped nuts, if desired. Heat milk to just below scalding point. Stir in any remaining honey and salt. Beat eggs in large bowl and gradually add milk mixture. Strain and pour into custard cups. Set cups in shallow pan of hot water, with water coming about ⅔ way up sides of cups. Bake in 325° oven about 50 minutes, or until knife inserted in center of custard comes out clean. Serve in cups, warm or cold. Serves 8.

Variation—Substitute carob syrup for honey. If you wish to unmold, use 5 eggs in custard mixture instead of 4.

■ **TOP-OF-STOVE CUSTARD**

Mix 1 beaten egg with 1 c. milk, 1 tsp. honey, ¼ tsp. vanilla, ½ tsp. salt. Pour in 2 custard cups. Place in pan of water so water comes up ⅔ way on cups. Sprinkle nutmeg over custard. Place tight lid over top of pan and cook over low fire 10-15 minutes, until point of knife comes out clean. Custard will cook after removing from fire, so do not over-cook. Chill. Serves 2.

Custards curdle when cooked at too high temperatures. If mixture begins to curdle, remove from fire, set in cold water and beat vigorously to redistribute particles of egg and milk solids.

■ CUSTARD RICE PUDDING

2 c. milk	2 eggs, beaten
1½ c. cooked brown rice	½ c. raisins
¼ tsp. salt	¼ c. honey
½ tsp. nutmeg	

Heat milk to near-scalding. Add washed raisins, turn heat low and cook 15 minutes. Add rice, honey, sugar and salt. Stir in beaten eggs. (Add a little hot pudding to eggs before combining with rest of pudding.) Pour in casserole, sprinkle nutmeg on top. Bake at 325° until it thickens; be careful not to bake too long. Serves 6.

■ PALM SPRINGS RICE PUDDING

1 c. brown rice	1 c. milk
3 c. water	1 c. pitted, chopped sun-dried
½ tsp. salt	dates

Wash rice thoroughly and cook in salted water about 20 minutes. Turn into double boiler, add milk and cook until liquid is absorbed. With a fork, lightly stir in dates. Let stand 5 minutes and serve warm with cream. This pudding is also delicious with a fruit sauce. Serves 4.

■ INDIAN PUDDING

2 c. milk	½ tsp. ginger
3 tbsp. cornmeal	½ tsp. cinnamon
1 egg, beaten	¼ tsp. salt
1 tbsp. unsulphured molasses	½ tsp. vanilla
¼ c. raw sugar	½ c. sun-dried dates

Place milk in upper part of double boiler with cornmeal, beaten egg, molasses and raw sugar. Add ginger, cinnamon and salt. Stir frequently until milk thickens; remove from fire, add vanilla and dates. Serve hot with cream. Serves 4.

■ WHEAT HONEY NUT PUDDING

1 c. wheat cooked in upper part of double boiler until tender. Do this the day before you intend to use it. Grind in a food grinder. To wheat mixture add ½-¾ c. sliced or chopped walnuts. Sweeten to taste with honey. Serve with top milk or cream. Serves 2.

■ **RICE CREAM TROPICALE**

1 c. cooked brown rice
1 c. whipped cream or
  whipped powdered milk
1 c. shredded drained pineapple

Juice and grated rind of ½
  lemon
½ tsp. vanilla

Fold whipped cream into cooked rice; blend lemon juice and vanilla with pineapple and stir gently into rice mixture. Heap into 6 sherbet glasses, chill and top with coconut just before serving. Serves 6.

■ **RICE WITH HONEYED MERINGUE**

3 tbsp. unbleached white flour
2 c. milk
3 egg yolks, beaten

1 tsp. vanilla
1½ c. cooked brown rice

Mix flour with just enough milk to make smooth paste. Blend with egg yolks, milk and rice; stir in vanilla. Pour into greased baking dish and bake at 325°, 20 minutes.
Honeyed Meringue: Beat remaining 3 egg whites until stiff; warm 2 tbsp. honey and fold into egg whites. Pile meringue on pudding, return to oven for a few minutes, to brown meringue. Serves 6.

■ **HONEY STEAMED PUDDING**

¼ c. butter
½ c. honey
1 egg, well beaten
1 c. milk
2¼ c. sifted flour (unbleached
  white or whole-wheat)

3½ tsp. baking powder
¼ tsp. salt
½ tsp. vanilla

Cream butter, add honey gradually and well beaten egg. Add sifted dry ingredients and milk alternately. Add vanilla. Fill buttered individual molds or custard cups ¾ full. Cover loosely with wax paper held in place with a rubber band. Place molds in a steamer for 30 minutes. Test with a toothpick. Serve hot. Makes 12 small molds.

■ **APPLE CRUMBLE**

8 tart apples
1 tbsp. cinnamon
½ c. water

1 c. brown sugar
¾ c. unbleached white flour

Peel and core apples; cut in thin slices and arrange in buttered 1½-qt. casserole. Sprinkle with cinnamon, adding more if desired. Sprinkle water over apple mixture. Work brown sugar and flour together with fingers until crumbly. Spread over apples and bake uncovered at 375°, about 45 minutes, or until apples are tender. Serves 8.

■ VANILLA PUFF

2 pkg. unflavored gelatin
½ c. milk, cold
3½ c. milk, heated to just below scalding
3 egg yolks, beaten
1 c. raw sugar or ½ c. honey
3 egg whites, beaten stiff
2 tsp. vanilla

Soften gelatin in cold milk. Combine with heated milk in top of double boiler. Combine beaten egg yolks with sugar or honey and add to gelatin mixture. Cook, stirring constantly until creamy and smooth. Remove from heat; fold in beaten egg whites and vanilla. Chill. Serves 6.

■ CHOCOLATE MOUSSE

1 pkg. unflavored gelatin
¼ c. water
1 pt. milk
1 square unsweetened chocolate, slivered, or 3 tbsp. cocoa or carob powder
⅔ c. raw sugar
2 egg yolks, beaten
2 egg whites, beaten stiff
1 tsp. vanilla

Soften gelatin in cold water. Heat milk in top of double boiler with slivered chocolate or cocoa, until mixture blends; do not bring to boil. Stir in beaten egg yolks and sugar, stirring constantly until creamy and smooth. Add gelatin, fold in egg whites and vanilla. Chill until set. Serve with cream. Serves 4.

■ CREAMY FRUIT COMPOTE

2-3 fresh pears, sliced
1 c. each sliced bananas, pineapple and oranges
½ c. walnuts or other nuts
1 egg, beaten
1 c. table cream or yogurt
1 tbsp. honey
Nutmeg or coriander

Prepare fruit and mix in bowl in which it will be served. Combine remaining ingredients and pour over fruit. Refrigerate 2-3 hours. Sprinkle with nutmeg or coriander. Serves 6.

■ **YOGURT-FRUIT DESSERT**

1 c. yogurt	1 c. diced raw apples, pine-
¼ c. uncooked rolled oats	apple or banana
6 tbsp. honey	¼ c. orange juice
½ c. raw cashew nuts	½ c. whipped cream
1 tbsp. lemon juice	

Mix yogurt with rolled oats and honey. Blend and place in refrigerator overnight. An hour before serving, mix in remaining ingredients. Serves 4.

■ **COCONUT CHEESE CAKE—UNBAKED**

1 tbsp. unflavored gelatin	1 c. unsweetened pineapple
¼ c. cold water	juice
¼ c. hot water	1 c. whipped cottage cheese
1 tsp. grated lemon rind	Freshly grated coconut
1 tbsp. honey	

Stir gelatin into cold water to soften. Dissolve in hot water. Add grated lemon rind, honey and unsweetened pineapple juice. Fold in cottage cheese which has been whipped to creamy consistency in blender or electric mixer.

Oil a 9-inch glass pie plate. Press freshly-grated coconut on bottom and sides of plate, leaving out some for top. Pour in cheese mixture. Sprinkle with remaining coconut. Chill. Serves 6.

■ **FRUIT WHIP**

1 c. dried apricots, prunes or peaches, unsulphured, and cut in pieces with kitchen scissors.	2 tbsp. honey 2 eggs, separated

Cover cut dried fruit with warm water and soak overnight. Keep refrigerated. Before serving, blend fruit until smooth, adding water from soaking and the honey. When smooth add egg yolks. Whip egg whites stiff and fold into fruit mixture. Serve in chilled sherbet glasses with whipped cream or yogurt. Serves 4.

■ **GELATIN SNOW**

Make your favorite fruit-flavored gelatin and chill until thick and syrupy. Beat 1 egg white; add to syrupy gelatin and beat until light and "snowy."

■ **SPARKLING GELATIN**

Make your favorite gelatin and just before serving, break it into small pieces and heap the sparkling bits in sherbet glasses.

■ **CAROB À LA CREME**

Carob candy may be bought at most health food stores. Allow 3-4 chunks per person; ½ tsp. butter per person; 2 egg yolks and 1 egg white per person. Melt carob candy in top of double boiler; add butter and blend. Cool, and stir in beaten egg yolks. Beat egg white stiff and fold into carob mixture. Fill individual custard cups and chill at least 2 hours.

■ **STRAWBERRY SNOW**

1 pkg. frozen sliced strawberries thawed	½ c. instant nonfat dry milk
	½ c. ice water
1 pkg. unflavored gelatin	1 tbsp. lemon juice

Drain thawed strawberries; measure juice, add water if needed to make 1 c. Soften gelatin in juice; dissolve over boiling water; stir in drained berries; chill until syrupy. Combine nonfat dry milk, ice water, and lemon juice in medium-size bowl; beat with rotary beater, or in electric mixer at high speed, until mixture stands in peaks. Fold syrupy gelatin mixture into whipped milk; pour into 4-c. mold; chill 2-4 hours, or until firm. Unmold, serve plain or with more strawberries. Serves 4.

■ **PLUM PUDDING**

1 c. raisins	½ tsp. cloves
1 c. currants	1 tsp. nutmeg
1 c. dates (chopped)	1 tsp. salt or substitute
½ c. dried figs	1 c. sour milk
⅓ c. citron, chopped fine	1 c. molasses
2 c. flour	1 c. suet, ground (put through
1 tsp. soda	meat grinder)
1 tsp. cinnamon	1 c. walnuts

Dredge fruits with 1 c. flour. Sift 1 c. flour with soda, cinnamon, cloves, nutmeg and salt. To flour mixture add sour milk and molasses. Work in ground suet. Add fruits and nuts and enough more flour to make a stiff dough. Pour in greased 1½-qt. mold, cover tightly, or pour in greased coffee can with lid. Steam 3 hours. Serves 6.

■ **DELICIOUS APPLE DESSERT**

2 eggs, separated	¾ c. sugar (raw or brown)
½ c. flour	1½ tsp. baking powder
½ tsp. salt	1½ c. apples, peeled and
½ c. chopped nuts	grated or chopped fine
1 tsp. vanilla	½ tsp. almond flavoring

To yolks add ¾ c. sugar, sifted flour, baking powder and salt. Add grated apples to batter with nuts, and flavorings. Fold in stiffly beaten egg whites. Bake in buttered 6 x 9-inch pan at 350°, 35-40 minutes. This pudding will have a meringue-like top. Serve with cream. Serves 4.

■ **PERSIMMON PUDDING**

½ c. honey	½ tsp. soda
½ tsp. salt	3 tsp. baking powder
1 c. flour	¼ c. milk
1 egg, beaten	1 c. persimmon pulp
2 tbsp. melted butter	½ c. raisins
½ c. chopped walnuts	

Sift flour, salt, baking powder and soda. Blend in other ingredients; pour into greased loaf pan; bake at 350°, 1 hour. Serves 4.

■ **FESTIVE FRUIT PUDDING**

1 c. ground raisins	1 c. granular honey
1 c. chopped dried figs	1 c. whole-wheat bread crumbs
1 c. chopped sun-dried dates	1 c. concentrated fruit juice (as
1 c. other dried fruits, chopped,	orange)
(as apricots, pears, prunes)	1 c. sunflower seeds

Mix in order given. Pack into oiled mold, or bread pan. Ripen, covered, in refrigerator several days. Turn out on platter. Serve with whipped sweetened cottage cheese or yogurt. Serves 6-8.

■ **DATE TORTE**

2 eggs	¼ c. unbleached white flour
1 c. sun-dried dates cut up	1 c. nuts, chopped

Beat whites and yolks of eggs separately. When beating whites, add 2 tbsp. water to make them less dry. Mix beaten yolks, dates, flour and nuts. Fold into egg whites. Bake at 350°, in buttered pan set in water, about 30 minutes. Serve in deep glasses; top with whipped cream. Serves 4.

■ BOSTON CREAM PIE

1¼ c. brown sugar	2 tsp. tartrate baking powder
6 tbsp. butter	½ tsp. salt
1 egg	1 tsp. vanilla
1⅔ c. unbleached white flour	⅔ c. milk

Prepare 9-inch layer cake pan by greasing and flouring. Cream together until fluffy: brown sugar and butter; add egg and beat well. Sift flour, measure and sift a second time with baking powder and salt. Add vanilla and milk. Blend well and pour into cake pan. Bake at 350°, 35-40 minutes. Split layer and fill with custard. Dust with powdered sugar.

Custard Filling for Boston Cream Pie

½ c. raw or brown sugar	2 c. milk
½ tsp. salt	2 beaten eggs
6 tbsp. cornstarch or arrowroot	1 tsp. vanilla

Mix sugar, salt and cornstarch in sauce pan. Gradually sur in milk and cook, stirring constantly over low heat. Cook until thickened. Stir a little of this mixture into 2 beaten eggs and return to first mixture. Cook over low fire, bring to boil, remove, cool and add vanilla.

Variation—Whipped cream, flavored with vanilla, may be substituted for custard filling.

FROZEN DESSERTS

Frozen Desserts, such as ice creams and sherbets, may often be made in freezing compartment of refrigerator. But the magnificent Custard Ice Cream in this section requires a good old-fashioned hand freezer or electric freezer to be at its best.

■ AVOCADO BANANA WHIP

Chop 4 frozen bananas; cut up ½ small avocado. Blend or whip together in cold bowl. Return to freezer to set. The avocado makes this a super-smooth creamy mix. It can be served plain as a salad or dessert. Honey, blended with chopped, fresh orange, lemon or tangerine, contrasts with the blandness of the banana and avocado. Serves 6.

■ **CUSTARD ICE CREAM**

1 qt. milk	⅛ tsp. salt
1 qt. cream	3 eggs, beaten
⅔ c. raw sugar	2 tsp. vanilla

Heat milk in top of double boiler; do not allow to boil. Stir in sugar. Beat eggs with salt. Add a little of hot milk mixture to eggs and blend, then add to remaining milk and continue cooking, stirring constantly until smooth and creamy. Strain if necessary. Pour in mixing bowl; add cream and vanilla.

In freezer, mix 1 part ice cream salt to 8 parts finely crushed ice, making sure salt and ice are well mixed. Turn, occasionally removing container to scrape down ice cream from sides. Continue until ice cream is creamy-smooth.

To adapt for freezer compartment, decrease sugar to ⅓ c. Freeze slowly to a mush; remove to bowl and beat until smooth, but not liquid. Return to trays and freeze. This just isn't quite as good as the kind made in hand-freezer or electric freezer.

Variations

1. Substitute for sugar, ½ c. honey blended with paste made of 4 tbsp. flour and enough cold milk to mix together.
2. Maple sugar or dark brown sugar may be used, for interesting change in flavor.
3. After ice cream is partly frozen, you may add 2 mashed bananas, blended with 1 tbsp. lemon juice, or 1 c. drained crushed pineapple, or 1 c. crumbled coconut macaroons.

■ **PAPAYA DATE ICE CREAM**

Pour into blender: 1½ c. papaya, ¼ c. pineapple juice, ½ lb. dates, pitted and chopped. Blend until thickened. Whip ½ pt. cream, then add: ½ tsp. vanilla. Fold papaya and date mixture into this. Pour into freezing tray and freeze. Serves 4.

■ **YOGURT PINEAPPLE SHERBET**

1 c. crushed pineapple	½ pt. yogurt

Put yogurt in freezing tray and freeze slowly to soft mush. Remove and stir in crushed pineapple and juice. Return to freezing compartment and freeze to soft mush. Stir or beat well and freeze until solid. Instead of crushed pineapple, vary by using sweetened mashed strawberries, raspberries, youngberries or other berries, finely diced peaches, apricot juice or Concord grape juice. Serves 2.

■ **EASY LEMON SHERBET**

1 large can evaporated milk, undiluted	¼ c. honey or ½ c. raw sugar
2 tbsp. lemon juice	⅔ c. (6-oz can) frozen lemonade or any frozen fruit juice

Chill milk in refrigerator, whip until stiff. Add lemon juice and whip until very stiff. Fold in honey and frozen lemonade. Pour in refrigerator tray and freeze until firm. Any mashed fruit may be used instead of lemonade if lemon juice is increased to ¼ c. Do not be discouraged if milk seems to take a long time to whip stiff. Serves 4.

■ **BANANA ORANGE FREEZE**

Mash 3 ripe bananas and mix with 1 12-oz. can frozen unsweetened orange juice until smooth. Then combine 1 c. powdered skim milk with 1 c. liquid skim milk; add to mixture 2 c. yogurt; mix well until smooth. Combine milks and fruits and mix thoroughly. Freeze. If still smoother texture is desired, mix a second time after first freezing and refreeze. Serves 6.

■ **CRANBERRY ICE CREAM**

½ lb. cranberries, cooked and strained	½ c. honey
	1 pt. heavy cream

Blend cranberries, honey and cream in blender. Pour in ice cube tray and freeze. Serves 4-6.

■ **MINT-TANGERINE SHERBET**

1 can frozen tangerine juice, unsweetened	2 tbsp. chopped lemon peel
2 tbsp. frozen orange juice	2 tbsp. powdered dry mint leaves
Juice of 1 lemon	½ c. honey

Blend juices, peel, mint and honey in blender. Pour in ice cube drawer and freeze. Serves 4. You may fold in 2 egg whites, beaten until light and fluffy, before freezing if a fluffier sherbet is desired.

■ **BANANA POPSICKLES**

Peel semi-ripe bananas and cut in half. Insert a wooden skewer in each half. Wrap in freezer paper and freeze. Children adore these "sickles."

Variations—Dip skewered bananas in thick carob or chocolate syrup before freezing, or roll in finely chopped nuts or coconut.

■ SOY ICE CREAM

Soy milk may be used in place of milk in ice cream recipes. Follow regular directions, substituting soy milk for milk and adding half and half. Part milk and part soy milk may also be used if desired.

■ BANANA ICE CREAM

Peel and freeze very ripe bananas.

2 c. mashed frozen bananas blended with ½ c. cream, whipped, then quick frozen, makes sweet, but sugarless ice cream. Toppings of honey and fresh fruit whips are good on this. Serves 4.

■ FROZEN BANANA WHIP

Peel and freeze very ripe bananas. Use 1 frozen banana for each person to be served. Chop, still frozen, and whip in a cold bowl or in the blender. Serve at once, or return to the freezer to set. Portions may be topped with nuts or whipped cream, but they are party food, even when plain.

■ ORANGE PEEL GARNISH

With kitchen scissors cut orange peels into thin slices. Dry in oven at 270° or in full sunlight. When dry, pulverize in blender or pound fine. Use as flavoring or garnish for frozen desserts.

■ CARROT ICE CREAM

3 c. fresh raw carrot juice	2 tbsp. lemon juice
2 c. certified raw milk	2 tsp. vanilla
½ c. spray-dried powdered milk	Honey to taste

Blend and freeze in hand or electric freezer. An intriguing garnish for fruit salad or with main course meat dish.

■ CULTURED MILK SHERBET

2 c. buttermilk, yogurt or Kefir milk	½ lemon juice and grated rind
½ c. honey	1 egg, separated
1 c. puréed fresh fruit or frozen orange juice	

Combine buttermilk, honey, lemon, rind and juice; add the fruit or juice and beaten yolk of egg. Freeze in refrigerator trays to mushy consistency. Remove, fold in beaten egg white and freeze again.

■ FRUIT SHERBET

Soften 1 pkg. gelatin in ½ c. any preferred fruit juice concentrate. Dissolve over hot water. Add 1 c. buttermilk and ½ c. fruit juice concentrate. Sweeten to taste. Pour into freezing tray and freeze until crystals form around edge. Beat until smooth and add ½ c. crushed (sweetened if desired) fruit. Return to freezer trays. Serves 4.

PIES AND PASTRY

A light touch is what you need most to turn out a pie crust, rich and delicate and coming from the oven with its top a pale golden brown, its surface blistery, its fluted edges sealing in the filling.

There are three kinds of pastry: *plain,* which includes pies, tarts and turnovers; *puff paste,* a rich, special-occasion pastry; *chou paste,* for cream puffs and éclairs.

Every cook has a pastry secret or two, a special, personal method for mixing, rolling and baking. For instance, using 2 dinner knives to cut in the shortening until the mixture is finely crumbled, then adding ice water by sprinkling on the dough and lightly tossing with a fork, will produce a tender pastry. For a 2-crust pie, divide the dough in half in the bowl, remove half for bottom crust, form in ball and roll very lightly from center outward. Some people use a sheet of oiled paper, lightly floured and placed on table or board. When the pastry is rolled on this waxed paper, you may invert your pie tin on top of it, then flip over the paper and peel it from the crust. For the top crust, lift paper containing rolled crust and invert on filled pie. It is a good idea to have the bottom crust overlap the edge, so it may be turned up over the top crust and fluted with fork or fingertips to make a tight seal.

It doesn't take a nationwide poll to prove that apple pie is dear to the heart of the American male. And there is no reason why pies and pastries should not be included in a good nutritional pattern of family eating. For calories' sake, try to serve pastry desserts only when the rest of the meal has been simple and fairly "lean" . . . and remember that a single-crust pie with lots of fruit filling is just as much fun and far better for you. If now and then the occasion demands a good old-fashioned double crust pie . . . well, you'll find that here, too, made with the best possible ingredients.

Some Pastry Problems and Their Causes:

Smooth surface: too much flour when rolling, and overhandling.

Pale color: underbaking.

Uneven edge: crust not rolled in even circle, and not carefully enough placed in pan.

Tough pastry: lack of sufficient shortening, too much water, too much flour on board and poorly handled.

Dry dough: too little water.

Soggy lower crust: pie may have been baked at too low temperature; a lack of steam vent in 2-crust pie; filling may be too thin; too little shortening may have been used. Some people brush lower crust with beaten egg and allow to dry before filling is added.

Dry, mealy: shortening cut in too finely, not enough liquid.

Too tender, falls apart: undermixing, not enough water or too much shortening.

Shrunken: stretched crust when easing into pan. Pastry should fall loosely over pan and be eased into corners.

Large air bubbles: not pricked well enough on bottom and sides.

Large air space under top crust of fruit pies: caused by shrinkage of fruit when top crust bakes. If apples are sliced thinly and packed tightly or cooked first, this will not happen. Other fruit must not be heaped too high to push up crust.

If lemon pie filling becomes thin, it is because the starch was not properly cooked and lemon juice added at wrong time. Cook the filling quickly over direct heat, then remove from heat to add lemon juice. For the pastry shell, you may substitute 2 tbsp. cold lemon juice for 2 tbsp. ice water.

Meringues weep or collapse: when not beaten enough or too much sweetening has been added; or not spread to edges of pie. Sweetening should be added gradually when beaten whites stand in soft peaks and continue beating until firm glossy peaks form.

■ **OIL PASTRY**

If you prefer not to use butter or other shortening, try this recipe, doubling the amount for a 2-crust pie.

1 c. unbleached white flour or whole-wheat pastry flour	**½ tsp. salt**
¼ c. salad oil, such as corn, peanut, soy or other seed oils	**2½ tbsp. ice water**

Sift flour, measure again and sift with salt. Combine oil and water and beat with fork until thick and creamy. Pour over flour, all at once, and mix lightly with fork. Form into ball and roll on floured board, oiled paper or between 2 pieces of pastry cloth. Fit into 9-inch pie pan, folding over edges and pressing between fingers to flute. Chill before baking. Prick shell with fork. Bake at 450°, 10-12 minutes.

■ OIL NO-ROLL PASTRY SHELL

For single crust sift 1½ c. unbleached white flour and 1 tsp. salt into pie pan. Combine ½ c. salad oil with 2 tbsp. cold milk and whip with a fork until creamy. Pour all at once over flour mixture. Mix with fork until dough is completely dampened. Press evenly and firmly with fingers to line bottom of pan and press dough up on sides and halfway over rim. Be sure dough is of uniform thickness. Do not make high fluted rim.

For 2-crust pie you can make another recipe and use it as a crumble crust over fruit or berries. Bake in hot oven 425°, 15 minutes. Reduce to moderate 350° and bake 30-40 minutes.

■ FLAKY PIE CRUST

2 c. unbleached white flour, or ½ c. rice flour mixed with 1½ c. whole-wheat pastry flour
1 tsp. salt
½ c. cold butter (add 2 more tbsp. butter if richer crust is desired)
4 tbsp. ice water

Sift flour, measure again and sift with salt. Cut butter into flour with pastry blender or 2 dinner knives until fat particles are size of small peas. Sprinkle in ice water, stirring lightly with fork; mix only enough to moisten ingredients. Divide into 2 equal parts for 2 single-crust pies. For double-crust pie, make 1 ball of dough slightly larger for bottom crust. Turn on lightly floured board, 1 ball at a time; or use floured waxed paper or pastry cloth. Press ball of dough lightly, into thick circle. Roll lightly, using outward motion from center to form a circle. For unfilled shells, prick with fork before baking. Prick top crust of filled pies. Chill before baking. Unfilled shells will bake in 10-12 minutes in 425° oven. Covered pies require 30-40 minutes in 425° oven.

■ BERRY PIE MILLET CRUST

Fill browned millet meal pie crust with raw berries or other fruit in season. Top with whipped cream, whipped dry milk or ice cream. Directions for whipping dry milk are in milk chapter.

■   **FRENCH PASTRY PIE CRUST**

Try this French pastry crust when planning an unbaked berry or fresh peach pie.

1 c. flour, unbleached	1 tsp. lemon peel
1 egg yolk	¼ tsp. salt
1 cube butter (½ c.) softened	

Put flour in bowl, make well in center and drop in softened butter, egg yolk. lemon peel and salt. Mix to smooth dough. If dough is too stiff, add few drops of cold water. Do not roll, but press into a 9-inch pie pan, fluting edges. Chill. Place another pie pan on top of crust; bake in a 350° oven, 30 minutes. Remove top pan, cool and fill with berries, or thinly sliced peaches. Cover with honey-sweetened whipped cream or whipped dry or whipped canned milk. Chill. Do not wait too long before serving.

■   **CRUMB CRUST**

Combine 1¼ c. graham cracker crumbs (16 crackers) with 3 tbsp. brown sugar, ¼ tsp. cinnamon and ⅓ c. melted butter or oil. Pat crumbs firmly on bottom and sides of a 9-inch buttered pie pan. Bake about 6 minutes or until lightly browned in 400° oven. Cinnamon may be omitted for plain crust.

Variation—Add 2 tbsp. honey to crumb mixture and pack well in pie pan. Chill about 2 hours and add filling. You need not bake this crust; it will cut nicely.

■   **COCONUT PIE CRUST**

¼ c. softened butter	1 8-oz. pkg. shredded coconut or coconut macaroon (about 3 c.)

Combine butter and coconut. Press evenly into buttered 9-inch pie pan. Build up sides. Bake in 300° oven, 25 minutes or until crust is golden. Cool.

■   **SEED OR NUT CRUST**

Add to the shortening type pie crust ¼-½ c. ground nuts or ground sunflower seeds. Decrease fat about 2 tbsp. as ground seeds and nuts make a rich, tender crust and must be handled carefully. Sesame seeds or poppy seeds need not be ground.

■ MERINGUE PIE SHELL

Butter 9-inch pie plate heavily. Beat 2 egg whites, ¼ tsp. salt and ¼ tsp. cream of tartar until foamy in large bowl. Add ½ c. sifted brown sugar, 1 tbsp. at a time, beating well after each addition. Continue beating until meringue stands in still peaks. Fold in ¼ c. finely chopped pecans and ¼ tsp. vanilla. Spread meringue over bottom and sides of pie plate; bring meringue up higher around edge, with depression in the center.

Bake in very slow oven, 275°, 50-60 minutes until shell is crisp. Cool before filling.

■ MERINGUE SHELLS

Individual meringues are made the same as the above recipe only dropped in larger spoonfuls and the center of each pushed down to make a well. They can be scooped out and filled with chopped fresh fruit or ice cream. Omit chopped nuts if desired.

■ HONEY MERINGUE SHELLS

Beat 2 egg whites until almost stiff enough to stand in peaks. Dribble ½ c. honey on whites as you finish beating. Add ½ tsp. vanilla. Drop by spoonfuls on ungreased cookie sheet. Make depression in center if you plan to fill them. ⅓ c. fine coconut may be folded into the whites for a different flavor. Bake in very slow oven, 275°, 50-60 minutes or until light brown in color. Cool before removing. Place on wet towel which will steam the shells from the pan.

■ FRUIT PIES

Prepare pastry for 2-crust pie. Line 9-inch pie tin with lower crust and chill while filling is being prepared.

Use 3-4 c. fresh sliced fruit or 2 c. canned fruit with ½ c. juice. Mix with ⅔ tbsp. unbleached white flour or whole-wheat pastry flour, ¼ tsp. salt and ½-⅔ c. raw sugar, depending on sweetness of fruit.

For fresh apple pie, add 1 tsp. cinnamon or nutmeg, or mixture of both, to sugar before mixing with fruit. When shell is filled, dot apples with butter. 1 tbsp. milk or cream may be sprinkled over apples before covering with top crust.

Be sure to prick top crust well with fork before baking.

Bake fruit pies at 425°, 8 minutes; then lower heat to 350° and continue baking 30-35 minutes.

■   **DEEP DISH HONEY APPLE PIE**

Follow procedure for Flaky Pie Crust, using the combination of rice flour and whole-wheat pastry flour rather than unbleached white flour. Bottom crust will require larger portion of the pastry, since it must fit a 2-inch deep baking dish, either 8-inch round or 6 x 10-inch rectangular. Fill with honey-apple mixture:

1½ c. quartered apples, peeled and cored	¼ c. rice flour or unbleached white flour
½ c. honey	1 tsp. cinnamon
1½ tsp. lemon juice	1½ tbsp. butter

Toss apples in bowl with flour and cinnamon. Arrange in baking dish. Blend honey and lemon juice and dribble over apples. Dot with butter. Cover with top crust, pricking well with fork. Bake at 425°, about 40 minutes, until golden brown on top.

■   **APPLE CRUMB PIE**

Peel, core and quarter 4 apples. Add ¼-½ c. raw sugar or honey, depending on tartness of apples. Place in kettle with as little water as possible and cook over very low heat until just tender. Arrange in 9-inch buttered pie tin and cover with mixture of ¼ c. finely chopped nuts and ¼ c. whole-wheat bread crumbs. Bake at 400°, about 15 minutes, or until browned on top.

Variation—Fresh strawberries may be substituted for the fruit, and honey may be used instead of sugar.

■   **APPLE OR PEACH SOUR CREAM PIE**

1 pkg. cream cheese	½ c. butter
1 c. flour	

Allow cheese and butter to become soft and blend. Mix lightly into flour. Form dough into a ball and chill. Roll out and line 8-inch pie pan. Mix together the following ingredients: 1 c. thick sour cream, ¾ c. brown sugar, ⅛ tsp. salt. Stir in 2 beaten egg yolks and 2 tsp. melted butter. Sprinkle 1 tbsp. flour over crust. Arrange thinly sliced peeled apples, or peaches on top, sprinkle with another tbsp. flour. Pour sour cream mixture over fruit. Bake in 425° oven, 15 minutes. Reduce heat to 350° and continue baking about 40 minutes longer.

■ **LEMON MERINGUE PIE**

1 c. raw sugar	2 eggs, separated
4 tbsp. cornstarch or arrowroot	⅓ c. lemon juice
¼ tsp. salt	1 tbsp. grated lemon rind
1½ c. boiling water	2 tbsp. butter

Combine sugar, cornstarch and salt in a sauce pan. Add 1½ c. boiling water, stirring constantly. Cook over low fire until mixture thickens. Separate eggs. Beat yolks slightly, pour some of the hot mixture over yolks and return to sauce pan; cook 2-3 minutes longer. Remove from fire, add lemon juice, lemon rind and butter. Cool and pour into baked 8-inch pie shell.

Beat whites stiff and dribble 1 tsp. honey over whites; fold in honey. Spread whites gently over lemon filling. Bake in slow 325° oven until meringue is brown.

■ **LEMON CHIFFON PIE**

1 pkg. unflavored gelatin	½ c. lemon juice
¼ c. cold water	½ tsp. salt
3 eggs, separated	1 tsp. grated lemon rind
⅓ c. raw sugar	⅓ c. raw sugar

Soften gelatin in cold water. Beat egg yolks; add sugar, lemon juice and salt. Place in top of double boiler and cook over hot water, stirring constantly until of custard consistency. Remove from heat. Add softened gelatin, stir until dissolved. Add grated lemon rind; chill until it begins to thicken.

Beat egg whites and fold in sugar and gelatin mixture. Pour into 9-inch baked pastry shell or Crumb Crust. Chill until firm; garnish with whipped cream or coconut.

■ **COCONUT CUSTARD PIE**

3 eggs	½ c. crushed toasted coconut or
⅓ c. honey	coconut macaroon
½ tsp. salt	1¾ c. milk
½ tsp. vanilla	

Beat eggs, add honey, salt, vanilla and coconut. Heat milk to blood temperature and add to above. Mix well. Pour into unbaked 9-inch Flaky Pie Crust. Place in hot oven, 450°, 10 minutes. Decrease heat to 325° until point of knife inserted in custard comes out clean. Sprinkle coconut over top.

■ **CUSTARD PIE**

3 eggs
⅓ c. honey or less (taste for sweetness)
½ tsp. salt

⅛ tsp. nutmeg
1¾ c. milk, heated to blood temperature
½ tsp. vanilla

Beat eggs, add honey, salt, nutmeg, milk and vanilla. Pour into unbaked 9-inch Flaky Pie Crust. Place in hot oven, 450°, 10 minutes to set crust. Decrease heat to 325° and bake until point of knife inserted in custard comes out clean.

■ **RAISIN AND CHEESE PIE**

1½ c. small curd cottage cheese
2 eggs
⅓ c. honey
2 tbsp. butter

1 lemon (grated rind and juice)
2 tbsp. cream
½ tsp. cinnamon
1 c. chopped raisins

Press cheese through sieve or ricer. Beat eggs, add honey and other ingredients. Fold in raisins. Pour in pastry-lined 9-inch pie pan. Bake at 450°, 15 minutes, then turn heat to 325° and bake until knife point comes out clean. Coconut or chopped nuts may be added to cheese instead of raisins.

■ **DATE-WALNUT PIE**

3 tbsp. butter
5 tbsp. brown sugar
2 tbsp. flour
1¼ c. light molasses or maple syrup
1 tsp. salt

¼ c. water
3 beaten egg yolks
1 c. dates
1 c. walnut meats
3 stiffly beaten egg whites

Cream butter with brown sugar and flour. Add molasses or maple syrup, salt, water and egg yolks. Stir in dates cut into large slivers and walnut meats broken into pieces. Fold in stiffly beaten egg whites and spoon mixture into uncooked 9-inch pastry shell. Bake in slow oven, 325°, 50 minutes. Serve cold with whipped cream.

■ **PUMPKIN PIE**

1¾ c. cooked pumpkin
⅔ c. brown sugar
1 tsp. cinnamon
½ tsp. ginger

1 tsp. salt
3 eggs, beaten
2 c. milk
1 tsp. vanilla

Mix in order given. Turn into 9-inch crust-lined pan and bake at 450°, 10 minutes; reduce to 325° and bake until silver knife in center comes out clean.

Pumpkin pie may be served with a topping of whipped cream flavored with cinnamon and sugar or rum-flavor.

■ CRUSTLESS PUMPKIN PIE

1 tbsp. unflavored gelatin	½ c. milk
¼ c. cold water	½ tsp. salt
3 eggs, separated	1 tsp. cinnamon
⅔ c. honey	¼ tsp. nutmeg
1½ c. cooked, mashed pumpkin	2 tbsp. honey

Soak gelatin in water to soften. Beat yolks of eggs and combine with honey, pumpkin, milk, salt, cinnamon and nutmeg. Cook in top of double boiler, stirring constantly until mixture thickens. Remove from heat and add gelatin. Beat egg whites until frothy; dribble in honey and continue beating until stiff. Fold into pumpkin mixture. Pour into oiled 9-inch pie pan and chill several hours.

■ MINCE PIE

3 apples, peeled, cored and chopped	2 tbsp. raisins or currants, if desired
2 c. prepared mincemeat	1 tbsp. apple cider or sherry

Line 9-inch pie tin with Flaky Pie Crust. Combine chopped apples with mincemeat; add raisins or currants, if desired. Mix in cider or sherry. Spoon into pie shell. Top with upper crust, making slits for steam to escape. Bake in 425° oven, about 35 minutes, until golden brown on top.

■ MOCK CHERRY PIE

2 c. cranberries	1 c. seedless raisins
1 c. raw sugar	

Wash and pick over cranberries. Cook in a little water until cranberries are tender; watch so they do not burn. Add sugar and raisins. Pour into 9-inch uncooked pastry-lined pan. Make lattice strips of remaining crust and cover top. Bake in 425° oven 10 minutes. Reduce heat and bake 30 minutes at 350°.

■   **STRAWBERRY YOGURT PIE**

Crumb Crust

1¼ c. zwieback or graham cracker crumbs	½ tsp. grated lemon rind
¼ c. sugar, brown or raw	¼ c. melted butter

Combine crumbs, sugar, and lemon rind in bowl; blend in melted butter. Press mixture in even layer over bottom and sides of 9-inch pie plate. Bake in moderate oven, 350°, 5-8 minutes. Cool.

Filling

1 tbsp. unflavored gelatin	¼ c. milk
¼ c. cold water	2 8-oz. pkgs. cream cheese
2 egg yolks	1 tsp. vanilla
¼ c. raw sugar or 2 tbsp. honey	2 8-oz. containers plain yogurt

Sprinkle gelatin over cold water in top of double boiler; dissolve over simmering water; remove from heat. Beat yolks slightly in bowl, gradually beat in sugar until mixture is thick and lemon colored; stir in milk; add to dissolved gelatin. Cook over simmering water, stirring often until mixture coats a metal spoon. Cool.

Blend cream cheese and vanilla in bowl; stir in yogurt, a small amount at a time, until smooth. Fold in cooled gelatin mixture and remaining yogurt. Pour into 9-inch Crumb Crust; garnish with sliced strawberries or any fresh sweet fruit.

■   **LEMON CHEESE CAKE PIE**

3 small pkgs. cream cheese	2 tbsp. white flour
2 tbsp. butter	⅔ c. milk
1 c. raw sugar	¼ c. lemon juice
1 egg	2 tbsp. grated lemon rind

Cream cheese, butter, and sugar together. Add egg and beat thoroughly. Then add flour, milk, lemon juice and rind. Beat again. Pour into unbaked 9-inch Crumb Crust. Bake in 350° oven, 35 minutes. Chill. Graham cracker crumbs may be sprinkled on top before baking. Crushed pineapple (drained) or crushed strawberries may be spread over top after pie is cold.

■ CREAM PUFFS

Chou Paste

1 c. boiling water	4 eggs
½ c. butter	
1 c. whole-wheat pastry flour or unbleached white flour	

Add butter to hot water; when boiling, add flour all at once, stirring until mixture makes a smooth, compact mass. Remove from heat. Break in 1 egg at a time; beat until mixed after each egg. Drop by spoonfuls on cookie sheet. Oven should be at 425°. Bake about 30 minutes, or until puffed, dry and golden brown.

Filling

Whipped cream, sweetened with honey may be colored pink with concentrated beet juice, or boiled custard firmed agar (vegetable gelatin) if you wish to prepare filling a longer time before serving.

Fresh berries or chopped fruit may be mixed with whipped cream or whipped skim milk.

■ BANBURY TARTS

Chop 1 c. raisins and mix with ½ c. honey or 1 c. raw sugar, juice and grated rind of 1 lemon, 4 tbsp. whole-wheat cracker crumbs and 1 beaten egg. Make Flaky Pie Crust; chill and roll out thin. Cut 4 x 4-inch squares of pastry. Put a spoonful of raisin mixture on pastry square. Fold into triangle. Wet edges with cold water and press with fork. Brush tarts with cream and bake at 400° until browned. Prick tops of each with fork before baking.

CHAPTER 7

Eggs

*E*GGS are a fragile food, to be cooked with a delicate touch. They rate high on your nutrition scale, too, being rich in protein and also supplying iron and Vitamins A and B$_2$.

The best eggs are those from hens which are not cooped up in cubicles. A fertile egg has important estrogenic hormones and so is more valuable than one without.

The test of a really good egg is an upstanding yolk, deep yellow or orange in color, with the white clinging tightly to the yolk. If you wash eggs, wait to do so until you are ready to cook them. A fresh egg has "bloom" on its shell; a stale egg is shiny. Eggs kept for 4 days in a warm market or kitchen, where temperatures are between 70° and 80° will lose as much freshness as those kept several weeks in a covered container in a refrigerator. Covering the eggs while under refrigeration keeps them from losing moisture and quality, and also from absorbing other food flavors.

Eggs, like all proteins, should be cooked over low heat. Coddling is best for both soft-cooked and hard-cooked eggs, and it means that the water has been kept below the boiling point during the cooking.

■   **SOFT-COOKED EGGS**

Use a deep saucepan, so that water covers eggs, with 1 pt. water for each egg up to 6, and ½ pt. for each additional egg. Bring water to boil, remove from flame, add eggs and let stand, tightly covered, 4-6 minutes, depending upon how soft you like them.

With care you can peel eggs which have been cooked 5-6 minutes, by immediately plunging them into cold water, then gently cracking and removing the shell. Peeled soft-cooked eggs are used in aspics and may also be served in thin white sauce to which you have added thinly sliced onions or mushrooms. These peeled eggs must be fairly firm on the outside and the yolk must be runny. Once you have mastered the trick of cooking them just right and peeling them, your own imagination is the only limit as to the variety of ways you may serve them.

■ **HARD-COOKED EGGS**

Place eggs in deep saucepan with enough cold water to cover. Heat slowly to just below boiling point. Cover tightly and let stand on stove, with heat turned off or very low, 30 minutes. Plunge in cold water. Tap each end and roll on hard surface. Shells will be easy to remove.

■ **POACHED EGGS**

Heat water to boiling point in oiled or greased frying pan. Add salt and a few drops of vinegar. Break each egg gently into saucer and slide into water. If water does not cover egg completely, dip water over it with a spoon until it is covered with white film. Remove with perforated ladle, draining water carefully.

Buttered muffin tins may also be used, with an egg dropped in each tin and the whole set in a shallow pan of water to poach.

A variety of egg poachers may also be used.

Serve poached eggs on buttered whole-wheat toast or in ring of fresh-cooked spinach; dropped into clear soup; as topping for corned beef or roast beef hash.

■ **POACHED EGGS DE LUXE**

Separate each egg, being careful not to break the yolk. Beat each white separately until stiff and slide into buttered ramekin or well of muffin tin. Place yolk in center and poach in shallow pan of hot water. Dot with butter, sprinkle with salt and pepper and serve with triangles of buttered whole-wheat toast.

■ **SCRAMBLED EGGS**

Beat eggs quickly and lightly, just before cooking. Season with salt and pepper, but do not add milk, water or any other liquid. Cook slowly in butter, in frying pan, stirring until soft and creamy.

Variation—Melt butter in casserole which has been placed in a pan of hot water over low heat. Pour in lightly beaten eggs, stir and allow to cook over slowly bubbling water until creamy.

■ EGGS IN RECIPES

The size of the eggs you use in a recipe can vary the consistency, so a good idea is to use a measuring cup. In general, you can depend upon the following equivalents:

2 medium eggs ⅓ c.
2 large eggs ½ c.
3 medium eggs ½ c.
3 large eggs ⅔ c.

Variations

1. Just before serving, stir in a little heavy cream and pieces of butter.
2. Sauté chopped tomatoes in butter and stir into eggs just before serving.
3. Add crumbled crisp bacon to egg mixture before scrambling.
4. Cook minced onions in butter until tender, but not brown and add to egg mixture before scrambling.
5. Add chopped, cooked mushrooms before scrambling eggs.
6. Stir cottage cheese into egg mixture before scrambling.
7. Add chopped stuffed olives to egg mixture before scrambling.
8. Marinate avocado cubes in lemon juice and stir in just before eggs are ready to serve.
9. Add minced sunflower seed sprouts before scrambling.
10. Add grated Cheddar or Swiss cheese before scrambling.
11. Add chopped green onions and tops, and chopped green peppers before scrambling.

■ SCOTCH WOODCOCK

Make rich scrambled eggs and serve on thin strips of hot, buttered whole-wheat toast. On each serving place 2 anchovy fillets, crossed. Sprinkle with freshly ground black pepper and minced parsley.

■ FRENCH OMELET (BASIC RECIPE)

2 whole eggs	**Butter**
2 tsp. water or milk	**Salt and pepper**

Break eggs into a bowl. Beat with a fork until well blended. Add water (or milk), salt and pepper. Mix well. Pour into hot, buttered skillet. As eggs cook at the sides and on the bottom, prick with a fork so that the soft egg on top goes down to the bottom of the pan. Do not break the cooked egg. When it is firm, slide onto a platter. Fold and serve immediately. Serves 2.

■ OMELET SOUFFLÉ (BASIC RECIPE)

4 eggs, separated	½ tsp. pepper
4 tbsp. milk	1 tbsp. butter
1 tsp. salt	

Beat egg whites until they stand in peaks. Beat yolks lightly and blend with milk. Add salt and pepper. Fold in egg whites. Melt butter in skillet over low heat. Pour in omelet mixture, which should be about 2-inches deep in pan. Continue cooking over low heat on top of stove, meanwhile pre-heating oven to 325°. With knife tip, determine when bottom of omelet is light brown. Remove from top of stove and bake in oven about 8 minutes, or until knife blade inserted in omelet comes out clean. Slide onto platter and fold in half. Serves 4.

Variations

See suggested variations under Scrambled Eggs and use any of these as filling for omelet, placing on half the omelet just before folding it over.

There are endless ways to make sweet omelets; using your favorite fruits as fillings and dusting top, after omelet is folded, with powdered sugar.

■ OYSTER-MUSHROOM OMELET

1 Omelet Soufflé Recipe (above)	½ c. fresh mushrooms, sliced
6 large oysters	½ tsp. salt
1 tbsp. butter	¼ tsp. celery salt
1 Thin White Sauce Recipe	¼ tsp. pepper

Melt butter in saucepan; add oysters and cook gently until edges curl. Remove and cut off hard section at end of oyster. This is known as "bearding." Sauté mushrooms in saucepan. Remove. Add white sauce to butter and mushroom liquor in saucepan; season with salt, pepper, celery salt and stir in liquor from oysters. Add mushrooms and oysters. Heat and pour over omelet.

Variation—¼ c. grated American cheese may be added to white sauce before stirring in mushrooms and oysters.

■ SHIRRED EGGS

The classic way to shir eggs is to use individual shallow pottery baking dishes. Melt 1 tsp. butter in each baking dish and add 2 eggs to each, being careful not to break yolks. Cook for 1 minute on top of stove, over low heat. Pour a little melted butter over eggs and bake in 350° oven until whites are milky, but still soft.

Variations—Just before putting in oven, add 1 tbsp. heavy cream to each baking dish. Or top eggs with thinly sliced tomatoes before baking; sprinkle with grated Parmesan cheese toward end of cooking time, and brown under broiler.

■ **EGGS BENEDICT**

Break English muffins in half, toast and butter while hot. On each serving, place thin slices of broiled ham and 1 carefully poached egg. Top with Hollandaise sauce.

■ **EGGS FLORENTINE**

Line individual buttered casseroles with hot, creamed spinach. Add 2 carefully poached eggs to each and pour over each casserole a rich white onion sauce. Top with grated Parmesan cheese and brown under broiler.

■ **EGGS IN ASPIC**

2 tbsp. plain gelatin	1 tbsp. minced parsley
½ c. water	½ tsp. celery salt
4 beef bouillon cubes	½ tsp. salt
4 c. water	¼ tsp. pepper
1 tbsp. grated onion	1 tbsp. white wine
1 tbsp. grated carrot	6 peeled soft-cooked eggs
1 tbsp. minced celery	

Dissolve gelatin in ½ c. water. Heat 1 qt. water and pour small amount over bouillon cubes to dissolve. Add to remaining hot water. Stir in vegetables and seasonings and simmer 20 minutes. Pour in gelatin mixture. Strain through colander which has been lined with cheesecloth. Be sure strained broth is clear. Add wine. Chill, and when aspic is still fairly liquid, pour into 6 chilled individual molds and into each mold add 1 peeled egg. Return to refrigerator.

Aspics should always be soft and light, but not "poury." Any well-seasoned stock may be used instead of bouillon cubes, but the resulting jelly must be clear so that the egg shines through. Aspics are always served cold and may be garnished with vegetables, fish or meat according to your fancy. You may also use 1 large mold, but be careful to place the eggs so that they are separated from each other and arranged so that the turned-out mold will be pleasing to the eye. To unmold, dip large or individual molds in warm water or surround mold with cloth dipped in hot water and wrung out. Invert mold on plate and it should slip out after a minute or so.

■ DEVILED EGGS

Cut hard-cooked eggs in half, lengthwise. Mash yolks and season with salt, pepper, prepared mustard, vinegar and melted butter. Refill whites with yolk mixture and top with sprigs of parsley.

You may vary deviled eggs to fit the occasion; add any of the following:

1. Minced ham.
2. Grated Cheddar cheese.
3. Mayonnaise and paprika.
4. Minced parsley and celery salt.
5. Crumbled crisp bacon.
6. Chopped nuts.
7. Minced mushroom caps.
8. Minced tuna fish.
9. Minced onion.

■ EGGS CURRIED

½ c. chopped onion	1 tsp. salt
4 tbsp. butter	2 c. milk
3 tbsp. flour	8 hard-cooked eggs
2 tsp. curry powder	

Sauté onion in butter until golden. Remove from heat and blend in flour, curry powder, salt and milk. Stir constantly over medium heat, let sauce thicken and boil 1 minute. Add hard-cooked eggs, quartered lengthwise, and heat through. Heavenly eating on hot waffles, toasted muffins or hot buttered toast.

■ BEAN SPROUT OMELET

1 tbsp. butter	2 tbsp. milk
1 c. bean sprouts	½ tsp. salt
2 eggs	¼ tsp. pepper

Melt butter in warm skillet. Stir in bean sprouts and cook gently until sprouts are limp, but not soggy. Remove to side dish.

Break eggs in bowl and beat with fork until yolk and white are blended. Add milk, salt and pepper. Melt 1 tsp. butter or oil in the skillet. Pour in egg mixture. As egg cooks at sides and on the bottom, prick with fork so that the soft egg on top goes to the bottom of pan. Spread slightly cooked sprouts over egg. Fold once, place in hot oven for a few minutes. Serves 2.

■ EGGS GOLDENROD

6 hard-cooked eggs	1 tbsp. minced parsley
2 c. medium white sauce	¼ tsp. paprika
6 slices hot, buttered whole-wheat toast	

Cut eggs in half, lengthwise, then cut whites in long slices and add to sauce. Add parsley and keep warm over low heat; meanwhile force egg yolks through sieve. Prepare toast and pour egg sauce over each slice. Sprinkle sieved yolk on top and dust with paprika.

■ EGG-BACON RINGS

Gently cook over low fire a strip of bacon for each egg to be served. Turn twice, keeping bacon limp. Coil tender bacon with fork into a ring. Drop egg into center of each ring, add a dash of salt and freshly-ground pepper. Cover skillet and cook eggs until white is cooked. Add dash of paprika to each egg and serve. Eggs may also be cooked inside toast frames. Pull out soft center of bread, lay on hot griddle, drop egg in center. Cover as for above.

CHAPTER 8

Herbs and Spices

HERBS

Shakespeare, Milton and a host of major and minor poets have praised the virtues of herbs; "rosemary . . . for remembrance"; rue, "the sour herb of grace." Generations of wise women have tended herb gardens and concocted herb teas as topics and appetizers. In the following brief Dictionary of Herbs I have included ideas for their use, and I have added a few other plants from which teas can be made.

HERBS

1. *Anise* is used as flavoring for licorice products and cough medicines. Anise seeds are a piquant topping for bread, rolls and cookies and the seeds also may be crushed and added to hot milk drinks to help induce sleep.
2. *Basil* belongs to the mint family. The leaves, fresh or dried, are used to flavor soups and stews. Basil is especially good with tomatoes and tomato sauce. Dried sweet basil is excellent sprinkled on pork chops before cooking. Basil also makes a fine marinade for meat or game.
3. *Bay leaves* are the smooth, shiny leaves of the bay tree. They are fragrant and pungent in flavor; a little goes a long way. Bay leaves add flavor to soups, especially tomato; they are also used in stews, meat loaf and with fish. A bay leaf may be floated in the water in which you cook vegetables such as onions, carrots or tomatoes.
4. *Camomile flowers* are dried and used to make a delicate tea.
5. *Caraway seeds* are a delicious companion to rye bread and may also be used on crackers or cookies. The whole seeds add a distinctive flavor to cottage cheese, sauerkraut, sausage and baked apples.

6. *Cardamon seeds* have a flavor kinship with coffee. They are pods from a bush and may be used in cookies, pastries, coffee cake, sausage and pickles.

7. *Celery seeds* come from a plant very similar to the celery we use as a vegetable. The oil in celery seeds has the tangy flavor and fragrance of fresh celery. Whole celery seeds are excellent in salads, pickles, stewed tomatoes and potato salad.

8. *Chervil,* used much as parsley is used, is good with greens, egg dishes, fish, fowl or sauces. Blend with cream cheese to stuff celery.

9. *Chives* are slender, onion-like sprigs. They grow easily and should be in everyone's garden, or potted in the kitchen window. They do wonders for salads, cottage cheese, eggs and sauces where a mild onion flavor is desired.

10. *Clover* (red clover) blossoms are used in herb teas. Clover honey is very desirable as are all flower honeys.

11. *Cumin* seed is a small dried fruit grown on a small plant. It is used to flavor almost all oriental meat cookery, and especially in Mexican national dishes. It is an appetite stimulator. The flavor is strong and it should be used carefully.

12. *Coriander* is the dried ripe fruit of a small plant, and its flavor is a combination of lemon peel and sage. It is used in pickling, meats, lentils and Spanish dishes. It is good in a wild game stuffing.

13. *Dandelion* leaves can be used in teas. The root has long been known for its tonic effect and has a flavor similar to ordinary coffee, especially when served with cream.

14. *Desert herb* tea is obtained from plants growing on rich mineral land and virgin soil, and the tea contains trace qualities of these natural elements. Do not steep too long in making tea as it may develop a bitter taste.

15. *Dill* is an annual of the parsley family and is used to flavor soups, salads, sauces, fish dishes, and obviously, in making dill pickles. Do use it fresh whenever possible. Chop leaves and add to cottage cheese or sprinkle over steaks before serving.

16. *Elder flowers* are used as an old-time medical remedy to purify the blood and can be used in herb tea. Use only a little as the flavor is pungent.

17. *Fennel* is a perennial of the parsley family. There are several kinds, bitter, sweet English and Italian. The bitter is used in soups and fish sauces; the sweet in pickles. The Italians like it on roast pork. The seed supposedly has medicinal value. The combination of crusty rolls and fennel seed is good.

18. *Fenugreek* seed is of Moroccan and Indian origin. The green seeds are sticky and when dried and made into a tea are soothing and appetizing.

19. *Garlic* is a bulbous annual belonging to the lily family. The edible part is the root made up of many small sections called cloves. It also has medicinal qualities. Its flavor is stronger than that of onions and is used in stews, salads and salad dressings. Fresh cloves of garlic are preferable as neither the powder nor the oil is as flavorsome.

20. *Geranium* leaves are very popular. Those most commonly used are strawberry, rose and lemon. It is used in fruity puddings and custards or fruit drinks. Use fresh leaves in salads or fruit cups. For hot drinks crush the leaves before using and for cold, float the leaf on the top.

21. *Horseradish* root is used fresh or dried. Fresh, it is very good with roast beef, in salad dressings, yogurt and cream cheese sauces, and in dips and spreads. For prepared horseradish use a distilled vinegar, as cider vinegar will tend to turn it dark; white wine vinegar may also be used. Bottle at once.

22. *Huckleberry* leaves from the commonly known plant, when brewed, make a very pleasant tea.

23. *Lemon verbena* leaves are used in salads, cold drinks, and to flavor cream cheese. Infuse the dried leaves in boiling water for a short time to make a hot tea.

24. *Linden* blossoms also make a delicious tea.

25. *Marjoram* is a member of the mint family and the leaves are used in an herb bouquet, to flavor soups, stews, stuffing, pork, lamb, tomatoes, and string beans. Use marjoram if stronger flavor of sage is not desired.

26. *Mint* is a well known leaf used for drinks, vegetables, pea soup, lamb, fruit salads, and for mint tea. The peppermint and spearmint leaves add a wonderful touch to most herb teas.

27. *Nasturtium* leaves can be used in salads or sandwiches or as a garnish. Chop the tender leaves and mix with cream cheese for canapes.

28. *Oat straw* is the dried oat plant, and is especially valuable for silicon and is used in herb teas.

29. *Oregano,* an herb of the mint family, is used in soups, chili and in tomato sauce. Use in marinades for meat or game, or in oil-vinegar salad dressing.

30. *Papaya* leaves from the tropical tree are used in herb teas. Its characteristic is the presence of an active enzyme called papain. Papaya juice is a good meat tenderizer.

31. *Parsley* is valuable for its vitamins and minerals. It is used in liquefiers to make green drinks, in salads, vegetables and meat, cheese, egg and other well known ways.

32. *Rosemary* leaves are from a small evergreen shrub. They are somewhat bitter in taste but give "bite" to foods. Used in sauces, greens, salads, turnips, or cauliflower, and in Italian sausage. Used fresh it is delicious in fruit cups or salad. Eggs or biscuits are improved with a little of this herb.

33. *Saffron* is the stigma of a crocus plant. It is expensive, but its flavor is so unusual that a little goes a long way. It is used in fancy rolls, coffee cakes, and with rice and chicken.

34. *Sage* leaves are gray with a strong fragrance. They are used fresh or dried with pork, stuffings, sausage, hamburgers, poultry, and fish. The leaves also make a pleasant, soothing tea. Blend a small amount with Cheddar, cottage or cream cheese for sandwiches or canapes.

35. *Sarsaparilla root* is used to make tea and to flavor iced drinks.

36. *Savory,* both winter and summer, is of the mint family and can be used in place of sage. Use with green beans, scrambled eggs, hamburgers and green salads.

37. *Strawberry leaves* make a fine drink which also has beneficial qualities. It is a good tea to drink with meals.

38. *Tarragon,* a plant used to flavor vinegar, is used with meats, sauces, salads, pickles, eggs, and chicken. Use it in marinades, Tartar sauce, or to flavor Hollandaise sauce.

39. *Thyme* is also from the mint family and has a fresh, aromatic odor. Among the many varieties, the most popular are French, English and lemon. It is used to season pea soup, in sauces and with meats, especially rabbit and poultry.

40. *Water cress* is well known and the peppery sprigs are used as a garnish, in salads, sandwich fillings, and finger salads where the cress is dipped in dressing. Use a few sprigs in vegetable drinks, also in biscuits and scrambled eggs.

41. *Yerba mate,* a drink from the leaves of the plant of that name, is a wholesome and flavorsome tea.

SPICES

The great spice caravans of ancient times crossed China and India to bring the prized cargo to Mediterranean and Persian Gulf ports and on to the market places of Rome and Athens, where they sold for fantastically high prices. It is said that pepper was part of the ransom price for lifting the siege of Rome in 408. Spices were part of the history of the Crusaders, of the great explorations to find new trade routes around Africa and across the Atlantic and Pacific Oceans. The powers of Europe were in bitter competition for monopolies of spice-producing areas all over the world. Spices gave a lift to the monotonous diet of medieval times and they were a useful disguise for foods which had spoiled! Now we use spices to enhance the natural flavor of foods, as well as for their health-giving properties. This short Dictionary of Spices will give you some ideas as to their varied use.

SPICES

1. *Allspice* resembles the flavor combination of cloves, cinnamon and nutmeg. It is used as a seasoning for pot roast, pumpkin pie, and as a pickling spice. A little adds interest to carrots or eggplant.

2. *Cayenne pepper* is much hotter than red pepper, and is used in curry powder as well as in meat dishes. Use a dash in barbecue sauce and in cream or cottage cheese spreads.

3. *Cinnamon,* the bark of a tree, is very aromatic. Its uses in cakes, cookies, apple sauce and pie are familiar and it may also be added to milk drinks or herb teas. Try it in baked squash.

4. *Cloves,* the unripe buds of the tree, are fragrant. Use with ham, pork, meats, spice cakes, gingerbread; and it is good in meat loaves.

5. *Ginger* is obtained from the root below the ground. The flavor is both strong and piquant. Used in cookies, meats, and drinks, it is wonderful on steak before broiling. Try it in pot roast and meat loaves.

6. *Mustard* seeds are small and hot. They are used in pickling, in cabbage and sauerkraut. Ground mustard is used in salad dressing, spreads, dips. It is also used medicinally as a poultice.

7. *Nutmeg* is the seed of its fruit, and *mace* the red outer covering. The flavor is fragrant and is used as is cinnamon. Try it on roast lamb.

8. *Paprika* pods are ground into a fine powder with a bland, but distinctive flavor. It is important for its Vitamins C and A.

9. *Black pepper* is the immature berry of the pepper vine, and *white pepper* is the berry left on the vine, fully matured. *Red pepper* is from the pod of the plant and because it is so hot, should be used sparingly.

10. *Poultry seasoning* is a mixture of herbs and spices. It can be added to biscuit dough for an interesting variation.

11. *Pumpkin pie spice* is a ready-mixed blend of spices. Try it sprinkled over steamed squash or pumpkin when served as a vegetable.

12. *Sausage seasoning* is a bland of herbs and spices including white pepper, coriander and nutmeg. It can be used in meat loaf, pork or veal birds.

13. *Turmeric* is the root of the ginger family, orange in color. It is an important ingredient of curry powder. It is used both whole and ground and can substitute for saffron for coloring cakes, breads or cookies. It is also good in rice dishes.

14. *Vanilla beans* are the dried, cured fruit of an orchid. Vanilla is used mostly in pure extract form, but the extract cannot compare with the bean itself.

CHAPTER 9

Meats

*T*HE word protein comes from the Greek and means "of first importance." And that's just how it is regarded today.

Our grandmothers lacked our scientific jargon, but if you remember their juicy roast chicken, redolent with sage dressing; their roasts of beef, seared brown on the outside, pink and tender within; sizzling chops and savory stews, you know they were nutrition experts by instinct. They didn't need to be told that protein is an essential part of every living cell, that without it the tissues of the body would starve to death because it is vital to growth and repair; that protein functions as enzymes, hormones, toxins, antitoxins, antigens and antibodies.

The human body can manufacture more than half the 22 amino acids which make up protein, but the other half must be supplied pre-formed, preferably altogether in a single food or combination of foods. Anyone who wishes to enjoy sustained vigor and a normal life expectancy, as well as contribute to the improvement of the race, must eat a liberal quantity of *good protein*. By liberal, I mean an amount well in excess of theoretical needs; an amount such as the more prosperous races have instinctively chosen over the years.

Meat, milk, cheese and eggs top the list of good proteins. Next best are nuts and soybeans. Grains, legumes and gelatin lack some amino acids and so are known as incomplete proteins. When high and low protein foods are combined, the incomplete ones are made more useful.

PROTEIN NEEDS

Nature has provided the young baby with protein containing the amino acids essential for growth, in the form of milk. Daily milk continues to supply a goodly portion of protein for the preschool and school child. By this time, too, he has many other protein foods in his diet. As he approaches adolescence, the spurt in his growth rate creates an increased need for protein.

The adult's major need of protein is for upkeep and repair. About 70 grams per day is the accepted minimum daily requirement. Below that, the standard of good health cannot be maintained.

Recent studies of nutritional needs of the aged indicate that older men and women have a need for more protein and seem to benefit from intakes that are 50% above the needs of young adults.

The protein needs of pregnant women are higher than the usual needs. Surveys at Harvard have shown that women consuming 83 or more grams of protein bear healthier infants than those receiving less. In lactation the need for amino acids is even greater, for now the woman must supply milk to feed a larger and rapidly growing baby.

Most of the body's ability to ward off disease may be traced to factors in the blood called antibodies. These are protein in nature, and there is a direct relationship between the adequacy of protein in the diet and the number of antibodies circulating in the blood. Well-fed test animals show a tremendous antibody response to invading bacteria; poorly fed ones exhibit only a halting response. Recently this has also been shown to be true of human beings.

■ GOING TO MARKET

It is not easy to be *sure* you are buying meats which contain the nutrients you need and desire. Of course the best way is to raise your own chickens, turkeys, cattle and pigs. Since this is not possible for the great majority, the next best procedure is to know exactly where your meat comes from. This is not as difficult as it sounds. Most communities now have excellent nutrition centers within easy driving distance, where the food sources are known and clearly defined. It is your job to locate such centers.

Marketing for meat can be quite a problem because of the many things which can be done to a carcass before you meet up with it in your butcher's case or super-market. After all, meat is simply a plant product brought to market through the animal's re-conversion. Since animals are such an important source of protein, they must feed on nitrogenous and mineral-containing foods. When cattle are allowed to range, they instinctively select the plants that are best for them. It follows that such range-fed cattle are best for human consumption. When the cattle are fattened in feeding pens, the nutritional value decreases due to the change in fat.

The factors which determine the grading of meat are con-formation, finish and quality.

Conformation implies plump or blocky carcasses as contrasted to rangy or angular. This means that the cuts should be shapely, with full muscles and a large percentage of good meat as compared to bone.

Finish refers to quality, color, and distribution of the fat. The best finish implies a smooth, even covering of creamy white, flaky fat over most of the exterior, and liberal deposits between the large muscles and muscle fibers, which is called "marbling."

Quality refers to characteristics of the flesh and the fat in the flesh. It relates to the firmness and strength of muscle fiber and connective tissue, since these affect the tenderness of the meat.

Texture of meat is related to quality. The round purple stamp seen on meat is the symbol of federal inspection and means only that the meat is from federally-inspected animals and is wholesome. The grading stamps (also purple) are to indicate:

1. U.S. Prime—Excellent quality, juicy, marbled, tender.
2. U.S. Choice—Acceptable quality, moderately fat.
3. U.S. Good—More lean, not so much fat.
4. U.S. Commercial—Older animal, not so tender.

How to judge beef: Moderate covering of fat over exterior, thinner over ribs. Liberal deposits of fat between large muscles and con-nective tissue and muscle fibers. Velvety, fine grain; bones porous and red in young animal—white and flinty in older animal.

How to judge veal: The lean should be light grayish-pink; fine grain, fairly firm and velvety; not much fat, but what there is should be clear, firm and white, with no marbling; bone porous and red, ends of same still pliable.

How to judge lamb: Age produces changes in character, color and consistency of the flesh and bone. The hardness and color of bones are good indications of age. One should look for the "break joint," the place where the fore-feet are taken off. In young lamb it is smooth, moist and red; in older animals it is hard and white. Flesh varies from light to dark pink. As the animal grows older the color deepens. The fat is soft and creamy white or slightly pink.

How to judge pork: Most pork comes from young animals 6 to 12 months old and is usually tender. The color is grayish pink, changing to delicate rose in older animals. The flesh is relatively firm and fine-grained, free from excessive moisture. The lean is well marbled and covered with firm white fat.

■ **HOW TO COOK FRESH MEAT**

The basic methods for cooking meat are by dry heat or moist heat, depending upon whether liquid is used in the cooking process. Each method has several variations.

Dry Heat methods are ideal for tender cuts.

Moist Heat creates steam which softens connective tissue and cooks the less tender cuts to juicy goodness.

Dry Heat Methods	*Moist Heat Methods*
Oven roasting	Braising
Broiling	Stewing
Pan broiling and pan frying	Simmering in water

■ **OVEN ROASTING**

1. Place meat, fat side up, in shallow roasting pan. Use rack under boneless cuts. Season with salt and pepper, if desired. Insert meat thermometer into thickest part of muscle, being careful bulb does not touch bone or rest in fat.
2. Do not add water. Do not cover. Place roast in 325° oven and roast to desired degree of doneness as registered on thermometer. Refer to timetable for approximate cooking time. Fat melts and "bastes" roast as it cooks.
3. Take roast from oven and allow to stand 15-20 minutes for easier carving. "Feather" bones may be removed from roast in kitchen. Carve meat across the grain toward the ribs, freeing slices with tip of knife along the bone.

■ BROILING

Steaks and chops should be cut at least 1-inch thick for best flavor results. They may be broiled frozen or partially or completely thawed.

Broiling is not recommended for fresh pork, which requires longer cooking time, or for veal, which is lacking in fat. However, *smoked* ham and bacon are often broiled.

1. Place steak or chops on rack in broiler pan. Slash fat edge of meat at 1-inch intervals to prevent cupping. Brush very lean meat with fat before broiling. If desired, use meat thermometer on thick steaks, inserting horizontally into thickest muscle.
2. Follow range manufacturer's directions for broiling. Place rack so that surface of meat is 2½-3 inches from source of heat (greater distance for thicker cuts). Broil for about half of time allowed in timetable. Season, turn and finish broiling. To turn, use tongs or fork inserted in fat.
3. Degree of doneness of steak depends upon individual preference but for best flavor, avoid over-cooking. Serve sizzling steak on hot platter, garnishing with tomato and onion slices and a bit of crisp greens. A thick Porterhouse weighing over 4 pounds will serve 4-6.

■ STEWING

1. Have meat cut into uniform cubes, 1-2 inches in size. Shake in seasoned flour in paper bag. (Flour may be omitted and meat seasoned with salt and pepper.)
2. Brown meat slowly and evenly in about 2 tbsp. hot oil in heavy kettle. Floured meat develops deeper brown—if not floured, it may be browned without added fat.
3. Add hot water, broth or other liquid, about 2 c., until it just covers the meat. Add desired seasonings, varying to enhance flavor of meat used.
4. Cover kettle tightly and simmer until meat is tender. Do not boil. Slow cooking over low heat makes meat tender and flavorful. Add more liquid if necessary.
5. Add vegetables during last part of cooking time, before meat is quite done. Do not overcook vegetables. Time depends on kind used and whether whole or cut.
6. Remove meat and vegetables and thicken liquid for gravy. Serve stew in individual ramekins or in large casserole. Or top with pastry or biscuit for meat pie.

■ COOKING MEATS IN WATER

1. Cover meat with hot water. Meat may be browned first, if desired.
2. Add seasonings and desired herbs, spices or "seasoning" vegetables, such as onion and celery.

3. Cover tightly and simmer until meat is tender. Do not overcook.
4. If meat is to be served cold, cool in stock in which it was cooked. Store in stock in refrigerator.
5. For "boiled" dinners, add vegetables to meat just long enough before meat is tender to cook them.

REFERENCE: American Meat Institute, 59 W. Van Buren St., Chicago, Ill.

■ HOW TO STORE FRESH MEAT

Before Cooking—
Storing in the Refrigerator: Meat should be placed at once in the meat compartment or in a very cold area of the refrigerator after purchase. Fresh meat wrapped in market paper should be re-wrapped loosely to allow circulation of air. Pre-packaged meat should have the wrapping loosened before the meat is refrigerated.

The best temperature for storing fresh meat is 38 to 40°.

Steaks, chops and small roasts can be held under good re-frigeration 2-3 days, larger roasts for slightly longer. Ground or cubed meat and variety meats should be used within 24 hours for best eating quality.

Storing in the Freezer: Meat for freezer storage should be fresh and in top condition. The meat should be carefully packaged in suitable packaging materials to protect against drying and freezer burn. Each package should be labeled with a statement of contents and packaging date.

Steaks, chops or ground beef patties should be separated with suitable packaging material to insure easy separation of the meat before cooking.

Freeze meat immediately after wrapping and allow space for air to circulate between packages which are being frozen. Avoid placing large quantities of unfrozen meat in a freezer at one time, as this usually overloads the freezer unit and may result in a slow-frozen product of inferior quality. It is desirable to freeze meat at sub-zero temperatures, −10° or lower.

In all cases frozen meat should be stored at 0° or lower, with as little fluctuation in storage temperature as possible. The ice cube compartment of a home refrigerator usually does not main-tain temperature as low as a freezer storage compartment or a home freezer and therefore should be used for only limited storage of frozen meats.

Freezer Storage Time: The following storage times should not be exceeded if the meat products are to be of high quality when consumed.

Product	Recommended Maximum Storage Time at 0° or Lower
Beef	6-8 months
Fresh Pork and Veal	3-4 months
Lamb	6-7 months
Ground Beef	3-4 months
Variety Meats (Liver, Heart, Tongue, etc.) . .	3-4 months

After Cooking—

Storing in the Refrigerator: Cooked meat should be allowed to stand at room temperature for about an hour to cool slightly. Then it should be covered or wrapped tightly to prevent drying and placed in the meat compartment or very cold part of the refrigerator. Meat will keep better if left in larger pieces and not cut until ready to use.

Under efficient refrigeration, cooked roasts and larger cuts of meat, if unsliced, will hold 4-5 days.

Storing in the Freezer: Cooked meat, if to be held for longer than 4-5 days, should be stored in the freezer or freezing compartment of the refrigerator. It should be tightly wrapped in moisture-vapor-proof paper, sealed carefully and labeled as to contents and packaging date. Frozen cooked meat will be at its best if used within 2-3 months after freezing. Once thawed, it should be used immediately and not re-frozen.

REFERENCE: American Meat Institute, 59 West Van Buren Street, Chicago, Ill.

■ HOW TO COOK FROZEN MEAT

Frozen meats may be cooked in the frozen state or after partial or complete thawing. When properly cooked, there is practically no difference in shrinkage or flavor. When cooked from the frozen state, additional time is necessary to allow for thawing during the cooking process. If the meat is partially thawed, cooking time will be only slightly longer, and if completely thawed, no longer than for fresh meat.

In preparing commercially frozen meat or meat products, follow package directions.

■ ROASTS

If cooked from the frozen state, large roasts usually require ½-again the time required for fresh roasts or frozen roasts which have been completely thawed. Small frozen roasts will require less additional cooking time depending on the size and shape of the cut. Cooking method is the same as for fresh roasts.

■ STEAKS AND CHOPS

Frozen steaks and chops require ½ to once-again the time required for similar cuts of fresh meat. They are broiled in the same way, except that the meat is placed at least 4 inches from the source of heat so that the exterior surface does not over-brown before the interior is cooked to desired degree of doneness. If rack cannot be lowered, the broiling temperature should be reduced.

If steaks and chops are to be *pan broiled* from the frozen state, allow ¼ to ½-again the time required for fresh or completely thawed meat.

In pan broiling frozen meat, it is important that the skillet be hot so that the meat browns quickly before it has a chance to thaw and "water" in the pan. A little fat should be added to the pan and the meat may be dusted lightly with flour for better browning. On thicker cuts, lower heat after browning, and cook slowly.

■ LESS TENDER CUTS

Frozen round steak intended for "Swissing" or braising and cubed boneless meat to be used in braised dishes should be at least partially thawed to facilitate pounding in or dredging in flour. Cooking time required is about the same as for fresh meat. Meats that require no flouring may be browned without thawing and require a little additional cooking time.

Ground meat frozen in bulk form should be thawed for shaping into meat loaves or patties. If frozen in pattie form, the patties may be broiled or pan broiled from the frozen state, partially thawed or completely thawed. Cooking time will be the same as for steaks and chops.

Frozen cuts that are to be simmered in water may be browned in the frozen state in a little hot fat, if desired, then covered with water and cooked slowly, covered, until the meat is tender. Or they may be cooked from the frozen state or after partial or complete thawing by covering with water and cooking slowly, covered, until meat is tender.

■   **THAWING FROZEN MEATS**

For best results, thaw frozen meats in the refrigerator. Meats thawed at room temperature will spoil readily if allowed to stand at room temperature for too long.

1. Leave meats wrapped while thawing.
2. Do not immerse meat in water for thawing unless meat is to be cooked in water after thawing.
3. Cook meat as soon as it is thawed.
4. Do not refreeze meat after thawing. Meat loses juices during thawing and deterioration is possible between the time of thawing and refreezing.

ORGAN MEATS

The meats most important nutritionally are liver, kidney, brain, spleen, sweetbreads or thymus, heart, tripe and tongue. Head, tails and feet are not organ meats, but they are good food and may be used imaginatively to add variety to your menus.

Liver contains an abundance of iron in the right form for use by the body and has a rich supply of Vitamins A and B. If the intake of protein, sugar and vitamins is more than the body needs, it is stored in the liver. Nutritionally it is the most outstanding meat.

Brains are one of the richest sources of the B vitamin Cholin. Kidney is a good source of vitamin A, B, and G. Sweetbreads are a good source of vitamins A and B. These meats have the function of carrying on vital life processes; therefore they contain proteins of the most superior quality and larger quantities of vitamins and minerals than do muscle meats.

Heart and *tongue* are muscular organs and their food value is very like that of lean beef.

The protein of *glandular meats* has an amino acid make-up similar to the amino acid content of the human brain, kidneys and glands; therefore the rare amino acids needed to protect, repair, or build the human glandular organs should come from animal source. The glandular meats are more perishable than other meats, so special care must be taken to refrigerate them. They should not be washed unnecessarily, as the B vitamins are soluble in water. There is a mineral loss too.

Meat	Preparation	Cooking
Liver	Do not soak or scald. Precook liver only when it is to be ground.	Pan-fry or broil veal or lamb liver. Braise pork or beef liver. May be baked with bacon, or ground for use in loaves, patties, etc.
Kidneys	Can be soaked or not. Wash, remove outer membrane, halve, remove fat and white veins.	Veal and lamb kidneys may be broiled. Braise pork and beef. Or grind, slice or chop for patties, loaves or kidney pie.
Hearts	Do not soak or precook. Trim out fibers at top. Wash thoroughly in cold water.	Heart cooked tender in water may be ground or diced for hash, meat pie, casserole. Beef, veal may be stuffed and braised. Pork and lamb may be braised whole or in slices.
Brains	Soak in salted cold water 15 minutes. Remove membrane. Precook in simmering water 15 minutes, then prepare for desired serving.	Cooked brains may be diced for use in scrambled eggs, creamed dishes, or sliced egg; and crumbed, and deep-fat or pan-fried.
Sweet-breads	Do not soak. Precook in simmering water 15 minutes. Remove loose membranes. Prepare for desired serving. Juice of two lemons in water for 3 pairs of sweetbreads.	Cooked sweetbreads may be braised, pan-fried, broiled, or baked whole. Use precooked sweetbreads diced in salads, creamed dishes; or slice, egg and crumb, and fry.
Tongue	Simmer fresh tongue in seasoned, salted water until tender. Then remove outer skin. Omit salt in cooking smoked tongue.	Slice and serve hot or cold. May be diced and used in casserole dishes or salads.
Tripe	Fresh or pickled honeycomb tripe may be bought precooked, ready for final cooking.	Brush with melted fat, broil five minutes each side. Tripe also may be pan-fried, braised, or served in a sauce.

■ **BRAINS**

The membrane is most easily removed while holding under cold running water. Brains may be broiled, creamed, baked, sautéed with eggs or as sandwich spread.

■ **BAKED STUFFED HEART**

1 beef heart or 2 veal hearts	¼ c. celery, chopped
2 slices bacon	1 tbsp. salt
2 c. bread crumbs	3 tbsp. flour
½ c. diced onion	3 tbsp. fat
¼ tsp. sage	1 tbsp. Worcestershire sauce

Cut out tough fibers, after cleaning heart. Simmer 2 hours in salted water or cook in pressure cooker 5 minutes at 15 lbs. pressure. Dice bacon and fry until crisp. Combine with bread crumbs, onion and 1 tsp. salt, ¼ tsp. sage and ¼ c. chopped celery. Season cavity with remaining salt. Fill with dressing; fasten with toothpicks to hold in dressing or tie with string. Dredge heart in flour, brown in fat in a heavy skillet. Add ½ c. water and Worcestershire sauce. Cover and cook slowly in a moderate oven 350° or simmer on top of stove 1½ hours, or until heart is tender.

■ **BEEF HEART PATTIES**

Trim a beef heart of all fat and sinews, then put it through food chopper, using the finest blade. For each lb., mix in 1 tsp. salt and ½ tsp. fresh ground pepper. Form into patties the size of hamburgers, sprinkle with tenderizer, if desired, and allow to stand overnight in the refrigerator. This keeps them from falling apart when cooking. Sauté in butter or oil. Do not overcook; they are best rare.

■ **WAYS TO SERVE LIVER**

To *braise* liver, dip ½-inch slices in flour. Season. Brown well in oil in heavy skillet. Add ⅓-½ c. water. Cover and cook over low heat 15-20 minutes. Should be pink on inside when done.

Brown ½-inch slices of liver in small amount of oil. Add 1 c. thin *barbecue sauce*. Cover and simmer 15 minutes.

For liver *brochettes,* combine 1-inch cubes veal or lamb liver, bacon squares, small boiled onions, and mushrooms on skewer. Brush with French dressing. Broil about 15 minutes, turning to brown evenly.

To prepare liver for *croquettes,* patties or liver loaf; cook liver in salted water until firm, then grind. Combine with a very thick white sauce, paprika, grated onion, lemon juice for seasoning.

■ **SWEETBREAD SUGGESTIONS**

Sweetbreads make delicious salads. Clean, cook, chill, and cube the sweetbreads. Marinate in French dressing 1 hour. Combine with any of the following:

1. Diced canned pineapple, orange sections, salad dressing.
2. Diced cucumber in chilled tomato cup.
3. Diced cooked chicken, toasted almonds, salad dressing.
4. Cooked peas, diced celery, diced green pepper, salad dressing.
5. Egg-and-crumb cooked sweetbreads. Brown in hot fat. Serve with orange sauce.
6. Thread cooked sweetbreads and 1-inch bacon squares alternately on skewer. Broil 10-15 minutes, until bacon is crisp.

■ **SWEETBREADS À LA KING**

1 lb. uncooked sweetbreads	⅓ c. chopped green pepper
¼ c. butter or oil	½ c. sliced mushrooms
¼ c. sifted flour	2 tbsp. butter or oil
2 c. milk	2 tbsp. chopped pimiento
1 tsp. salt	

Simmer sweetbreads in salted water using 2 tsp. salt per quart of water, 15-20 minutes. Drain. Cool. Remove all loose membrane. Dice sweetbreads. Make a white sauce of butter, flour, milk and salt. Sauté green pepper, mushrooms, pimiento; add sweetbreads to sauce. Heat slowly 5 minutes. Stir to prevent burning. Serve on toast points, corn bread, or in pastry shell. Serves 4.

■ **KIDNEYS CREOLE**

Cut kidney in half, soak 1 hour in slightly salted water. Remove every trace of white tubes from kidneys. Dice into ¾-inch cubes and mix well with 2 tsp. vinegar; put into a paper bag and shake with 3 tbsp. whole-wheat pastry flour. Sear kidneys about 3 minutes in oil. Turn on paper towel. Sauté 5 minutes in same utensil 1 chopped onion, diced pimiento or green pepper to taste, 1 minced clove garlic, 1 chopped celery stalk with leaves. Add:

1 c. tomato purée or canned tomatoes	¼ tsp. freshly ground pepper
1 tsp. salt	¼ tsp. basil, savory or thyme

Simmer 10 minutes; add kidneys and reheat. Serve over steamed brown rice. Serves 4-6.

■ **STEAK AND KIDNEY PIE**

1 lb. round steak
½ lb. lamb kidneys or 1 medium veal kidney
¼ c. flour
½ tsp. salt and ¼ tsp. pepper
4 tbsp. oil
1 c. chopped onion
½ c. peas

1 bay leaf or ¼ tsp. oregano
2 tbsp. chopped celery leaves
2 tbsp. chopped parsley leaves
2 c. water
½ c. mushrooms (stems and pieces)
½ c. sliced carrots

Cut steak in 1-inch cubes. Remove all white membrane from kidneys and cut in small pieces. Combine flour, salt and pepper and roll kidney pieces in flour mixture. Heat oil and brown the meat and onion. Add water, bay leaf, celery, parsley. Cover tightly and simmer 1 hour. Add mushrooms, carrots and peas. Make whole-wheat biscuit dough, and roll out thin. Line a shallow baking dish with part of dough. Pour in meat mixture. Roll out remaining dough, cutting slits for steam to escape, and cover pie. Bake in hot oven 425° for 30 minutes or until pastry is brown. Serves 4-6.

■ **KIDNEY SAUTÉ**

1 beef kidney
1 slice ham
Whole-wheat flour

Salt and pepper
2 medium onions, sliced

Cut kidney in half and soak 1 hour in slightly salted water. Brown ham. Cut kidney into 1-inch squares and drop into briskly boiling water, 1 minute; drain and rinse. Roll in flour, salt and pepper. Quickly fry with sliced onions and serve with the ham. Serves 6.

■ **TRIPE**

Simmer pickled tripe about 2 hours in 1 c. water and 2 tbsp. vinegar and fresh tripe about 3 hours or until a cut piece looks clear on the edge. Cooked tripe may be used in Philadelphia pepper pot soup; braised and served with creole sauce; baked in a casserole with carrots, onions, green peppers and Worcestershire sauce; stewed and served with slices of apple or tomatoes. Tripe can also be cooked with 1 tsp. cloves, minced garlic, onions, allspice or marjoram and 1 tbsp. vinegar.

■ SWEETBREAD BROIL

Simmer sweatbreads in water about 15 minutes; remove any loose membrane. Cut in 1-inch cubes. Thread sweetbreads on skewer, alternating each cube with 1-inch uncooked bacon strip. Broil 10-15 minutes, turning to crisp the bacon.

■ TONGUE WITH DILL OR HORSERADISH SAUCE

Place 1 beef tongue or 6-8 lamb tongues (washed) in pan with tight lid. Add 1 inch water with 1 tsp. tenderizer, 1 tsp. each of rosemary, thyme, basil, savory, marjoram, 1 tsp. salt substitute. Simmer 2 hours, or until tender, adding more hot water as needed. Top with dill sauce: to 2 c. cream sauce, add 2 tbsp. or more to taste of dill or dill seed. May substitute horseradish instead of dill for another good sauce. Serves 6-8.

LAMB *

■ ROAST LAMB

Select a small leg of lamb, about 5 lbs. Sprinkle meat with salt. Place fat side up in an open roaster. Make several slits in roast about ½-inch wide and insert thin slices of garlic. Baste frequently with unsweetened pineapple juice, papaya juice, or apple juice. A little hot bouillon or consommé may be used, or dry white wine. Roast in slow oven, 325° 1½ hours for rare; 2 hours for medium and 2½ hours for well done. If lamb is not at room temperature when roasting begins, allow 30-40 minutes more. Serves 4-6.

■ ROAST LEG OF LAMB WITH HERBS

Lard generously with garlic, tenderizer and papaya powder. Rub with juice of 1 lemon. Roast as above. Baste with the following mixture:

1 tsp. rosemary	1 tsp. sweet basil
1 tsp. thyme	1 tsp. marjoram
1 tsp. savory	½ c. dry white wine or water

Start at 250°; cut to 175° oven temperature. Baste often.

* Diagrams showing how to carve lamb will be found following page 183.

■ LAMB SHANKS

Sprinkle 4 lamb shanks with 2 tsp. liquid tenderizer; brown in oil at very low temperature. Add 1 bay leaf, 1 tsp. rosemary, 1 tsp. oregano seasoning. Cook 1 hour. Add 3 carrots and 2 sticks of celery to the pan during last 15 minutes of cooking. Serves 4.

■ LAMB SAUSAGE

5 lbs. lean shoulder, ground	¾ c. leaf sage
1 tsp. cardamon seed or coriander	2 tsp. papaya powder
	1 tsp. thyme
2 tsp. oregano	1 tsp. marjoram
2 tsp. basil	

Mix, shape in patties and fry as for sausage. Serves 8.

■ LAMB STEW

1½ lbs. lamb shoulder	¾ tsp. ginger
1 tbsp. salad oil	12-14 small onions, peeled
½ c. chopped celery with leaves	4 small carrots
⅓ c. minced parsley	4 c. water
½ bay leaf	¼ c. flour mixed with ¼ c.
2 tsp. salt	water
½ tsp. rosemary	

Cut meat into 1½-inch pieces. Brown in salad oil. Add chopped celery, minced parsley, bay leaf, salt, rosemary, ginger, peeled onions, carrots cut in 2-inch pieces, and 4 c. water. Cover and cook about 1 hour on simmer, or until vegetables are done. Mix flour and water and stir into hot stew. Cook for 2 minutes. Serve over cooked brown rice or with dumplings. Serves 6.

■ ROASTED LAMB RIBS

4 lbs. lamb ribs	2 cans tomato sauce
6 slices unsweetened pineapple	¼ c. molasses
¼ c. brown sugar	4 garlic cloves, minced
1 tsp. dry mustard	1 tsp. papaya juice
1 tbsp. organic seasoning or "seasoned salt"	

Place ribs in roasting pan and top with pineapple slices. Make sauce by blending dry ingredients with tomato sauce, molasses and papaya juice. Pour over meat and bake 1 hour at 300°. Lower heat to 250° and bake 2 more hours, turning ribs occasionally. Serves 6.

■ MINT GARNISH FOR LAMB

Heat 1 c. unsweetened pineapple juice to boiling point; stir in 1 c. crushed fresh mint leaves and simmer 15-20 minutes. Soften 1 tbsp. unflavored gelatin in ½ c. unsweetened pineapple juice; add 1 tsp. lemon juice. Stir in mint mixture and sweeten to taste. Refrigerate until mixture jells and serve with roast lamb or mutton.

■ LAMB CHOPS, CREAM GRAVY

6 shoulder or round-bone lamb chops	1 c. consommé or 1 cube of beef bouillon
Piece of garlic	1 c. hot water
¼ c. minced onion	2 tbsp. chopped chives
2 tbsp. flour	2 tbsp. chopped parsley
½ tsp. salt	¼ tsp. thyme
Dash of Tabasco	1 bay leaf
¼ c. light cream or yogurt	

Rub lamb chops with piece of garlic and brown both sides in a little oil in skillet. Add minced onion and flour. Stir until flour is blended with fat. Pour in consommé or cube of beef bouillon dissolved in hot water. Add chopped chives and chopped parsley, salt, thyme and bay leaf. Add a dash of Tabasco. Put chops back into gravy, add light cream or yogurt and cook over low heat for 30 minutes or until tender. Serves 6.

■ CURRY OF LAMB

1½ lb. lean lamb (about 2 c.)	3 tomatoes, cut in pieces
2 tbsp. butter	2 c. water or consommé
⅓ c. chopped onions	1 tsp. salt
1 tbsp. curry powder	⅛ tsp. pepper
1 minced clove of garlic	3 tbsp. flour
1 grated peeled apple	

Cut lamb in 1-inch cubes; brown in butter with chopped onions. Add curry powder, minced garlic, grated apple and tomatoes. Add water or consommé, salt and pepper. Simmer covered about 1½ hours until lamb is tender. Remove lamb, thicken sauce with flour mixed to a smooth paste in cold water. Return meat to sauce. Serve with rice pilaff. Serves 4-6.

Variation—Leave out tomatoes, increase apples to 3, add 2 tbsp. lemon juice and ½ tsp. grated lemon rind, ½ c. raisins and 2-3 cloves. Proceed as in above recipe.

■ **POT ROAST OF LAMB**

4 lbs. shoulder of lamb	5 medium potatoes, pared and
1 tsp. salt	halved
½ tsp. pepper	5 medium carrots, cut in halves
3 tbsp. whole-wheat flour	5 medium onions, cut in quar-
3 tbsp. oil	ters
½ c. water	1 tsp. Worcestershire sauce

Mix salt, pepper and flour. Dredge meat in flour and brown on all sides in hot oil. Place meat and water in large covered pan and roast at 325°, 45 minutes per lb. During last 45 minutes, add vegetables. Remove meat and vegetables to platter and make gravy of liquid in pan, adding 1½ c. water. Make paste of 3 tbsp. flour and ⅓ c. water. Pour into gravy and stir until thick. Season and add Worcestershire sauce. Serves 6-8.

■ **LAMB BREAST, SPANISH SAUCE**

2 lbs. breast of lamb	¼ tsp. chili powder
1 medium onion, chopped	1 tbsp. vinegar
½ c. chili sauce	1 c. water
1 tsp. salt	¼ tsp. pepper

Cut lamb in 6 serving pieces. Place in hot skillet and brown fatty sides. Pour off excess fat. Season with salt and pepper. Mix other ingredients and pour over lamb. Cover and simmer 1½ hours, then remove lid and cook until sauce is nearly absorbed. Serves 6.

BEEF *

■ **MEAT LOAF**

2 lbs. ground beef	1½ tsp. salt
1 egg	2 c. soft bread crumbs or 1½
1 c. tomato juice or milk	c. rolled oats
½ c. finely chopped onion	¼ tsp. oregano or thyme
¼ c. finely chopped parsley	½ tsp. chopped garlic

* Diagrams showing how to carve beef will be found following page 183.

Beat egg and add liquid. Add remaining ingredients and mix well. Form into loaf and place in shallow baking pan. Place a few cloves and bay leaf on top. Bake in moderate oven 350° for 1½ hours. Serves 4-6.

Variation: Meat mixture may be ½ beef, ¼ veal and ¼ pork.

■ CARROT MEAT LOAF

2 c. cooked carrots, mashed	1 small onion, minced
1 lb. ground beef	2 tsp. salt
1 egg, beaten	¼ tsp. pepper
¾ c. soft whole-wheat crumbs	

Mix all ingredients thoroughly and bake in greased loaf pan 1 hour at 350°. Serves 6.

■ MEAT PORCUPINES

1 lb. hamburger	¾ tsp. salt
¾ c. brown rice, uncooked	¼ tsp. pepper
1 tbsp. oil	1 tbsp. minced parsley
1 small onion, minced	2 c. tomato juice
1 tsp. thyme	

Blend all but tomato juice. Form into balls about 1½-inches in diameter, press firmly in shape. Brown in a little oil. Cover with tomato juice and cook slowly, covered, for 1 hour. Add enough more juice to keep balls from sticking, as needed. Serves 4-6.

■ CABBAGE OR SWISS CHARD MEAT BALLS

12 large leaves Swiss Chard or cabbage	½ tsp. celery salt
	⅛ tsp. pepper
1 lb. ground lamb or lean beef	1 tsp. salt
1 c. cooked brown rice	2 tbsp. salad oil
½ c. minced, peeled onion	1 c. water
1 egg, slightly beaten	2 c. tomatoes

Wash chard or cabbage; cut off stems; cover leaves with boiling water; let stand 1 minute; drain. Combine meat, rice, onion, egg and seasoning. Shape into 12 balls; wrap in chard or cabbage leaves, fastening with toothpicks. Heat oil in skillet; brown rolls on all sides. Add tomatoes and water; sprinkle with salt and pepper; cover, and simmer 40 minutes, turning once. Remove toothpicks. Serves 4.

■ **STUFFED STEAK**

1 flank or round steak, cut ½-inch thick	1 tbsp. chopped onion
	½ c. chopped celery
1 c. crumbs	2 tbsp. chopped parsley
½ c. water	2 small carrots, diced
1 tsp. salt	1 can mushroom soup or sauce
¼ tsp. pepper	

Have steak scored. Wipe steak, remove skin, lay meat flat on a board. Make a dressing of crumbs, water, salt, pepper, onion, celery and parsley and spread it on meat. Roll steak with the grain and fasten with toothpicks, if necessary. Place diced carrots in roasting pan with the rolled steak. Add 1 c. water, cover and bake at 350°, 1 hour, or until tender. Remove from pan. Add 1 can mushroom soup or sauce and heat. Pour over stuffed steak. Serves 4.

■ **SWISS STEAK**

Purchase 2 lbs. round steak, 1-inch thick. Place on board and season with salt, pepper and oregano. Sprinkle 2 tbsp. flour over steak and pound in with side of small pie pan. Turn on other side and repeat. Place 2 tbsp. oil in skillet and brown steak on both sides. Half cover steak with hot water and simmer 1½ hours. Remove steak to hot platter, thicken liquid with a little flour and pour over steak. Sprinkle chopped parsley over all. Serves 6.

■ **BEEF STROGANOFF**

Buy 1½ lbs. lean beef; remove all fat and gristle; cut with kitchen scissors into narrow strips about 2½-inches long, ¾-inch wide and ¼-inch thick. Sprinkle strips with salt and freshly ground pepper. Set aside for about 2 hours in cool (not cold) place. When ready to prepare the meat, melt 1 tbsp. butter in a heavy skillet and sauté 1 c. sliced fresh (or canned) mushrooms until tender, about 10 minutes. Remove from skillet and set aside. In same butter, sauté a thinly-sliced onion until brown; remove from skillet and set aside. Add 1 tbsp. butter to skillet and, when hot, put in strips of beef and sear on all sides, but leave rare. Remove beef and set aside. Add 2 tbsp. flour and blend into remaining butter. Slowly add 2 c. beef bouillon, stirring well to form a smooth gravy. Next, add 3 tbsp. sherry or cider, 1 tsp. dry mustard; blend all well. Add to sauce the strips of beef, onions and mushrooms; simmer over low heat, 20 minutes. About 5 minutes before serving, add ⅔ c. commercial sour cream; blend; when hot, serve. Serves 6.

■ NEW ENGLAND BOILED DINNER

A 4-5 lb. corned-beef brisket will serve 4 people for 2 meals.

Place meat in large kettle with 4 peppercorns, 1 bay leaf and ¼ tsp. thyme. Cover with cold water. Bring slowly to boiling, simmer covered, 3-4 hours. Skim if necessary. About 45 minutes before meat is done, add 6-8 small potatoes, pared, 8 small peeled white onions, and 6-8 scraped small carrots. Cook about 30 minutes; then place 1 small head of cabbage, cut in quarters, and 8 small turnips, peeled and sliced thin, on top and cook 20 minutes longer. Lift meat onto platter, place vegetables around sides and sprinkle minced parsley over the meat.

■ BEEF RAGOUT

2 tsp. butter	4 quartered, peeled tomatoes
1 lb. boned chuck, cut in 1-inch cubes	12 small white onions
1 tsp. salt or substitute	1 c. sliced mushrooms or canned stems and pieces
1 bouillon cube	4 stalks celery, sliced
6 pared small carrots in ½-inch chunks	2 tbsp. snipped parsley

In hot butter in large skillet, brown meat well on all sides about 5 minutes. Add boiling water to cover, salt and bouillon cube. Simmer, covered, 30 minutes or until meat is almost tender. Skim off fat. Add carrots, tomatoes, onions, mushrooms, celery. Cook, covered, 30 minutes or until vegetables are fork-tender. To serve, ladle into soup plates; sprinkle with parsley. Serves 6.

■ BROWNED SHORT RIBS

1 c. minced raw vegetables	2 c. beef bouillon
1 clove garlic, minced	½ tsp. dried basil
2 tbsp. oil	1 bay leaf
3 lbs. short ribs	2 tbsp. minced parsley, fresh

Mince any raw vegetables (onions, peas, celery, carrots, fresh pepper, beans—all are good). Brown with garlic in oil. Remove with a slotted spoon. Salt, pepper and flour ribs and brown them in same pan, adding more oil if necessary. Return browned vegetables to pan. Cover meat with broth, add dried herbs and simmer gently, 2-2½ hours. Add parsley. Serve with rice and green beans. Serves 4.

■ **BEEF CURRY**

3½ lbs. top round or top sir-loin	4 c. water
1 c. flour	1 c. seedless raisins
3 tbsp. curry powder	2 cooking apples
1 c. chopped onion	¼ tsp. cayenne
1 c. water-chestnuts, if de-sired	1 tsp. salt
¼ lb. butter	2 lbs. sliced fresh mushrooms or 1 large can stems and pieces
3 cloves garlic, minced	

Cut steak into bite-size pieces. Mix flour with curry powder. Add more for really hot curry. Dredge meat thoroughly in flour mix and shake it a little in a wire sieve so not too much flour clings. In deep skillet or Dutch oven, melt butter, add garlic minced, and brown meat, stirring often. When meat is browned, add water, raisins, peeled, cored and chopped apples, chopped onion and water-chestnuts, if desired. Cover. Lower heat and cook until meat is tender, about 1 hour. *Don't overcook* or meat will fall apart. Add salt or substitute and a dash of cayenne, and mushrooms. Remove from heat. Can be re-heated on top of stove or in oven, served in casserole or chafing dish. Serves 6.

Serve with the following condiments: Separate small bowls of chutney; 4 chopped, hard-cooked eggs; 1 c. pecans or walnuts cut in small pieces.

■ **POT ROAST**

Brown 4-5 lbs. chuck, rump or brisket slowly in a heavy kettle, turning often. Add 2 tsp. salt, 2 stalks chopped celery, 3 carrots cut up in chunks, 1 clove garlic, sliced, 3 small peeled onions, 2 bay leaves, ⅛ tsp. rosemary, thyme or basil. Add 1 c. cider or water. Cover tightly and cook over low heat, 3-4 hours, or until meat is tender. Turn meat frequently, adding more water if necessary. Serves 8.

■ **MEAT PIE WITH BROWN BISCUITS**

1½ lbs. lean beef, chuck, round or rump	2 tsp. salt
3 tbsp. unbleached white flour	⅛ tsp. pepper
1 tbsp. oil	3 medium carrots, quartered
3 c. water	10 small white onions
2 tbsp. chopped celery	3 sprigs parsley

Cut beef in 1-inch pieces. Roll in flour. Brown in oil. Add water, celery and salt. Cover; simmer about 2 hours until meat is almost tender. Add carrots, onions and parsley. Cover and cook about 20 minutes, or until carrots are tender.

Make whole-wheat biscuit dough, rolling about ¼-inch thick. Bake with biscuit topping. Serves 4-6.

■ PARSLEY MEAT BALLS FOR SPAGHETTI

Soak ¾ c. whole-wheat bread crumbs in ½ c. milk. Grate 2 onions and stir into bread. Add the following: 2 lbs. ground chuck, 1 c. minced parsley, 2-3 small cloves garlic, minced, 1½ tsp. salt, ¼ tsp. pepper, ¼ tsp. oregano, a few dried or fresh mint leaves, and 2 egg yolks or 1 whole egg. Blend and roll into small balls. Heat ¼ c. salad oil or butter in skillet and brown balls on all sides slowly. Makes about 3 dozen small balls.

These may be served by themselves for hors d'oeuvres or as a main dish. Make them smaller for hors d'oeuvres.

■ HAMBURGERS

Broil or pan-fry meat patties. Broiling is recommended, but patties may also be pan-fried. To do so, heat pan so a drop of water dances. Sprinkle salt or substitute over the bottom of frying pan. Place patties in pan, reduce heat and cook slowly until done. They should be rare inside and brown outside. Salt need not be added if pan is hot and "burgers" are watched carefully.

Variation—To 1 lb. ground beef add 1 beaten egg, ½ tsp. salt or substitute and ¼ tsp. freshly ground pepper. Any of the following may be added:

¼ tsp. oregano	½ chopped small onion
1 minced garlic clove	¼ c. tomato sauce or catsup
½ c. moistened bread crumbs	1 tbsp. chopped green pepper
1 tbsp. chopped parsley	½ c. Cheddar cheese, cut in
Dash of Tabasco	small pieces
½ pkg. dried onion soup	

1 lb. of meat will make 4 medium patties or 3 large ones. Serve with chili beans; mushroom sauce; in hamburger buns; on toasted whole-wheat muffins; with cheese sauce; or pan gravy.

Warning: Ground meat spoils quickly. Do not keep longer than a day unless frozen.

■ **CORNED BEEF WITH MUSTARD SAUCE**

4-6 lbs. corned beef, rolled and tied	1 tbsp. prepared mustard
A few peppercorns and a clove of garlic	⅓ c. catsup or stewed tomatoes
4 bay leaves	⅓ c. brown sugar or ¼ c. molasses
12 whole cloves	3 tbsp. vinegar
	3 tbsp. water

Put corned beef in large kettle, cover with water. Add peppercorns, garlic and bay leaves. Cook until water boils. Reduce heat and cook gently until meat is tender when pierced with a fork. Allow 30 minutes per lb. Start oven at 300°. Transfer beef to shallow baking pan. Stud fat side with cloves. Pour mixture of mustard, catsup, brown sugar, vinegar and water over meat. Bake with fat side up, 1 hour, basting occasionally. Serves 4-6.

■ **BAKED SPARE RIBS**

4 lbs. beef spare ribs	2 cans tomato paste
¼ c. brown sugar	¼ c. unsulphured molasses
1 tsp. dry mustard	4 garlic cloves, minced
1 tbsp. organic seasoning or "seasoned salt"	1 tsp. papaya juice

Blend dry ingredients with tomato sauce, molasses and papaya juice. Place meat in roasting pan and pour over sauce. Bake uncovered at 300°, 1 hour. Lower oven to 250°; bake 2 more hours, turning ribs from time to time. Serves 6.

■ **FATLESS GRAVY**

Pour all the fat possible from the pan under the roast. You can add ice cubes to make fat particles congeal, then they can be spooned out.

Mix 2 tbsp. flour with ½ c. cold water. Stirring constantly, add flour paste to remaining meat drippings. The drippings hold the flavor. Cook until thickened.

VEAL

■ **VEAL STEW**

2 lbs. veal rump or shoulder. Wipe meat with a damp cloth and cut into 2-inch cubes. Brown in heavy saucepan in 2 tbsp. oil. Add 1 tbsp. lemon juice, 1 tbsp. chopped onion, ½ tsp. rosemary, and 2 c. water. Cover tightly and simmer about 40 minutes. Add ½ c. chopped celery, 3-4 carrots cut in pieces, 4 new potatoes, or 2 medium potatoes pared and cut in cubes. Simmer 20-25 minutes or until vegetables are tender. Gravy may be thickened with ¼ c. flour and ¼ c. cold water mixed into a paste and added. Season with salt, pepper and Worcestershire sauce. Serves 4.

■ **VEAL SCALLOPINI**

1½ lbs. thin veal steak	2 tbsp. flour
¼ c. salad oil	1¼ tsp. salt
1 small clove garlic, minced	¼ tsp. pepper
¾ c. thinly sliced onion	1 c. water
½ c. white wine or ¼ c. lemon juice	
¼ lb. mushrooms sliced or 1 medium can stems and pieces	

Cut meat into serving pieces. Heat oil in large heavy skillet. Add meat and garlic and brown on both sides. Lift out meat. Brown onion and mushrooms in the drippings. Blend flour, salt and pepper into fat. Add wine or lemon juice gradually, then stir until thickened. Place meat in gravy, add water, cover and cook over low heat until meat is tender. Serves 4-6.

■ **VEAL SMOTHERED IN MUSHROOMS**

1¼ lbs. veal cutlet pounded thin	2 tbsp. oil
1½ tsp. Kitchen Bouquet	3-oz. can mushrooms
1 tsp. salt	2 tsp. cornstarch
⅛ tsp. marjoram	2 tbsp. cold water

Cut meat in 8 strips and place in mixing bowl. Sprinkle with Kitchen Bouquet, salt and marjoram. Stir with fork to coat meat evenly. Brown meat lightly over moderate heat in oil. Add mushrooms. Cover tightly and cook over low heat until meat is tender, about 30 minutes. Blend together cornstarch and cold water; stir in. Bring to boil, stirring constantly. Serve immediately. Serves 4.

■   **BREADED VEAL CUTLETS**

Use sirloin tips or round of veal steak. Cut in pieces for serving. Sprinkle with salt, dip in crumbs, then in egg and in crumbs again. Fry until well browned. Set pan in oven and cook slowly 1 hour or more, until tender.

■   **WIENER SCHNITZEL**

6 veal steaks, cut thin	3 tbsp. oil or butter
1 tsp. salt	Juice of 1 lemon
½ tsp. pepper	1 tbsp. flour
2 eggs, beaten	1 c. commercial sour cream
1 c. whole-wheat flour	6 lemon slices

Pound veal steaks to about ¼-inch thickness. Season with salt and pepper. Dip into eggs, then into flour. Brown in fat; cover and cook over low heat about 1 hour, until meat is tender. Sprinkle with lemon juice and place on hot platter. Blend flour with fat in pan, add sour cream and cook over low heat, about 3 minutes. Season with salt and pepper and pour over chops. Garnish with lemon slices. Serves 6.

■   **DEVILED VEAL CUTLET**

2 lb. thin veal cutlets	1 c. minced onion
2 tbsp. oat flour or whole-wheat flour	1 bouillon cube
	1½ c. boiling water
1 tsp. salt	Pinch of dry mustard
1 tsp. paprika	1 tsp. horseradish root
2½ tbsp. butter	½ c. commercial sour cream

Cut veal into serving-size pieces; roll in flour mixed with salt and paprika. In hot butter in skillet, sauté onions, remove and set aside. In same skillet, brown veal well. Dissolve bouillon cube in boiling water; pour over veal. Add sautéed onions, mustard, horseradish; simmer, covered, 25 minutes or until veal is tender. Remove meat to serving dish. Gradually stir sour cream into gravy, spoon over meat. Serve at once. Serves 6.

■   **JELLIED VEAL LOAF**

4 pieces veal shank or knuckle of veal	1 sliced carrot
	1 bay leaf
1 tbsp. salt	6 peppercorns
1 medium onion, chopped	2 tbsp. cider vinegar

Place veal in large kettle of boiling water; add salt, onion, carrot, bay leaf, peppercorns and vinegar. Cover and simmer about 2½ hours, until meat is tender. Remove meat and cool broth. When meat is cold, run through coarse blades of food chopper. Drain broth through fine sieve or cheesecloth. Cool. Skim fat from broth. There should be 1 qt. broth; if more, cook down to 1 qt.; if less, add necessary water. Add ground meat. Taste to determine whether additional seasoning is required. Pack into 9 x 5 x 3-inch loaf pan. Cover with freezer paper and refrigerate overnight. Unmold and slice. Serves 6-9.

■ VEAL BIRDS

2 lbs. veal cut ¼-inch thick, or 2 steaks	3 tbsp. oil
2 tsp. salt	2 c. tomato juice
¼ tsp. pepper	¼ tsp. thyme
2 c. bread stuffing	¼ tsp. oregano
4 tbsp. flour	¼ c. minced parsley

Season veal steak with salt and pepper. Spread stuffing evenly over steak, and roll. Fasten with toothpicks or tie with string. Roll in flour and brown in hot oil. Add ½ c. tomato juice, thyme and oregano. Cover tightly and simmer about 1½ hours. Turn occasionally. To serve, remove skewers or string, place on serving platter. Add remainder of tomato juice which has been mixed with flour and juices in pan. Cook until thickened and pour over meat. Sprinkle with parsley. Serves 4.

■ LEMON VEAL CUTLETS

¾ lb. veal, sliced thin and pounded	1 c. fine whole-wheat crumbs
Rind of 1 lemon, grated	¼ c. whole-wheat flour
Juice of 2 lemons	1 tsp. salt
1 egg, beaten	¼ tsp. pepper
	4 tbsp. butter

Veal sliced to ½-inch thick should be pounded to ¼-inch thickness.

Place veal in shallow dish and sprinkle with grated lemon rind and juice. Let stand for 1 hour, turning meat frequently. Dip veal in egg, then in crumbs seasoned with salt, pepper and flour. Lay slices on waxed paper and let stand 30 minutes, until crumb coating dries. Melt butter in heavy skillet and brown meat. Serves 4.

■   **VEAL CHOPS WITH HERBS**

Brown 4 veal chops in melted butter or oil. Then add 1 tsp. salt, ¼ tsp. pepper, ¼ tsp. each of thyme, oregano, basil and rosemary. Add a small onion chopped, 1 clove garlic, minced, and pour in 1 c. consommé. Cover and cook slowly for 30 minutes or until tender. Pour over 1 can sliced mushrooms. Stir into gravy. Serves 4.

■   **VEAL AND EGGS**

1 lb. veal, cut in strips	½ c. top milk
1¾ c. water	Dash of cayenne
2 tsp. salt	⅛ tsp. nutmeg
1 onion, chopped	Salt to taste
Few celery leaves	3 hard-cooked eggs
Few whole black peppercorns	2 tbsp. sherry (optional)
2 tbsp. whole-wheat pastry flour	Rice pilaf or Chinese rice

Cover veal with 1¾ c. water. Add salt, onion, celery leaves and peppercorns. Simmer until meat is tender. Remove peppercorns. Make paste of flour and milk and stir into the meat. Add seasonings, taste for salt. Press egg yolks through sieve into meat and add whites cut in narrow lengthwise strips. Cook until thickened. Add sherry. Serve over rice. Serves 4.

PORK

Although pork is "in season" 12 months of the year, the period when supply is greatest and price most economical is between November and March. Since this coincides with the colder months when appetites are heartiest, it follows that more fresh pork is served then. Cured pork products are used in both warm or cool months. Pork sausage finds great favor in the cold months.

■   **COOKING FRESH PORK**

All Pork is Cooked Well Done: One general rule applies to the cookery of all fresh pork. Cook it well done. This means that an internal temperature of 185° or more should be reached. The easiest way to tell when pork has reached the well done stage, if no thermometer is available, is to see whether all the *pink color* has disappeared, the meat itself whitish tan in color and the meat juice clear. Well done pork has the maximum flavor in both meat and fat. Cured and smoked pork, like ham and bacon, have reached fairly high temperatures in the smoking, and therefore need less cooking at home, either for flavor, tenderness or safety. Roasting, braising, and cooking in water, are the three major methods of cooking fresh pork. Broiling is not recommended, as the meat becomes hard and dry before it is well done. Since pork has considerably more fat than other fresh meats, the fat drippings will be in larger amount.

■ ROAST PORK

6-lb. pork loin	2 onions, sliced thin
½ tsp. pepper	2 tbsp. flour
1 tsp. salt	
1 tsp. sweet basil or 1 tsp. ground ginger, if desired	

Wipe meat with damp cloth; rub in seasonings and sift flour over roast. Place in roasting pan in 425° oven until meat browns. Reduce heat to 350° and place onions around pork; add 1 c. water and roast about 3 hours, basting frequently. Remove roast to hot platter. Carefully stir 2 tbsp. flour into liquid in pan; add 1½ c. water and cook over low heat, stirring constantly until mixture thickens. Serve in gravy boat along with roast. Serves 8.

■ STUFFED PORK CHOPS

Have butcher cut shoulder chops about ½-inch thick, for rolling and stuffing. Serve 1 chop per person. Make bread dressing, allowing a generous handful per chop. Combine soft whole-wheat bread crumbs with finely chopped celery, salt, pepper, minced onion and just enough water to moisten. Place handful on each chop, roll and fasten with toothpicks or tie with string. Place in baking pan. Add water or milk to nearly cover chops. Bake at 350°, about 1 hour, or until meat is thoroughly done.

■ PORK CHOP CASSEROLE

Allow 1 loin pork chop per person. Season with salt and pepper and brown quickly on both sides in frying pan. Remove to casserole and pour over 1 can cream of mushroom soup. Cover and bake 40 minutes at 375°.

■ **PORK, BEEF AND HAM LOAF**

¾ lb. smoked ham, ground	¾ c. non-fat dry milk solids
½ lb. lean pork, ground	3 tbsp. chopped onion
½ lb. beef, ground	1 c. dry bread crumbs
½ tsp. salt	1 egg, beaten
1 c. water	

Combine all ingredients in large bowl. Mix lightly until well combined. Pack in well greased loaf pan. Bake in moderate oven, 350°, 1¾ hours. Serve with sour cream or yogurt mixed with 2 tbsp. chili sauce or tomato catsup. Serves 8.

■ **PORK AND HAM LOAF**

1 lb. ham, ground	1 egg
1 lb. pork shoulder, ground	¾ c. milk
1 c. whole-wheat bread crumbs	1 small can tomato sauce

Use 1 tbsp. tomato sauce; mix ham, pork, crumbs, egg, milk. Place in a loaf pan. Cover with remaining tomato sauce. Cover and bake at 325°, 2 hours. Serves 8-10.

■ **BREAKFAST SCRAPPLE**

½ c. chopped ham, salt pork or bacon	2 c. whole-kernel corn, ground, or yellow cornmeal
1 tbsp. each, chopped onion and celery	1 tsp. salt
6 c. boiling water	¼ tsp. paprika

Fry meat and vegetables in a small amount of oil until brown. Add boiling water and cook five minutes, then stir in cornmeal. Season and cook about 1 hour. Place in loaf pan. When cold, cut in slices, roll in flour and sauté.

■ **SCALLOPED HAM AND POTATOES**

1 slice center-cut ham or 2 c. leftover baked ham	2 c. milk
8 medium potatoes, sliced	4 tbsp. butter or oil
4 tbsp. flour (unbleached)	½ tsp. salt
	Dash of pepper

Make white sauce of melted butter, flour, salt and milk. Place ½ of sliced potatoes in bottom of a well greased 3-qt. casserole. Cover with ½ of ham, add remaining potatoes and top with ham. Pour white sauce over top. Bake for 1½ hours at 350°. Serves 6-8.

■   **SWEET-AND-SOUR PORK**

Cook 2 lbs. fresh pork, cut in 2-inch pieces, in enough water to cook tender in about 20 minutes. Remove and cool.

Make sweet-and-sour sauce of ¾ c. brown sugar, ¼ c. soy sauce, ⅓ c. vinegar, 3 tbsp. cornstarch, and about ¾ c. water. Cook, stirring constantly until thickened. Remove from fire.

Sauté ¼ c. onion and ¼ c. crushed pineapple in 2 tbsp. oil. A medium cucumber, peeled and sliced; or green pepper, sliced, may be used instead of the pineapple. Cook 1-2 minutes.

Dip pork in mixture of 2 tbsp. soy sauce and 2 tbsp. wheat germ or cornstarch. Heat oil for deep-fat frying (365°) and fry meat until crisp and brown. Combine meat and vegetables and pour sweet-and-sour sauce over all. Serves 6-8.

HAM *

Hams may be purchased as fresh leg of pork, cured, smoked ham, cured ham, and cooked, canned ham.

Smithfield and Tennessee hams differ only in that they have a heavier cure and need to be soaked and parboiled before baking.

Smoked hams are marketed as cook-before-eating-hams, ready-to-eat (flavor is improved by further cooking), fully cooked (usually canned). Smoked ham may be purchased bone in or whole, cut into butt or shank ends, or center slices.

Rolled hams are boneless and skinless, and tied into rolls.

Picnic hams are the lower section of the shoulder or foreleg, or shoulder butt. They are sometimes boned and skinned.

When considering cost, uncooked hams are usually less expensive and cooked hams with bone in are less expensive than boned and skinned hams. But it figures out about the same when you consider the edible portions.

The butt end costs more than the shank, and the center slices are choice, so most expensive.

A good buy is a heavy shank end. Have butcher cut off 1-2 slices and cut ham down the center to within 4-5 inches. Use bone for baked beans or split pea soup. Bake the heavier piece of the two remaining and cut up the smaller piece for a casserole dish.

* Instructions for carving ham will be found following page 183.

Refrigeration is important: With the new, mild cure now used in processing hams, they must be handled just like fresh meat. Keep them in the refrigerator before and after cooking and until used. After cooking, the remaining ham may be cut from the bone and stored in smaller space in the refrigerator. In this case, make split pea soup or bean soup from the bone at once. Do not try to keep ham any longer than you would fresh meats. Large sized canned hams, 6¾-12 lbs. are cooked in the can, but are not sterile. They must be refrigerated at all times.

Bacon should be wrapped in the wrapper in which it comes, or freezer paper. Keep in refrigerator (not necessarily in the coldest part). Do not try to keep bacon more than 2 weeks as it loses its finest flavor and tends to dry when cooking.

■   **TO BAKE HAM**

Place ham fat side up on rack in open baking pan. Do not add water or cover pan. Bake in slow oven 325°. Insert meat thermometer through fat side into center of thickest part of meat, being careful not to touch the bone.

> *Cooked (ready-to-eat) ham* will take—whole—10 minutes per lb.
> —half —14 minutes per lb.

The meat thermometer will register 150° when done; or depend on your timing.

> *Uncooked ham* must be baked—whole—18-20 minutes per lb.
> —half —20-25 minutes per lb.

The meat thermometer will register 160° when baked.

When a *picnic ham* is baked with the bone, it will take 3-4 hours and the thermometer will be 170° when done.

About 45 minutes before ham is done, remove from oven, cut away skin on top, pour off drippings, score fat surface of ham and stud with whole cloves. Spread with any of the following glazes and return to oven. Bake at 400° until done.

1. **1 c. honey mixed with frozen pineapple or orange concentrate or fresh juice.**
2. **1 c. brown sugar mixed with ½ c. crushed pineapple or apple sauce.**
3. **1 c. unsulphured molasses mixed with 1 tsp. dry mustard.**

Fresh leg of pork is placed on rack in open roasting pan and cooked at 325°, 35 minutes per lb., or until meat thermometer registers 185°.

About ½ hour before ham is done, remove from oven, pour off drippings, take off rind, score fat and stud with cloves. Use any of the glazes listed for smoked ham and return to 400° oven to finish baking.

A *smoked boneless butt* is best simmered, but small ones can be baked. Place butt in deep kettle, cover with water, add 1 sliced onion, bay leaf, 2-3 peppercorns, 1 tsp. celery salt and ½ c. vinegar or lemon juice. Cover and simmer over low heat. Allow about 50 minutes per lb. Slice and serve.

HOW TO COOK A HAM SLICE

Thickness	Weight (approx.)	Method	Time
2 in.	2½-3 lbs.	Bake	1½-1¾ hours
1½ in.	2 lbs.	Bake	1-1¼ hours
		Broil	25-30 minutes
¾ in.	16-24 oz.	Broil	15 minutes
		Fry	12 minutes
½ in.	9-12 oz.	Broil	10 minutes
		Fry	8 minutes

Baking: Place thick slice in covered casserole and bake in 325° oven, 1-1¾ hours; for a 1½ in. slice 1-1¼ hours. Brown sugar and cloves, fruit juice or mustard and milk may be used over the ham during baking. Uncover the last 15-20 minutes for browning.

Broiling: Score fat edges and lay on broiler rack. Set 3½ inches under moderate heat and broil for time specified above, turning only once.

Frying: Score fat edges of ham slice and place in pre-heated fry pan. Fry over moderate heat for time specified above.

■ SAUSAGE

Buy well-seasoned pork sausage links or meat, allowing about ⅓ lb. per person. Sage may be added to sausage meat if desired. Broil links of sausage meat, formed into patties, on rack 4 inches from flame. Turn so that sausage is uniformly browned.

Sausage may also be pan-fried. Place in unheated frying pan and cook over low heat, turning to brown; drain on brown paper.

Sausage is excellent with apple slices browned in pan in which sausage has been fried.

■   **TOASTED SAUSAGE ROLLS**

6 sausage links   6 slices whole-wheat bread
                                   with crusts removed.

Roll cooked sausage links in bread slices, fastening with tooth-picks. Place under broiler until bread is golden-brown.

■   **FRANKFURTERS**

Wieners, frankfurters or hot dogs may be all beef, or all pork. The most popular are made of pork. They are cooked when you buy them, but are usually cooked again if only to warm them. They do not require long cooking and it must be at a low temperature. They may be heated by steaming in ¼ c. water with tight lid on pan or by broiling or pan frying. Care must be taken that they do not get too hot and shrivel. Wieners which do not contain pre-servatives are available in most markets.

They may be served in the following ways:

1. Split, and filled with barbecue sauce or chilli sauce; heat 5-10 minutes.
2. Split, and filled with bread dressing; wrap with bacon or fasten with toothpicks and bake until brown.
3. Cut in pieces and served with scrambled eggs.
4. Placed in cabbage last 5 minutes of cooking.
5. Placed in baked beans last 5 minutes of cooking.
6. Placed in sauerkraut and heated through.
7. Steamed and served with cheese sauce.
8. Rolls may be hollowed, wiener placed in center and toasted under broiler.
9. Biscuit dough may be wrapped around a wiener and baked for 15 minutes.
10. Sliced wieners may be placed in macaroni or Spanish rice dishes.
11. Sliced wieners may be cooked with beans.

■   **BACON**

Broiled: Place bacon slices on rack and broil 4 inches from heat, about 2 minutes on each side, until brown and crisp.

Pan-Fried: Place bacon slices in unheated frying pan and brown on both sides, over low heat, until crisp. Remove to brown paper to drain. Eggs may be fried in remaining bacon fat, breaking each egg on a plate and sliding gently into pan.

Baked: Remove broiling pan; place bacon slices on rack and bake in 400° oven, about 12 minutes, until brown and crisp. Slices do not have to be turned.

■ GLAZED PARTY HAM

Soften 1 pkg. unflavored gelatin in ½ c. apricot nectar, cold. Add ½ c. hot apricot nectar to dissolve. Chill to consistency of unbeaten egg whites and brush about half the mixture over a cold cooked ham. Keep remaining gelatin in warm place so it will not stiffen. Chill ham until gelatin glaze is firm. Garnish ham with fruit slices, sliced hard-cooked eggs or sliced olives. Coat fruit, eggs or olives with gelatin. This makes a stunning luncheon platter.

Variation—Use lemon-flavored gelatin as a glaze for cold tongue or pressed veal; garnish as desired with gelatin-glazed fruit or sliced hard-cooked egg or olives.

POULTRY *

A plump chicken coming to table, its skin crackly brown, the fragrance of sage and thyme floating from the stuffing, a bowl of creamy gravy at its side, mashed potatoes light as a summer cloud . . . this is part of almost everyone's Sunday memories.

But now that poultry of all kinds is available the year round, it should be served often and in an exciting variety of ways. It is an excellent protein. If you do not raise your own poultry, be sure that the bird you buy has not been given stilbestrol to induce quick weight and antibiotics to keep it alive in an unnatural environment. Dr. Clive McKay, Professor of Nutrition at Cornell University, has found that residues are left in poultry thus fed, and that test animals given such poultry failed to reproduce normally.

Chicken, turkey, duck, goose, capons and Cornish rock hens may be purchased fresh-killed, frozen or canned. Poultry cut in pieces may be either fresh or frozen.

"Dressed Weight" means what the bird weighs when only the feathers have been removed. "Ready to Cook" means that the giblets have been removed and separately wrapped and that the lungs and other internal tissues have been taken out and all pinfeathers removed. There is no waste in "Ready to Cook" poultry, so the cost is slightly higher.

Frozen poultry will keep for months in your freezing compartment. After thawing, do not refreeze and do not try to keep in refrigerator more than a day.

* How to carve roast poultry is explained following page 183.

Methods of thawing frozen poultry:

1. Place poultry in original wrapper in regular food compartment of refrigerator, allowing about 4 hours per lb. This averages overnight for a frozen chicken and 2-3 days for a large turkey.
2. Place whole bird in cool running water until just pliable enough to handle. Do not leave in water after bird is thawed.
3. Place cut-up chicken on a rack, in shallow pan until parts can be separated.

You should plan on about 1 lb. of poultry per person.

Broiling chickens are 2½-3½ months old and average 1½-2 lbs. dressed. Skin should be smooth and white.

Frying chickens are 3½-5 months old, frying roosters 5-9 months. They vary in weight according to breed.

Roasting chickens are about the same age as fryers and should weigh 4-5 lbs. Chickens older than a year will have yellow skins and tougher meat, and should be used for stewing or soups.

■ ROAST TURKEY, CHICKEN, OR DUCK

Clean the bird thoroughly; singe, remove pin feathers. Wash inside to remove blood or loose pieces of lungs or entrails. Pat dry with paper towels. Stuff not too tightly, place in 325° oven on an open rack. Cover for first 2-3 hours with a clean cloth saturated with butter or oil. Remove to brown the bird. Poultry is done when the leg joints move freely in a firm grasp.

> **Roast turkey**-20-25 minutes per lb. at 325°.
> **Roast chicken**-40 minutes per lb. at 325°.
> **Roast duck**-30 minutes per lb. at 325°.

If necessary to draw poultry, insert hand in cavity, loosen the entrails and remove. Reach in and pull out windpipe, lungs and kidneys. Cut out the oil sac on back of the tail. From breastbone cavity remove any part of windpipe remaining. Pull back skin from neck and cut off neck. When separating heart, gizzard and liver, be very careful not to break the gall bladder. Remove it and destroy.

After stuffing bird, fold the wing tips back under the first joint. Flatten out neck skin and fold back, fastening with wooden or metal skewer. After stuffing main cavity, draw skin together and insert skewers. Now lace with strings. Bring ends of drumsticks and tail together, wrap cord around them and tie at back.

Never stuff a chicken or turkey with warm dressing, then hold overnight without roasting. Never partially roast a bird one day and expect to continue the next.

Remove dressing from the bird after serving and do not hold more than 24 hours unless thoroughly heated again.

Never let gravy, dressing or cooked poultry stand at room temperature for even a few hours. Put in refrigerator. If cooked poultry is too big for refrigerator, disjoint it, wrap loosely and then refrigerate.

Cooked poultry absorbs flavors quickly, so must be covered in the refrigerator. Do not try to keep cooked poultry more than a few days.

■ **TRADITIONAL STUFFING**
   (*Sufficient for 12-lb. turkey*)

3 qts. whole-grain bread crumbs	¾ c. chopped celery
Chopped giblets	¾ c. butter or ½ c. oil
6 tbsp. chopped onion	1 tbsp. chopped parsley
¾ tsp. poultry seasoning	1 tbsp. salt
1½ c. broth from cooking giblets	¼ tsp. pepper

Add only enough broth to make crumbs stick together when squeezed in the hand. Too much liquid makes a soggy dressing.

The addition of 1 c. chopped chestnuts, boiled and peeled, is an old-time favorite.

1 or 2 c. corn bread crumbs may be substituted for an equal amount of wheat-bread crumbs.

■ **BRAZIL NUT STUFFING**

⅔ c. oil or butter	4 stalks celery, chopped
1½ c. shelled Brazil nuts	½ c. chopped parsley
2 medium onions, chopped	2 tsp. salt
2-day-old whole-wheat bread cubes (about 3 qts.)	¼ tsp. pepper
1½ tbsp. poultry seasoning, or thyme, sage or other herbs to taste	½ c. liquid from cooking giblets, or use water

Place nuts in boiling water for 5 minutes. Drain well and cut in thin slices. Chop onion and celery in fine pieces. Heat oil, add onions and celery and cook until tender, but not browned. Stir in salt, pepper and seasonings. Combine vegetables and bread cubes. Stir in nuts. Add liquid and parsley. Mix thoroughly. Makes enough for 12-16-lb. turkey.

■   **RICE STUFFING**

For a change of flavor in preparing stuffing for fowl, use cooked brown rice, mixed with any of the following: cooked, chopped mushrooms; toasted sesame seeds; toasted whole-wheat bread crumbs; pignolia nuts; soy grits; flaked almonds or pecans.

■   **BROILING POULTRY**

Broiled chicken, ducklings, and small turkeys or ½ turkeys are delicious. Some table-dressed broilers come split down the back and need only to be cut through breast to separate the halves.

Have meat dealer split turkeys for broiling, removing back-bone; slip wing tip in back of shoulder joint and skewer wing to body.

Duckling must be split the same way, removing neck and backbone.

Braising chickens or turkeys is done the same as for frying; then finish cooking in a closely covered frying pan or casserole.

■   **TO BROIL**

Place chicken or turkey on broiler rack, skin-side down, with meat 4 inches from heat unit. Brush with butter or barbecue sauce; broil for about 15 minutes. Turn poultry, brush with sauce again and continue broiling until tender. Turkeys should be placed 7 inches from heat and will take about ½ hour on each side.

■   **OVEN-COOKED YOUNG CHICKEN**

Toss each piece of chicken in flour mixed with salt and pepper. Do this in a paper bag. Place chicken pieces in a well-buttered casserole. Pour either melted chicken fat or ⅓ c. melted butter over chicken. Cover tightly and bake at 325° for 1 hour. Remove lid, turn pieces and continue baking until chicken is brown.

■   **CHICKEN PIE**

Simmer 1 stewing chicken until tender in enough water to cover. Cool, remove meat from bones in as large pieces as possible. Thicken remaining liquid, add salt to taste and 1 c. milk, to which has been added 1 beaten egg. Place chicken pieces in a large pan or casserole and cover with thickened stock. Add ½ c. chopped parsley. Cover with biscuits made with 2 c. flour, 2 tsp. baking power, ¼ tsp. salt and 2 tbsp. butter; blend and add ⅔ c. buttermilk and ¼ tsp. soda. Roll to ½-inch thick. Cut with biscuit cutter and lay over chicken. Bake in hot oven, 400°, until brown.

■ STEWED CHICKEN

Cut up 1 stewing chicken, cover with boiling water, add 2 tsp. salt, 1 carrot, 1 onion, 1 stalk celery. Simmer for 2½ hours or until tender. Remove chicken from bones. Remove vegetables from broth. For each c. broth, mix 2 tbsp. flour with a little cold water to make a thin paste.

Chicken and gravy may be served over biscuits, brown rice or cornbread. Dumplings or noodles may be cooked in the gravy.

■ FRIED CHICKEN

Place pieces of cut-up young chicken in paper sack to which ½ c. flour, 2 tsp. salt and ⅛ tsp. pepper has been added. Shake well. Melt half butter/half oil in frying pan (about ½ c. in all). Brown pieces slowly, turn heat low, continue frying 30 minutes.

■ CHICKEN WITH FRUIT JUICE

2½ lb. fryer	1 3-oz. can sliced mushrooms
1 medium onion	2 tbsp. fresh or bottled lemon
¼ c. flour	juice
2 tsp. salt	½ c. canned apple juice
¼ tsp. pepper	¼ tsp. marjoram
3 tbsp. butter	

Have chicken cut in pieces at market. Chop onion fine. Wash chicken, drain and dry. Mix flour, salt, pepper. Dip chicken in seasoned flour. Melt butter; brown chicken; add onions. Cover and cook 3 minutes. Add mushrooms and remaining ingredients. Cover and cook slowly, 45 minutes. Serve with brown rice. Serves 4.

■ CHICKEN CREOLE

1 large onion	1 No. 2½ can tomatoes
1 green pepper	½ tsp. oregano
3 lb. fryer	⅛ tsp. Tabasco
½ c. salad oil	1 tsp. salt
¼ c. flour	¼ tsp. pepper

Cut chicken in pieces. Cut onion in thin slices. Chop green pepper in small pieces. Wash and dry chicken. Heat salad oil in deep skillet. Dip chicken in flour, add to fat and brown well. Remove chicken. Add onions, green pepper and cook until tender, but not browned. Pour off fat. Return chicken to skillet. Add remaining ingredients. Cover tightly and cook over low heat, 30 minutes. Uncover and cook 30 minutes longer. Serves 4-6.

■ **CHICKEN CACCIATORA**

1 frying chicken (about 3 lb.) cut in serving-size pieces	2¼ c. (1-lb. 4-oz. can) tomatoes
1 clove of garlic, peeled	1 can tomato paste
¼ c. flour	6 small white onions, peeled
1 tsp. salt, for chicken	1 tbsp. minced parsley
⅛ tsp. pepper	1 tsp. salt, for sauce
¼ c. olive oil or salad oil	1 bay leaf

Wash chicken; drain; dry well. Save neck and giblets to make soup for another meal. Rub chicken well with garlic. Mince garlic; save for later on. Combine flour, salt (for chicken), and pepper in large paper bag; shake chicken pieces in bag until well coated. Heat oil in Dutch oven, add chicken, a few pieces at a time; brown well on all sides; drain on unglazed paper. Pour off any oil remaining in pan. Return chicken to Dutch oven; add minced garlic, tomatoes, tomato paste, onions, salt (for sauce), and bay leaf. Simmer, covered, basting occasionally with sauce in pan, about 1 hour, or until chicken is tender. Serves 6.

■ **CHICKEN NOODLE OR RICE CASSEROLE**

1 5-lb. chicken, cut up	½ tsp. salt
2-3 stalks celery	1 c. whole-wheat noodles or
Parsley	1 c. brown rice
½ c. butter	2 c. boiling salted water
½ c. white flour	1 medium can mushrooms,
1 qt. milk	stems and pieces
Buttered crumbs	1 tsp. Worcestershire sauce
¼ c. slivered almonds	½ c. sliced stuffed olives

Cook cut-up chicken until tender in water to cover. Add celery, a little parsley, and about ½ tsp. salt. When chicken is tender, remove from bones and save liquid for soup. Discard celery and parsley. When liquid is cold, skim off fat and save. It is good in making molasses cookies. Cook 1 c. whole-wheat noodles or 1 c. brown rice in 2 c. boiling salted water until done (about 45 minutes). Make 1 qt. of white sauce by melting butter in saucepan; add white flour and stir in slowly 1 qt. of milk. Cook, stirring constantly, until thick. Combine white sauce and chicken with mushroom stems and pieces, Worcestershire sauce, sliced stuffed olives. Pour into greased casserole. Cover with buttered crumbs and slivered almonds. Bake at 350°, about 45 minutes, until set and brown. Serves 6-8.

■ CORNISH GAME HENS

These plump little chickens are the result of crossing the white Malayan game cock with a domestic hen. They are ready for market when a few weeks old and will weigh 1 lb. or less, dressed. Each person should be served a whole hen.

They may be stuffed and roasted whole, sautéed or broiled. To broil, split down the back and flatten. Brush with olive oil, salad oil or melted butter, and broil first with skin side up over glowing coals. Turn several times and baste with fat each time. They will take 25-35 minutes.

■ GAME HENS, ROASTED

Wash and prepare hens for roasting. Sprinkle cavities lightly with seasoning, such as salt, pepper and marjoram. Stuff and truss hens. Roast uncovered, 1-1½ hours, or until tender, at 325°, basting now and then with melted butter, added to the pan drippings.

Roast parboiled small whole onions and potatoes along with the birds. Turn as they brown.

■ CHINESE DUCKLING

1 5-lb. duckling	2 tbsp. fat
½ small onion	1 c. water
2 tbsp. soy sauce	1 medium green pepper
2 tbsp. honey	1 No. 1 can sliced pineapple
1 tsp. salt	2 tbsp. cornstarch
Dash of pepper	

Cut wing tips from duckling. With sharp-pointed knife, cut skin from neck to vent; first along breast of duck and then along backbone. Loosen skin by running knife underneath close to flesh of duck. Peel skin back off duck. Wash thoroughly; cut into serving pieces. Chop onion fine. Mix soy sauce, honey, salt, pepper, onion in large bowl. Add duck. Let stand for 45 minutes. Roast in 350° oven for 2 hours, turning and basting.

Cut pepper in 1-inch strips. Drain pineapple, save syrup. Cut pineapple in quarters; add with green pepper to duck. Cover and cook 15 minutes longer. Mix cornstarch and pineapple syrup. Add to duck and cook, stirring constantly until sauce thickens. Serves 6.

■   **ROAST GOOSE**

It is best to select a young goose for roasting; geese older than 4-5 months should be braised. Singe the goose, remove pinfeathers and wash it in warm water. Wash it a second time in cold water and draw; then clean thoroughly inside. Stuff with any desired dressing, truss and place in roasting pan and bake at 475°, 40 minutes. Remove from oven, pour off fat, sprinkle with salt and pepper and add 1 c. water to the pan. Return goose to pan; reduce heat to 375°. Baste goose often, allowing 20 minutes per lb. for a young goose. Remove goose from pan, add 1 c. hot water and thicken the gravy. Garnish with parsley.

If goose is not fat, lay thin slices of pork across breast.

Wild geese are prepared the same way, although sliced apples or onions are often used for stuffing. Roast in hot oven, 400°, for 2 hours, or until done.

■   **GUINEA FOWLS**

Guinea fowl has a slightly gamey flavor. They may be roasted or prepared in any of the ways chickens their age are prepared. The meat is dark and the preferred method of cooking is to roast the fowl. Fill cavity with cooked wild rice or cooked brown rice. Cover breast with a slice of fat bacon. Have oven at 500° for first 15 minutes, then reduce heat to 350°. Allow 40 minutes per lb. for medium-sized bird.

GAME

Furred and feathered

Wild game animals include deer, rabbit, and squirrel. Opossum, moose, porcupine and hedgehog also are killed for food, but so infrequently that I have not included recipes for them here.

Ways of cooking old or young wild game differ, as they do for domestic animals, so judge the age of your kill before deciding on the recipe.

The flesh of wild game is dark in color and strong in flavor. Old tough meat is made more tender by hanging. Hares and rabbits should not be drawn before hanging.

Hang in cool place, or freeze for several days before cooking.

Before cooking rabbits, hares or squirrels, soak in luke-warm water to draw out any blood pockets. All game may be marinated to advantage, unless very young.

■ **MARINADE FOR GAME**

⅓ c. vinegar or lemon juice   1 bay leaf
1 c. water   a few peppercorns
1 chopped onion

Mix, bring to boiling and cook 5 minutes. Cool; pour over rabbit, squirrel, tough venison or opossum. Turn pieces frequently and marinate 10-12 hours.

■ **VENISON**

Deer meat is dry and improves with marinating or frequent basting while cooking. It is hung in the hide for about a week before cooking.

Venison steaks, chops or loin cutlets are marinated for 2 hours before broiling. Wipe dry and brush with oil or butter, broil 3-5 minutes longer than beefsteak. Serve on hot platter, sprinkle with salt, pepper and paprika and spread with butter.

■ **FRIED VENISON STEAK**

Season steak with salt and pepper, dip in whole-wheat flour and cook until brown in ½ c. oil. Make gravy of whole-wheat flour and water stirred into drippings. Add 2 tbsp. plumped dried currants to the sauce.

■ **ROAST VENISON**

Wipe meat and pull off the dry skin. Season and lard the meat with bacon or salt pork strips. Make little incisions all over the meat and insert small pieces of pork or bacon and a few thin slices of garlic. Place in very hot oven, 500°, and when fat begins to run, baste with 1 c. water, fruit juice or wine; baste every 15 minutes. Reduce heat to 400° after 15 minutes. Roast about 1¾ hours for a 10-lb. haunch; if liked rare, allow only 1½ hours.

■   **FRICASSEE OF RABBIT**

If rabbit is old, cut up and put in hot water and cook until tender, about 2 hours. If a very young rabbit, cook 1 hour. Cut in pieces, roll in flour. Heat butter or oil in frying pan, put pieces of rabbit in pan and brown on all sides. Season with salt and pepper. When brown, remove pieces and pour off most of the fat. Stir into remaining fat, 3 tbsp. flour and when thick and smooth, add 1½ c. of the liquid in which the rabbit was cooked. If not enough liquid, add milk to make 1½ c. Stir until thick and pour over browned pieces of rabbit.

Rabbit or hare may be steamed after marinating; when tender, dip in flour and brown in fat or oil.

Domestic rabbit may be purchased, cleaned and cut in pieces. Cook as for fried chicken. The meat is white and delicious.

■   **ROAST HARE OR RABBIT**

Wipe the meat, fill with a good wheat-crumb stuffing. Sew up. Lay piece of beef suet over the rabbit for the first ½ hour. Remove and baste frequently. Cook at 500° for first 15 minutes, then reduce heat to 350°. Takes about 2 hours.

■   **HARE OR RABBIT CASSEROLE**

Scald in enough water to cover; drain, season, dip in egg and wheat-cracker crumbs. Season with salt and pepper. Brown pieces in fat. Place meat in casserole; pour gravy made from drippings over the meat. Cover and bake until tender.

■   **BRUNSWICK STEW**

3 squirrels, cut in pieces	6 potatoes, peeled and diced
1 tbsp. salt	2 tsp. pepper
2 onions, chopped	2 tsp. sugar
2 c. lima beans	3 c. tomatoes, diced
2 c. corn, fresh or frozen	¾ c. butter, diced

Bring 4 qts. water to boil, add salt, squirrel, onions, beans, corn, potatoes and pepper. Simmer, covered, 2 hours. Add sugar and tomato; simmer 1 hour. Roll diced butter in flour; add 10 minutes before serving. Boil up; add salt and pepper if needed; serve from tureen. Serves 8.

■ GAME BIRDS

Game birds should be hung in their feathers, as soon as possible after being shot, in a cool, dry place, for not longer than a week.

Birds are not scalded, but dry-picked, wiped with a damp cloth. Shot and entrails are removed. If birds are to be kept 7 days, it is best to draw them after the third day.

Most birds are dark meat, but quail and partridges are white and must be thoroughly cooked, but not dry. The dark-meat birds, as ducks, pigeons or squabs, partridges, pheasant and quail, are cooked rare. The youngest and fattest are best for grilling.

■ BROILED BIRDS

Clean the birds and split down the back; rub with salt and pepper, dust with flour and, if desired, wrap in bacon slices. Lay the inside next to the fire and place over low flame. Quail will cook in about 10-15 minutes, while partridges and pheasants will take 30-40 minutes. Turn often, and baste if the birds are not fat, using melted bacon grease or butter.

Young ducks are treated as the above birds except they are broiled over or under a hot fire, turning once or twice.

■ PARTRIDGES AND PHEASANT

Young partridge and pheasant can be grilled. They are cleaned, split down the back, brushed with butter and dusted with salt and pepper. Grill 15-20 minutes. Turn often.

The age of a pheasant can be determined by the last big wing feather, which is pointed when bird is young, and round when old.

Partridge and pheasant can be roasted; if old they should be parboiled first. Most partridges need be roasted only ½ hour. A buttered cloth, placed over the bird for the first 15 minutes, will help to insure a more juicy bird. Take off cloth to brown bird.

■ QUAIL AND GROUSE

Clean and wipe with damp cloth. Rub with butter and sprinkle with salt and pepper. Place a large oyster in cavity, if desired. On each bird lay thin slices of bacon, covering well. If roasting, grouse and quail should be basted frequently. Cook in a hot oven, 450°, 15-30 minutes. When done, remove bacon, brush with bacon fat or butter, dust with flour, and place in oven again only long enough to brown. The liquor in the pan is thickened and used for gravy.

Young quail and grouse may be grilled.

■ ROAST DUCK

Ducks dry out very quickly and must be basted and served with a sauce. When ducks are to be roasted, some cooks place a carrot in the cavity and cook in boiling water 10-15 minutes before roasting. Then they are wiped dry, rubbed inside and out with salt and a little black pepper and stuffed with bread stuffing or chopped celery. The bread and celery stuffing should include a small chopped onion. Apples, prunes, and wild rice also are popular stuffings for ducks.

Place duck in roasting pan and, if not fat, cover breast with thin slices of salt pork. Roast in hot oven, 500°, 15-30 minutes, depending upon rareness desired. Reduce heat to 400° after 15 minutes.

Young wild ducks are usually not stuffed except for 1 small apple, chopped, 2 cut-up prunes, chopped orange with rind or chopped onion.

■ PIGEONS AND SQUAB

Squabs are usually broiled, but can be roasted if placed closely together in a pan. Cover completely with bacon strips or place in buttered paper, closing around the bird. Foil may be used. Serve in juices that have run into paper or foil. They need only about 20 minutes cooking at 450°.

Old pigeons require slow cooking and are usually served in stews or pie. Clean and cut pigeons in small pieces and simmer 1 hour, or until tender, in beef broth, or consummé. Add water as needed. When tender, season liquor with salt, pepper, cream and ½ c. mushrooms. Arrange on platter and pour sauce over all. Add chopped parsley and serve.

Pigeon may be served over buttered toast.

TIME AND TEMPERATURE CHART
FOR COOKING FRESH MEAT

Roasting—Use oven temperature of 325° F.

Cut	Weight Range	Internal Meat Temp.	Approximate Total Time— (Hours)
BEEF			
Standing Ribs (3)	8-9 lbs.	140° rare	2¼-2½
		160° med.	2¾-3
		170° well done	3½-4
Standing Ribs (2)	6-6½ lbs.	140° rare	1¾-2
		160° med.	2¼-2½
		170° well done	3-3¼
Rolled Rib	4-5 lbs.	Same as for 3 Standing Ribs	
Rolled Rump	5-7 lbs.	170° well done	2½-3½
Sirloin Tip	3-3½ lbs.	160° med.	2-2½
VEAL			
Leg (Center Cut)	7-8 lbs.	170°	3-3½
Loin	4½-5 lbs.	170°	2½-3
Boned Rolled Shoulder	5-6 lbs.	170°	3½-4
Boned Rolled Shoulder	3 lbs.	170°	3
LAMB			
Leg (whole)	6-7 lbs.	175-180°	3½-3¾
Leg (half)	3-4 lbs.	175-180°	3-3½
Boned Rolled Shoulder	4-6 lbs.	175-180°	3-4
Bone-in, Stuffed	4-5 lbs.	175-180°	2½-2¾
FRESH PORK			
Fresh Ham	10-14 lbs.	185°	6-7
Fresh Ham (half)	5-6 lbs.	185°	3½-4
Loin	4-5 lbs.	185°	3¼-3½
Loin End	2½-3 lbs.	185°	2¼-2½
Shoulder Butt	4-6 lbs.	185°	3½-4

Broiling

Cut	Thickness	Weight	Approximate Total Time (Minutes)		
			Rare	Medium	Well Done
BEEF					
Rib Steak	1 inch	1½ lbs.	8-10	12-14	18-20
Club Steak	1 inch	1½ lbs.	8-10	12-14	18-20
Porterhouse	1 inch	1½-2 lbs.	10-12	14-16	20-25
	1½ inch	2½-3 lbs.	14-16	18-20	25-30
	2 inch	3-3½ lbs.	20-25	30-35	40-45
Sirloin	1 inch	2½-3½ lbs.	10-12	14-16	20-25
	1½ inch	3½-4½ lbs.	14-16	18-20	25-30
	2 inch	5-5½ lbs.	20-25	30-35	40-45
Ground Beef					
Patties	¾ inch	4 oz. each	8	12	15
Tenderloin	1 inch	—	8-10	12-14	18-20
Cube Steaks	¼ inch	4 oz. each	2-4	4-8	8-10
LAMB					
Rib or Loin					
Chops (1 rib)	¾ inch	2-3 oz. each	—	—	14-15
Double Rib	1½ inch	4-5 oz. each	—	—	22-25
Lamb Shoulder					
Chops	¾ inch	3-4 oz. each	—	—	14-15
Lamb Patties	¾ inch	4 oz. each	—	—	14-15

Pan Frying

Cut	Thickness	Weight	Heat	Approximate Total Time—Minutes
Frozen sandwich-type steaks	—	3-8 ozs.	High	3
Calf's or Beef Liver	¼ inch	—	Medium	10-12
Individual steaks— Club, Rib or Tenderloin	1 inch	—	Medium	8-12 Rare to Medium
Hamburgers	¾ inch	4 ozs.	Medium	8-12 Rare to Medium
Cube Steaks	¼ inch	4 ozs.	Medium	4-8

REFERENCE: American Meat Institute, 59 West Van Buren Street, Chicago, Illinois.

Braising

Cut	Weight Range	Approximate Time
Beef Pot Roast, Chuck, Rump or Heel of Round	3-5 lbs.	Brown then simmer 3½-4 hours
Swiss Steak (round) 1 in. thick	2 lbs.	Brown then simmer 1½-2 hours
Flank Steak	1½-2 lbs.	Brown then simmer 1½ hours
Beef Short Ribs	2-2½ lbs.	Brown then simmer 2-2½ hours
Ox Tails	1-1½ lbs.	Brown then simmer 3-4 hours
Rolled Lamb Shoulder Pot Roast	3-5 lbs.	Brown then simmer 2-2½ hours
Lamb Shoulder Chops	4-5 oz. each	Brown then simmer 35-40 min.
Lamb Shanks	1 lb. each	Brown then simmer 1½ hours
Pork Rib or Loin Chops	4-5 oz. each (¾-1 inch)	Brown then simmer 35-40 min.
Pork Shoulder Steaks	5-6 oz. each	Brown then simmer 35-40 min.
Veal Rolled Shoulder Pot Roast	4-5½ lbs.	Brown then simmer 2-2½ hours
Veal Cutlets or Round Steak	2 lbs.	Brown then simmer 45-50 min.
Veal Loin or Rib Chops	3-5 oz. each	Brown then simmer 45-50 min.

Simmering in Water

Cut	Weight Range	Approximate Total Time
Fresh Beef Brisket or Plate	8 lbs.	4-5 hours
Corned Beef Brisket Half or Whole	4-8 lbs.	4-6 hours
Cross Cut Shanks of Beef	4 lbs.	3-4 hours
Fresh or Smoked Beef Tongue	3-4 lbs.	3-4 hours
Pork Hocks	¾ lb.	3 hours

Stewing

Cut	Weight Range	Approximate Total Time
Beef—1-1½ inch cubes from neck, chuck, plate or heel of round	2 lbs.	2½-3 hours
Veal or Lamb—1-1½ inch cubes from shoulder or breast	2 lbs.	1½-2 hours

HOW TO CARVE

LEG OF LAMB

STANDING RIB OF BEEF

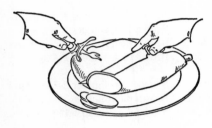

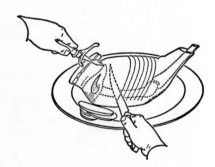

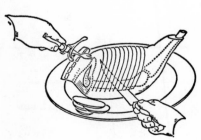

Courtesy National Live Stock and Meat Board

POT ROAST   ## PORTERHOUSE STEAK

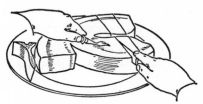

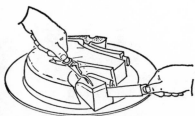
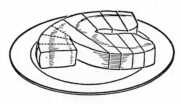

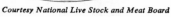

Courtesy National Live Stock and Meat Board

HAM

1. Cut a lengthwise slice from side of ham opposite cushion side. This will form a flat base on which to stand the ham for carving from the cushion side.

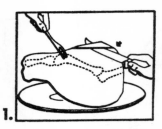

2. Turn ham on platter so that shank end is to the right of the host, and stand on the cut side. Hold ham firm with a carving fork placed securely through meaty part of ham. Make first cut straight down to bone about 6 inches from shank end.

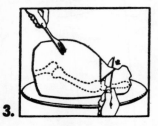

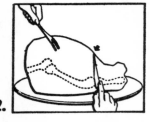

3. Make next cut on an angle to remove wedge of meat near shank end, thus exposing the first cut.

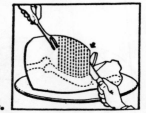

4. Slice from right to left, cutting clear to bone and making enough slices to serve all guests. Then loosen all slices at once by a horizontal cut. Later, the ham may be turned and cut from the other side.

Courtesy Armour and Co., Chicago

ROAST POULTRY

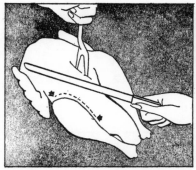 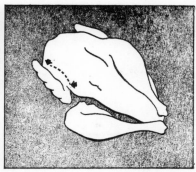

1. Place platter in front of carver so that neck of bird is to the left and feet to the right. Stick tines of carving fork deep into breast at the tip of the breast bone. With sharp knife, separate leg and thigh from nearest side by cutting at the thigh joint and pressing the leg away from the body.

2. Separate nearest wing in same manner, cutting around the joint to locate the exact dividing point of joint.

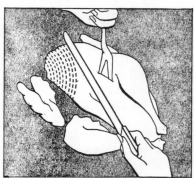 

3. Slice breast meat thin, starting at an angle from tip of breast bone and cutting toward the wing joint.

4. & 5. Separate thigh and leg at the joint. Slice thigh and leg lengthwise for turkey. Leave whole for small birds—turn platter and repeat process for second side of bird.

Courtesy Armour and Co., Chicago

HOW TO USE CHOP STICKS

STEP "A"— Place one chopstick in hand as shown in Figure "A"— this chopstick should be held stationary in a fixed position and firm.

STEP "B"— Keeping the first chopstick in position, place second chopstick in hand as you would hold a pencil as shown in Figure "B."

STEP "C"— Now with the tips of the thumb, second finger and index finger manipulate the second chopstick to meet the first, as shown in Figure "C."

CHAPTER 10

Sea Foods

---

*F*RESH-CAUGHT fish make marvelous eating. They should be bright of eye and shiny of scale, with the tang of the sea in their firm, tender meat. Fresh-water fish are delicious, too, and for those who live far from ocean, lake or stream, excellent frozen fish is available. Some kinds of fish, notably tuna and salmon, are very good canned, and there are dried and smoked fish as well.

Cooking fresh or frozen fish is a delicate art. Overcooked, dried-up or mushy fish can alienate your family to what ought to be an eagerly anticipated part of the regular eating pattern.

Fresh and frozen fish comes whole, in fillets, steaks or fish sticks. Baking, broiling, pan-frying and boiling are the accepted cooking methods.

Oysters, clams and mussels are bought by the count in the shell, and by the pint or quart out of the shell; or in frozen package servings. Soft-shell crabs and scallops also are bought by the count, although fresh scallops also are sold by the pound, as are shrimps, crabs and lobster. These sea foods come by the package when frozen. There are smoked canned oysters, canned crab meat and canned clams and clam juice.

Fish gives you about the same amount of protein as meat and eggs. However, it is lacking in Vitamin A, which is stored in the inedible liver. It is a rich source of phosphorus, and ocean fish and sea foods are excellent sources of iodine. Ocean fish brings you valuable minerals absorbed from the sea water.

Fresh fish should always be refrigerated at once and should not be kept uncooked for more than a day or two. Frozen fish must not be thawed and refrozen. Fresh fish should be wrapped and kept in freezing compartment or coldest place in refrigerator.

When buying canned fish, be sure to read the label to see if it has been inspected and guaranteed safe.

■ HOW TO CLEAN FISH

Your fish market will usually prepare fresh fish for you as you wish, in fillets or steaks, or simply split and cleaned. However, it is a good idea to know how to deal with that inevitable fish that arrives from somebody's catch.

Wash slimy fish in warm water and rinse salt-water fish in fresh water. Lay fish on several layers of newspaper or paper towels. Remove scales first by drawing dull knife over fish, beginning at the tail and working toward the head; wipe off scales occasionally. Head and tail need not be removed if fish is to be cooked whole. Trout and other small fish are often served with head and tail left on.

If fish is to be skinned, cut off head, tail and fins. Kitchen scissors work better than a knife. Slit skin down the backbone and lengthwise along center of abdomen. Loosen skin from gills, cutting when necessary down each side. Cut the length of the abdomen and remove vital organs. Rinse under cold running water or wash carefully to remove all blood clots. Pat dry at once with paper towels. To bone the fish, run a sharp knife under the flesh close to the backbone along the entire length; turn and remove flesh from other side.

To prepare fish steaks, clean the fish, remove head, tail and organs and slice with sharp knife across the fibers.

■ PREPARING LOBSTER

Live lobsters are first plunged tail-first into a large kettle of boiling water, to which ⅓ c. salt has been added. Allow water to come to boiling point before the addition of each lobster. Lobster must be entirely covered with water. Cover and boil 20 minutes. Place on backs to cool. Open lobsters by removing large and small claws; separate tails from the body. Crack shells with a hammer or nutcracker; remove meat from claws, tail and body. Remove small intestinal vein, stomach and liver. Rinse in running water. Kitchen shears are often handy here.

■ SHRIMP

Shrimp, if purchased raw, should be boiled until pink. Shell and cut out black vein which is the intestine. Shrimp may be washed and shelled before cooking, but are best cooked first for most recipes.

HOW TO EAT LOBSTER

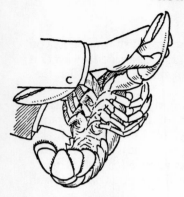

1. Twist off the claws.

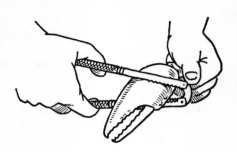

2. Crack each claw with a nutcracker, pliers, knife, hammer, rock or what have you.

3. Separate the tail-piece from the body by arching the back until it cracks.

4. Bend back and break the flippers off the tail-piece.

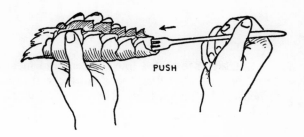

5. Insert a fork where the flippers broke off and push.

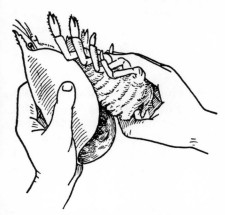

6. Unhinge the back from the body. Don't forget that this contains the "tomalley", or liver of the lobster which turns green when it is cooked and which many persons consider the best eating of all.

7. Open the remaining part of the body by cracking a p a r t sideways. There is s o m e good meat in this section.

8. The small claws are excellent eating and may be placed in the mouth and the meat sucked out like sipping cider with a straw.

■   **CRABS**

Crabs are boiled like lobsters and meat removed from claws and body. Soft-shelled crabs are those that have just cast off their shells and after cleaning they are fried whole, and are simply delicious.

■   **CLAMS**

Clams should be purchased alive in the shell. Wash thoroughly, changing the water several times. Put into a large kettle, add ½ c. hot water to about 4 qts. of clams; cover tightly and steam until shells partially open. If not to be used at once remove meat from shells and drop into cold water. Large clams should have their stomachs opened with kitchen scissors and the contents emptied.

■   **CLAMBAKE**

Clambakes are popular on the East coast. To bake clams outdoors, first wash them in sea water. Pile stones in a shallow pit, burn wood on stones until they are hot, remove ashes, place thin layer of seaweed on the stones, then the clams and more seaweed and cover all with canvas to retain steam. Steam until clams begin to split open. Corn wrapped in husks can be placed on the stones also and cooked along with the clams.

■   **COOKING FISH**

Fish must be cooked at low temperatures, as for other protein foods. The connective tissue in fish softens rapidly during cooking and it is easy to overcook it. So cook fish lightly and not too long. You can tell when it has cooked enough as the fish loses its transparency and flakes easily when fibers are separated with a fork, but the flesh will be firm, moist and tender, with a delicate flavor.

■   **BROILED FISH**

Broiling is one of the best and easiest ways to cook fish. Select fillets, steaks, split small whole fish, or shrimps, lobster, or soft-shell crabs.

Brush fish before broiling with a sauce made of 2 or 3 tbsp. melted butter or salad oil, 2 tsp. lemon juice, salt and pepper. Other seasonings may be added to this basic sauce such as: 1 tsp. Kitchen Bouquet, Worcestershire sauce, prepared mustard, horseradish, catsup, white wine or relish, herbs or sour cream. Fish may be placed in this marinade for ½ hour in refrigerator before broiling.

Preheat broiler and grease racks. Place foil in bottom of pan to facilitate washing of the pan. Fish need not be turned during broiling, unless whole. Fillets and steaks are placed about 2 inches from moderate heat, and thick fish from 4 to 6 inches. Baste several times to bring out flavor.

The broiling time will vary with thickness. Serve the fish with lemon, or a good sauce.

Fish may also be broiled on a heat-proof platter or wooden plank.

■ BROILED FILLETS OR STEAKS

Thaw quick-frozen fillets or wipe fresh fish with damp cloth. Brush fish with the basic sauce of lemon juice and butter; then during the last 2-3 minutes of cooking, spread with any of the following sauces:

SOUR CREAM SAUCE

Melt 2 tbsp. butter in small pan; add 1 tbsp. minced onion, parsley and ¼ tsp. paprika. Cook over medium heat, 3-4 minutes. Add 1 tsp. lemon juice, ½ tsp. salt, pepper and ½ c. sour cream, or yogurt.

BARBECUE SAUCE

Sauté ¼ c. minced onion, 3 tbsp. butter or salad oil, salt, 1 c. catsup or tomato sauce, ⅓ c. vinegar, 1 tsp. honey, ½ c. water, 1 tsp. prepared mustard, and 2 tbsp. Worcestershire sauce. Simmer 10-15 minutes. 3 tbsp. chili sauce may be substituted for catsup.

■ PAPRIKA FISH FILLETS

1 pkg. frozen fish fillets, thawed, or 1 lb. fresh fillets	3 drops Tabasco
4 tbsp. salad oil	2 tsp. lemon juice
2 tsp. Worcestershire sauce	½ tsp. salt
	½ tsp. paprika

Cut fish in 4 serving pieces and place in broiling pan. Blend oil, Worcestershire sauce, Tabasco, lemon juice and seasonings. Brush fish with half the sauce and broil, about 4 inches from flame, about 8 minutes. Turn fish and brush with a little more of the sauce, retaining some to pour over before serving. Broil about 8 minutes. Serve on hot platter. Serves 4.

■ BAKED FISH

Many fish are fine for stuffing and baking whole, including bluefish, sea bass, cod, haddock, mackerel, shad, weakfish and whitefish. If fish are fairly small, do not try to stuff them, and allow about 20 minutes baking time. Larger stuffed fish should be baked about 20 minutes per lb. Experiment with your favorite bread stuffings and sauces. Several combinations are suggested in the recipes to follow.

Place greased parchment or heavy paper, or foil, on bottom of greased baking dish or pan. Brush fish inside and out with butter and baste occasionally while baking. White wine used for basting adds a delightful flavor.

For larger fish, bake for first 20 minutes at 425°, then lower to 325°. Do not overcook.

Before serving, sprinkle fish with a little salt, paprika and chopped parsley, and surround with lemon wedges.

■ PLANKED FISH

The same kinds of fish used for baking may be planked.

Fish should be brushed inside and out with butter or oil and placed on an oak plank, broiler pan or heat-proof platter. Any of the following foods, or a combination of several, may be arranged around the fish. Large fish require about 20 minutes baking per lb. Have oven at 425° for first 20 minutes, then lower to 325° and finish baking. Do not overcook. Wooden plank or platter may be brought to table. If broiler pan is used, remove fish to heated platter and rearrange vegetables around it.

Garnishes for Planked Fish:

1. Tomato halves brushed with butter and seasoned with salt and oregano, or tomato slices topped with buttered whole-wheat crumbs or grated cheese.
2. Mashed potato patties brushed with butter and sprinkled with paprika.
3. Buttered cooked carrots cut in rounds and seasoned with salt and pepper.
4. Cubes of cooked banana or acorn squash brushed with butter and seasoned with salt and pepper.
5. Onion rings, first sautéed in butter or oil and seasoned with salt and pepper.
6. Mushroom caps, placed rounded sides down; ½ tsp. melted butter in each cap; season with salt and pepper.
7. Sliced eggplant brushed with butter and seasoned with salt and pepper.

■ BOILED FISH

Boiled fish may be served hot or cold. Cold boiled salmon with mayonnaise is a classic luncheon dish for warm weather, but many other fish are ideal for boiling, including cod, flounder, mackerel, red snapper, halibut, sole, haddock and large lake or sea trout.

Adding ¼ tsp. marjoram or sweet basil to the water will give the fish a subtle and intriguing flavor.

To help keep the shape of the whole boiled fish, insert a carrot before cooking. Fish will also keep its form better if tied to a strainer with twine.

Both shape and flavor are retained by using a steamer for cooking. Serve with your favorite butter or Hollandaise sauce and garnish with water cress or chopped parsley and lemon slices.

Fish which do not have much flavor in themselves are excellent boiled in a court bouillon.

■ COURT BOUILLON

1 carrot, chopped	2 cloves
1 onion, chopped	1 small bay leaf
2 stalks celery, chopped	1 tsp. salt
2 tbsp. butter	2 tbsp. vinegar
¼ c. minced parsley	2 qts. water
5 peppercorns	

Cook carrot, onion and celery in butter until tender; add parsley and other seasonings. Add water and boil about 10 minutes, covered. Place raw fish in broth and simmer, covered, about 10 more minutes. Remove to heated platter and serve with your favorite fish sauce, or allow to cool in broth if to be served cold.

Variations

1. Substitute 2 c. white wine for 2 c. of the water.
2. Substitute 2 c. fish stock for 2 c. of the water.
3. Substitute 2 qts. bottled clam juice for the water.

■ BAKED FILLETS OR STEAKS IN SOUR CREAM

Cover bottom of baking pan with thin slices of lemons or onions; arrange fish on top. Sprinkle with salt and pepper, cover and bake until easily flaked. Uncover and spread with sour cream and sprinkle lightly with paprika. Serve at once.

■   **BAKED STUFFED FISH**

3-4 lbs. white fish, pike or lake trout	**1 onion**
3 tsp. salt or substitute	**½ c. butter or oil**
1½ c. bread crumbs	**½ c. cornmeal**
¾ c. milk	**½ c. light cream**

Split and clean the fish. Mix bread crumbs, seasoning, milk, grated onion with 3 tbsp. butter or oil and stuff the fish. Fasten opening with toothpicks and roll outside of fish in remaining melted fat, then in cornmeal. Grease a baking pan and arrange fish in pan. Bake 20 minutes in 350° oven. Add cream and bake 30 minutes longer. Baste with juices or soy oil. Serves 6.

■   **NEW ORLEANS BAKED FISH**

Red snapper, mackerel or other white fish—about 3 lbs.	**½ c. chopped parsley**
¼ c. butter or oil	**1 tsp. thyme**
1 c. chopped onion	**2 drops Tabasco**
½ c. chopped green pepper	**2 bay leaves**
1-2 cloves garlic chopped	**Pinch of oregano**
2 tbsp. flour	**Salt and pepper to taste**
3 c. tomato sauce or purée	

Remove head, scales and tail from cleaned fish. Wash and dry. Melt butter or oil in fry pan. Add onion, green pepper, garlic; cook until pepper is tender. Stir in flour, tomato sauce or puréed tomatoes, parsley, thyme, Tabasco, bay leaves and oregano. Salt and pepper to taste. Cook over low heat, 30 minutes. Place fish in a greased pan; pour some of the sauce inside fish and rest over top. Bake 1 hour in slow oven, 325°. Serves 4.

■   **FISH WITH VEGETABLES**

Fish may be served on cooked onions, tomatoes, mushrooms, or these vegetables may be cooked with the fish, as follows:

Melt butter in skillet, add onions; place fish on top of onions, and tomatoes and chopped parsley on the fish. Pour court bouillon around fish. Cover and cook over medium heat, 5-10 minutes. Remove to oven-proof platter. Pour over fish rich cream sauce made of ⅓ c. cream, 1 tbsp. butter, and salt to taste. Put under broiler until golden brown.

Mushrooms, thin sliced carrots, or thin slices of lemon may be substituted for tomatoes.

■ **BLOCK ISLAND "TURKEY"**

Make rich cream sauce of 2 c. milk. Add 2 c. steamed, flaked codfish. Add wedges of 3 hard-cooked eggs and ¼ tsp. curry, cayenne, pepper and ¼ c. crumbs or ¼ c. sliced pimientos. Bake in greased casserole in moderate oven, 350°, about 40 minutes. Serves 4-6.

■ **HALIBUT WITH SAUCE**

½ c. chopped green pepper	½ tsp. garlic salt
½ c. chopped onion	Salt to season
2 tbsp. butter	2 small bay leaves
½ c. catsup	1¾ lbs. frozen halibut steaks

Divide halibut into 4 servings; cut a piece of heavy paper to wrap each piece. Cook green pepper and onion in butter until tender, but not brown. Add catsup, garlic, salt, bay leaves. Simmer 10-15 minutes. For each person, place 1 serving of halibut on parchment or heavy paper, just off center; sprinkle with salt. Pour ¼ of the sauce over each serving. Fold each of the 4 packages, place on shallow pan and bake in 500° oven, 15-20 minutes.

The fish also may be placed in greased baking dish and sauce poured over the top. Bake in 325° oven uncovered about 40 minutes. Top with chopped parsley. Serves 4.

■ **BOILED LOBSTER**

Place live lobsters in kettle of boiling hot water. Kettle should be large enough to accommodate lobsters, leaving about 3 inches of water covering them on top. Add ⅓ c. salt, cover immediately. When water comes to boil again, cook 20 minutes. Serve hot or cold, allowing 1 small lobster or ½ large to each person. Serve hot with side dishes of melted butter. Serve cold with melted butter or mayonnaise.

■ **BAKED LOBSTER**

Place lobsters on their backs; cross large claws; hold firmly and with very sharp knife cut quickly the entire length of body and tail, starting at a point between the two large claws. Remove craw and intestinal vein, leaving the green liver (or tomalley). Top with dressing (below).

Allow 1 small or medium cooked lobster per person.

■   **DRESSING FOR BAKED LOBSTER**

1 c. whole-wheat crumbs	¼ tsp. pepper
¼ c. melted butter	¼ c. milk
½ tsp. salt	2 tsp. sherry

Mix butter, crumbs, salt and pepper, add milk and sherry. Stuff lobsters with mixture. Top with:

4 tbsp. melted butter	6-8 lettuce leaves
4 tbsp. grated Parmesan cheese (optional)	

Pour butter over stuffed lobsters. Add cheese if desired. Cover lobsters with lettuce leaves and bake in hot oven, 400°, 30-40 minutes. Remove lettuce leaves. Serves 4.

■   **MAINE LOBSTER CROQUETTES**

3 c. cooked lobster meat	¼ c. whole-wheat crumbs
¼ lb. butter	1 c. bread crumbs
½ c. finely chopped onions	3 eggs
½ c. finely chopped celery	1 oz. sherry
1 c. rich cream sauce	

Sauté onions and celery in butter until tender-crisp. Add lobster meat. Simmer 3-4 minutes. Remove from heat; add cream sauce, bread crumbs and sherry. Cool, shape into balls. Dip in eggs; roll in ¼ c. bread crumbs. Brown in hot oil in skillet, turning frequently. Makes 12 croquettes.

■   **SWORDFISH WITH MUSHROOMS**

1 lb. swordfish	1 c. whole-wheat bread crumbs
½ c. butter	2 tbsp. minced parsley
2 tbsp. lemon juice	8 sprigs water cress
1 tbsp. Worcestershire sauce	16 mushroom caps

Sauté swordfish in butter. Pour on lemon juice. Remove from fire and keep warm in oven. Lightly brown mushrooms in warm butter, in same skillet as fish was cooked in. Add Worcestershire sauce, bread crumbs and parsley. Pour over fish and add sprigs of water cress. Serves 4.

■ POACHED FISH

The gourmet believes that the most delicious fish is that which has been poached, because the delicate flavor and nutrients are more easily retained. Use milk, wine, water or broth.

Fish must be poached in the skillet in which it is to be served. The following fish are recommended to poach and serve hot: sole, perch, haddock, halibut, cod, sea bass, pompano.

Crab, lobster, and salmon may be simmered in court bouillon, 6-10 minutes per lb. and allowed to cool in the broth. Before serving, drain, place carefully on platter, garnish with water cress and lemon wedges. Serve with mayonnaise which may be tinted pale green with vegetable coloring.

To successfully poach fish, use a foil cover with a hole in the center to allow steam to escape. Paper covers may also be used.

■ CODFISH—DOWN-EAST SYTLE

2½ c. salt codfish	¼ tsp. salt
4 tbsp. butter, melted	¼ tsp. pepper
4 tbps. flour	1 egg, slightly beaten
2 c. milk	Dash of Worcestershire sauce

Blend melted butter and flour, add milk and stir over low heat until thickened. Add egg, salt, pepper and Worcestershire sauce. Stir, but do not bring to boil. Place fish, broken in small pieces, on a heated platter, cover with sauce and serve at once. Excellent with steamed brown rice or mashed potatoes. Serves 4-6.

■ BAKED FISH TURBOT

2½ c. cooked, flaked cod, halibut or tuna	½ c. buttered whole-wheat crumbs
4 tbsp. flour	¼ c. grated Cheddar cheese or
4 tbsp. butter, melted	¼ c. finely chopped cashew
2 c. milk	nuts (optional)

Blend flour and melted butter; add milk and stir over low heat until thickened. Place fish in oiled casserole, cover with the white sauce and top with crumbs. Add cheese or nuts if desired. Bake ½ hour in moderate oven, 375°. Serves 4.

■ **SALMON MOLD**

1 8-oz. can salmon   1 egg
⅓ c. chopped parsley   2 tbsp. milk
¼ c. chopped onion   ½ tsp. salt, dash of pepper
2 tbsp. butter or oil
1 c. soft whole-wheat bread
   crumbs

Drain and break up salmon; beat egg and add milk. Mix salmon, parsley, onion, and bread crumbs; combine with egg mixture; add melted butter. Pour into greased casserole or mold; cover tightly; place on rack in pan of hot water. Bake in 350° oven for 45 minutes. Serves 2-3.

■ **SALMON LOAF**

½ lb. can salmon   ⅓ c. milk
⅓ c. soy flour   1 beaten egg
¼ tsp. salt

Sift soy flour and salt. Combine beaten egg and milk and gradually stir into dry mixture. Break salmon into small pieces and add with juice. Bake in greased small loaf pan in moderate oven, 350°, until loaf is firm, about 1 hour. If you want a molded loaf, line pan with freezer paper. Serves 2.

■ **TUNA CASSEROLE**

¼ c. butter   2 tbsp. chopped stuffed olives
¼ c. flour   1 small onion, minced
2 c. milk   1 clove garlic, minced
1 tsp. salt   ⅓ c. parsley
2 tsp. paprika   ½ pkg. or 4-oz. noodles
2 tbsp. Worcestershire sauce   2 7-oz. cans tuna
¼ c. catsup
1 4-oz. can mushroom pieces
   and stems

Cook noodles and drain. Make cream sauce of butter, flour and milk; add seasonings, mushrooms, olives, onion, garlic and parsley. Combine with cooked, drained noodles and drained tuna. Pour in greased casserole. Bake 30 minutes, at 350°. Serves 6.

■ **CREAMED BAKED FILLETS**

Buy 2 lbs. fillet of sole or some other thin fish. Allow to thaw, if frozen. Roll up each fillet and place, rolled, in a shallow baking pan. Pour 1½ c. milk over fillet, add 1 tsp. salt and sprinkle with pepper and paprika. Bake 25 minutes at 350°; if thick they may take longer. Test for flaking.

Melt 2 tbsp. butter in saucepan, add 3 tbsp. flour and mix well. Remove milk from fillets, being careful not to disturb fish rolls. Add this milk slowly to the butter-flour mixture, stirring constantly until it thickens. Add ½ c. grated Cheddar cheese, 2 tsp. Worcestershire sauce, and 2 tsp. lemon juice. Pour over fillets and place under broiler to brown. Top with minced parsley.

■ **CREAMED FISH**

2 c. canned or cooked fish (tuna, shrimp, crab, lobster, halibut, salmon, or cod)	2 c. milk
	2 eggs, beaten
	Salt and pepper to taste
¼ c. butter or salad oil	Parsley
¼ c. unbleached white flour	

Make white sauce of butter or salad oil, flour, milk, salt and pepper. Add fish and cook until heated. Add beaten eggs and cook 1 minute. Add parsley and more salt and pepper to taste. Serve over any of the following:

1. Cooked brown rice.
2. Cornbread squares.
3. Whole-wheat noodles to which a little minced onion has been added.

■ **SALMON CASSEROLE**

2 c. cooked whole-wheat macaroni	½ c. water
	2 8-oz. cans salmon
¼ c. chopped ripe olives	⅓ c. grated Cheddar cheese
¼ tsp. salt	¼ c. whole-wheat bread crumbs, buttered
¼ tsp. mayonnaise	
1 c. cream of tomato soup	

Add macaroni, olives, salt and mayonnaise to soup and water. Place layer of macaroni mixture in bottom of greased casserole, then layer of salmon. Cover with remaining macaroni and buttered crumbs. Sprinkle grated cheese on crumbs. Bake 30 minutes at 350°. Serves 6.

■ TUNA-CHIP CASSEROLE

1 large pkg. potato chips or whole-wheat cracker crumbs	1 egg, beaten
½ pkg. whole-wheat or soy noodles, cooked	1 c. milk
	1 can mushroom soup
	1 7-oz. can tuna fish chunks

Pour potato chips or crumbs on half of kitchen towel, fold other half to cover chips; crumble chips roughly with rolling pin or palm of hand. Cover bottom of greased 2-qt. casserole with half the crumbled chips. Blend milk and egg; add mushroom soup and pour mixture over noodles. Alternate layers of noodle mixture and tuna, sprinkling each with crumbled chips. Top with remaining chips and bake at 375° about 20 minutes. Serves 4-6.

■ TUNA CROQUETTES

1 c. thick white sauce	½ tsp. pepper
1 7-oz. can tuna fish, flaked	1 egg, beaten with 2 tbsp. water
1 tbsp. chopped onion	
2 tbsp. lemon juice	1 c. fine whole-wheat crumbs
½ tsp. salt	

Mix tuna with white sauce, onion, lemon juice and seasonings. Shape into 8 small croquettes; dip in egg, then roll in crumbs. Brown 3-5 minutes in deep fat, heated to 365°. Serve with cheese sauce. Serves 4.

■ TUNA SOUFFLÉ

1 can mushroom soup, undiluted	4 eggs, separated
⅓ c. milk	⅓ c. mild Cheddar cheese, grated
2 c. peas, cooked	¼ c. minced parsley
1 7-oz. can tuna, drained	

Mix mushroom soup with milk, peas and tuna. Beat egg yolks until lemon colored and fold in grated cheese. Beat whites of egg until they stand in peaks and carefully fold into yolks with parsley. Add soup, tuna and peas, folding just enough to lightly mix. Pour all into greased 1½-qt. casserole. Bake in 400° oven, only until top is brown. Serves 4.

■ **PAN-FRIED SARDINES**

1 egg	2 3¼-oz. cans sardines
1 tbsp. milk	½ c. salad oil
1 c. whole-wheat cracker	
crumbs	

Combine egg and milk, beat well. Dip sardines in egg and then in crumbs. Heat oil in heavy fry pan. Fry on each side until golden brown. Serves 4.

■ **FISH LOAF**

2 tbsp. butter or salad oil	1 tbsp. lemon juice
2 tbsp. chopped onion	⅓ c. chopped parsley
2 c. flaked white fish or tuna,	1 c. whole-wheat bread crumbs
or 1 lb. can of salmon,	1 egg, beaten
drained and flaked	¼ c. milk

Melt butter or oil in 2-qt. saucepan; add chopped onion and cook until soft. Remove from heat, add flaked fish, mix in bread crumbs, egg, milk, lemon juice and chopped parsley. Pour into greased baking dish and bake in moderate oven, 375°, about 40 minutes. Let stand a few minutes and turn out on a platter. Serve with a tart sauce. Serves 4.

■ **AVOCADOS WITH SEA FOOD**

4 ripe avocados	1 tbsp. minced onion
1 tsp. lemon juice	1 small clove garlic, minced
2 tbsp. butter	1½ tsp. salt
2 tbsp. flour	2 c. cooked crab meat, tuna,
1 c. milk	salmon or lobster flakes
½ tsp. Worcestershire sauce	½ c. grated Cheddar cheese
Dash of Tabasco	

Cut avocados in half, remove seed from each and sprinkle with lemon juice. In top of double boiler, blend butter and flour, add milk and cook, stirring, until smooth. Add seasonings, onion and garlic. Stir in sea food. Fill avocado halves with mixture, top with cheese. Place in baking pan and pour in water to about ½ inch. Bake at 350°, 15 minutes. Serves 4.

Variation

Substitute 4 acorn squash for avocados. Cut in half, remove seeds and parboil until tender before stuffing. Omit lemon juice. Add ¼ tsp. nutmeg to seasonings if desired.

■ SEA FOOD CREOLE

2 lbs. fresh shrimp, deveined	1 tsp. salt
1 7-oz. can flaked lobster or crab	½ tsp. paprika
	⅛ tsp. cayenne pepper
3 tbsp. butter or oil	½ tsp. Worcestershire sauce
2 onions, chopped	¼ tsp. thyme
2 chopped green peppers	¼ tsp. basil
2 c. canned tomatoes or stewed fresh tomatoes	6 c. cooked brown rice, hot

Combine shrimp and lobster or crab. Sauté onions and peppers in butter or oil until tender. Add tomatoes and seasonings. Stir in sea foods and cook in top of double boiler about 15 minutes to thoroughly blend flavors. Serve over rice. Serves 6.

■ SALMON PATTIES

1 1-lb. can salmon, flaked	½ tsp. pepper
¼ c. dampened fresh-ground cornmeal	½ c. tomato catsup
	2 tbsp. lemon juice
1 onion, chopped	1 egg, beaten
1 tsp. salt	⅓ c. minced parsley

Drain liquid from salmon into measuring cup; add water to fill. Pour into saucepan and gradually add cornmeal, stirring constantly. Cook over low heat until mixture thickens; remove from heat. Mix salmon in bowl with onion, salt, pepper, catsup, lemon juice, egg and parsley. Blend with cornmeal mixture and form into patties. Fry in hot oil until golden brown on both sides. Serves 4-6.

■ SHELL FISH

Shell fish is available fresh, frozen or canned. The frozen or fresh are preferred, as there is less loss of the valuable nutrients. All shell fish are especially rich in minerals.

■ SAUTÉED SCALLOPS

1 pt. scallops	¼ tsp. paprika
½ c. fine whole-wheat crumbs	¼ c. minced onion
½ tsp. salt	⅓ c. butter or oil
⅛ tsp. pepper	

Mix crumbs, salt, pepper and paprika. Toss scallops in mixture until well covered. Heat butter or oil in frying pan. Add scallops, onion and any remaining crumbs. Sauté until golden brown. Serves 3-4.

■ BAKED SCALLOPS

1 c. fine whole-wheat crumbs	4 tbsp. melted butter
½ tsp. salt	1 qt. scallops
⅛ tsp. cayenne pepper	½ c. minced parsley
1 egg, beaten with 2 tbsp. water	

Mix salt, pepper and crumbs. Dip each scallop in egg-water mixture, then in crumbs. Place in greased casserole, pour melted butter over scallops and top with parsley. Bake in 450° oven about 25 minutes, until golden brown. Serves 6.

■ OYSTER STEW

¼ c. butter	Pepper to taste
1 pt. drained oysters	Pinch of thyme
1 qt. milk	1 tsp. paprika
1½ tsp. salt	

Melt butter, add drained oysters and cook a few minutes, until edges begin to curl. Add milk and seasonings. Do not allow to boil; serve as soon as stew is hot, with whole-wheat crackers on the side. Serves 4.

■ SCALLOPED OYSTERS

Melt ½ c. butter or heat ½ c. oil. Add 2 c. soft whole-wheat bread crumbs, 1½ tsp. salt and pepper. Drain 1 pt. oysters and place alternate layers of crumbs and oysters in a greased baking dish. Should make 2 layers only. 2 tbsp. oyster liquor and 1 tbsp. cream may be added before baking. Bake 15 to 20 minutes in hot oven, at 450°. Serves 4.

■ **PAN-FRIED OYSTERS**

¼ c. butter or salad oil   Dash of Tabasco
2 doz. shucked large oysters ¼ c. top milk
1 tbsp. minced onion   1 tbsp. minced parsley
1 tsp. salt   Whole-wheat toast, buttered
⅛ tsp. pepper

Melt butter or salad oil in fry pan. Add shucked oysters, onion salt, pepper and Tabasco. Cook over low heat until oyster edges begin to curl, about 5 minutes. Add top milk and minced parsley. Serve on buttered toast. Serves 4-6.

■ **BAKED OYSTERS ÉMINCE**

1 qt. oysters   ½ tsp. salt
¼ c. celery, chopped   2 c. soft whole-wheat bread
2 small onions, chopped   crumbs
2 tbsp. butter   1 egg, beaten
2 tsp. lemon juice   ½ c. fine toasted whole-wheat
¼ tsp. thyme   crumbs
½ tsp. paprika

Drain oysters and chop fine, saving liquor. Gently sauté celery and onions in butter, not allowing to brown. Mix in lemon juice and thyme. Moisten bread crumbs with a little oyster liquid; squeeze to remove excess liquid. Stir lightly into celery mixture. Cook over low heat about 20 minutes to blend flavors; do not allow to burn or stick to pan. Stir in oysters, salt and paprika; add beaten egg, mix well; place in buttered casserole or individual clam or scallop shells. Top with fine crumbs and bake about 20 minutes at 425°. Serves 4-6.

■ **SOFT-SHELL CRABS**

6-8 medium soft-shell crabs   1 tbsp. lemon juice
⅓ c. melted butter   ¼ tsp. salt

Cut off head of each crab behind eyes. Fold top of shell back on each side and scrape out soft matter. Turn crab and remove "apron" (a small pointed piece in the center). Brush with butter and lemon. Broil shell side down for 5 minutes under moderate heat. Turn and brush with butter and lemon juice again and broil 5 minutes more. Pour remaining butter and salt over crabs before serving. Serves 6-8.

■ DEVILED CRAB

1½ lbs. crab meat	1 tsp. mustard
1 c. onions, chopped	2 tbsp. mayonnaise
1 c. celery, chopped	2 tbsp. catsup
Butter or oil	¼ tsp. nutmeg
½ c. unbleached white flour	½ c. whole-wheat cracker
1 pt. top milk	crumbs

Sauté onions and celery in butter or oil to a light brown. Mix flour, milk, mayonnaise, catsup, mustard, nutmeg and cracker crumbs. Stir into skillet slowly so as not to lump flour. Add crab meat. Cover and cook about 1 hour, stirring frequently. Serve on cleaned clam shells (optional). Serves 6.

■ SHRIMP AND VEGETABLES

1 c. uncooked shrimp	1½ c. sliced onions
2 tsp. soy sauce	1 c. celery, cut in 2-inch pieces
¼ tsp. salt	1 small can water chestnuts,
1 tsp. fresh or dried ginger	sliced lengthwise
root	3 c. fresh sprouts
1 tbsp. sherry (optional)	1 tsp. cornstarch
4 tbsp. salad oil	½ c. bouillon

Shell and clean shrimp; dip in mixture of soy sauce, salt, ginger and sherry. Heat 2 tbsp. oil in skillet and sauté shrimp. Remove from pan. Add remaining oil and lightly sauté onions, celery and water chestnuts. Add fresh sprouts and shrimp. Mix cornstarch with small amount of bouillon; stir smooth, add remainder of bouillon and pour over shrimp mixture. Good with steamed brown rice. Serves 6.

■ FRIED SHRIMP

½ c. unbleached white flour	⅓ c. milk
¼ tsp. salt	2 doz. cleaned, cooked shrimp
1 egg, slightly beaten	(or canned)
½ tsp. lemon juice	Oil for frying

Sift flour and salt together. Mix egg, lemon juice and milk. Combine mixtures, stirring until smooth. Dip shrimp in this batter. Pour oil into frying pan, to come up ½ inch on sides; do not heat above 360°. Brown shrimp on both sides; drain on heavy paper or paper towel. Serves 4.

■ **BUTTERFLY SHRIMP**

Plan on 6-8 shrimps per person; medium, not jumbo. If raw, cook shrimps in boiling water a few minutes, until they turn pale pink. Cool, remove shells, slice down back and remove veins. Wash and pat dry on towel. Dip each shrimp in the following batter (sufficient for 24 shrimps): 1 lightly beaten egg; 1 c. unbleached white flour sifted with 1 tsp. baking powder, 1 tsp. salt. Blend egg with flour and slowly add 1 c. ice water, stirring to make smooth batter. Drop batter-covered shrimps in deep fat, hot enough to sputter when water is sprinkled on top. Cook about 10 minutes, turning when golden brown on one side. Do not cook too many at a time, as they should stand apart in the hot fat. Drain and serve.

■ **SHRIMP COCKTAIL**

You may use fresh or frozen shrimp. Serve in sherbet glasses or sea food cocktail glasses. For each person, allow 4 Jumbo shrimp or 6 medium shrimp or ¼ c. very small shrimp. In each glass, put 1 tbsp. Sea Food Cocktail Sauce; add more shrimp and sauce until glass is filled. Garnish with lemon wedges.

Variation—Use ½ quantity of shrimp and for remainder, substitute peeled, sliced avocado.

■ **SEA FOOD COCKTAIL SAUCE**

¾ c. tomato catsup	2 tbsp. lemon juice
¼ c. prepared horseradish	¼ tsp. salt
6 drops Tabasco	

Mix all ingredients and chill until ready to serve. Makes enough for 6 shrimp cocktails. Experiment with this sauce to find out how hot you like it, increasing or diminishing horseradish and Tabasco.

■ **CLAM CASSEROLE**

2 c. milk	24 whole-wheat crackers
2 7-oz. cans minced clams	4 eggs, beaten
¼ c. minced onion	1 tsp. salt
¼ tsp. pepper	⅓ c. chopped parsley

Pour milk over crackers. Add all other ingredients and pour into greased 1½-qt. casserole and bake in moderate oven, 350°, about 45 minutes, until knife inserted comes out clean. Serves 4-6.

■ **SHRIMP MEXICAN**

1 lb. fresh or thawed frozen shrimp	¼ c. butter
¼ c. chopped onion	1 small clove garlic, finely chopped
1 No. 2 can or 2½ c. tomatoes	1 tsp. chili powder
¼ c. chopped green pepper	⅛ tsp. marjoram
2 tsp. salt	Pepper and bay leaf

Remove vein from shrimp. Simmer all other ingredients for 10 minutes. Add shrimp and cook 10 minutes more. May be served over cooked brown rice or wide whole-wheat noodles (cooked). Serves 4-6.

■ **CURRIED SHRIMP**

1 can frozen shrimp soup	1 pkg. frozen uncooked shrimp
½ can evaporated milk	
3 tsp. curry powder	3 tbsp. sherry or 2 tsp. lemon juice
½ tsp. prepared mustard	
1 tsp. Worcestershire sauce	2 beaten egg yolks
2 drops Tabasco	4 c. cooked brown rice
1 pkg. frozen cooked shrimp or	

Thaw shrimp. If uncooked, place in boiling water until pink and tender, about 2 minutes; shell and devein. Combine shrimp soup with milk and seasonings and simmer until ingredients are blended. Remove from heat and stir in egg yolks and sherry or lemon juice. Add shrimp. Keep warm in chafing dish or warming oven. Do not allow to boil. Serve over rice. Serves 4-6.

■ **CRAB STEW**

2 tbsp. butter	¼ tsp. pepper
6 whole-wheat crackers	½ tsp. salt
3 c. fresh crab meat	⅔ c. top milk, or half cream, half milk
½ c. hot water	
1 qt. milk	¼ c. minced parsley

Melt butter slowly in kettle in which you plan to make the stew. Roll crackers very fine. Combine crumbs and crab meat in butter, add water; allow to bubble 1 minute. Pour in milk, stir gently until small bubbles appear. Do not boil. Add salt and pepper. Add top milk or half cream, half milk, and heat slowly. Do not boil. Serve at once. Top each bowl with parsley. Serves 4-6.

■   **CLAM CHOWDER**

Anyone from New England will tell you that it amounts to national treason to permit a tomato to come within tasting distance of a true clam chowder. In New York and other parts of the Eastern seaboard, people insist on Manhattan's version, complete with tomatoes. So here are both ways.

■   **NEW ENGLAND CLAM CHOWDER**

½ c. diced salt pork	3 c. milk
1 small onion, minced	1 tsp. salt
1 c. hot water	¼ tsp. pepper
2 c. diced raw potatoes	¼ tsp. thyme
2 c. minced clams, fresh or canned	6 buttered whole-wheat crackers

Brown salt pork gently in saucepan; add onions, water and potatoes. Cook over low heat until potatoes are tender. If fresh clams are used, heat slowly in their own liquor. Add clams, milk and seasonings; do not allow to come to boil. Serve at once, either adding crackers to chowder or serving separately. Serves 6.

■   **MANHATTAN CLAM CHOWDER**

Follow above recipe, except instead of milk, use 1 c. stewed tomatoes and 1 c. light cream. Chopped green peppers may be added to onions and potatoes before cooking.

■   **NEW ENGLAND BOUILLABAISSE**

⅔ c. salad oil	2 doz. shrimp, cooked and cleaned
1 minced carrot	¼ c. chopped parsley
2 minced onions	2 tsp. salt
1 clove garlic, minced	½ tsp. cayenne pepper
3 lbs. fish fillets	2 tbsp. lemon juice
1 can tomato paste	⅔ c. canned shrimp soup
1 can bouillon	¼ c. sherry (optional)
2 cans clam chowder	
1 doz. raw oysters	

Heat oil in large skillet; cook carrots, onions and garlic 5 minutes. Cut fish fillets in small pieces and cook with vegetables, 5 minutes. Add tomato paste, bouillon and clam chowder. Lower heat and simmer 15 minutes. Stir in shrimp, oysters, parsley and seasonings. Add shrimp soup and wine. Heat and pour over buttered croutons. Serves 8.

■ CLAM FRITTERS

1 pt. clams	⅓ c. milk or juice drained from
2 eggs, beaten	clams
1⅓ c. unbleached white flour	Salt and pepper to taste
2 tsp. baking powder	

Drain clams and chop. Beat eggs until light; add milk or clam juice. Sift flour, baking powder, and salt; add to egg mixture; add clams and season to taste. Drop by tablespoons into a little hot fat or salad oil in skillet. Sauté until golden brown on each side. Drain on paper towels. Serves 6.

■ FISH IN CASSEROLE

Shrimp, crab, tuna, or flaked lobster may be used. To ½ c. of the fish, add 1 c. finely diced celery. Butter thin slices of whole-wheat bread. Alternate layers of fish and bread in a 1½-qt. greased casserole. Combine 3 beaten eggs, 2¾ c. milk, 2 tsp. Worcestershire sauce, dash of Tabasco, and pour over mixture. Bake in 350° oven, 45 minutes. Serves 4.

■ LOBSTER, CRAB OR SCALLOPS NEWBURG

1 pkg. frozen lobster, crab or	Nutmeg
scallops	3 tbsp. chopped parsley
3 tbsp. butter	1 tbsp. Worcestershire sauce
3 tbsp. flour	¼ c. sharp Cheddar cheese,
1¾ c. half cream and half milk	grated
1 tsp. salt	4 or 6 tbsp. sherry or 1 tbsp.
½ tsp. paprika	cider vinegar

Thaw shell fish in saucepan over low heat. Stir lightly. Drain and cool. Make white sauce of butter, flour and half-and-half. Season with salt, paprika and nutmeg. Add parsley and Worcestershire sauce; then mix in shell fish. Add cheese and sherry and cook over low fire until cheese melts. Serve over toast or cooked brown rice. Serves 4.

■ SCALLOPS—BAKED IN CLAM SHELLS

1 pt. scallops	1 tbsp. minced onion
½ c. butter or salad oil	Black pepper to taste
1½ tsp. chopped chives	1 tbsp. minced parsley
1½ tsp. parsley flakes	Buttered crumbs
1 clove garlic, minced	

Melt butter, add chives, parsley flakes, garlic, onion, parsley and black pepper. Cook about 3 minutes. If scallops are large, cut into small pieces. Place some of butter mixture in cherrystone clam shells on baking pan. Put 3-4 pieces of scallop in each shell. Sprinkle with buttered bread crumbs. Bake 5 minutes, at 350°. May be served as hors d'oeuvres; or in larger clam shells or shallow baking pan as a main dish.

■ **FINNAN HADDIE WITH EGGS AND MUSHROOMS**

2 lbs. finnan haddie, boned and filleted	4 hard-boiled eggs
	½ lb. mushrooms or 2 c. sliced
1 qt. cream sauce	mushrooms

Simmer finnan haddie in water for 20 minutes. Drain and break into large flakes. Make cream sauce of ⅓ c. each flour and butter, 1 qt. milk, salt and pepper to taste. Combine with the fish, hard-boiled eggs, sliced, and mushrooms which have been sliced and sautéed in 2 tbsp. butter for 5 minutes. Serve over whole-grain toast. Serves 6-8.

■ **SAUTÉED SHAD ROE**

Ever since Colonial times, the East Coast has known the joys of shad and shad roe in the spring. Shad roe should be sautéed gently in butter in a covered skillet, about 3 minutes. Test with toothpick for doneness, but avoid overcooking. Add more butter if pan tends to dry out. Just before serving, pour over the juice of a large lemon and ¼ c. chopped parsley. Serve on hot triangles of whole-wheat toast, and pour over remaining lemon-butter from pan. The ideal accompaniment food is spring asparagus, served with Hollandaise or vinaigrette.

■ **PLANKED SHAD**

Shad for planking should weigh 4-5 pounds, and may be purchased already boned and split. Wash and dry the fish and place skin side down on lightly oiled broiling pan, about 4 inches from heat. Leave in broiler 5-6 minutes, then remove to hot, oiled plank, with skin side up. Brush fish with 2 tbsp. melted butter and place in 400° oven, 10 minutes. Arrange around edges 2 c. fluffy mashed potatoes. Brush tops of potatoes with 1 beaten egg and broil until potatoes are lightly browned. Garnish with chopped parsley and wedges of lemon.

■ SEA MUSSELS

Sea mussels are delicious and should be more appreciated in this country. Wash and rinse the mussels and open by steaming or with a knife. They must be alive before cooking. The hairy beard must be discarded.

Allow 6-8 mussels per portion. Canned or frozen mussels are also obtainable.

Mussels, like oysters and clams, become tough when over-cooked.

Mussels may be served in a thin cream sauce, in soup plates. They may also be chopped and added to scrambled eggs.

Bake mussels in shallow pan, sprinkled with salt, pepper and a little chopped onion. Crisp crumbled bacon and grated cheese may be sprinkled over the mussels. Bake at 350°, 15-18 minutes.

CHAPTER 11

Milk, Cheese and Milk Products

MILK is a valuable food and people who do not drink it often show deficiencies of protein, calcium, and the B vitamins. The best milk is clean certified raw milk from tested cows that graze on green pastures.

When milk is exposed to light there is a great loss of Vitamin B. It must be kept in a refrigerator or cooler and heated in a covered pan. Milk should always be heated at low temperatures in order to reduce the loss of nutrients.

■ **KEFIR MILK**

Kefir milk is a cultured milk beverage sold by some dairies. Your health food store can get the cultured grains for you if you wish to make it yourself.

The culture is a combination of milk-fermenting yeasts and bacteria. The cultured grains are placed in 1 qt. fresh certified raw milk. Allow to stand at 70° or room temperature until it reaches the degree of sourness desired. The grains you strain out of the milk may be used indefinitely.

Kefir milk is used in recipes calling for sour milk or buttermilk. It may be warmed to 115°. The poured-off whey and the remaining soft curd may be used as you would use a soft, mild cheese.

■ **DRIED MILK**

Dried milk, both whole and non-fat, is very useful in many recipes, as it will increase the nourishment without increasing the liquid. Dry milk has many advantages, one of the most important being the fact that it will keep indefinitely in its dry state. It is a life-saver when you run out of liquid milk. Be sure to purchase spray-dried powdered milk as there is less destruction of nutrients.

Because of its high protein content, dry milk will increase protein as much as 50% of solid to liquid without interfering with palatability of the food. Dry milk is also rich in calcium and most of the B vitamins.

People on reducing diets can get their required nutrients through non-fat dry milk, without increasing their calorie intake. The protein content of many recipes in this book has been increased by the addition of non-fat dry milk powder.

■ WHEY

In the making of cheese a pale amber liquid remains after the curd of cheese forms. This is whey. It contains nearly all the lactose and appreciable amounts of the proteins, minerals and soluble vitamins of whole milk. This liquid whey has been evaporated under low-heat methods. Some companies have transformed part of the lactose into betalactose, the type found in human milk and through ion exchange eliminated the bitter taste that characterizes some of the minerals.

Whey helps regulate the acidity and bacterial count of the digestive tract. It also is a help to those who cannot use the casein and fat of whole milk. Because of this lack of fat those who wish to eliminate animal fat from their diets find that whey provides most of milk's nutritional benefits.

Powdered whey is delicious. It can be eaten direct from the container or mixed with milk or fruit juice for added nourishment. It can be sprinkled over fruits, berries, cereals, or included as part of the dried milk in any recipe, thereby increasing the nourishment with fewer calories.

■ YOGURT

Yogurt, a famous Bulgarian milk product, was brought to North America by the Rosell Institute of La Trappe Monastery in Canada. The microbes that gave yogurt its distinction were separated and named Bacillus Bulgaricus. This culture is shipped all over the country and made into a delicious food, which has the consistency of custard when cooled. You can get this culture by mail or at a health food store and make your own appetizing yogurt. The prepared yogurt or culture is added to warm milk and the acid formed changes the milk to a thick custard which should be chilled at once to stop the bacterial growth and keep it from becoming too sour.

Yogurt is a superior nutritional product, as its bacteria breaks down milk sugar into lactic acid in the intestines and harmful bacteria cannot live in that acid medium. Some believe that the B vitamins thus produced in the intestinal tract are responsible for the long life of the Bulgarian people who eat quantities of yogurt.

There are yogurt recipes in nearly every chapter of this book, because yogurt lends itself to such a pleasing variety of uses.

Ways to Serve Yogurt:

1. Sweeten yogurt with honey or brown sugar to taste and sprinkle cinnamon over top. Chill and serve.
2. Mix 2 tbsp. undiluted frozen orange juice and 2 tsp. honey into 1 c. chilled yogurt for a quick dessert.
3. Blend 1 c. yogurt with 1 can undiluted, heated tomato or mushroom soup. Season to taste with salt, herbs, and serve as sauce over meat loaf.
4. Blend 1 c. cold yogurt with ½ c. chili sauce, ¼ c. drained sweet relish, chopped parsley, and salt to taste. Serve as a salad dressing for tossed green or vegetable salad.
5. Combine 1 c. cold yogurt, 3 tbsp. honey, ⅛ tsp. nutmeg or cinnamon and salt to taste. Serve with fresh fruit cup. Honey may be omitted if tartness of yogurt is not objectionable.

To Make Yogurt:

First, be sure to get fresh yogurt culture for starter. Warm 2 qts. certified raw milk to 115°; cool to 100° before adding starter; add 2 tbsp. yogurt for each pt. of milk. Shake to break up the milk solids. Pour into sterilized pint jars. Place in large kettle of warm water in oven. The pilot light usually provides enough heat to incubate the yogurt, but 105° should be maintained. Leave in warm place 3 hours or until set. Put in refrigerator to cool. To make thicker, add ⅓ c. per qt. of spray-dried powdered milk before pouring into glass jars.

Bleu Cheese Yogurt Salad Dressing:

Mash 1½ oz. Bleu cheese. Add 1 c. yogurt and beat. Then fold in 1 c. whipped cream and 1 clove crushed garlic.

■ NON-FAT DRY MILK

To make into liquid skim milk: Follow this chart to make the amount of liquid milk you need:

Dry Skim Milk	Add Water	Makes Liquid Skim Milk
3 tbsp.	1 c.	1 c.
6 tbsp.	2 c.	1 pt.
¾ cup	4 c.	1 qt.

Mix and shake powder and water in a jar or beat smooth in bowl.

To use as dry skim milk: Add it to recipes that call for milk and a generous measure of dry ingredients. Stir or sift measured dry skim milk with dry ingredients such as flour and salt; then use water as liquid in place of milk. For example: If your recipe calls for 1 c. milk, mix and sift 3 tbsp. dry skim milk with the dry ingredients, then continue with the recipe exactly as directed, but instead of the 1 c. fresh milk called for, use 1 c. water.

■ HOW TO WHIP DRY SKIM MILK

Combine ½ c. cold water, 2 tbsp. lemon juice and 1 tsp. vanilla in 1 qt. bowl. Sprinkle ½ c. dry skim milk over top. Beat with rotary beater about 8 minutes; with electric beater about 4 minutes, or until mixture is stiff. Gradually beat in 3 tsp. honey, continuing to beat about 2 minutes more until mixture is smooth and creamy. For best flavor, chill 30 minutes before serving. Use as a dessert topping. Makes about 1½ c.

To Make Sour Milk from Sweet Milk:

Add 1 tbsp. vinegar or lemon juice to 1 c. sweet milk.

■ CHEESE

Cheese may be divided into 2 general classes—those in which the curd is produced through the action of rennet, and those in which it is formed by means of lactic acid. When rennet comes in contact with milk, the milk casein coagulates, drawing together in a semi-solid mass. This is called curd. The watery substance remaining is the whey. The differences among the varieties of cheese are due to source of milk, whether from the cow, goat or sheep, the temperature and conditions of ripening, harmless organisms such as mold and bacteria added to help development of flavor and texture. Cheese furnishes calcium and Vitamin B_2. It is not hard to digest, but remains in the stomach until its proteins are digested to a liquid.

Almost all varieties of cheese are produced by the rennet method except cream cheese, which is usually produced by the lactic acid method. This means that pure cultures of lactic acid are added to milk to start the conversion of lactose (milk sugar) to lactic acid.

Cheese may also be divided into hard and soft types. The difference between them is the amount of moisture or whey left in the curd, the bacteria or mold used to produce their characteristic flavor, and their method of curing. The common types of hard cheese are *Cheddar* and *Swiss*. The soft types are *Cream, Brie, Camembert*. Between these two groups are varieties which may be described as semi-soft, such as *Brick, Muenster* and *Bleu Cheese*.

American, Cheddar or just plain cracker-barrel cheese is one of the best you can buy. You can get wedges varying in color from pale yellow to deep orange, and in flavor from mild to very sharp. It is an all-purpose, full-flavored, natural, good-keeping cheese.

Swiss cheese is at the top of the preferred list of cheeses. It is pale yellow, has a mild nut-like flavor and big, even, round holes.

Bleu cheese is a strong, salty-flavored, soft cheese with blue mold veins running through it. It is the American version of Roquefort. Serve it as a spread, sprinkle over green salad, add to French dressing or serve with fruit.

Gouda cheese is a flattened sphere-shape, with a bright red coat that peels off when cut. It is creamy yellow with a salty nut-like flavor. Excellent for sandwiches or for dessert with fruit or crackers.

Provolone is a smoky pungent cheese, pear-shaped, yellow-tan in color and with rope marks. Good for appetizers.

Camembert is a foil-wrapped single-portion triangular-shaped cheese, just soft enough to spread easily and tangy enough to have character.

Limberger cheese has a very strong flavor. It is eaten as a sandwich snack and with fruit.

Romano and *Parmesan* are hard Italian-style cheeses, excellent for grating. For best flavor, grate only as needed.

Sapsago is a hard Swish cheese flavored with herbs and comes in a small conical shape. Grate and use like *Parmesan*.

■ MORE FACTS ABOUT CHEESE

Use low heat when cooking cheese as it is a protein food and, like other proteins, is toughened by high or prolonged heat.

Melt in a double boiler rather than over direct heat.

To keep natural cheese from molding, spread cut surface with soft butter.

½ lb. bulk cheese, grated, will make about 2 c. Use your blender to grate dry cheese. Keep covered in glass jar in refrigerator.

Because of the versatility of cheese it can be used any time of the day. At breakfast, grated Cheddar cheese is wonderful on scrambled eggs while cream cheese may be spread on bread or toast.

Cheese is a popular spread or filling for sandwiches, either hot or cold.

Cheese may be the principal ingredient of dips and spreads for the cocktail hour or served with crackers as hors d'oeuvres.

Cheese is suitable for the main dish at lunch or dinner. It is important in many casserole dishes.

Cheese may be used as a sauce (such as rich cheese sauce for baked potatoes) or it can be used as a garnish sprinkled over vegetables or entrées.

Cream cheese, cottage cheese and hoop cheese are delightful with fruit, vegetable and tossed green salads. Grated or slivered cheese, such as Swiss or Cheddar, are very good as a topping for Chef's salad, vegetable and tossed green salads.

Bleu and Roquefort cheese add zest to many salad dressings.

A classic gourmet dessert is fresh fruit served with assorted cheeses, such as apples and pears with Gouda and Camembert.

Keep soft cheese tightly covered. Wrap hard cheese and place in a covered container in the refrigerator.

Farmer-style cottage cheese and hoop cheese are excellent for weight watchers. The low-calorie cottage cheese and hoop cheese are de-fatted, fine-grain and frequently unsalted, and being high in protein, they are also nutritious and satisfying.

Recipes using cottage cheese appear frequently in this book and I will include a few hoop cheese recipes here. Cream cheese or farmer-style cottage cheese put through a sieve may be used instead of hoop cheese. Well blended cream cheese may be used instead of whipped cream.

■ LOW-CALORIE CHEESE PANCAKES

1 egg	1 tsp. honey
1 c. hoop cheese	¼ tsp. salt
3 tbsp. whole-wheat flour	

Beat egg and add hoop cheese, mixing in well. Stir in flour, honey and salt; beat until batter is smooth. Fry on well-greased griddle or skillet, using low heat, until edges are brown and bubbles form. Turn to other side to brown. Serve with honey.

■ LOW-CALORIE STUFFED CELERY

⅓ c. hoop cheese or farmer-style cottage cheese	¼ tsp, marjoram
1 tbsp. mayonnaise	Dash of Tabasco
½ tsp. salt	4-6 crisp celery stalks

Mix cheese and mayonnaise together, add seasonings and whip until smooth. Stuff celery stalks. Serve with salads, or cut in 1-inch pieces and serve as appetizer.

■ LOW-CALORIE CHEESE-RICE CASSEROLE

2 tbsp. minced onion	1 c. hoop cheese or farmer-style cottage cheese
1 can mushroom stems and pieces	⅓ c. milk
¼ c. parsley, chopped	1 tsp. salt
2 c. cooked brown rice	

Combine onion and mushrooms; add cheese, parsley, milk and salt. Mix thoroughly and bake in greased casserole in 350° oven, 14 minutes. Serves 4-6.

■ CHEESE-STUFFED APPLES

½ c. hoop cheese or farmer-style cottage cheese	4 apples, cored
⅓ c. chopped dates or raisins	¼ c. chopped nuts
	¼ c. lemon or pineapple juice

Mix cheese with dates or raisins; add nuts, mix and stuff into centers of cored apples. If apples have been sprayed with a poison spray, they should be peeled. Cut apples in slices, sprinkle with lemon or pineapple juice and serve on crisp lettuce leaves. Serves 4-6.

■ CHEESE-SQUASH CASSEROLE

6 medium zucchini or summer squash	1 tsp. salt
1 egg, beaten	Dash of Tabasco
¼ c. whole-wheat crumbs	½ c. buttered whole-wheat crumbs
½ c. hoop cheese	1 tsp. paprika
¼ tsp. marjoram	

Cook squash or zucchini in boiling water until tender. Cut in small pieces; blend with egg, ¼ c. crumbs, cheese and seasonings. Pour into greased casserole; top with crumbs, sprinkle with paprika. Bake at 350°, 20 minutes. Serves 4-6.

■ CHEESE CUSTARD LUNCHEON PIE

Pastry shell	3 eggs beaten
4 slices bacon	¼ tsp. pepper
2 tbsp. fat	1 tbsp. minced parsley
⅓ c. chopped onion	2 c. shredded sharp Cheddar cheese
2 tbsp. green pepper, chopped	
1½ c. milk	

Prepare pastry from any favorite recipe and fit into a 9-inch pie pan. Chill. Fry bacon until crisp and chop. Pour off all but 2 tbsp. fat. Cook onion and finely-chopped green pepper in remaining bacon fat until tender. Heat milk to scalding and add slowly to beaten eggs. Add bacon and onion mixture and pepper. Add parsley and cheese. Pour into cold pastry and bake in slow oven, 325°, 45 minutes, or until set. Serve at once. Serves 6.

■ COEUR À LA CREME

1 lb. creamed cottage cheese	1 tsp. salt
1 c. heavy cream	

Put cottage cheese in mixing bowl; add salt. Add cream to cheese gradually and beat until smooth as possible. Use electric mixer or use rotary beater. Line a sieve with cheesecloth and pour in cheese mixture and let stand overnight in refrigerator to drain. Unmold next day and serve with fresh fruit or frozen fruit sweetened with honey.

■ **CHEESE-MACARONI CASSEROLE**

2 tbsp. powdered milk	¼ tsp. salt
¼ c. cooked whole-wheat mac-	2 c. grated Cheddar cheese
aroni	2 eggs
½ c. rolled oats	1½ c. milk
¼ c. soy grits	A little grated onion or
¼ c. wheat germ	chopped green pepper

Mix dry milk with liquid milk. Mix all ingredients and pour over top. Bake in moderate oven at 350°, 40 minutes. Serves 4.

■ **CHEESE-HAM SOUFFLÉ**

¼ lb. cooked ham	2 tbsp. butter
¼ lb. Swiss cheese	3 tbsp. flour
½ small onion	¾ c. milk
4 sprigs parsley or ¼ c.	1½ tsp. salt
chopped parsley	⅛ tsp. pepper
4 eggs, separated	¾ tsp. dry mustard

Chop ham into small pieces. Grate cheese on coarse grater. Chop onion and parsley fine. Separate eggs. Melt butter. Stir in flour. Slowly stir in milk. Cook over low heat, stirring constantly until thickened. Remove from heat. Add grated cheese, stir until cheese melts. Add ham, onion, parsley, salt, pepper, mustard. Beat whites of egg until they hold a stiff peak. Gently stir cooled cheese mixture into whites of egg. Pour into ungreased 1½-qt. casserole. Bake in 325° oven, 50 minutes. Serves 4-6.

■ **WELSH RAREBIT**

4 tbsp. butter	½ tsp. dry mustard
1 lb. sharp Cheddar cheese	Dash of Cayenne pepper
⅔ c. milk	2 eggs
½ to 1 tsp. salt	2 tsp. Worcestershire sauce

Melt butter in top of double boiler over direct heat. While it melts, cut cheese in cubes and add to fat, still over very low direct heat. Stir frequently until cheese melts. Now place pan over hot (not boiling) water. Stir milk, salt, dry mustard, Cayenne pepper and eggs together slightly in a bowl and, when cheese is melted and well mixed with fat, pour in egg mixture and Worcestershire sauce. Stir until heated through and slightly thick. Serve immediately over toast, or cover and let stand over the hot water until needed. Serves 4.

■ **MEATLESS CHILI WITH CHEESE**

2 tsp. minced onion or 1 tbsp.   ½ c. milk
   dry onion soup mix   3 tsp. chili powder
1 tbsp. salad oil   1 c. freshly-grated cheese
1 5-oz. can tomato sauce   2 beaten eggs

Brown minced onion or dry onion soup mix in salad oil. Add tomato sauce, milk, chili powder. Simmer, but do not boil, for 15 minutes. Add cheese, eggs, and season to taste. Serve on toast.

■ **CHEESE CROQUETTES**

1 c. dried whole-grain bread   ⅛ tsp. black pepper
   crumbs   Dash of Tabasco
2 c. grated Parmesan or sharp 1 egg, well beaten
   Cheddar cheese   2 tbsp. top milk
1 tsp. prepared mustard   Dried bread crumbs

Soften bread crumbs with enough water to shape. Mix with grated cheese, mustard, salt, pepper, Tabasco, egg, and milk. Shape into 6-8 conical croquettes, roll in additional dried bread crumbs. Fry in deep hot oil (or in ½-inch of oil in skillet), turning often. Drain on brown paper and serve with tomato sauce.

■ **CHEESE SOUFFLÉ**

2 tbsp. butter   3 eggs, separated
2 tbsp. flour   Salt and pepper to taste
½ c. milk   Dash of Tabasco
1 c. grated Cheddar cheese

Melt butter, stir in flour until smooth, add milk and cheese. Cook 1 minute. To this add beaten yolks of 3 eggs, salt, pepper and Tabasco. Cool. Add beaten whites of eggs. Fill greased casserole or custard cups ¾ full. Put in pan of hot water. Bake 15-25 minutes at 350°. Serves 3-4.

■ **MACARONI IN CHEESE SAUCE**

1¾ c. whole-wheat macaroni   2 c. rich cheese sauce
2 qt. boiling water   Paprika and chopped parsley
Salt

Boil macaroni in boiling, salted water. Drain, reheat in cheese sauce. Serve with paprika and parsley. Serves 4.

■   **CHEESE SAUCE**

4 tbsp. butter or oil	**¼ tsp. nutmeg**
4 tbsp. flour	**1 tbsp. grated onion**
¼ tsp. pepper	**2 c. milk**
½ tsp. salt	**1 c. grated Cheddar cheese**

Melt butter or oil in medium-size saucepan. Blend in flour, onion, salt, pepper and nutmeg. Slowly stir in milk. Cook over low heat, stirring constantly until sauce thickens and boils, about 1 minute. Add grated cheese. Continue to cook over low heat, stirring constantly until cheese melts. Serve over baked potato, macaroni, broccoli or tuna and salmon croquettes. Makes 2 c.

■   **COTTAGE CHEESE MADE FROM SOUR MILK**

Place 2 qts. certified raw milk in a large pan. Cover and keep at room temperature until it sours naturally, 12-24 hours. Set pan of clabber over lowest heat. Use thermometer. Bring to 110°. It is ready when the curd first appears solid. Pour into cheesecloth bag or clean flour bag and hang on sink faucet, or where it can drain. The length of time it hangs determines the kind of cheese; a day and a half should be enough. Place curd in dish, break up with a fork and season with salt and top milk or cream. This may be beaten in a blender or mixer if velvet-smooth product is desired.

■   **COTTAGE CHEESE MADE WITH RENNET**

Heat 2 qts. milk to 90°. Dissolve 1 junket tablet in 1 tbsp. warm water and stir into warmed milk. Cover bowl and let stand until set, possibly all night. Cut through curd with silver knife several times. Place bowl in large pan of hot water. Bring curd to 110° for soft cheese and to 118° for farmer-style cheese. Mix curd once or twice while heating. Pour into strainer lined with cheesecloth, or into cloth bag. Squeeze out whey or drain until whey is removed. Mash the cheese with a fork; add 1 tsp. salt and enough sweet or sour cream or yogurt until you get the desired consistency. Blend for whipped cottage cheese or cream cheese.

■   **CHEESE SPREAD OR MOLDS**

Put into blender 2 c. cottage cheese and a little yogurt or some cream. Add any of the following, depending on how you wish to serve it. Pack into oiled mold or glass jar.

2 tsp. caraway seeds, crushed   1 tbsp. chopped parsley
1 small wedge Roquefort   ½ pkg. dry onion soup mix
cheese

■ CHEESE THINS

2 c. sharp Cheddar cheese,   1 green pepper, minced fine or
grated   ½ c. minced sweet red pep-
½ c. butter   per, or ½ c. chopped canned
2 c. unbleached white flour   pimiento

Cream cheese and butter thoroughly. Add flour gradually and add pepper or pimiento. Shape into a roll. Wrap in parchment paper or oiled paper. Chill in refrigerator several hours. Just before serving, slice and bake on cookie sheet, at 400°, until lightly browned.

■ CHEESE PUFFS TO SERVE WITH COCKTAILS

1 lb. cream cheese   ½ c. grated onion
3 egg yolks   ¼ c. minced parsley
1 tsp. salt   1 tin smoked oysters or ½ c.
½ tsp. Cayenne pepper   minced lobster or crab meat
Whole-wheat crackers

Have cream cheese at room temperature. Beat yolks, add salt, Cayenne pepper and onion. Drain oysters and cut into tiny bits, or mince crab meat or lobster. Add to yolk mixture, then stir into the softened cream cheese.

Spread on crackers and brown under broiler until slightly puffed. Serve hot, with parsley sprinkled on top.

■ CHEESEBURGERS, MEATLESS

2 8-oz. pkgs. cottage cheese   1 tbsp. minced parsley
1 beaten egg   ¾ tsp. salt
¾ c. whole-wheat bread   1 tsp. Worcestershire sauce
crumbs   ¼ c. chopped walnuts
2 tbsp. minced onion   1 c. fine bread crumbs

Combine cottage cheese with egg, bread crumbs, onion, parsley, salt, Worcestershire sauce and walnuts. Form into 6-8 cakes and coat with fine bread crumbs. Fry in butter or oil until brown on both sides. Serve with bottled chili sauce.

■   **OLIVE-CHEESE TURNOVERS**

Pastry rounds	**⅓ c. chili sauce**
⅔ c. grated Cheddar cheese	**Chili powder to taste**
⅔ c. chopped ripe olives	**Cumin powder**

Prepare 1 recipe of your favorite pastry, roll into 2-inch rounds. Mix grated cheese with olives, chili sauce, chili powder and dash of cumin. Place 1 tsp. of filling on each pastry round, moisten edges, fold over half and pinch edges together. Place on cookie sheet. Chill. When ready to serve, bake 10-12 minutes, at 475°. Serve hot, as hors d'oeuvres.

CHAPTER 12

Raw Foods

*T*HE attainment of optimal health throughout life is the goal of us all, and there are many of us who believe the only way to achieve this is by a return to more natural nutrition. This means eating food elements that have been built up by the sun's rays, not destroyed by man's processing; foods containing more life-giving substances.

Everyone knows how delicious fruits and vegetables can be when freshly picked from an organic garden, not needing rich sauces, added sugar, or seasoning. But raw fruits and vegetables must be very carefully selected, in the market, for the nutrients believed to be there, may not be, if the food was not grown on organically prepared soil and free from poison sprays.

According to Dr. Royal Lee, nutritionist, "Cooking of food reduces its nutritional value in animal feeding tests at least one-third, judging from weight gains produced." He also says that cooking destroys some amino acids, enzymes and vitamins. The amount of food value lost depends upon the type of food, method of preparation and degree of temperature used in cooking.

As Doctor Sherman of Columbia has pointed out, whole foods with their original content of enzymes, minerals, vitamins, proteins, unsaturated fatty acids and natural carbohydrates, are first to be considered in our meal planning. These whole foods have factors both known and unknown.

Many believe that man's digestive organs have been conditioned by a long period of eating cooked foods, so that weak stomachs and flaccid intestines cannot properly assimilate and utilize food unless it is carefully broken up. So some preparation of raw food is necessary; otherwise people accustomed to cooked foods may rebel at a return to plain, unseasoned raw food. Anyhow, no one wants to sit down to a meal of cabbage leaves, raw whole beets, or other large raw vegetables, served without thought of the aesthetic and psychological effect upon the digestive juices. As Dr. Harold Hawkins puts it, "Perhaps nothing contributes more to the general health and happiness of a family than properly prepared and served meals. Every article of food must be evaluated separately as to the best method of preparation."

■ **FRUITS AND VEGETABLES, LIQUEFIED**

To obtain these juices, a juicer or liquefier is necessary. The liquefier or juicer will remove the fiber and produce only the juice, whereas a blender reduces food to a fine purée consistency. The juicer is an excellent way to obtain nutritional substances from a large amount of material without the necessity of eating so much bulk. The blender can provide extra vitamins and minerals for your family, as well as delicious and nutritious drinks, soups, sauces, spreads, dips, batters and desserts. Food may also be shredded, ground, chopped or blended, depending on how you wish to use them.

When liquefying fruits or vegetables, always start with a liquid base of milk, buttermilk, yogurt, soy milk, coconut milk, fruit or vegetable juice, or other liquid. Use enough to cover the agitator blades. If a thick mixture is desired, to be eaten with a spoon, use less liquid. Always have the ingredients chilled, for delicious flavor. A thick fruit base mixture when cold, is like sherbet; sprinkled with ground nuts, shredded or powdered coconut, or toasted sesame seeds, makes a heavenly dessert. The vegetable purées can be used as soup or dips, used with gelatin to make salads, or as a vegetable.

Water cress is very rich in organic minerals and vitamins and has an abundance of Vitamin E, and more iodine than most plants. Do not use too much, since it is quite nippy.

Cabbage leaves may also be used. They are a rich source of Vitamins A, B, C, and G, and contain chlorine, calcium, sodium and iron.

Cucumbers are a medium source of A and B, and rich in vitamin C. They also have potassium, iron, magnesium, and a high percentage of silicon and chlorine.

Kale is a good source of vitamin A, rich in calcium, riboflavin, and B vitamin.

Turnip tops when juiced are a valuable source of iron and have 3 times more vitamin C than oranges or tomatoes.

Lettuce has an abundance of potassium, sodium, calcium, magnesium, iron, and folic acid.

Pea pods when fresh, can be juiced to advantage.

Parsley leads the list of vegetables in iron and is also rich in blood-building copper and manganese. Parsley also ranks high in vitamin B_1 and is low in starch. It is so potent that only a few leaves are used in each drink.

Alfalfa roots delve deep into the soil, as much as 25 or 30 feet, to get organic phosphorus, chlorine, silicon, aluminum, calcium, magnesium, sulphur, sodium, and potassium. The United States Department of Agriculture has reported that the protein content of alfalfa is about 1½ times as much as wheat or corn.

Carrots are nature's miracle food and carrot juice has been called liquid gold. In recent years carrots have been recognized as one of the most valuable and best balanced vegetables from the standpoint of vitamins and minerals. Raw carrots contain nearly all the minerals and vitamins required by the human body. They are an exceedingly rich source of vitamin A, carotene being the vegetable form. There are moderate amounts of vitamins B and C in carrots, and carrot juice taken daily is one of the finest foods obtainable.

Celery is a rich source of vitamins A and B, calcium, sodium, potassium, phosphorus and iron, and has an alkaline reaction in the body. It is advisable to use every part of the plant to get the most benefit from its nutrients.

Potato juice is an excellent vegetable source of nutritious protein. It is high in vitamin C and contains a lot of the tyrosinase fraction, the organic copper blood-builder. Potato juice should be made just before it is to be consumed, as it darkens by oxidation. Some lemon juice squeezed over the pieces will arrest this.

Coconut milk has often been the only source of liquid available in some tropical regions. To get the milk, punch the eyes on the shell with an ice-pick and drain out the liquid. Put the whole coconut into a hot oven until you hear it crack, which means the meat will be loosened. The brown skin need not be removed for juice-making. Cut up the meat and put it in the blender, and then in the juicer.

To make *soy milk,* soak soybeans in several changes of water, keeping them refrigerated. Liquefy the soaked beans in a blender, then pour the purée into a juicer to set the milk. This may be diluted and used as any milk. Good soy powder may be purchased in health food stores and made into milk.

The most popular friut juices are the following:

Apple juice which is rich in magnesium, iron, silicon, and potassium. Apples also contain malic acid which is most beneficial.

Tomato juice is a good source of vitamin C and many of the minerals.

Orange juice is also an excellent source of vitamin C. When juicing oranges, it is important to get as much of the white part of the orange as possible, because of the valuable bioflavinoids and protopetins which it contains.

Pineapple juice, unsweetened, is a nutritious and delicious drink. It is important for vitamins, minerals, natural sugar, and is a digestive factor.

Grape juice is one of the most healthful of juices and has been used for centuries for grape cures. It is an almost neutral juice and extremely important because of its minerals, vitamins, and natural sugars.

■ BLENDER COMBINATIONS

Your imagination is the only limit to the possible blender combinations you can make with fruits, vegetables, fresh or dry milk, powdered whey, soy milk, dried fruits, seeds, nuts, wheat germ, molasses, honey, herbs, carob powder, rice polish, powdered yeast. If nuts or grains are to be used they must be ground first, before the liquid is added. Fruit and vegetable juices used in a blender must be freshly squeezed or frozen, to retain important vitamins. Never put whole fruit or vegetables in your blender. They must be cut into small pieces of 1-2 inches, and leafy vegetables should be broken up.

The delicious milk, fruit and vegetable drinks which can be made quickly in a blender are a most important contribution to our meal planning. Try some of these suggested combinations, and do not hesitate to experiment to discover others for yourself.

To 1½ c. fruit juice, add any two or three of the following:

1. **1 medium apple (peeled if it has been sprayed) cut into small pieces, or 1 medium banana.**
2. **1 orange, without yellow rind, cut up.**
3. **¼ c. nuts (almonds, cashews, pecans, pignolias).**
4. **⅓ c. raisins, figs, or other dried fruit.**

5. ¼ c. sesame, sunflower, or squash seeds.
6. ½ c. powdered skim milk.
7. ¼ c. powdered whey.
8. ¼ c. raw wheat germ.
9. ¼ c. rice polish.
10. 2-3 chopped dates.
11. 1 c. fresh fruit or berries.
12. 1 c. melon cubes.
13. ¼ c. raw honey.
14. 3 tbsp. cottage cheese.

To 1½ c. carrot juice add any two or three of the following:

1. ⅓ c. unsweetened pineapple juice.
2. 1 c. fresh alfalfa leaves with ¼ c. parsley leaves.
3. ¼ c. almonds.
4. ¼ c. raisins or dates, or 1 small orange without yellow rind.
5. ¼ c. wheat germ.
6. 1 small onion.
7. 1 stalk celery.
8. 3-4 string beans.
9. ½ c. spinach.
10. 1 small cucumber.
11. 1 small piece green pepper.
12. ¼ tsp. vegetable salt.

To 1½ c. tomato juice (or use 2-3 fresh tomatoes) add any two or three of the following:

1. 1 small onion.
2. Sprig of parsley.
3. ¾ c. sauerkraut juice.
4. 1 slice lemon.
5. Pinch of basil and marjoram.
6. ¼ tsp. vegetable salt.
7. Few celery tops or beet leaves.
8. 2-3 cabbage leaves.
9. 1 small avocado.

To 1½ c. liquid milk, soy milk, or yogurt, add 2 or 3 of the following:

1. ½ c. orange, pineapple, or berry juice.
2. ¼ c. frozen fruit.
3. ½ c. skim milk powder.
4. ¼ c. dry whey.
5. A few almonds, pignolias, pecans, peanuts.

6. ¼ c. fresh fruit or berries.
7. A few dates or raisins.
8. 1 banana, cut up.
9. 1 apple (peeled if sprayed), cored and cut up.
10. ¼ c. carob powder.
11. ¼ c. powdered yeast.
12. Sunflower seeds.
13. ¼ c. molasses or honey.
14. 1-2 eggs, separated, the white folded in after the mixture has blended.

There are various ways of preparation: squeezing, cutting or grating into small pieces, and mixing in various ways. All raw fruits and vegetables must be carefully selected. First, obtain them from organic orchards or gardens; next, cut off parts that are not fresh or indigestible; and lastly, thoroughly clean by washing under running water. Never soak vegetables, as the water-soluble vitamins are lost.

■   RAW VEGETABLES AS A MAIN DISH

Raw vegetables should be chosen for variation in color, texture, and flavor, and then arranged attractively with a delicious dressing or seasoning added. For example, any of the following combinations are good, and you will think of many more.

1. Finely cut lettuce, sliced tomatoes, grated carrots, cucumber circles, celery strips.
2. Endive, grated raw peeled beets, cashew nuts, bean sprouts, parsley sprigs.
3. Romaine lettuce finely cut, green pepper strips, quartered tomatoes, cauliflower flowerettes, sliced yellow turnips.
4. Grated red and green cabbage, young onions, carrot curls, green corn sliced from the cob.
5. Shredded spinach, diced celery, mashed tomato and diced cucumbers, minced onion, green peas.
6. Water cress, radishes, turnips, carrots and beets grated, celery fans, almonds.

Suitable dressings include:

1. Seed meal dressing: To ¼ c. lemon juice add ½ c. soy, sesame, or peanut oil, ¼ tsp. vegetable powder, and 2 tsp. sesame or sunflower meal.
2. French dressing: Mix and beat with ½ c. oil, ¼ c. lemon juice or vinegar, 1 tsp. honey, ¼ tsp. paprika, ¼ tsp. garlic powder and onion powder (freshly grated onion and garlic are even better) ¼ tsp. vegetable salt.
3. Tomato dressing: ¼ c. tomato juice, vegetable salt to taste, ¼ c. lemon juice or cider vinegar, ½ c. sesame or soy oil.

4. **Horseradish dressing.** 1 tbsp. horseradish, 4 tbsp. soy or peanut oil, 4 tbsp. lemon juice, finely chopped parsley.
5. **Mayonnaise:** Break an egg yolk into a bowl, add 2 tsp. lemon juice or cider vinegar, 1 tsp. honey, 1 tsp. vegetable salt. Slowly, drop by drop, add 2 c. olive, sunflower, sesame, or soy oil, beating with a rotary beater. Keep everything cool and refrigerate.

SEEDS, NUTS DATES, HONEY AND MOLASSES

Most civilized food has gotten away from the delectable and nutritious factors found in many seeds, and only now are we becoming aware of what we have been missing. It is the consensus of many scientists that because the seed is the means of survival of the species, its chemical composition does not vary as widely as does the composition of other foods. The quality of seeds will remain constant though the quantity varies. Seeds are also not as much affected by the use of poison sprays, as are the leaves and stalks of plants. The seeds and leaves, however, complement each other, and together make a satisfactory meal. The most important nutritive elements of seeds are probably vitamins B and E, unsaturated fatty acids, minerals and proteins.

Of all the seeds the *soybean* is by far the most important. It is the most highly concentrated natural food known and has about 43% of perfect protein. It has about 2½ times as much protein as lean beef, 3½ times as much as eggs or cheese and more than 12 times as much as whole milk. In addition, it contains well known vitamins. Thirteen minerals are also present in a natural relationship similar to the body needs, as well as a very large amount of lecithin (over 2%) combined organically with phosphorus and choline, all essential for normal body functions. People allergic to animal milk, meats, cereal foods, eggs or sugars, as well as strict vegetarians, will find that the soybean will supply most of the deficiencies met with in a restricted diet. The soybean is used principally in the form of flour and oil, but there are also other products such as soy grits, soy nuts, canned soy beans, and soy lecithin spread. They are delicious when eaten fresh. Soy flour should be added to all bakery goods, and in amounts under 15% there will be no flavor, yet the protein will be greatly increased. Because of its non-gluten content, soy flour should be mixed with other flours when used for bread.

Lentils are among the oldest vegetables cultivated having protein, minerals, and some vitamins, and they can be used for many recipes calling for dried beans.

Sunflower seed is extremely popular in Europe, but is far less known in this country as food for humans. The seeds are rich in vitamins B, A, and D, and niacin, and in bone-forming calcium and trace minerals. They are outstandingly rich, over 50% in high-quality, easily digested protein. They may be used in salads, desserts, quick breads, casserole dishes, with meats, and are popular in milk drinks. The seeds can be ground or put in a blender and made into a paste. This paste is very good with bananas, pineapple, apricots, prunes, raisins, in quick bread, or in milk drinks. Or it may be mixed with ½ c. shredded carrots, 2 tbsp. chopped raisins, and 2 tbsp. yogurt for an individual salad. The paste may also be mixed with cottage cheese and yogurt, and used to stuff softened prunes. The whole or chopped seeds are good in vegetable or tomato soup. But the most popular way to eat sunflower seeds is either raw or lightly toasted and a few eaten each day is claimed by some to constitute a miracle food.

The Indians of the Americas have long eaten *squash* or *pumpkin seeds*. Either toasted or plain, a mixture of sunflower seeds, pumpkin seeds, and pignolia kernels is a delicious dessert. *Beans* and *corn* have also been an important food of the Indians. Beans when young and tender can be eaten raw, and young corn cut off the cob is excellent uncooked.

Sesame seed is one of the first recorded seeds eaten by man. It is high in protein, especially methionine, also in calcium and phosphorus, and a good source of vitamin B, niacin or nicotinic acid. Another vitamin present in sesame seeds is vitamin E. Sesame seed oil has the property of preventing rancidity in other oils, and contains lecithin which is very important for the chemical work to be done by the liver. The seeds are small, sweet and oily, and add a pleasing taste to many foods. They have been consumed mostly in the Mediterranean area, but are now finding a ready market in America. Large quantities are used in candy and by bakers as a topping on breads, rolls and cookies. They can be purchased crushed into a paste. This product can be converted into milk, which stays fresh for a long period, and is easily digested.

A wide variety of seeds can be used as seasoning.

Caraway is used in rye bread, applesauce, soups and stews.

Cardamon, an oriental herb, is used in cakes, and cookies.

Celery seed is a delicious adjunct to soups, casseroles, and salads.

Cariander seeds are crushed and used in cakes, breads, cheese, poultry, and sausage.

Cumin seeds are hot to the taste and used where highly seasoned dishes are desired. They are one of the ingredients in curry powder.

Dill seeds are added to pickles, salads, and some vegetables.

Mustard seed, used in pickles, is also used in powdered form, combined with horseradish root for a spread.

Nutmeg contains another spice, *mace,* and both are used in cakes and cookies, with apples, or whenever an extra spicy flavor is needed.

Poppy seeds obtained from the pod of the flower, are used on breads, cakes and cookies and can be sprinkled over salads.

Anise seed is obtained from an herb of the carrot family. It is very aromatic and is used in baking and in the making of certain liqueurs.

Nuts have long been a valued food. The almond has been cultivated since Roman times, but other nuts (in any quantity) only in recent times. The American Indians used nuts of the pine, horse-chestnut and hazel extensively in their diet, and those of the oak and beech have been used in other parts of the world. The pecan is the best native nut in this country, and the coconut is the most widely used tropical nut. Nuts are high in proteins, fats, vitamin A, thiamin, B vitamin, and minerals. Among the nuts containing excellent proteins, but not complete, are butternuts, pecans, filberts (hazel), Brazil nuts, English walnuts, black walnuts, almonds, pine nuts (pignolias), chestnuts, and coconuts.

Coconuts are large seeds and because they grow close to the sea, are rich in minerals. They have beneficial natural bulk, unsaturated fatty acids, and are high in vitamins. Powdered coconut is delicious when sprinkled on cereals, desserts, fruit salads or dressings, or mixed in fruit or vegetable drinks.

Malted coconut has a special enzyme added, and is most delicious.

Almonds have been used extensively in the Orient as well as in Europe. A milk is made of them which, because of its high protein content, promotes growth in children. Almond meal or paste is frequently used in cakes and candies.

Pine nuts or *pignolias* as they are more often called, grow in the wild and are excellent food because they have not been subjected to poison sprays or chemical fertilizers. Many American Indian tribes made a ritual of gathering these precious nuts and storing them for winter use. They are equally good as snacks, on salads, added to fruits or vegetables, or made into cakes or nut loaves.

Walnuts first grew in Persia many centuries ago, and were planted on the shores of the Mediterranean by the ancient Greeks and Romans. They were first brought to California by the Spanish padres, but commercial planting was not started before 1867. Walnuts have an acid reaction in the body, so they should be used with milk or other alkaline food.

Peanuts are not truly a nut, but the seeds of a leguminous plant. Peanut flour contains over 4 times the amount of protein, 8 times the amount of fat, and 9 times the amount of minerals found in wheat flour. It can be used in most recipes instead of wheat flour, but it should not be used in making bread.

Dates are probably man's oldest cultivated fruit. They are a clean, natural food and as a natural sweet they are unsurpassed. Dates are a good source of chlorine, potassium, manganese and magnesium, and a fair source of vitamins A, B, D, and G. Though generally eaten out of hand, they are also available as crunchies, crystals, granulated, date sugar and as creamed dates. They lend themselves to all kinds of baking, milk shakes, sandwich spreads, candies and desserts. Be sure dates are sun-dried.

Honey is a natural, unrefined food and since Biblical times has been prized for its health-giving properties. New therapeutic uses are being found all the time. Seventy-five percent of the composition of honey is sugar, primarily monsacharides or simple sugar, requiring no digestive change before being absorbed. Levulose, or fruit sugar, predominates in the chemical composition, and because it is almost twice as sweet as cane sugar, one can tolerate a smaller amount of honey than the refined sugars, making it particularly desirable from the nutritional standpoint. It is the natural dextrose in honey that forms crystals. Honey has been found to be a mild laxative, natural diuretic, and mild stimulant. It is a good source of readily-available energy and because bacteria cannot live in honey, it is considered a safe food if obtained from plants not sprayed with poison sprays. There are several kinds of honey available on the market; liquid, comb, chunk, solid, and creamed.

The flavor of honey depends upon the flowers from which the bees gather nectar. Because of this, you must know whether the nectar was obtained from blossoms that have not been sprayed. Honey from natural sources such as wild plants, will in most cases prove safer. Be sure that you get only blossom honey, for some bees are fed sugar and glucose during the winter months. The darker honey will usually have more minerals, vitamins and enzymes. Avoid storing honey in damp places, because it has the property of absorbing and retaining moisture. It does not require refrigeration. If the honey has granulated, place it in a bowl of warm water or in a warm place on the stove (but not on a burner). Because of its moisture-retaining qualities, cakes and cookies made with honey retain their keeping quality and stay moist longer. Whenever possible avoid pasteurized honey because it has been heated, so that some enzymes and possibly vitamins may have been destroyed. It is better to buy raw honey, and melt the crystals if they form, at low temperature.

■   **MOLASSES**

Molasses has been a standard commodity in all our kitchens from the early times of our country. The first sailing vessels trading with the sugar-producing West Indies brought back the rich, flavorsome black molasses. (In England it is called treacle.) There are two kinds of molasses, sulphured and unsulphured, the latter being preferable. Sulphured molasses is a by-product of sugar-making, mostly from areas other than the West Indies. Where the ripening season is not long enough to mature the cane properly, the green cane is treated with sulphur fumes during the sugar-extracting process. Obviously where sulphur fumes have been used in refining, sulphur will be present in the molasses. Sulphur destroys the B complex which molasses contains. It is possible to get good molasses made from the juice of sun-ripened cane, and not just as a by-product. There are 4 different kinds of acceptable molasses: first-run, second-run, third-run (blackstrap), and Barbados light. The first-run and the Barbados are delicious used as topping, in milk drinks and uncooked candy. Most nutritionists recommend blackstrap as an ingredient of energy-producing drinks. For really rich, old-fashioned gingerbread, ginger drop cakes, and cookies, dark molasses is preferred.

■ **ROASTED OR RAW ALMOND BUTTER**

Grind or place in blender ⅓ c. almonds. Leave on brown skins.

Mix with mayonnaise or cream cheese.

■ **NUT BUTTER**

Other nut butters may be made in blender or grinder. If using blender, pulverize 1-2 c. raw nuts. Add vegetable salt if desired and enough oil to make a paste. When using grinder, use the blade for crushing and put through grinder 2-3 times. Add salt to taste and oil to make a paste. Place in glass jar and refrigerate.

■ **FATS AND OILS**

With all the hullabaloo about fats, oils and calories, I have been besieged by people wanting to know the answers. As you know if you've been getting acquainted with this book, there is no *one* answer to good nutrition, no wonder-food, no panacea. It all takes doing, and is worth it. Generally, here's what you need to know about fats and oils:

The two principal types of fats are the saturated and the unsaturated. Animal fats, in general, have a higher percentage of saturated fatty acids, and the vegetable oils have more unsaturated fatty acids. The unsaturated fatty acids are linolenic acid, linoleic acid, and arachidonic acid. Human milk is rich in these unsaturated fats. The saturated fats are all solids at room temperature, and the unsaturated ones are liquid.

There are desirable unsaturated oils on the market whose raw products were grown with organic fertilizer and no sprays used. The raw seeds have been pressed in an expeller and the oil forced out without heat or the use of chemical solvents. Some of these good oils are corn, rice bran oil, soy, saf-flower seed, wheat germ, sesame, peanut, and sunflower seed.

Coconut and olive oils are low in the scale of unsaturated fatty acids.

Rice bran oil has linoleic acid, lipase, an enzyme and other important factors. It can be used in salads or whenever the use of an oil is indicated.

Sesame oil is high in unsaturated fatty acids. Sesame seeds, ground into butter, are good for bread or cookies. Since it is one-half oil, twice as much should be used as of other fats.

This sesame butter, also known as Tahini, is the basis for a candy, pleasant to taste and high in nutritional value. It can be used successfully for pie crust, waffles and pancakes, as well as for ice cream.

Sesame oil has a bland, intriguing flavor which is excellent in salad dressings and as a cooking oil. Some people have to acquire a taste for both the oil and butter, and here are some get-acquainted ideas:

■ TAHINI CANDY

Mix 1 tbsp. sesame butter with 1 c. powdered milk, ⅓-½ c. honey and ⅓ c. carob powder. Knead into a roll, chill and slice.

■ TAHINI MILK SHAKE

Blend 2-4 tbsp. sesame butter with 1 c. powdered milk and ¼ c. honey. Combine with 2 c. water; shake or blend until smooth.

CHAPTER 13

Salads and Salad Dressings

A SALAD can be something very special, bringing color to your table and zest to your meals in addition to providing the fresh, crisp greens needed for good nutrition.

Salads may be served in 6 different ways:

1. *Garnish salads* are the small and decorative additions to your main dish. They may be radish roses, carrot curls, sprigs of parsley or water cress, little lettuce cups filled with a fruit or vegetable salad, or tiny molded gelatin salads. Dressings should be used sparingly and ought to be piquant.

2. *Appetizer salads* are served as the first course and should look and taste especially good, since they are appetite-teasers. Keep the portions small. Crisp raw vegetables are excellent, as are sea food and fish salads, either molded or plain; fruit sections or avocado slices are also fine appetizer salads. Dressings should be on the tart side rather than bland. These small salads may also be served as hors d'oeuvres.

3. *Main-course salads* constitute the major part of the meal and should, therefore, provide all the necessary nutrients. Their variety is limitless, including combinations of cooked or raw vegetables with meat, poultry, fish, eggs or cheese, as well as combinations of fruits and cheese. Molded gelatin salads are a favorite main course for summer luncheons.

4. *Accompaniment salads* are just what the name implies. They are served with the main course and in general ought to be cold and crisp for contrast. Greens, raw vegetables and well-seasoned dressings provide a taste contrast for the rest of the hot meal.

5. *Dessert salad* is usually colorful and dainty. It is served as a light dessert for a meal, or may be the main food at a party. The dessert salad may be gelatin molds of fruits, frozen-fruit salads, fresh fruit, berries or melon. Cheese, nuts, nut-meal, coconut, sunflower seeds or dried fruits are used generously. If served as a party refreshment, fancy, small sandwiches, tiny, hot muffins or rolls usually accompany the salad.

6. *Slaws* are often classed alone because they are served in so many different ways, such as garnish, appetizer, main dish, accompaniment salad, as a relish or the salad in a salad sandwich. They are red or green shredded cabbage combined with any of the following: carrots shredded, shredded apples or pineapple, chopped celery, olives, green peppers, fruits, peanuts or other nuts, or hard-cooked eggs. A smooth, well-seasoned dressing, yogurt or sour cream is used as a blender.

SALAD GREENS

Greens are the basis for almost every salad and therefore are most important. The best are those that are very green, as they have more chlorophyl, vitamins and minerals.

The following are cultivated or wild greens, and the choice is yours:

Romaine—dark green, large spear-like leaves that may be used as a base, a garnish, served alone or in a tossed green salad. Romaine has a sharper taste than leaf lettuce.

Leaf Lettuce—long, loose, dark green leaves often with rust-colored crimped edges.

Bib Lettuce or *Boston Lettuce*—is shaped like a green rose. The leaves are very tender and mild in flavor. Their cup-like leaves make very pretty salads.

Iceburg Lettuce—is compact and crisp but, because it is not dark green to the core, is not so desirable from a nutrition viewpoint.

Endive—has flat green, tightly-curled leaves and is mild to bitter in taste. The very curly endive has a white center. It is also called chicory. Very decorative.

Escarole—is broad-leafed endive, deep green, sharp in taste, best used when chopped with other greens.

Water cress—can be used in many ways, as a basis for a salad, in tossed green salad, as a finger salad, as a garnish, or chopped in sandwiches. It is very important for its vitamin and mineral content, and has a nippy flavor.

Spinach—is best used when the leaves are young, in a tossed green salad.

Parsley—is usually a garnish, but can be chopped and served in green salads, in sandwiches or on hors d'oeuvres, as well as sprinkled over meat-salads.

Mint Leaves—are used as a garnish for cocktails, main dishes, accompaniment salads or desserts.

Celery Tops or *Beet Tops*—when young and tender are an addition to potato salad, green salads and vegetable salads.

Swiss Chard—when very young can be used in a green salad.

Chinese Cabbage—has long, wide leaves with a white center section and somewhat strong flavor. The stiff white center can be cut out and cooked as a vegetable. Flavor is like cabbage.

Nasturtium Leaves—use as green background for fruit salads.

Green Cabbage—is often mixed with green salad, raw vegetables, fruits, or served alone.

Wild Greens—such as *Lamb's Quarters, Dandelion or Mustard,* are nutritionally important and will add interesting flavor and texture to your tossed salads. Use only when young and tender.

Here are some things to remember when making salads:

1. Greens should be washed lightly and quickly, then drained in French salad basket or placed in towel and gently patted. To drain a large quantity of washed greens, try whirling them in an old muslin pillow case. They may be stored in refrigerator in towel or plastic bag.
2. Salads should be kept cold until serving time.
3. Create a center of interest with a fat ripe strawberry, a slice of fresh fruit, hard-cooked egg or stuffed olive; sliced date, a few raisins, anchovy fillet, pimiento strip, dash of paprika, etc.
4. Be sure salad ingredients are compatible in flavor and have interesting contrasts in color and texture.
5. Dressing should not be added to tossed salads until just before serving.
6. To vary your cooked or raw vegetable salads, try adding thin slivers of cheese. Slivers of ham, fish, chicken or veal are excellent with green salads, while chopped green or ripe olives go beautifully with fruit, vegetable, meat or fish salads.
7. Frozen fruit salads are very good with a piquant horseradish dressing.
8. Perfect your own versions of the three basic dressings: French, mayonnaise and boiled dressing, adding flavor variations as you please.

■ TOSSED GREEN SALADS

Time was when men considered salads "sissy" . . . but now the man of the house frequently brags about his ability to toss a mean green salad. He is watching his waistline as carefully as his wife watches hers and more often than not, his lunch consists of a salad bowl. At dinner, he may happily settle for a tossed green salad with his meat instead of those calorie-heavy potatoes.

A wooden salad bowl can be satin-smooth inside if you "ripen" it by wiping it clean after every usage, instead of washing it. A wooden salad fork and spoon are ideal for tossing greens in the bowl, and they, too, should be carefully wiped clean rather than washed. You may store your bowl, fork and spoon in a clean cloth bag.

Salad greens should never be soaked in water. They should be torn apart, rather than cut, and the stiff stems, hard midriffs and marred outer leaves should be removed. Always keep them cold and crisp.

Cheese to be used in salad may be kept in freezing compartment. It is then easier to grate or to slice off in fragments.

About 5 minutes before tossing with dressing, place salad bowl and greens in deep freeze. They will emerge wonderfully crisp.

Vary your tossed green salads with any of the following:

1. Bleu cheese crumbled over greens just before serving.
2. Toss in ½-1 c. toasted buttered whole-wheat bread crumbs.
3. Grated carrots, beets, turnips or cabbage, tossed in along with dressing.
4. For a simplified Caesar salad, stir 1 egg gently and pour over greens, then add small cubes of whole-wheat bread and slivers of chicken, pork, veal or anchovy fillets. Toss along with dressing.
5. If you must use left-over vegetables, such as peas, green beans, carrots or beets, they may be added to salad greens before tossing.
6. Small wedges of tomato, alternated with slices of peeled avocado may be arranged on tossed salad after dressing has been mixed in.
7. Sliced hard-cooked egg or thin slices of radish make a good topping.
8. Grated raw beets, red cabbage, young turnips or thinly sliced cucumber, green or red bell peppers, or tender young peas or string beans are all good toppings for green salads.

GARNISH OR APPETIZER SALADS

Tomato Flowers: Choose small, firm tomatoes. Peel or not, as desired. With small, sharp knife, divide each tomato into sixths or eighths, cutting just to the base, but not quite through. Spread into petalled shape and fill with deviled egg, or mixture of tuna celery and mayonnaise or mashed avocado with lemon juice, or your favorite cream cheese mixture. Garnish with black olives and serve on crisp lettuce leaves if desired.

Cheese Apples: Use cream cheese, tinted with red vegetable coloring. Shape into tiny apples and insert a few cloves at blossom and stem ends. Use pale green coloring and shape into pears, or orange coloring for carrot shapes. Tuck parsley sprigs at top of shaped cheese carrots. Artificial coloring of vegetable origin is harmless. Do not use synthetic colorings. Color may be brushed on cream cheese instead of being blended in. Egg yolk, hard-cooked and grated, and sieved spinach have been used successfully to color cream cheese.

Celery Curls: Use crisp green stalks, fairly large. Cut into 2-inch pieces. Make lengthwise slits, close together, from both ends of each stalk, leaving about ½ inch uncut in center. Soak about 1 hour in ice water to make the split ends form curls.

Radish Roses: Cut off root and stem ends. Make lengthwise slits through radish, but leave bottom uncut. With point of knife, press into open petals. Chill in ice water to make petals unfold. For radish accordions, make slits horizontally, almost through radish, and chill in ice water.

Fringed Cucumbers, radishes, carrots or beets are scored lengthwise with a fork, then sliced.

French-cut Tomatoes: Slice very thin, not horizontally, but from stem to blossom end. There is less loss of juice and they are easier to eat.

Carrot Curls are made by thinly scraping large carrots with vegetable peeler. (Carrots should be at room temperature.) Fasten with toothpick, place in cold water to chill and *set* curl.

Pitted Olives may be filled with celery or carrot sticks, almonds or cream cheese. Roll in oil to bring back shine.

Celery or *Carrot Stick Ends* may be dipped in paprika to resemble matches. Cut celery and carrot sticks about 3 inches long with a sharp knife. Slice off outside bulge so they lie flat, then cut lengthwise into match strips. Tie into a bundle tightly so they won't curl, and drop in ice water.

Melons and *Avocados* may be cut into balls with a ¼-measure teaspoon or a melon-ball tool; may be threaded on kabobs with chunks of pineapple, berries or chunks of other fruits. Serve raw.

Stuffed Olives and *Pitted Large Green or Black Olives* are most attractive garnishes. Stuff olives with blanched almonds, pearl onions, Cheddar or cream cheese, peanuts or other nuts.

Pimientos or *Green Peppers* may be cut into shapes or initials.

Cream Cheese, softened with a little cream, may be used to stuff celery, carrots, peppers, cucumbers or avocados, and these cut into rings are most attractive. Cheese may be seasoned with herbs, seeds, ground nuts, minced parsley or fresh horseradish.

Dried Vegetable Broth can be mixed with cream cheese or grated nuts for different taste in fillings for vegetables.

Cream Cheese Balls. Shape and roll in finely minced parsley, celery leaves, finely chopped chipped beef, ground nuts, sesame or poppy seeds. Season balls with herbs, seeds, minced raw vegetables, fine coconut, or meat or fish paste.

Carrot Ring Holders: Choose large carrots (at room temperature). Wash, scrape, cut into 3-inch lengths. Core each piece with apple corer, then cut into rings about ½-inch wide. Chill, serve with chilled green onions, celery straws or string beans.

Egg Chains: Cut hard-cooked eggs crosswise in thin slices. Remove yolk, cut a slit in half of the white rings and link the rings together to form a chain around the edge of the platter. Do this on the platter used in serving, as you can't transfer it.

MAIN DISH SALADS

On a hot summer's day, nothing is so refreshing as a cold, crisp salad served as the main course. Main dish salads are good in cooler weather too, preceded by a cup of soup and served with piping hot rolls. Berries or fruit with cheese are the perfect dessert.

■ FRESH FRUIT PLATTER

A small ice cream scoop of cottage or cream cheese is a splendid companion for a fruit platter, either topping the fruit or placed on the side. A bowl of yogurt on the side is another favorite complement. Salad dressings with a tang of mint or cheese are an imaginative touch. Here is a good combination as a starter to the many cool and colorful platters you will dream up for yourself:

Alternate on each salad plate fan-shaped banana slices, wedges of orange, melon balls, pineapple slices, whole strawberries, canned or fresh peach halves. Garnish with sprigs of water cress or cream cheese balls rolled in minced parsley or chopped pecans, or black cherries, purple grapes or raspberries. Serve with yogurt as dressing, or sweet whipped cream flavored with honey or mint.

■   **GREEN PEA SALAD**

  1 c. fresh green peas   1 small bunch green scallions
  2 stalks crisp green celery   1 green pepper
  1 heart of green celery   2 small tomatoes

Dice celery stalks and heart, scallions, pepper and tomatoes. Mix with peas and serve on lettuce with your favorite dressing. For a change in taste, try dressing made of peanut butter thinned with lemon juice.

■   **SUMMER SUPPER SALAD**

  1 pkg. frozen mixed vegeta-   1 sliced cucumber, unpeeled if
  bles, cooked until tender   grown organically
  5 c. mixed salad greens   3 tomatoes, cut in thin wedges
  3 green onions or scallions,   1 c. cubed Cheddar cheese
  finely chopped   1 c. chopped sprouts
  ½ lb. cold boiled ham, cooked
  chicken, tuna or salami, slivered, hard-cooked eggs

Mix cooked vegetables with sprouts. Drizzle ⅓ c. French herb dressing over vegetables and sprouts; chill about 30 minutes. Add to salad greens and toss lightly. Arrange slivers of meat, cucumber, tomatoes and cheese on top. Drizzle 2 more tbsp. French herb dressing over salad before serving. Serves 6-8.

ACCOMPANIMENT SALADS

Fruit Combinations—

Pineapple-Banana: 1 can unsweetened sliced pineapple, 1 large ripe banana cut in thirds and sliced lengthwise in thin sticks, 1 orange, peeled and sliced thin. Arrange fruits on 4 salad plates. Top with dressing made of non-homogenized peanut butter blended with a little mayonnaise, or use plain mayonnaise or other salad dressing. Color may be added by centering each salad with a preserved cranberry.

Fruit and Cottage Cheese: Mix 1 pt. cottage cheese (2 c.), with 1 tbsp. chopped chives or minced parsley. Roll in balls or use small ice cream scoop and serve on 6 individual salad plates with combinations of fresh pineapple and fresh black cherries, pitted; or fresh peaches, sliced, with fresh red raspberries; or fresh strawberries with melon balls.

Pears, peeled and cut in half may be served with a spreading of cream cheese. Canned pears are best for this salad and may be combined with banana sticks and topping of finely chopped nuts.

Melon Balls are ideal to mix with other fresh fruits, chilled and topped with yogurt or sour cream and slivered almonds.

Orange slices or grapefruit cut in pieces may be mixed with fresh or canned pineapple chunks and topped with grated coconut.

Sliced apples should be dipped in lemon juice to prevent discoloration. They are very good combined with chopped dates, sunflower seeds or chopped nuts and topped with yogurt. Diced fresh apricots may be served in the same way.

Vegetable Combinations—

Tomato Slices may be alternated on individual salad plates with thin slices of sharp Cheddar cheese, topped with a little mayonnaise or served with small scoops of cottage cheese and topped with minced parsley.

Stuffed Tomatoes should be carefully cut at stem ends and enough of the center removed to make a hollow. Fill with any fresh, crisp raw vegetable, finely chopped and topped with mayonnaise. Chopped apples may be combined with chopped cabbage, or grated apple, cabbage and carrot may be used. Radishes, finely chopped, can be combined with grated carrot, chopped celery and cabbage. French dressing may be substituted for mayonnaise.

Whole Tomatoes, prepared as above, may also be stuffed with chicken, diced and mixed with chopped celery, or flaked crab mixed with chopped celery. Top with mayonnaise. Stuffed tomatoes are a separate course in themselves. They add color and zip to a vegetable plate, but should be served on individual salad plates, separated from the hot vegetables.

Green Beans may be slivered and served raw if very young and tender. Otherwise, cook beans until just tender and cut in slivers. Marinate in French dressing and serve with sliced tomatoes.

Beets may be grated and served with rings of sweet onion and French dressing. Pickled beets may be used if desired.

Asparagus Tips may be served raw if very young and tender. Otherwise cook until just tender and serve only the tips, marinated in French dressing and garnished with grated hard-cooked egg. Very good with chilled, sliced tomatoes.

Green Peas are also delicious served raw if very young and tender. Otherwise, cook until just tender. Mix with finely chopped celery and onion and cubes of Swiss or Cheddar cheese. Top with French dressing.

■   **CLASSIC CAESAR SALAD**

Advance preparations: Chop 3 garlic cloves into 1 c. olive oil and let stand several hours at room temperature. Toast 2 c. tiny cubes of whole-wheat bread crumbs in stove oven until brown and crisp.

½ c. seasoned oil (above)	1 tsp. salt
½ c. grated Parmesan cheese	½ tsp. pepper
¼ c. crumbled Bleu cheese	2 eggs
1 tbsp. Worcestershire sauce	½ c. lemon juice
½ tsp. dry mustard	

This is enough for a large salad, containing about 3 qts. of crisp greens. Pour above ingredients over greens in order given, breaking eggs over greens just before adding lemon juice. Dip toasted crumbs in remaining seasoned oil, toss with salad and serve at once while crumbs are crunchy. Serves 8.

■   **STUFFED TOMATO SALAD**

Dip firm tomatoes in boiling water or hold over fire to loosen skins, peel and chill. Cut out cone-shaped center. Scrape out remaining pulp and turn upside-down to drain. Place on lettuce leaf and fill with any meat or vegetable mixture to which salad dressing has been added. Place cone-shaped core on top as a hat, with pompom of cream cheese or salad dressing.

■   **TOMATO-AVOCADO SALAD**

2 stalks celery, diced	4 tomatoes
1 green pepper, finely chopped	Juice of 1 lemon
1 onion, finely chopped	2 tbsp. honey
1 avocado, peeled and mashed	

Mix diced celery, pepper and onion; add mashed avocado. Scoop out tomato pulp, cut fine and add to mixture. Add lemon juice or ½ yogurt and ½ mayonnaise for dressing. Fill tomatoes and serve with yogurt or mayonnaise.

■   **STUFFED TOMATO AND SHRIMP**

Quarter a medium-size peeled tomato, not quite cutting through at the bottom. Fill with chunks of boiled shrimp or lobster, or both. Place on crisp lettuce and cover with chilled Creole dressing.

■ TOMATO-CHEESE MOLDED SALAD

Soak 1½ tbsp. gelatin in ½ c. cold water. Dissolve in 1 can undiluted tomato soup, heated. Soften 1 3-oz. pkg. cream cheese with a little soup. Add cheese, ½ c. chopped celery, ½ c. chopped cucumber, 1 small grated onion, ½ c. chopped parsley and ½ c. salad dressing. Stir well and chill. Serves 6.

■ EASY TOMATO ASPIC

1 pkg. unflavored gelatin	¼ tsp. salt
1¾ c. tomato juice	Dash of Tabasco
1 tbsp. lemon juice	

Sprinkle gelatin into ½ c. of the tomato juice to soften. Cook in double boiler until gelatin is dissolved. Stir in remaining tomato juice, lemon juice, salt and Tabasco. Pour into 4 individual molds or 1 medium sized mold; chill until firm. Invert to unmold and garnish with water cress.

Variation—Double above recipe and pour into ring mold. Chill until firm. Invert on platter to unmold and fill center with sea food salad.

■ TOMATO ASPIC

2 c. tomato juice	¼ c. cold water
½ bay leaf	1 tbsp. onion juice
½ tsp. salt	1 tbsp. vinegar
1 stalk celery or leaves	1 c. sliced celery
1 envelope unflavored gelatin	

Boil together for 10 minutes, tomato juice, bay leaf, stalk or leaves of celery and salt. Sprinkle gelatin on top of cold water and add to mixture. Stir until gelatin is dissolved. Add onion juice and vinegar. Strain and cool. When it begins to set, add sliced celery. Allow to set firmly. Avocado slices may be added, sliced stuffed olives or black olives. Serves 4.

■ CRANBERRY-ORANGE SALAD

Soften 1 tbsp. unflavored gelatin in ¼ c. cold pineapple juice. Heat 1¼ c. pineapple juice and dissolve gelatin in juice. Add 1 c. raw, ground cranberries, 1 orange ground (skin and all), ¼ c. honey and ½ c. nuts. Pour in oiled mold. Excellent as a garnish.

■   **TOMATO ASPIC IN GREEN PEPPER SHELLS**

Make Tomato Aspic, omitting celery. Select 6 large, perfect green peppers. Cut small circle around tops and remove seeds, taking care not to break sides. Rinse out with cold water and turn upside down to drain. Then fill with unjelled tomato aspic; set upright in shallow pan, so aspic will not spill; cover with foil or other wrap and refrigerate until aspic is set. To serve, cut thick slices of aspic-filled peppers and serve on crisp lettuce leaves, garnished with sliced black olives. May be topped with a little salad dressing, if desired, such as mayonnaise blended with cottage cheese or cream cheese whipped with mayonnaise. Serves 6.

■   **STUFFED EGGS IN TOMATO ASPIC**

Slice 6 hard-cooked eggs lengthwise. Remove yolks and mash with 1 tsp. horseradish, 1 tbsp. mayonnaise, ½ tsp. onion juice, ½ tsp. salt, ½ tsp. pepper. Stuff sliced whites with this mixture. Press halves together to resemble whole hard-cooked egg. Make tomato aspic, omitting celery. Pour in 6 molds, filling about halfway. Place egg in each mold and fill with aspic. Chill, unmold and serve with slices of cucumber or avocado. Serves 6.

■   **MAIN-DISH ASPIC**

Prepare Easy Tomato Aspic according to directions. Chill until mixture is the consistency of unbeaten egg white. Fold in 1 c. cut-up cooked shrimp, ½ c. diced celery and ¼ c. diced green pepper. Turn into a 3-c. mold; chill until firm. Unmold and garnish as desired. Serves 4-6.

■   **WALDORF SALAD**

1 c. diced apple	Mayonnaise
1 c. diced celery	Cherries (optional) or pitted
½ c. broken walnut meats	dates, halved
Lettuce leaves	

Fold together apple, celery and nuts with just enough mayonnaise to coat lightly. Serve on lettuce leaf with 1 cherry or ½ date on top for center of interest. Serves 4.

■   **PINEAPPLE AND COTTAGE CHEESE SALAD**

1 9-oz. can crushed pineapple	3 pkg. unflavored gelatin
2 c. pineapple juice	soaked in ½ c. cold water
1 pt. Farmer-style cottage cheese	

Heat juice and dissolve soaked gelatin. Add crushed pineapple and cottage cheese. Mix well. Pour in oiled mold. Serve with fruit salad dressing or plain. Serves 8.

Variations—Cottage cheese may be added to any fruit jello, or cream cheese may be rolled into balls and placed in the salad. Cream cheese may also be rolled in chopped pecans or almonds. Arrange chopped pecans between fruits and use black cherries, grapes or raspberries as garnish.

The dressing may be yogurt or sweet whipped cream tinted pale green, flavored with honey and mint, or 2 c. cottage cheese mixed with ¼ c. salad dressing and flavored with chopped fresh mint leaves.

■ **POTATO SALAD**

3 potatoes, steamed or boiled until tender, peeled and cubed	1 c. chopped celery
	2 tsp. celery seed
	¾ tsp. salt
1 small bunch green onions, chopped	¼ c. chopped parsley
	2 hard-cooked eggs, sliced

Save 1 sliced egg for garnish. Gently mix other ingredients with mayonnaise or the following dressing:

½ c. sour cream or yogurt	1 tsp. lemon juice or cider vinegar, if desired
1 tsp. raw sugar or honey	

Mix sour cream or yogurt with sweetening. Lemon juice or vinegar makes a tarter dressing. Mix with potato salad and garnish with egg slices. Serves 4-6.

■ **COLE SLAW**

4 c. finely shredded cabbage	¼ c. honey
1 c. finely shredded carrots	1 c. sour cream or yogurt
¼ c. finely chopped green pepper, if desired	¼ tsp. salt
	2 tsp. celery salt
¼ c. lemon juice or cider vinegar	

If sour cream is used it should be beaten to creamy thickness. Yogurt should be used as is, not beaten. Mix all ingredients together and chill before serving. Serves 8-10.

Variations—Add any of the following: chopped chives, minced parsley, finely diced pineapple or apple.

■ **CABBAGE-PEANUT SALAD**

½ medium head shredded   1 c. chopped peanuts
   green cabbage   ½ c. chopped stuffed olives
4 c. chopped tart apples

Stir together gently and mix with sour cream or mayonnaise. Dressing may be thinned with lemon juice, if desired, and nut butter may also be added. Serves 8.

■ **RED AND GREEN COLE SLAW**

Shred 1 small head green cabbage and 1 small head red cabbage. Add 1 medium onion, chopped; 6 green onions or scallions, chopped; 1 tsp. minced parsley. Mix lightly with cabbage. Blend ⅓ c. salad oil with 3 tbsp. vinegar and 1 tbsp. celery seed. Top each serving with 1 tbsp. sour cream and a dash of paprika. Serves 8-10.

■ **CAULIFLOWER SALAD**

½ head uncooked cauliflower, with outer leaves removed; cut in paper-thin slices. Mix together ½ c. finely chopped green pepper, ½ c. finely chopped celery, 1 tsp. salt. Toss with cauliflower slices. Break ½ large head lettuce or 1 small head, into small pieces and toss with cauliflower mixture. Top each serving with minced parsley. Serves 6.

■ **GARDEN VEGETABLE BOWL**

An iced bowl of garden-fresh vegetables is perfect with almost any meal, passed along with the main course or served just beforehand, accompanied by a bowl of dressing for dunking, and crisp whole-wheat crackers. Fill a big glass or china bowl with finely chopped ice and stick in all sorts of vegetables, such as celery sticks, carrot or turnip strips, cauliflower buds, green onions, rings of green pepper, cucumber and tomato wedges.

■ **DRESSING FOR VEGETABLE DUNK**

1 c. cottage cheese   ¼ tsp. pepper
¼ c. crumbled Bleu cheese   ¼ c. yogurt, mayonnaise or
¼ c. grated onion   sour cream
½ tsp. salt

Mix all ingredients together gently, chill and pass in separate small bowl, along with Garden Vegetable Bowl.

■ WILTED DANDELION SALAD

This is an old favorite from the Pennsylvania Dutch country. Choose only young, tender dandelion leaves, 3-4 c.; wash thoroughly, drain and place in towel or cellophane bag in refrigerator to crisp. Dice 3 slices bacon and fry crisp. Remove bacon bits and add to drippings ½ c. hot water, ⅓ c. apple cider vinegar, ½ tsp. salt, ¼ tsp. pepper. Heat to boiling point, add bacon bits and pour over crisp greens. Serve at once. Serves 4.

Variations—Use half dandelion greens and half chopped lettuce; add ½ green pepper cut in thin strips and 3 green onions, diced. Serve cold with French dressing.

Dandelion greens may also be served cold and crisp with wedges of tomato, sliced hard-cooked egg and slivers of Swiss cheese, topped with French dressing.

■ STUFFED AVOCADO SALAD

Peel 2-3 medium avocados. Pour 3-4 tsp. lemon juice over all surfaces. Mix 2 3-oz pkgs. cream cheese with ⅓ c. finely-chopped celery, 1 tsp. minced parsley and 1 tsp. minced onion. Add top milk to make the cheese of whipped cream-like consistency. Season with a vegetable salt. Fill avocado halves, put back together, wrap in oiled paper, chill and slice. Place 2 crossway slices on each salad plate, serve with orange or grapefruit sections. Serves 4-6.

■ RAW SPINACH SALAD

1 c. raw spinach	2 small onions
4 ripe tomatoes	

Cut up all vegetables. Mix together and serve on green lettuce leaves. For dressing, use lemon juice or minced ripe avocado and lemon juice. Serves 2.

■ LETTUCE WITH HOT DRESSING

4-6 slices bacon	¼ tsp. freshly-ground pepper
¼ tsp. paprika	3-4 tbsp. vinegar
¼ tsp. salt	¼ c. boiling water
¼ tsp. dry mustard	1 tbsp. honey

Fry bacon and break into small pieces. Add seasonings, vinegar, honey and water. Pour over large bowl of cleaned, broken lettuce. Serve at once.

■ **RAW VEGETABLE SALAD COMBINATIONS**

1. Carrot, celery, raisins or nuts and lettuce. French dressing.
2. Spinach, grated carrots, grated apple. Yogurt dressing.
3. Red cabbage, celery and a few green onions. French dressing.
4. Cucumbers, onions, tomatoes. French dressing.
5. Cauliflower flowerettes, ripe olives, shredded carrots. Mayonnaise.
6. Green peppers, cabbage, carrots. French dressing.
7. Bean sprouts, celery, cabbage and onions. Yogurt dressing.
8. Sliced cauliflower, grated carrots, shredded lettuce, sliced radishes, nuts. French dressing.

■ **BEAN SPROUTS IN SALAD**

1 c. chopped celery	1 tbsp. Sesame seeds
1 c. grated carrots	1 c. fresh bean sprouts
½ c. cashew or pignolia nuts, chopped	

Mix and serve with French dressing. Serves 6.

■ **SPROUTED WHEAT SALAD**

1 c. sprouted wheat	2 avocados, peeled and sliced
½ c. green onions, chopped	1 pkg. cream cheese
1 c. chopped celery	¼ c. minced parsley

Combine wheat, onions and celery. Arrange on salad plate with avocado slices. Roll cream cheese in small balls, then roll in parsley. Arrange on plates and garnish with crisp lettuce leaves. Serves 4.

■ **CUCUMBERS IN SOUR CREAM**

2-3 cucumbers, thinly sliced	½ tsp. powdered dill
3 tbsp. chives or young green onion, chopped	Salt and pepper to taste
1 c. sour cream mixed with 3 tbsp. vinegar or lemon juice	

Mix cucumbers with chives or onions; stir in dill and dressing; chill. Serves 4-6.

■ **ARTICHOKE HEART SALAD**

Place freshly-cooked or canned artichoke hearts on plate of greens. Add wedges of tomatoes and black olives. Serve with French dressing.

■ FINGER SALADS

Finger salads should be colorful combinations of raw vegetables. They may be arranged on a large platter as hors d'oeuvres or on individual salad plates, served as a first course or as an accompaniment salad. Try combining chilled strips of carrot and celery with crisp radish roses, or thin strips of cucumber with green pepper rings and tender flowerettes of young cauliflower marinated in French dressing. Thin slices of peeled young turnip are good as well, as are little cherry tomatoes and canned sliced artichoke hearts. You may go on from here, dreaming up your own delectable finger salads according to season and the contents of your refrigerator.

■ FRUIT SALAD

Combine cantaloupe balls, berries, seedless grapes, sliced oranges. Cherries may be used instead of berries. Spoon carefully on salad greens and cover with shredded nuts and coconut. Serve with sour cream or yogurt dressing. This salad may also be used as a dessert.

■ MELON-CHEESE SUMMER SALAD

Fill centers of cantaloupe rings with cottage cheese. Top with chilled, honeyed raspberries. Serve with French dressing, sour cream or yogurt. This salad is utterly delicious if filled with chopped fresh fruit, seedless grapes and berries, and served with sweet or sour cream or honey-sweetened yogurt. A few chopped nuts or coconut over top add nutrients and interest. Serve on salad greens.

■ DATE-CARROT SALAD

½ c. chopped firm dates	¼ c. (or more) of mayonnaise
1 c. finely-shredded raw carrots	½ c. chopped nuts
½ c. finely-chopped celery	¼ tsp. salt and dash of paprika

Combine all ingredients. Chill and serve on lettuce. Serves 6.

■ BANANA-APRICOT NECTAR SALAD MOLD

2 c. apricot nectar	2 pkgs. unflavored gelatin
2 c. pineapple juice	soaked in ⅓ c. cold water

Heat 1 c. juice and dissolve soaked gelatin in the hot juice. Add rest of juice and cool. Add 2 sliced bananas. Pour in oiled mold. Serve with fruit-salad dressing. Serves 6.

■ **TOMATOES FARCIE**

Carefully spear each tomato with fork and hold over flame until skin cracks. Then peel and score out centers, handling gently so that sides do not break. Unpeeled tomatoes may be cut in eighths, using sharp knife and not cutting clear through, so that sections may be spread in petals and filling placed in center. The following will fill 6 medium tomatoes:

Sprout Filling: 2 c. chopped sprouts, 1 small, chopped green pepper, 2 medium stalks chopped celery, 1 tsp. salt, ½ tsp. pepper, ¾ c. mayonnaise. Mix lightly, stuff tomatoes and sprinkle with paprika or minced parsley, if desired.

Egg Filling: 4 chopped, hard-cooked eggs, 1 c. chopped celery, 3 tbsp. minced onion, ¼ c. sliced, stuffed green olives; 1 tsp. salt, ½ tsp. paprika. Mix together lightly with ½ c. mayonnaise.

Tuna Filling: 1 c. flaked tuna fish, drained well (7-oz. can); 2 chopped, hard-cooked eggs, ½ c. chopped celery, ¼ c. finely chopped parsley, ¼ tsp. salt. Mix lightly with ½ c. mayonnaise. Stuff tomatoes and sprinkle with paprika, if desired.

Variation—For color-interest, stuffed tomatoes may be topped with a slice of black olive, hard-cooked egg or small rosette of cream cheese sprinkled with minced parsley or paprika.

■ **GOURMET BUFFET BOWL**

3 c. cooked, chopped turkey	½ c. olive oil
2 avocados, peeled and sliced	1 tsp. kelp, powdered
1 c. raw mushrooms, sliced	1 tbsp. frozen orange or pine-
1 c. chopped celery	apple juice
½ c. chopped water cress	½ c. chopped walnut meats
1 c. whole water cress	1 lemon, sliced very thin
Juice of one lemon	

Toss together turkey, avocado, mushrooms, celery and chopped water cress. Blend lemon juice, oil, kelp, orange or pineapple juice. Add to salad mixture the walnut meats and lemon slices and toss lightly with dressing. Place in big salad bowl and garnish with whole water cress. Serve chilled. Serves 6-8.

■ FRUIT LUNCHEON PLATE

¼ c. pecans
1 3-oz. pkg. cream cheese
2 large oranges
1 large grapefruit
1 bunch grapes
4 peach halves
4 pear halves
4 slices pineapple

4 whole apricots, or 2 pears peeled, cored and quartered
2 large bananas
Salad greens
Berries (in season)
Mayonnaise or salad dressing
Salad greens

Chill fruits well. Chop nuts fine. Mash cream cheese and add a little cream or milk to soften. Form into 8 small balls and roll in chopped nuts. Peel orange and grapefruit; section the fruits. Cut bananas in slices. Arrange fruits and cheese on salad greens. Serve with mayonnaise which has been mixed with a little strawberry or concentrated orange juice for color. Serves 4-6.

■ CHICKEN SALAD ALMONDINE

1 3½-lb. cooked chicken or 2 5½-oz. cans chicken
⅓ c. blanched almonds, toasted to golden brown in oil and slivered
4 medium stalks celery, thinly sliced

1 c. seedless green grapes, cut in half
⅓ c. chopped fresh coconut or canned coconut
1 tsp. salt
¾ c. mayonnaise

If cooked chicken is used, remove meat from bones and cube. Mix with other ingredients and serve with small, crisp lettuce leaves or on a bed of crisp water cress.

■ VEGETABLE PLATE À LA FRANCAISE

1 c. sliced cooked carrots
1 c. cooked peas
1 c. cooked asparagus or cauliflower
1 c. French dressing
2 medium tomatoes, cut in wedges

2 hard-cooked eggs, cut in eighths
1 head lettuce
1 c. slivered cooked ham, chicken tongue or bologna

Marinate carrots, peas and asparagus or cauliflower in French dressing about 30 minutes. Chill. Serve on lettuce and garnish with tomato and egg wedges. Arrange meat slices on top. Serves 4-6.

■ **TUNA-TOMATO ROSE SALAD**

6 medium tomatoes	2 hard-cooked eggs, sliced
1 7-oz. can tuna chunks	¼ c. chopped ripe olives
¾ c. chopped celery or finely-grated cabbage	1 tbsp. chopped parsley
¼-⅓ c. salad dressing or mayonnaise	1 tbsp. lemon juice

Peel tomato by holding over high heat on a fork, rotating tomato until skin splits. Peel and cut out stem; chill. Drain tuna, separate into flakes, and add lemon juice, parsley, celery and olives. When ready to serve, add salad dressing. Cut tomato into 8 wedges, but do not cut all the way down. Spread tomato wedges apart and fill with tuna mixture. Top with 1 tsp. salad dressing, sour cream or yogurt. Stick slice of hard-cooked egg into each section. Place slices of stuffed olive on top. Serves 6.

Variations—Chicken, veal, 1½ c. veined, cut-up shrimp or crab meat may be used instead of tuna.

Soften cream cheese with a little top milk. Form 2 rows of petals on each tomato by pressing level teaspoons of softened cheese against side of tomato, drawing spoon down in curving motion. Sprinkle center of each tomato with hard-cooked egg yolk pressed through strainer. Serve on crisp water cress.

■ **RAW VEGETABLE LUNCHEON SALAD**

Grate 3 small beets, 2-3 small carrots, small head of cabbage and 1-2 sweet turnips. Fringe (peel and draw fork down sides) and slice 1 cucumber. Cut 8-10 sticks of celery and 8-10 radish roses. Place bib lettuce cups on 6 dinner plates. Put small serving of grated vegetables on each plate and a whole tomato (cut from center to represent a rose) in middle of plate. Alternate grated vegetables with celery, radishes, cucumbers. Pour small amount of French dressing on grated vegetables. Fill center of tomato with finely chopped black olives and yogurt or mayonnaise.

■ **BUFFET GREEN SALAD À LA SCHUYLER**

1 head crisp lettuce	2 cucumbers, sliced thin
1 large bunch water cress	3 tomatoes, cut in wedges
1 head curly escarole	2 tbsp. lemon peel
2 Belgian endive	

Toss together all greens with sliced cucumbers. Toss with dressing made as for Gourmet Buffet Bowl, stirring lemon peel into dressing. Use tomato wedges for garnish. Serve chilled. Serves 8-10.

■ **SENATE SALAD LUNCHEON**

1½ c. cracked crab meat	Lettuce or Romaine
¼ c. chopped green onions	2 medium avocados, peeled
1 c. diced celery	and halved
2 medium tomatoes, peeled, cubed	Sliced ripe olives
Sections from ½ grapefruit or 1 medium orange	

Mix crab meat, onions, celery, tomatoes and grapefruit sections in a bowl. Break up lettuce and place on 4 large salad plates. Place an avocado half on center of each plate. Fill with crab meat mixture. Garnish with sliced ripe olives. Serve with French dressing.

■ **SALAD À LA REINE**

1 c. tuna fish or crab flakes, or diced chicken	½ c. cooked peas
	½ tsp. salt
2 hard-cooked eggs	¼ c. minced parsley
½ c. finely chopped celery	½ tsp. paprika

Mix together lightly, chicken, tuna or crab with 1 hard-cooked egg, finely chopped, celery, peas and salt. Slice remaining egg for topping. Serve on crisp salad greens, topping with sliced eggs, parsley and paprika. Serves 2.

■ **CHICKEN OR TURKEY SALAD**

½ c. mayonnaise	2 tbsp. heavy cream
1 tbsp. fresh lemon juice	Ripe olives
¼ tsp. salt	Tomato slices
⅛ tsp. pepper	3 c. chicken or turkey, chopped
⅛ tsp. dried marjoram	in large pieces

Combine mayonnaise with lemon juice, salt, pepper, marjoram and cream. Dip chicken or turkey pieces in this dressing, or mix dressing with chopped chicken or turkey. Arrange on dinner plate with olives and tomatoes. Serves 4.

■ GELATIN SALADS

Gelatin is an easily digested animal protein. It is not quite as valuable, nutritionally, as meat, milk or eggs since it is incomplete in amino acid.

Both flavored and unflavored gelatins contain instructions on the package. In general, gelatin powders should be soaked in cold water, then dissolved in hot water or other liquid.

For molded salads, chill the gelatin until slightly thickened before adding fruits, vegetables or other solid ingredients. Also, pour a little of the thickened gelatin into the mold and chill before adding the rest.

You may use almost any liquid you wish with gelatin, except fresh pineapple juice, which tends to "digest" the gelatin protein.

1 tbsp. unflavored gelatin will bind up to 2 c. food solids. The solids, such as fruits, meats, nuts, vegetables, may be crushed, diced or even left whole if they are not too large.

In making layer salads in mold, such as a layer of lemon gelatin, then a layer of cottage cheese, then a layer of tomato aspic, be sure the bottom layer is firm before you add the next one.

To unmold gelatin salad, loosen edges with warm knife, then dip mold quickly in warm water. Invert mold on serving dish. If the mold is a large one, you should also dampen the surface of the gelatin and the center of the serving plate before inverting.

Vegetable gelatins may be used in the same proportion as those of animal source, but must be boiled in 1 c. liquid, 1-3 minutes, before other liquids and ingredients are added. Vegetable gelatin is made from seaweed and has practically no food value. It is used in low-calorie diets, since 6 c. contains only about 2 calories. It is also used as a jelling agent when animal gelatin is not desired. It jells very rapidly.

■ BASIC RECIPE

Dissolve ½ c. vegetable gelatin in 1½ c. cold water for 5 minutes. Boil gently until dissolved, about 1-3 minutes. Remove from fire and add 2 c. fruit or vegetable juice, or chicken broth. Sweeten fruit with honey to taste. Pour into mold.

If fruits, vegetables or meats are to be added, wait 10 minutes until jell begins to set before combining mixtures. Serves 6-8.

■ SOUFFLÉ SALAD

1 pkg. lemon gelatin or 1 pkg.	¼ tsp. salt
plain gelatin	½ to 1 tsp. chopped onion
½ c. cold water	1 c. diced cooked ham, fish or
1 c. hot water	chicken
2 tbsp. lemon juice or vinegar	1 c. diced celery
½ c. mayonnaise	1 c. cooked peas

Put gelatin in a bowl, add cold water until gelatin softens. Dissolve in hot water. Add lemon juice, mayonnaise and salt. Blend with rotary beater until foamy. Turn into freezing tray. Chill until sides begin to harden. Scrape into a large bowl, beat until fluffy. Fold in onion, meat or fish and ½ c. chopped celery. Pour into 1-qt. ring mold and chill until firm. Combine peas and remaining celery. Unmold on large serving plate. Fill center with peas and celery. Serves 4-6.

■ LAMB AND MINT LOAF SALAD

1 pkg. unflavored gelatin	2 tbsp. vinegar or lemon juice
1 c. boiling water	1½ tbsp. chopped fresh mint
½ c. cold water	¼ tsp. salt
1-⅓ c. cold lamb, cut fine	

Soak gelatin in ½ c. cold water. Dissolve in 1 c. boiling water and add mint, vinegar and salt. Chill until it begins to thicken. Add lamb. Mold and chill until firm. Leftover cooked veal or chicken may be used instead of lamb. Serves 4.

■ CHICKEN MOUSSE

1 pkg. unflavored gelatin	1 tsp. minced onion
1 tsp. salt	½ c. chopped celery
⅓ c. cold water	¼ c. chopped green pepper
¾ c. mayonnaise	1 tbsp. chopped sweet pickle or
½ c. cooked, minced chicken	green olives, if desired

Soften gelatin in water. Dissolve in double boiler, remove from heat and blend in mayonnaise, minced chicken and other ingredients. Pour into pint mold and chill until firm. Unmold and garnish with water cress, if desired. Serves 4.

Variation—Substitute for chicken ½ c. minced cooked ham or tongue.

■ **ORANGE CREAM VEGETABLE GELATIN**

1 tbsp. vegetable gelatin	2 tbsp. honey
¼ c. cold water	½ c. top milk or cream
½ c. boiling water	2 small bananas, sliced
½ c. orange juice	

Soften 1 tbsp. vegetable gelatin in ¼ c. cold water, 5 minutes. Add ½ c. boiling water and gently boil 1 minute until dissolved. Cool, add juice and honey. Stir in cream and bananas. Pour in mold.

■ **SEA FOOD SALAD RING**

2 pkgs. unflavored gelatin	Salt and pepper to taste
½ c. cold water	2 cans or 2 c. crab meat
½ c. boiling water	2 cans or 2 c. lobster meat
1½ c. mayonnaise	2 tbsp. lemon juice
¾ c. seasoned tomato sauce	Crisp water cress
4 hard-cooked eggs, chopped	Sliced black olives or slices of
1 green pepper, chopped	avocado

Soften gelatin in cold water; dissolve in boiling water. Stir in mayonnaise, which has been mixed with tomato sauce, eggs and green pepper. Salt and pepper to taste. Chill until mixture thickens, then spoon into lightly-oiled ring mold. Chill and set. Drain crab and lobster, cut in small pieces, and mix with lemon juice; chill. Turn salad ring onto bed of water cress. Pile sea food mixture in center. Garnish with sliced black olives or avocado slices. Serves 6.

■ **MOLDED SHRIMP SALAD**

2 pkgs. unflavored gelatin	½ tbsp. salt
¾ c. cold water	½ c. salad dressing
1½ c. tomato juice	1 c. cooked brown rice
2 tbsp. lemon juice	4 tbsp. chopped parsley
1 tsp. honey, if desired	1 c. chopped celery
2 tbsp. horseradish	½ c. chopped cucumber
1 small onion, grated	1 lb. cooked shrimp

Soften gelatin in cold water; dissolve over boiling water. Combine gelatin, tomato juice, lemon juice, honey, horseradish, grated onion, salt and salad dressing. Blend well with rotary beater and pour into ice cube tray. Chill until firm about 1 inch from edge, turn into bowl and whip until fluffy. Fold in rice, parsley, celery, cucumber and chopped shrimp. Pour into 1-qt. mold. Chill until firm, unmold and garnish with parsley. Serves 6-8.

■ **SHRIMP SALAD**

2 c. cleaned cooked shrimp
1 c. French dressing
½ c. mayonnaise
2 hard-cooked eggs, chopped

½ c. chopped celery
½ c. pignolia nuts or cashew
  nuts
3 tbsp. chopped ripe olives

Cut shrimp in small pieces and marinate with French dressing. Drain and add rest of ingredients. Serve on lettuce. Serves 4-6.

■ **MOLDED SALMON SALAD**

1 pkg. unflavored gelatin
½ c. cold water
1 c. boiling water
½ tsp. salt
¼ tsp. paprika
1 tbsp. lemon juice

¾ c. mayonnaise
2 c. salmon, flaked
½ c. chopped celery
1 small green pepper, minced
1 tsp. chopped parsley

Soak gelatin in cold water, dissolve in boiling water. Add salt, paprika, lemon juice, and chill until it begins to thicken. Beat in mayonnaise. Fold in remaining ingredients; mold in tube pan. Chill until firm and turn out on large plate. Place sprigs of water cress around sides. Serves 6.

■ **ORANGE JUICE SALAD**

2 pkgs. unflavored gelatin
2¾ c. cold water
1 6-oz. can frozen concentrated
  tangerine or orange juice
2 tbsp. honey
⅛ tsp. salt

2 tbsp. lemon juice
½ c. grated raw carrot
½ c. finely-chopped celery
1 c. cottage cheese
1 9-oz. can drained crushed
  pineapple

Soften gelatin in 1 c. cold water in top of double boiler; dissolve over hot water. Remove from heat. Stir in tangerine or orange juice, 2¾ c. water, honey, salt and lemon juice.

Chill one-half until syrupy; keep other half at room temperature. Fold carrot and celery into syrupy gelatin, pour into 6-c. mold; chill until almost set.

In order for second layer to stick, first layer must be slightly sticky. Chill second half of gelatin until syrupy, fold in cottage cheese and pineapple. Spoon on top of almost firm gelatin; chill until firm. Turn out on platter and serve with mayonnaise or yogurt. Serves 6-8.

■ **MOLDED TOMATO-CHICKEN SALAD**

2 pkgs. unflavored gelatin	Dash of Tabasco
1 10½-oz. can condensed bouil-	2 5-oz. cans chicken, diced
lon	1 c. chopped celery
1 17½-oz. can tomato juice	½ c. chopped cucumber
½ tsp. salt	¼ c. chopped stuffed green
2 tbsp. lemon juice	olives

Sprinkle gelatin on 1 c. of bouillon to soften. Heat in double boiler, stirring until gelatin is thoroughly dissolved. Add remaining bouillon, tomato juice, salt, lemon juice and Tabasco. Chill until consistency of unbeaten egg white. Fold in diced chicken, cucumber and olives. Turn into 6 c. mold and chill until firm. Unmold on crisp salad greens. Serves 6-8.

DESSERT SALADS

■ **FRUIT SALAD**

2 c. white cherries, halved and	2 eggs
pitted	1 tbsp. honey
2 c. diced pineapple	¼ c. light cream
2 c. orange sections	Juice of 1 lemon
2 c. quartered marshmallows	1 c. heavy cream, whipped
or cubed bananas	
¼ lb. blanched, slivered al-	
monds	

Combine well-drained fruits; add marshmallows or bananas and nuts. Beat eggs until light; gradually add honey, light cream and lemon juice. Mix and cook in double boiler until smooth and thick, stirring constantly; cool. Fold in whipped cream. Pour over fruit mixture and mix lightly. Chill 24 hours. Serves 8-10.

■ **FRUIT GELATIN SALADS**

Unflavored gelatin may be used with all fruit combinations. For a fresh fruit dessert of shimmering splendor, watermelon and cantaloupe balls may be combined with grape halves and peach slices and chilled in a lime or lemon juice base. Other fruit combinations may be orange and grapefruit sections with blueberries and strawberries; or raspberries, peaches and bananas. All the fresh, natural flavors of these fruits are enjoyed in the molded dessert, as unflavored gelatin blends without flavor competition.

Lime or lemon juice and water are the liquids used in the basic recipe with unflavored gelatin. However, orange or canned pineapple juice may be substituted. If creating your own recipe, the formula for using unflavored gelatin in this: 1 pkg. plain gelatin will jell up to 2 c. liquid and up to 2 c. diced, drained fruits. If sugar is used to sweeten the juice and fruits, count it as part of the liquid. Sugar goes into solution and thus must be counted as part of the liquid for a perfect jell; honey also must be counted.

The dessert should be chilled until firm—about 4 hours. To unmold, dip mold in warm water to depth of the gelatin; loosen around edge with tip of a paring knife. Place serving dish on top of mold and turn upside down. Shake, holding serving dish tightly to the mold. Lift off mold.

■ **MOLDED SUMMER FRUIT**

2 pkgs. unflavored gelatin
2¾ c. cold water
⅔ c. raw sugar or ⅓ c. honey
⅛ tsp. salt
½ c. lime or lemon juice

4 c. mixed fresh fruit—peach slices, halved white grapes, watermelon pieces and cantaloupe balls

Sprinkle gelatin on 1 c. cold water to soften. Place over boiling water and stir until gelatin is thoroughly dissolved. Add sugar and salt; stir until sugar is dissolved. Add to remaining water and lime or lemon juice. Arrange a small amount of the fruit in bottom of mold to form a design. Spoon on just enough of the gelatin mixture to cover bottom of mold; chill until almost firm. Chill remaining gelatin mixture until consistency of unbeaten egg white; fold in remaining fruit. Spoon on top of almost-firm layer; chill until firm. Unmold on platter. Serves 8-10.

■ **MELON, CHERRY SALAD**

1 cantaloupe and 1 watermelon, chilled
2 c. fresh cherries, pitted
1 head lettuce

½ c. Cottage cheese, yogurt or sour cream, mixed with mayonnaise

Cut balls from watermelon, using French ball cutter. Pare cantaloupe and cut crosswise into thin slices; cut slice into halves. Tear lettuce into pieces and place in salad bowl. Dribble a little dressing over lettuce. Arrange cantaloupe slices, melon balls, cherries on lettuce. Top with dressing and a cherry. Red raspberries or strawberries may be used. Serves 8.

■ FROZEN FRUIT SALADS

A frozen fruit salad may be served as dessert or as the main course of a summertime luncheon. You may use any combination of fresh or canned fruits and your favorite nuts, coarsely chopped. Here is the basic procedure:

1 tbsp. unflavored gelatin	⅔ c. heavy cream, whipped
¼ c. lemon juice	¼ c. honey
1 3-oz. pkg. cream cheese	2 c. mixed fruits; drain if
¼ c. mayonnaise	canned fruits are used
½ tsp. salt	½ c. chopped nuts

Soften gelatin in lemon juice; dissolve in double boiler. Remove from heat and stir in cheese which has been blended with salt and mayonnaise. Fold honey into whipped cream and stir in fruits and nuts. Combine with gelatin mixture and place in ice cube tray, which has been lined with waxed paper. Freeze until firm. Turn out on platter; remove paper. Serve plain or with water cress. Serves 4-6.

■ FROZEN CHEESE SALAD

½ c. evaporated milk, chilled several hours in refrigerator	½ c. chopped dates
2 tbsp. lemon juice	½ c. crushed, drained pineapple
3-oz. pkg. cream cheese	
¼ c. mayonnaise or salad dressing	

Whip chilled milk, add lemon juice, and beat until very stiff. Mash cream cheese and add mayonnaise; blend until smooth. Fold into whipped milk; add fruit and mix lightly. Turn into cold freezing pan and place in refrigerator until firm. Serve without salad dressing, but with chopped or ground nuts. Serves 4.

■ FROZEN FRUIT-NUT SALAD

½ c. evaporated milk, chilled several hours in refrigerator	1 medium sliced banana
1 tbsp. lemon juice	¼ c. crushed, drained pineapple
½ c. salad dressing or mayonnaise	½ c. seedless or seeded grapes
3 tbsp. chopped pecans	¼ c. softened dried apricots, cut up
1 small orange, cut in small pieces	

Whip chilled milk; add lemon juice and continue beating until mixture is very stiff. Fold in salad dressing, nuts and fruits. Turn into cold mold and place in freezing section of refrigerator, 2-5 hours. Serve on crisp lettuce leaves and sprinkle macaroon coconut over top. Serves 4-6.

■ **AUTUMN FRESH FRUIT SALAD**

1 head lettuce	Chopped nuts
½ fresh pineapple, pared and sliced, or 1 small can	¼ lb. Tokay grapes, seeded
1 grapefruit, peeled and sectioned, or 1 can	1 persimmon, peeled, sectioned
	1 orange, peeled, sectioned
½ red apple, sliced	1 c. whipped cream
2 bananas cut in chunks	¼ c. mayonnaise
Honey or lemon juice	Date crystals

Line salad bowl with lettuce. Divide bowl into 4 sections with half-slices of pineapple. Arrange alternate sections of grapefruit and apple slices in 1 division. Dip bananas in honey or lemon juice and roll in nuts; fill 1 division. Use other fruits for remaining divisions. Fill center with 1 c. whipped cream to which ¼ c. mayonnaise is added. Sprinkle date crystals over cream. Serves 4-6.

■ **PINEAPPLE BASKETS**

1 large ripe pineapple	1 c. heavy cream, whipped
2 c. mixed fresh fruits, such as orange sections, raspberries, strawberries, blueberries	

Cut pineapple in half, lengthwise. Remove eyes and carefully cut out meat with grapefruit knife, or shred with fork. Do not break pineapple shells. Cut shells in half again, to form 4 baskets. Mix pineapple with other fruits and pile in baskets. Top with whipped cream. Serves 4.

Variations—Garnish filled baskets with prunes stuffed with cream cheese, or sliced ripe figs, or cooked halves of dried apricot.

■ **PINEAPPLE BASKET TROPICALE**

Prepare pineapple as above. Combine cubed or shredded pineapple with 2 c. mixed orange and grapefruit sections and ½ c. cubed papaya or avocado. Mix whipped cream with 1 c. mayonnaise and top baskets with chopped almonds, pecans or cashews.

SALAD DRESSINGS

Your own salad dressing can be a pride and joy. Men who fancy themselves as creators of salad bowls are usually the tossed-salad type and will have a splendid time mixing their own dressings. Don't interfere. But do try your own wings when it comes to experimenting with the many delicious seed oils on the market, such as sesame, soy, safflower, sunflower seed, peanut, as well as the classic corn and olive oils.

There are delightful vinegars to add an exciting tang to salad dressings. In addition to the traditional cider vinegar and red wine vinegars, there are rosé, tarragon, white wine and herb vinegars.

Salt, pepper, mustard, onion, garlic and paprika are basic seasonings. But think of the glorious varieties of herbs you have to choose from, as well as the array of fancies, such as diced pimiento, dehydrated soup mixes, onion flakes, dried celery, parsley or a touch of soy sauce, tomato catsup or chili sauce.

Then there are the exotic flavor-texture additions to be achieved with nut butters, whipped skim milk, yogurt, mashed avocado, powdered coconut, whipped sweet cream or sour cream. Try combining cream cheese with tomato paste.

Well, the choice is yours. Keep your pepper mill at hand. Have fun and if one of your inspirations doesn't work, toss it out and try again!

■ **BASIC FRENCH DRESSING**

Measure out 1½ c. of your favorite salad oil, soy, peanut, olive or whatever. Season with 1 tsp. salt, ½ tsp. fresh ground black pepper, ½ clove minced garlic. Fold in 1 tsp. honey; add ½ c. wine or cider vinegar, dash of Tabasco, ½ tsp. paprika, 1 tsp. dry mustard. Pour into jar with lid, cover tightly and shake well. Keep in refrigerator. Remove 10 minutes before using and shake again before serving.

Variations—Substitute ¼ c. lemon juice for vinegar. Add 2 tbsp. chili sauce or chopped anchovies. Add 1 tsp. catsup or Worcestershire sauce. Add 1 tsp. of your favorite fresh, chopped herbs.

■ **SALAD DRESSING HINTS**

1. To marinate: Allow fruits, vegetables or meats to absorb a piquant French dressing, before draining and replacing with another dressing.

2. To combine or blend a salad mixture for body and smoothness: Salad ingredients must be well drained before the boiled dressing or mayonnaise is added.
3. As a center of interest or as a topping, add this dressing last for "looks" and taste: 1 tsp. whipped cream, sour cream, yogurt, boiled dressing or mayonnaise.

■ FRUIT SALAD DRESSING

Soften 1 3-oz. pkg. cream cheese with a little top milk. Whip 1 c. cream or canned milk and fold in creamed cheese mixture. A little honey or crushed nuts may be added for different flavor.

■ MOLASSES FRENCH DRESSING

¼ c. soybean oil	¼ c. blackstrap molasses
¼ c. vinegar	A few drops Worcestershire
1 tbsp. grated onion	sauce
1 tsp. salt	

Shake well in glass jar to blend.

■ SOUR CREAM HOLLANDAISE

2 3-oz. pkgs. cream cheese, blended with ¼ c. thick sour cream. Add 2 egg yolks, beaten; dash of salt and mace. Cook over *very low* fire or in double boiler for about 10 minutes. Lemon juice may be substituted for sour cream.

■ COOKED SALAD DRESSING

2 eggs, well beaten	1 tsp. flour
2 tbsp. vinegar or juice of 1 lemon	1 tsp. mustard
	½ tsp. raw sugar
2 tbsp. salad oil or melted butter	

Mix eggs with vinegar or lemon juice and oil or butter. Add dry ingredients last and cook in double boiler until stiff, stirring constantly. Thin with cream.

■ COTTAGE CHEESE DRESSING

1 8-oz. carton cottage cheese	1 tbsp. honey, if desired
Grated rind of 1 lemon	½ tsp. nutmeg or ginger

Blend cheese with other ingredients. Good on green salad.

■ **BASIC MAYONNAISE DRESSING**

1 egg yolk	½ tsp. dry mustard
1 tsp. honey	2 tbsp. vinegar
½ tsp. salt	1 c. salad oil
⅛ tsp. paprika	

Combine egg yolk, seasonings and 1 tbsp. vinegar in a deep bowl. Beat until blended. Continue beating and add salad oil 1 tbsp. at a time, beating thoroughly after each addition until ½ c. is used. Then add remaining vinegar and continue adding remaining oil, beating in a little at a time.

■ **APRICOT CREAM DRESSING**

1 3-oz. pkg. cream cheese	1 tbsp. lemon juice
½ c. apricot nectar	⅛ tsp. salt
¼ c. mayonnaise or salad dressing	

Soften cream cheese and blend in apricot nectar; beat until smooth. Add lemon juice, mayonnaise, salt and mix well. Wonderful with fresh fruit salad.

■ **WHIPPED COTTAGE CHEESE DRESSING**

Put 1 pt. cream-style cottage cheese in a blender and let whip 5-10 minutes, or until very smooth. Serve on fruit or on any salad where you do not want a high-calorie dressing.

■ **CREOLE SALAD DRESSING**

½ tsp. onion, finely minced	½ c. cider vinegar or lemon juice
¼ tsp. freshly-ground pepper	
1 tsp. dried vegetable broth	1½ c. salad oil
½ tsp. raw sugar or honey	⅓ c. tomato catsup
½ tsp. salt	Dash of Tabasco

Mix all ingredients in a jar and shake well.

■ **FRUIT FRENCH DRESSING**

4 tbsp. grape juice	½ tsp. seasoning to taste
2½ tbsp. salad oil	⅛ tsp. paprika
1 tbsp. lemon juice	1 tbsp. honey

Put all ingredients in a covered jar and shake well. Serve ice-cold with fruit salad.

■ ITALIAN SALAD DRESSING

Crush 1 clove garlic in ⅓ c. olive or other salad oil. Mix well with salad greens. Add ¼ c. wine vinegar, salt, coarse black pepper to taste. Mix again. Add fresh sweet basil if available. For flavor-lift, add oregano.

■ VINAIGRETTE DRESSING

¾ c. salad oil	1 tsp. minced onion
1 tsp. pepper	1 tbsp. minced celery
1 tsp. salt	Grated white of 1 hard-cooked
3 tbsp. raw sugar	egg
2 tbsp. lemon juice	1 tbsp. chopped dill pickle
½ c. white vinegar	1 tbsp. minced parsley
2 tbsp. capers	1 tbsp. chopped chives
1½ tbsp. cottage cheese	1 tsp. chopped basil

Pour salad oil in bowl and mix in pepper, salt, sugar, lemon juice, vinegar and capers. Stir together and gradually add remaining ingredients. Chopped thyme, chervil or tarragon may be substituted for basil. Delicious with coarse fresh greens or cold, filleted white fish.

■ MARDI GRAS DRESSING

¼ c. honey	½ tsp. salt
⅔ c. evaporated milk	¼ tsp. dry mustard
¼ c. lemon juice	1 tsp. paprika
2 tbsp. chopped chives	

Beat together honey, milk and lemon juice; add chives and seasonings and beat thoroughly. Refrigerate until slightly thickened. This is wonderful for slaw or raw vegetable plates.

Variation—Use blender and add to above ingredients ¼ c. diced raw carrots, ¼ c. diced green pepper, 1 tbsp. chopped chives.

■ YOGURT LOW-CALORIE DRESSING

1 8-oz. container yogurt	1 tsp. Worcestershire sauce
¼ c. catsup or chili sauce	Salt to taste
⅛ tsp. pepper and celery salt	Dash of Tabasco (if desired)
1 tsp. grated onion	

Blend yogurt with other ingredients. Good with tossed green salad.

■ **BUTTERMILK-HONEY DRESSING**

2 tbsp. melted butter	**2 tbsp. lemon juice**
2 tbsp. honey	**¼ c. powdered milk**
½ c. buttermilk	**Season to taste**

Melt butter, add honey and buttermilk. Alternate drops of lemon juice and powdered milk, beating constantly. Good on cole slaw.

■ **EGGLESS MAYONNAISE**

Mix ¾ tsp. salt, ¼ tsp. paprika, ¾ tsp. dry mustard, a few grains celery salt and cayene, dash of garlic powder. Beat in ½ c. seed oil and ¼ c. nut butter. Add ¼ c. lemon juice last.

■ **HONEY FRENCH DRESSING**

½ c. honey	**½ tsp. salt**
1 c. soy or other oil	**⅓ c. chili sauce**
½ c. cider vinegar or lemon juice	**1 medium grated onion**
	1 tbsp. Worcestershire sauce

Place all ingredients in a quart jar and shake well. Serve this dressing on lettuce with fresh or frozen fruit salad.

■ **LEMON FRENCH DRESSING**

½ c. lemon juice	**½ tsp. salt**
½ c. salad oil	**Pepper to taste**
1 tbsp. honey	**¼ tsp. paprika**

Combine all ingredients in a small jar with screw top; shake well until blended.

■ **ONE-EGG COOKED SALAD DRESSING**

1½ tbsp. flour	**1 egg**
1 tsp. salt	**¾ c. milk**
3 tbsp. sugar or 2 tbsp. honey	**4 tbsp. vinegar**
1 tsp. dry mustard	**1 tbsp. butter**

Blend flour, salt, honey and mustard in top of double boiler. Add egg and stir until smooth. Add milk, mixing well; add vinegar slowly, stirring constantly until thick. Remove from fire and add butter.

■ **GARLIC DRESSING**

1⅓ c. sesame oil, soy or other salad oil
¼ c. lemon juice or cider vinegar

1½ tsp. salt or substitute
1 tbsp. honey
1 tbsp. dry mustard
4 sliced garlic cloves

Cover and shake well. Let stand overnight. Strain out garlic. Keep refrigerated and shake before serving.

■ **AVOCADO DRESSING**

1 large ripe avocado
3 tbsp. lemon juice
½ c. light cream

1 tsp. prepared mustard
2 oz. sieved Bleu cheese

Sieve peeled avocado and immediately add lemon juice. Stir in remaining ingredients. Blend well. Chill and serve.

■ **BACON DRESSING**

4 slices bacon, diced fine
½ small onion, chopped

¼ c. vinegar or lemon juice
1 tsp. salt

Fry bacon until crisp. Remove bacon, cook onion in bacon fat until tender. Add remaining ingredients. Heat and pour over lettuce or spinach.

■ **SHARP FRENCH DRESSING**

¼ c. (1 oz.) crumbled Bleu or Rocquefort cheese
½ tsp. dry mustard
½ tsp. paprika

Seasoning to taste
Dash of Cayenne pepper
½ c. salad oil
3 tbsp. lemon juice

Combine and shake in covered jar.

■ **WESTERN SALAD DRESSING**

1 c. sour cream
2 tbsp. finely-minced green onions
½ tsp. salt and pepper to taste
½ c. Rocquefort or Bleu cheese, mashed

2 tbsp. mayonnaise or salad dressing
2 tbsp. lemon juice

Blend all and season to taste. Serve on lettuce or other greens.

■   **THOUSAND ISLAND DRESSING**

1 c. sesame oil   1 onion, chopped
1 c. tomato purée   1 tsp. paprika
⅓ c. lemon juice   1½ tsp. powdered vegetable
Garlic powder to taste   broth
¼ c. honey

Combine and shake well in covered jar.

CHAPTER **14**

Sandwiches and
Sandwich Spreads

A FAMOUS restaurant in Denmark has a menu featuring several hundred different kinds of sandwiches; tall ones, short ones, rolled, folded, cut in triangles and circles, with a dazzling variety of fillings. Using this chapter as a sort of blueprint, you can go ahead and be your own sandwich chef.

You may serve a three-decker sandwich as the main dish at luncheon, or the many attractive open sandwiches. The traditional one, named for the Earl of Sandwich, has two slices. When served at tea or cocktail time, the slices should be thin and the crusts removed. Crusts also should be removed from fancy sandwiches served at parties.

But the great thing is the taste of the homemade bread, buns and rolls you use. Try such innovations as waffle-sandwiches or sandwiches made from muffins, biscuits or even pancakes. Your sandwiches will never have a humdrum sameness if you use a variety of breads, such as whole-grain wheat, millet, oat, soy or a mixture of these grains; rye, pumpernickel, fruit bread such as raisin, date, orange, banana, apple sauce; nut breads and steamed brown breads, cold corn breads and breads made of unbleached white flour.

■ **TIPS ON SANDWICH MAKING**

1. Butter should be creamed thoroughly, so that it spreads smoothly.
2. For a sweet-tooth sandwich, cream equal amounts of butter and honey.
3. Add to creamed butter any of the following: curry powder, horseradish, chopped parsley or chives.
4. Most sandwiches need crisp greens, such as lettuce or Romaine. Greens may be chopped, sliced or shredded.
5. Cookie cutters may be used to cut fancy sandwiches into different shapes.

■   **TIPS ON SANDWICH MAKING—CONT'D**

6. One definition of a sandwich is "two slices of meat with a slice of cheese
   for a filler." So try, occasionally, stacking thin slices of meat and cheese,
   pressing down firmly and cutting in wedges or strips.
7. Sandwiches prepared ahead of time may be frozen, provided they are not
   filled with hard-cooked eggs or raw vegetables. Greens should be added
   after sandwiches are thawed. Sandwiches for freezing should be lightly
   buttered and have very little mayonnaise or salad dressing. It is a good idea
   to wrap together a pair of like sandwiches and print the name of the filling
   on each package.

■   **SANDWICH FILLINGS**

Ground Liver: Mix 1 c. ground cooked liver with 1 tsp. finely
chopped onion, 2 tsp. chopped pickle, 1 tbsp. pickle juice, 4 tbsp.
mayonnaise, salt and pepper.

Carrot-Nut: 1 medium carrot, ground with ⅓ c. walnuts or ½ c.
peanuts and mixed with ½ pkg. cream cheese softened with 2 tbsp.
top milk or with 1 tbsp. salad dressing.

Water Cress: 1 large bunch water cress washed, stems removed
and leaves chopped. Spread bread with butter or cream cheese and
press water cress between bread layers.

Cheddar Cheese: Mash or grate ½ lb. Cheddar cheese, add ½
cube butter, ½ tbsp. Worcestershire sauce, ¼ tsp. mustard and a
little paprika. Serve on thin-cut sandwiches.

Sardine and Celery: Remove skins and bones from 1 can sardines,
add 3 hard-cooked eggs, chopped, mix with mayonnaise. Spread
on buttered bread and sprinkle with thinly sliced celery.

Olive-Nut: Mix in blender or chop fine ½ c. stuffed olives, ¼ c.
almonds or cashews, 2 tbsp. mayonnaise, 1 tsp. lemon juice.

Tuna Fish, Pickle: Mix in blender or in bowl, ½ c. mayonnaise,
½ tsp. minced onion, ¼ tsp. prepared mustard, 1 tbsp. chopped
pickle, dash of garlic powder. Add 1 can drained, flaked tuna. Mix
chopped celery and green pepper with tuna.

Cheese, Egg: Mix in blender or bowl 1 c. shredded cheese, 1 hard-
cooked egg, chopped, ¼ c. salad dressing, ¼ c. chili sauce and
¼ tsp. Worcestershire sauce.

Cheese, Nuts, Dates: Blend softened cream cheese with chopped
dates and nuts. Blend cottage cheese with chives, spread on peanut butter. Add chopped dates, nuts, bacon bits or sunflower seeds
to cottage cheese.

Carrots grated, mixed with finely grated cabbage, raisins, salad dressing. Grated carrots with chopped hard-cooked eggs and salad dressing.

Tomato and Crisp Bacon Bits, with cream cheese or salad dressing.

Liverwurst and chopped hard-cooked eggs mixed with salad dressing.

Bologna, ground and mixed with pickle relish or finely chopped sweet pickles.

Peanut Butter or other nut butters, spread with mayonnaise.

Lettuce, Bacon and Tomato with salad dressing.

Cucumber or sliced radishes, lettuce, cream cheese, spread with salad dressing.

Meat: Left-over roast, meat loaf, cold cuts, canned meats, dried meats, as dried beef, dried smoked fish. Mix any of the above meats, chopped with any of the following: salad dressing or mayonnaise, chili sauce, pickle relish, prepared mustard, canned mushroom sauce, chopped green olives.

Cheddar Cheese, grated and added to French dressing, in which any of the following vegetables are marinated: sliced tomatoes, diced ham or chicken, diced green peppers, sliced radishes, flaked salmon or tuna, chopped hard-cooked eggs, left-over meat as beef or veal, chopped stuffed olives, chopped walnuts and celery.

Cheddar Cheese-Vegetable Spread: 1 c. grated Cheddar or Tillamook cheese, 1 can pimientos, ½ c. chopped green onions and celery. Moisten with pimiento juice and sour cream.

Date Spread: Any of following moistened with salad dressing: date crystals and orange marmalade; date crystals with coconut, figs and nuts; with finely cut celery and nuts; with peanut butter; with cheese.

Low-Calorie Spreads: (a) Spread 2 slices lean meat with a little cottage cheese and place 1 thin slice soy, millet or rye bread in the middle. (b) Spread 2 slices chicken or ham with cottage cheese and place slice raw apple in middle.

Ham and Olives: 1 c. ground cooked ham, ½ c. sliced stuffed olives, 1 tbsp. Worcestershire sauce, 1 tbsp. prepared mustard, 2 tbsp. salad dressing. Mix and spread on rye or whole-wheat bread. For change, mix ham with red pepper relish and mayonnaise.

Egg Salad: 6 chopped hard-cooked eggs, ¼ c. chopped ripe olives, salt, pepper, 1 tsp. prepared mustard, ⅓ c. mayonnaise or salad dressing.

■   **SANDWICH FILLINGS—CONT'D**

Fish: tuna, chopped pickles or hard-cooked eggs, mayonnaise. Or smoked salmon and slice of Swiss cheese with salad dressing. Or sardines blended with cottage cheese or left whole with pickle relish.

Orange and Peanut Butter: Peel skin from orange. Put orange in blender or through food chopper. Mix with ½ c. chunky peanut butter and ¼ c. salad dressing. Dried currants or raisins may be added.

Peanut Butter (non-homogenized) can be mixed with any of the following:

1. **Cream cheese, pickles, chopped.**
2. **Crumbled bits of bacon and chili sauce.**
3. **Raisins and chopped walnuts.**
4. **Finely chopped celery and stuffed olives, chopped.**
5. **Chipped beef and chili sauce.**

Southern Egg Butter Spread: ½ c. sorghum or molasses and ⅓ c. honey. Heat to near boiling point; beat 2 eggs; add hot syrup to eggs slowly; return to fire; cook over low heat to consistency of marmalade; cool slightly; then add ½ c. peanut butter and ½ c. dry skim milk; stir well to make a thick spread.

■   **OPEN-FACE SANDWICHES**

Whole-Wheat Bread: Butter, place any of the following on bread in this order: 1. lettuce or water cress; 2. slices of chicken, roast beef or cold boiled ham; 3. slices of Swiss cheese, Cheddar or Jack cheese; 4. slice of tomato and hard-cooked egg; 5. top with strip of crisp bacon.

Rye Bread: Butter, place any of the following on bread in this order: 1. lettuce or Romaine; 2. slice of salami, ham, cold tongue, tuna fish or pastrami; 3. slice of Cheddar, Jack or Swiss cheese; 4. slice of tomato, pickles or hard-cooked egg; 5. top with finely chopped parsley, chopped black or green olives.

Fish: Tuna, lobster, crab, halibut, minced and mixed with chopped celery and mayonnaise or chopped ripe olives.

Anchovy: blend 2 tbsp. Parmesan cheese, add 1 anchovy and a little dill.

Ham and Dill Pickles: Slice dill pickles, mix with minced ham and salad dressing.

Scrambled Eggs may be placed on half of toasted bun, sprinkled with cheese, then melted under broiler.

Fruit Sandwiches without bread: (a) Slice a banana lengthwise, spread one side with crunchy peanut butter and cover with other side of banana. To make ahead of time, dip banana sandwich in lemon or pineapple juice, wrap and chill. (b) Apple: Wash, core and, if fruit has been sprayed with insecticide, pare and slice in ¼-inch horizontal slices. Dip in fruit juice if not to be eaten right away. Slice Cheddar cheese in ⅛-inch slices and place between apple slices.

Apple: Peel and grate apple, then mix with crumbled Rocquefort or Bleu cheese and butter to get a smooth paste. Good on French bread.

Sprouts: Pumpernickel bread, cream cheese, water cress and sprouts. Millet bread, cucumber, and alfalfa seed sprouts.

■   HOT SANDWICHES

Cheese and Beans: Melt 2 tbsp. butter in frying pan. Add 1 can baked beans or 1 c. left-over home-baked beans. Add ¼ c. tomato sauce and cook about 5 minutes. Grate ½ c. Cheddar cheese and stir into beans until cheese melts. Pour over slices of whole-wheat toast. Serves 6.

Toasted Cheese: Spread bread with softened butter and place thin slices of Cheddar cheese on bread; top with remaining bread. Toast on electric grill or griddle on range. A large frying pan may be used by adding enough oil to keep from sticking. Cook until brown. Slices of tomato may be placed on cheese before topping with bread.

Toasted Vegetable Sandwich: Combine ½ c. grated carrots, ½ c. finely chopped celery, ½ c. grated cabbage, ¼ c. minced parsley, 1 tbsp. minced onion with 1 tbsp. chili sauce and 2 tbsp. mayonnaise, salt to taste. Spread on buttered bread slices. Toast until golden brown on both sides.

French Toasted Sandwich: Between slices of whole-wheat bread, place a slice of chicken, beef or ham. Add slice of cheese, and 1 tbsp. chili sauce if desired. Dip each sandwich in batter made of 2 eggs beaten with ¾ c. milk. Fry in melted butter or oil until brown on both sides, but cook slowly so filling is heated through. Other fillings are: deviled ham, chopped ripe olives, flaked salmon, crab or tuna, mixed with mayonnaise; peanut butter and crisp bacon bits; chopped walnuts and cream cheese mixed with mayonnaise.

■   **HOT SANDWICHES—CONT'D**

Grilled Ham: Combine 1 c. finely chopped cooked ham, 2 tbsp. finely chopped sweet pickle, 2 tsp. sweet-pickle juice, ½ tsp. prepared mustard, 2 tbsp. salad dressing. Spread on bread slices and cover with remaining slices. Mix 1 beaten egg with ¼ c. milk and ¼ tsp. salt in a pie plate. Place oil or fat on griddle, being sure the fat covers the grids or griddle. Dip both sides of sandwich in egg mixture, being careful that the bread is just moistened. Toast until brown, 3-5 minutes on each side. Beef, tongue, lamb or tuna may be used instead of the ham.

Grilled Hamburgers: 1 lb. ground beef, mixed with ½ tsp. salt, ¼ tsp. pepper, 1 tbsp. dried onion soup, ¼ tsp. chili powder. Divide into 8 even portions and form into patties ½-inch thick. Melt 1 tsp. fat on each grid or griddle. Cook until brown, turn, cook 5-7 minutes. Toast buns; spread with butter or mayonnaise. Place hamburger on bun and garnish with onion rings, slices of tomato, lettuce, relish, peanut butter, sliced cheese or bacon slices.

Bacon Cheeseburgers: 1½ c. grated Cheddar cheese, 2 tbsp. minced onion, 4 slices crisp bacon, crumbled; ¼ c. tomato catsup, 1 tbsp. prepared mustard, 6 whole-wheat hamburger buns. Combine cheese, onion, bacon, catsup and mustard. Cut buns in half and place on cookie sheet, cut sides up. Spread cheese mixture over six of the halves and lightly butter the remaining halves. Place all under broiler until golden brown. Top cheese buns with toasted halves and serve.

Supper Sandwiches: Dilute 1 can mushroom or tomato soup with ½ can evaporated milk. Stir in 1 can cooked shrimp and 1 c. peas; ½ tsp. salt and ½ tsp. pepper to season. Heat over low flame and pour over 4 slices hot, buttered whole-wheat toast. Top with grated Swiss cheese and minced parsley.

Surprise Sandwiches: ½ lb. frankfurters, chopped; 6 small sweet pickles, chopped; ¼ lb. Cheddar cheese, diced; 1 onion, chopped; 1¼ tsp. dry mustard, 1 tbsp. mayonnaise, 1 tbsp. horseradish, 1 tbsp. softened butter. Combine all ingredients except butter; put through food grinder. Cut tops from 12 frankfurter buns and from bottom halves, scoop out centers to form hollows. Butter insides of buns and fill with frankfurter mixture. Replace tops. These may be wrapped and stored in freezer compartment. To serve, place on cookie sheet and bake about 30 minutes in 375° oven. If used before freezing, bake only 20 minutes.

■ PARTY SANDWICHES

Brick: Remove crusts from day-old uncut loaf of whole-wheat bread. Slice horizontally into 3-4 long slices about ¾-inch thick. Spread each slice with creamed butter, then with a good sandwich spread, such as chopped deviled egg, avocado mixed with lemon juice and mayonnaise, cream cheese with chopped chives or your favorite meat spread. Stack slices, wrap firmly and chill several hours. Cut in thin slices and serve.

Rolled Sandwiches: Trim crusts from a loaf of fresh bread. Spread a thin layer of butter on end of loaf, cut off 1 slice as thin as possible. Spread with any of above fillings. Roll up as for jelly roll, fasten with toothpick if necessary. Repeat until loaf is sliced. Place rolls on clean napkin or paper pulled tightly around sandwiches. Chill. Remove toothpicks before serving.

Checkerboard Sandwiches: Trim crusts from same size whole-wheat and unbleached loaves of bread and slice. Put 4 slices together, alternating white and whole-wheat, having spread with thin butter and filling. Cut each stack in 4 slices. Put these 4 slices together with creamed cheese as a binder. Arrange so a white strip of bread is over a whole-wheat one. Wrap tightly in paper and chill. Cut across in ½-inch slices to serve.

Pinwheel Sandwiches: Trim crusts from a loaf of bread and cut lengthwise in thin slices. Spread with colorful filling, as hard-cooked egg mixed with salad dressing. Roll as for jelly roll, lengthwise. Wrap tightly in linen napkin or paper. Cut crosswise in ½-inch slices. Fillings for these sandwiches might be any of the following: Cream cheese mixed with a little salad dressing and colored with egg yolk or beet juice or green coloring. Cream cheese mixed with minced ham or chopped pimientos. Cream cheese mixed with chopped pickles or olives. Peanut butter. Mashed avocado. Minced dried beef or fish.

Stuffed Rolls: Make or buy whole-wheat buns or French rolls. Cut slices off 1 end. Pull out soft crumb center (toast for crumbs). Mix the following: 2 3-oz. pkgs. cream cheese with ground ham, liver or salami. Add dash of Worcestershire sauce and Tabasco and ¼ c. mayonnaise. Salt to taste. Pack into rolls, wrap tightly in paper, chill several hours. Cut crosswise in ¼-inch slices. If ground liver, heart or tongue is used, add 1 tbsp. finely minced onion and 1 tbsp. finely minced parsley. Pimiento cheese may be used instead of cream cheese, or cottage cheese mashed through a sieve first.

■ **PARTY SANDWICHES—CONT'D**

Ribbon Sandwich Loaf: Remove crusts from 1 loaf unbleached white bread, unsliced, and 1 loaf unsliced whole-wheat bread. Cut each loaf lengthwise into ½-inch slices. Start with whole-wheat slice and spread with butter and egg filling (hard-cook 3 eggs, mash yolks and chop whites fine, add vinegar, salad dressing to taste, salt, pepper). Place white slice next. Spread with softened cream cheese (add a little top milk until consistency to spread). Over the cheese put layer of deviled ham. Next add whole-wheat slice. Spread with softened butter and mixture of peanut butter and bacon bits (fry bacon crisp). Add white slice of bread, the underside of which you have spread with cream cheese and finely chopped water cress. Avocado may be used instead of peanut butter. Wrap in paper and chill overnight. Foil may cover the paper. When ready to use, frost top and sides with cream cheese moistened with top milk. Garnish with slices of ripe olives and pimiento strips.

Variations—Cottage cheese and dried vegetable broth; finely chopped green peppers, celery, carrots or cucumbers with cottage cheese; chopped chives and cottage cheese.

■ **TACOS**

2 medium potatoes, grated	1 bunch green onions, chopped
1 lb. hamburger	1 can Las Palmas or other
1 tsp. salt	Spanish sauce
1 tsp. chili powder	½ head lettuce, shredded
½ tsp. cumin powder	2 fresh tomatoes, sliced
2 cloves garlic, chopped	½ lb. sharp cheese, grated
1 doz. tortillas	Oil for browning

Brown hamburger in small amount of oil. Use coarse grater for potatoes, adding them to browned hamburger along with salt, chili powder, cumin, garlic and onions. When potatoes are tender, keep mixture warm, but do not cook further. In another frying pan, lightly oiled, place tortillas in pan, fold and brown on both sides, removing to brown paper to drain. Fill each tortilla with hamburger mixture, top with sauce, add shredded lettuce, tomato slice and 1 tbsp. grated cheese. Serves 6.

Hot, steamed tortillas, unbrowned, may also be filled with this spicy mixture.

■ **MEAT-CHEESEBURGERS**

1 medium chopped onion	Salt, pepper, tumeric powder
1 tsp. oil	to taste
1 lb. ground beef	8 whole-wheat hamburger
½ c. chopped black olives	buns
¼ c. tomato catsup	Grated Cheddar cheese

Cook onions in oil in fry pan until limp. Add meat and sauté until brown. Add olives, catsup and seasonings. Hollow out centers of whole-wheat buns and butter. Fill with meat mixture. Cover with grated cheese. Place in broiler about 6 inches from flame and cook until cheese melts and buns begin to brown. Serve 2 halves to each person. Serves 8.

For lunch box, place halves together and wrap tightly.

■ **CORNISH PASTIES**

Crust for Pasties

2 c. unbleached white flour	¼ tsp. celery seed
½ tsp. salt	Ice water
⅓ c. oil	

With dinner fork, lightly stir in seasonings and oil. Add ice water a few drops at a time until soft dough is formed. Pat dough into ball and roll out to ⅛-inch thickness on floured board. Cut into squares, about 4 x 4 inches. On half of each square, spread pasty filling.

Filling for Pasties

1 c. diced raw potatoes	½ tsp. pepper
¼ c. minced parsley	½ lb. chopped round or chunk
¾ c. onions, minced	steak
½ tsp. salt	

Lightly mix potato, onion, parsley, meat and seasonings. Spoon mixture onto half of each square and fold over other half, dampening edges and pressing tightly together so filling will not ooze through. Prick tops of each pasty with fork to allow steam to escape. Bake 10 minutes in 400° oven, then reduce heat to 325° and bake 30 minutes. Serve hot, with tomato sauce on side if desired. Pasties are very good served cold in lunch boxes or at picnics.

■ **NUTBURGERS**

3 slices whole-grain bread	¾ c. milk
2 c. walnuts	¼ c. chopped fresh parsley
1 egg	1 tsp. salt or substitute
1 tbsp. chopped onion	Soy oil

Crumb bread. Chop nuts fairly fine in blender, add remaining ingredients and blend. Combine with bread crumbs, mix well and shape into patties. Brown in soy oil or butter about 5 minutes on each side. Serve with hot tomato or mushroom soup, undiluted.

■ **SANDWICH SPREADS**

Sandwich spreads should be soft enough to spread easily, and bread slices should be covered right to the edges so that bread will not pick up moisture from the filling. Good old-fashioned bread and butter, especially when the bread is home made and the butter a good fresh country brand, makes wonderful eating. And there is practically no limit to the number of intriguing spreads you can concoct. Here are a few ideas:

1. ½ c. butter blended with ⅓ c. salad oil. This stretches the butter as well as giving you increased poly-saturated fats.
2. Blend ½ c. butter with 1 tsp. minced parsley, 1 tbsp. grated lemon rind. Spread on bread and use chopped olives as filling.
3. Blend ½ c. butter with ½ tsp. ground sweet basil and 1 tsp. lemon juice. Good as a spread for tomato and cucumber sandwiches.
4. For roast beef sandwiches, use spread of ¼ c. butter blended with ⅛ tsp. salt and 1 tbsp. prepared horseradish.
5. For ham, tongue or liverwurst sandwiches, use spread of ¼ c. butter blended with 1 tbsp. prepared mustard.
6. Blend non-homogenized peanut butter with shredded carrots or finely chopped celery.
7. Chicken sandwiches are good with a spread made of 2 tbsp. butter blended with 1 3-oz. pkg. cream cheese, ½ tsp. onion juice and ½ tsp. celery salt. Also good with shredded cabbage sandwiches.
8. Mashed avocado blended with lemon juice and minced onion makes a delectable spread for meat or sea food sandwiches, with sliced radishes as a garnish.
9. A piquant spread is made with ¼ c. chili sauce blended with 1 3-oz. pkg. cream cheese, ½ tsp. salt, ⅛ tsp. cumin powder, ½ tsp. onion juice. Bread spread with this mixture is good with baked beans or raw vegetables.

■ HONEY-SWEETENED RED RASPBERRY OR BOYSENBERRY JAM

Honey-sweetened jams require the use of commercial fruit pectin. Follow all directions, step by step. Use exactly the same amount of honey as other sweeteners for correct jam consistency. Jam prepared with honey is wonderful for people on low sodium diets.

6 level c. prepared fresh or frozen unsweetened raspberries	1 pkg. or 3½-ozs. commercial pectin 8½ c. honey

Crush or coarsely grind fruit. Place in large 6-8 qt. kettle. Add pectin, stir well. Grease measuring cup before measuring honey and it will slide out of cup easily. Place fruit and pectin mixture over high heat; bring to boil, stirring constantly. Gradually pour honey into fruit; return to full rolling boil, stirring. When mixture is boiling all over, allow it to cook exactly 4 minutes. Remove from heat, skim and stir 5 minutes. Pour into 14 medium-sized jelly glasses. Allow ½-inch of head room for paraffin coating.

■ HONEY AND ORANGE MARMALADE

6 medium-sized oranges (2 lbs. sliced) 6 c. water 9½ c. honey	½ c. lemon juice 1 pkg. or 3½-ozs. commercial pectin

Slice oranges very thin, discard the end sections. Add water and lemon juice to fruit, simmer in large kettle until very tender, about 1 hour. Measure the cooked ingredients. Add additional water to make total cooked peel and juice exactly 7 level c. Add pectin and bring to boil. Add honey gradually, stirring until mixture returns to full rolling boil. Boil exactly 4 minutes. Remove from heat, skim and stir for 5 minutes. Pour into prepared glasses. Seal with fresh paraffin coating. Yield: approximately 16 glasses.

■ APRICOT JAM, UNCOOKED

Soak 1 c. dried apricots in enough water to cover, for 3 hours, until water is absorbed and apricots soft but firm. Put through medium blade of meat grinder. Mix this apricot purée with ½ c. creamed honey (do not use liquid honey). Makes ¾ c.

■ **PINEAPPLE-APRICOT JAM**

½ c. unsweetened crushed   1 tsp. lemon juice
   pineapple   ⅛ tsp. salt
2 tsp. creamed honey   ⅓ c. uncooked apricot jam

Drain crushed pineapple and place in blender with honey, lemon juice and salt. Combine with apricot jam.

Variations—Other dried fruits, such as peaches, pears, prunes may be used instead of apricots. Make only a small amount of uncooked jam at a time and keep in refrigerator to use when you feel the need of a sweet spread. Excellent on plain cake, pancakes or waffles.

CHAPTER 15

Sauces

WHITE OR CREAM SAUCES

A roux is the best method for making white or cream sauces. The roux is a blend of butter, or other fat, with flour, to which the liquid is added and stirred over very low heat or in top of double boiler. Such sauces should be cooked slowly for 5 minutes to achieve the best flavor.

If cornstarch is used as a thickener, a longer cooking time is needed; 10-15 minutes over low heat, then allowed to stand 30 minutes over hot water in double boiler.

Brown sauce is made with basic white sauce recipes, except that the fat is allowed to reach golden-brown before flour is added.

Seasonings should be added just before serving.

■ BASIC WHITE OR CREAM SAUCES

1 *Thin White Sauce*

1 tbsp. flour	1 c. milk
1 tbsp. butter	

Blend flour and butter together over low heat; add milk slowly and stir, cooking about 5 minutes or until sauce is smooth and creamy, or cook in top of double boiler. Season to taste.

If carelessness produces a lumpy sauce, it may be strained. However, a strained sauce is never quite as good.

2 *Medium White Sauce*

2 tbsp. flour	1½ c. milk
2 tbsp. butter	

Use same cooking method as for No. 1

■   **BASIC WHITE SAUCES—CONT'D**

3   *Thick White Sauce*

3 tbsp. flour   **1½ c. milk**
3 tbsp. butter

Use same cooking method as for No. 1, but be careful to stir constantly so that it does not become lumpy.

Thin white sauces are best for cream soups.

Medium white sauces are suitable for creamed vegetables and for many casseroles where such sauces are used as a base.

Thick white sauces are a good base for croquettes and are often used for macaroni-cheese dishes, as well as for meat and fish.

Variations

Any of the white sauces may be used as the basis for an endless variety of additions. The following are gauged for 1 c. sauce.

1. 4 tbsp. chopped capers.
2. ¼ c. cooked celery, chopped.
3. ¼ c. grated cheese and ¼ tsp. mustard. Blend with white sauce over hot water in double boiler.
4. Substitute same amount of meat drippings for butter in Thin White Sauce recipe. Season with salt and pepper for a traditional Cream Gravy.
5. 1 hard-cooked egg, chopped. 1 tbsp. chopped parsley as garnish.
6. For Golden Sauce, add 1 lightly beaten egg to Thin White Sauce recipe and continue cooking until smooth and creamy.
7. ½ c. cooked lobster or crab, flaked; ½ tsp. paprika on top.
8. ½ c. canned mushroom tops and stems, sliced.
9. 2 c. oysters heated in own liquor until edges curl, then added slowly to Thin White Sauce.
10. 4 tbs. pimiento, finely chopped; 1 tbsp. onion, minced.
11. ½ c. cooked shrimp, chopped.

OTHER SAUCES

■   **HORSERADISH SAUCE**

4 tbsp. prepared horseradish   **½ tsp. pepper**
1½ tbsp. lemon juice   **½ tsp. paprika**
½ tsp. salt   **½ c. whipped cream or yogurt**

Combine horseradish with lemon juice and seasonings. Fold in whipped cream or yogurt.

■ DRAWN BUTTER SAUCE GOURMET

½ c. butter	½ tsp. pepper
4 tbsp. flour	1 tbsp. lemon juice
2 c. boiling water	1 tbsp. chopped parsley
½ tsp. salt	2 egg yolks, slightly beaten

Blend 4 tbsp. of the butter and flour in skillet and gradually add boiling water, stirring over low heat until sauce is smooth and thick. Slowly stir in remaining butter. Add lemon juice and parsley, then beaten egg yolks and seasonings. Stir over very low heat, not allowing to come to a boil.

■ TRADITIONAL BREAD SAUCE

1½ c. fresh bread, crusts removed and cubed	½ tsp. pepper
	1 onion
2 c. milk	5 whole cloves
1 tsp. salt	3 tbsp. butter

Pour milk over bread cubes in skillet; stick cloves in whole peeled onion and place in center of bread mixture. Add butter and cook over low heat about 10 minutes. Add seasonings and a little more butter to taste.

■ HOT SPICY SAUCE

Combine in small saucepan ½ c. catsup, 1 tsp. chopped onion, ⅓ c. finely-cut celery and leaves, ⅛ tsp. dry mustard, 1 tsp. curry powder, 1 tsp. Worcestershire sauce. Cook about 10 minutes. Pour over broiled, pan-fried or baked fish.

■ SOUR CREAM SAUCE

Melt 3 tbsp. butter in saucepan. Add ¼ c. chopped onions or scallions, ¼ c. chopped green pepper or sweet red peppers. Cook over moderate heat about 5 minutes. Add ½ tsp. salt, pepper, 1 tsp. lemon juice and ¼ tsp. thyme. Fold in ⅓ c. minced parsley and 1 c. sour cream. Heat a few minutes and pour over broiled or pan-fried fish.

■ TARTAR SAUCE

Mix 1 c. mayonnaise, salad dressing or yogurt with 1 tsp. minced onion, 1 tbsp. chopped parsley, 1 tbsp. chopped pickle relish, 1 tbsp. chopped green olives and 1 tsp. capers.

■ **LOW-CALORIE TOMATO DRESSING**

Mix well, ½ c. tomato juice, 2 tbsp. lemon juice, 1 tsp. grated onion, ½ tsp. Worcestershire sauce, ½ tsp. dry mustard.

■ **SEA FOOD COCKTAIL SAUCE**

2 tbsp. prepared horseradish	2 tbsp. vinegar
2 tbsp. tomato catsup	4 tbsp. lemon juice
1 tsp. salt	¼ tsp. Tabasco
¼ c. chopped ripe olives	

Mix together, add a few chopped celery leaves and a few sprigs chopped parsley. Let stand for seasonings to blend. Serve over fish, on sea food cocktails or avocado.

■ **HOT SOUP SAUCES**

Heat undiluted mushroom, spinach or celery soup with 1 tsp. lemon juice and ½ tsp. prepared mustard. Serve over broiled, baked or pan-fried fish.

■ **HOLLANDAISE SAUCE**

Melt ¼ lb. butter. Beat 2 egg yolks until thick, add ½ tsp. salt, dash of paprika and 3 tbsp. melted butter. Blend completely; it will be stiff. Continue beating, adding a few drops of lemon juice (about 1½-2 tbsp. in all) and rest of melted butter, slowly, alternating butter and lemon juice. Makes 1 c. To use sauce, heat over hot water, stirring constantly. Serve at once.

■ **EASY HOLLANDAISE SAUCE**

1 8-oz. pkg. cream cheese	⅛ tsp. salt
2 tbsp. cream or top milk	2 tbsp. lemon juice
2 egg yolks	

Soften cream cheese with cream. Add egg yolks, 1 at a time, beating well after each egg. Add lemon juice and salt; mix thoroughly. Heat in upper part of double boiler. Do not let water boil in lower part. Takes about 20 minutes.

■ **BLEU CHEESE CREAM SAUCE**

4-oz. Bleu cheese, crumbled (about 1 c.)	½ c. sour cream
	2 tbsp. chopped chives

Combine and serve as sauce over hot baked potatoes. Serves 8.

■ HOT SAUCE MEXICALI

1 clove garlic, minced	¼ tsp. thyme
1 medium onion, chopped	½ tsp. cumin
¼ c. minced parsley	¼ tsp. curry
¼ c. salad oil	1½ tsp. salt
¼ c. vinegar or lemon juice	1 8-oz. can tomato sauce
Dash of Tabasco	2 tbsp. Kitchen Bouquet or
½ tsp. oregano	Worcestershire sauce

Sauté garlic and onion with oil a few minutes. Add remaining ingredients and simmer 15-20 minutes. Serve on hamburgers, in tacos, or brush on steak.

■ GUACAMOLE

1 large avocado, peeled and mashed	1 tbsp. lemon juice
	1 tsp. Worcestershire sauce
1 small, or ½ large, firm ripe tomato, chopped	1 tsp. olive oil
	½ tsp. salt
4 green onions, chopped, tops and all	

Mix all ingredients. Chill 1 hour. Serve as a dip for fresh vegetables or crackers; as a spread for bread or topping for vegetable salad.

■ CRANBERRY-ORANGE SAUCE, OR RELISH

2 oranges, quartered (leave peel on if organically grown)	4 c. fresh cranberries (1 lb.)
	1 c. honey

Put oranges, including rind, and cranberries through food chopper, using coarse blade. Fold in honey. Chill several hours to develop flavor. Store in refrigerator. Serve with turkey or, if a tart sauce is liked, it is good on vanilla ice cream or on fruit salads. ½ c. chopped walnut meats may be added.

■ LEMON BUTTER

¼ c. butter	1 tbsp. minced parsley
1½ tbsp. lemon juice	Fresh herbs may be added,
½ tsp. salt and paprika	(about 1 tsp.)

Melt butter, add remaining ingredients and serve over broiled or pan-fried fish.

■ **PARSLEY BUTTER OR MAITRE d'HOTEL BUTTER**

Beat 3 tbsp. butter to a cream, then add 1 tbsp. lemon juice, 1 tbsp. chopped parsley, ½ tsp. salt and ⅛ tsp. pepper. Beat these ingredients into the butter. Spread on cooked fish or mix with new potatoes using only 1 tsp. of lemon juice.

■ **GARLIC BUTTER**

Cream 4 tbsp. butter with 2 cloves of garlic, minced. May use 1 tsp. minced sweet basil or thyme. Use as a spread.

SWEET SAUCES

■ **SAUCE FOR ICE CREAM**

Mash banana with a touch of lemon juice and beat to a cream. Chill. Melt ¼ c. butter with ⅓ c. carob powder. Add ½ c. honey and ½ c. hot water. Simmer until thick as syrup. Add 1 tsp. vanilla and chilled banana.

■ **NUT CREAM**

Put ½ c. almonds or cashew nuts in liquefier with enough pineapple juice to form a thick creamy substance when thoroughly mixed. For variation, a pinch of mint may be added, or a bit of cinnamon and nutmeg, or ginger, depending on how you wish to use the sauce. Good on fresh pineapple, baked apples, or pumpkin pie.

■ **EXCEPTIONAL SAUCE FOR FRUIT**

Combine following ingredients in blender:
1 egg yolk
1 pkg. cream cheese (small), broken in small pieces
1 c. sour cream
1 c. whipping cream
1 tsp. sugar or honey

Blend at low speed for 10 seconds. If blender is not used, whip cream and mix cheese, sour cream and egg yolk. Fold both together until smooth.

■ **HONEY HARD SAUCE**

Cream ¾ c. honey and ⅓ c. butter until completely blended. Add 1 tsp. lemon juice or vanilla and chill.

■ **HONEY BUTTER**

Blend together equal amounts of butter and honey. Store in glass jar in refrigerator. Serve on hot waffles, pancakes or French toast.

■ **HONEY PUDDING SAUCE**

Blend in double boiler ¼ lb. butter, ¾ c. honey and ⅓ c. cream, dash of salt. Stir over hot water until smooth and hot. Add 1 tsp. vanilla. Serve hot or cold on any steamed pudding.

■ **SAUCE FOR FRESH FRUIT**

Whip or put 1 c. cottage cheese through sieve. Add ½ c. sour cream or yogurt.

■ **LEMON SAUCE**

⅓ c. honey or ½ c. raw sugar	1 c. water
1½ tbsp. flour	2 tbsp. lemon juice
2 tbsp. butter	1 tsp. grated lemon rind

Mix sugar and flour together. Add water and cook on low fire, stirring constantly until thickened. Remove from heat and add flavoring and butter.

Variations

1. *Vanilla Sauce*—Add 2 tbsp. vanilla to above recipe and omit lemon juice and rind.
2. *Orange Sauce*—Substitute 1 c. orange juice for 1 c. water in lemon sauce recipe.
3. *Pineapple Sauce*—Substitute 1 c. grated pineapple or juice for water in lemon sauce recipe.
4. *Peach Sauce*—Substitute 1 c. peach nectar, juice or mashed fresh peaches for 1 c. of water.
5. *Cherry Sauce*—Substitute 1 c. cherry juice for 1 c. water.
6. *Apricot Sauce*—Substitute 1 c. apricot nectar for 1 c. water.

■ **CHOCOLATE-HONEY SAUCE**

Melt 2 pkgs. chocolate bits in top part of double boiler. Drizzle 2 tbsp. honey and ½ c. undiluted evaporated milk or cream into melted chocolate. Add ¼ tsp. salt and ½ tsp. vanilla. Serve warm over your favorite ice cream or wedges of Angel Food.

■ **HONEY-CREAM DRESSING**

1 3-oz. pkg. cream cheese	**2 tbsp. honey**
1 tbsp. fresh lemon juice	**¼ tsp. salt**
3 tbsp. fresh orange juice	

Whip all ingredients together until well blended, but cream cheese remains in little lumps. Fold into diced fruits or over gelatin salad.

■ **HONEY-SOUR CREAM DRESSING FOR FRUIT**

2 eggs	**½ pt. commercial sour cream**
⅓ c. honey	**⅓ c. fresh lemon juice**

Slightly mix eggs in a saucepan. Combine lemon juice and honey. Put lemon juice into measuring cup, then add honey; it will flow easily when added to egg mixture. Stir well while adding to mix. Cook over low heat, stirring until mixture resembles soft custard. Remove from heat, cool and fold in sour cream. Delicious over fresh peaches, bananas, apples. About 15 servings.

■ **CAROB SYRUP**

4 tbsp. carob powder	**¼ tsp. vanilla**
2 tbsp. brown sugar, or honey	**1 tbsp. butter**
1 c. water	

Cook over moderate heat until thick as syrup. Good on ice cream and in milk drinks.

Carob powder may replace chocolate in most recipes. Add an extra 2 tbsp. oil when substituting carob powder in baked recipes. The delicious carob bean has a natural sugar content of approximately 50% and resembles chocolate in flavor. It is an alkaline food, easily assimilated and a natural source of calcium, phosphorous, potassium and many more important minerals and vitamins. Carob can be used in many ways; for hot or cold milk drinks, in baking, puddings and custards. Children will probably invent new ways to use carob, so that they may replace their craving for chocolate with this wonderful natural food.

CHAPTER 16

Soups

■ RAW VEGETABLE SOUPS

Delicious soups can be made in almost no time with raw frozen vegetables. They retain most of their nutrients and garden-fresh flavors. They should, of course, be organically grown.

An easy way to divide a package of frozen vegetables in half is to strike the center of the package against the side of sink, loosening the vegetables so that you can cut through the package easily, and return the other half to your freezer for later use.

Place contents of half-package in your blender; add 1 c. milk, warmed to blood temperature. Blend and season with sea-salt. Top with bacon bits, grated cheese or chopped parsley. Serve hot or cold. Serves 2.

Variations—For milk, try substituting any of the following:

1 c. tomato juice
1 c. carrot juice
1 c. mixed vegetable juice

1 c. any other raw vegetable juice of a flavor compatible with frozen vegetables used.

■ DRIED VEGETABLE SOUPS

All the dried vegetable mixes on the market make excellent soups. Follow package directions, or try adding 1 c. warm milk, vegetable juice or water to 2 tsp. vegetable mix. Season if desired.

For appetizing dips, combine dried vegetable soup mixes with cream cheese, yogurt, mashed avocado or cottage cheese.

■ RICH VEGETABLE BROTH

Blend 1 tbsp. butter with 1 tbsp. soy powder, ¼ c. powdered yeast and 2 c. water. Add 3 tsp. vegetable broth mix and ⅛ tsp. garlic powder if desired. Serve with croutons. Serves 2.

■ **VEGETABLE-RICE SOUP**

½ c. brown rice
2 qts. water
1 tsp. salt
1 c. sliced green beans
1 c. chopped tomatoes
2 small onions, chopped

2 tbsp. soy oil
1 tsp. salt
1 tsp. chopped parsley
1 tsp. soy sauce
½ tsp. oregano

Cook rice in 1 qt. salted water until just tender; drain and keep warm in double boiler. Cook chopped vegetables in remaining quart of water until tender. Combine with oil, soy sauce, oregano and parsley. Mix with rice, heat and serve at once. Serves 6.

■ **GREEN SUMMER SOUP**

1 qt. water
1 tsp. salt
2 medium zucchini, chopped
2 c. chopped spinach
2 tbsp. chopped onion

¼ c. green pea flour or lima bean flour
2 tbsp. soy oil
2 tbsp. minced parsley

Bring water to boil, add salt, cook zucchini, spinach and onions until just tender, about 10 minutes. Blend flour with oil and add salt. Add small amount of soup mixture and stir smooth, then add to remaining soup mixture and stir. Top with parsley. Serves 4.6.

■ **CREAM SOUP—PEA OR LIMA**

½ c. green pea flour or lima bean flour
½ c. powdered milk
1 medium onion, chopped

1 qt. water
½ tsp. thyme
½ tsp. oregano
1 tsp. vegetable salt

Mix flour with powdered milk. Stir in water slowly until mixture is smooth. Add to remaining water, with onions and seasoning. Heat over low fire. Serve with buttered croutons of toasted wholewheat bread. Top with bacon-flavored yeast if desired. Serves 4.

■ **POTATO SOUP**

4 c. milk
4 medium potatoes, boiled
1 c. chopped onion
4 medium stalks celery, chopped

¼ c. chopped celery leaves
4 tbsp. chopped parsley
1 tsp. salt or substitute
2 tbsp. butter

Scrape potatoes slightly and chop. Liquefy all vegetables, add milk, heat to just below boiling point, until soup thickens a little. Add butter, let it melt, and serve. Serves 4.

If made without a blender, mash potatoes and finely chop onions, celery and parsley. Proceed as above.

■ ONION SOUP HABITANT

1 c. thinly sliced onions	½ tsp. black pepper
¼ c. melted butter	¼ c. grated Parmesan cheese
¼ c. salad oil	2 slices whole-wheat toast, cut
2 c. beef bouillon	in circles

Lightly brown onions in butter in deep skillet or saucepan. Add oil and water or bouillon; add seasoning. Simmer over low heat, 15 minutes. Float toast circles in each serving, top with cheese. Serves 2-3.

■ EASY BORSCH

1 c. minced onion	1 clove garlic, crushed
2 tbsp. butter	3 tsp. lemon juice
3¾ c. beef consommé	¼ tsp. ground cloves
2 c. grated beets	¾ tsp. salt

Sauté onion until golden brown. Add consommé, beets, garlic, lemon juice and seasonings. Simmer 10 minutes, until flavors blend. Top each serving with 1 tbsp. sour cream. Serves 4-5. Makes a zestful lunch when served with buttered rye bread, apples and Camembert cheese.

■ LENTIL SOUP

2 c. lentils, covered with cold water; soak 2 hours	1 medium onion, chopped
	⅓ c. minced parsley
3 diced carrots	6 c. water
1 medium green pepper, diced	2 tsp. salt
4 medium stalks celery, diced	½ tsp. pepper

Drain soaked lentils; add to diced vegetables in large soup kettle; add water and seasonings. Bring to boil and simmer 30 minutes. Bits of crisp crumbled bacon or thin slices of frankfurter may be added. Serves 6.

■   **CREAM OF TOMATO SOUP**

3 fresh tomatoes, chopped, or	2 c. water
1 medium can tomatoes, chopped	1 qt. milk
	1 c. thin white sauce
¼ tsp. basil	½ tsp. freshly ground black pepper
2 tbsp. chopped onion	
½ tsp. salt	1 tbsp. butter

Mix tomatoes with basil, onion and salt. Stir with water in large soup kettle; cook 30 minutes over medium heat. Press through sieve and return to pan. Stir in milk, white sauce, pepper and butter. Heat carefully, not allowing to boil. Serve at once. Serves 4-6.

■   **TOMATO BROTH**

8 fresh tomatoes, chopped, or 4 c. canned tomatoes, chopped	1 c. water
	1 tsp. salt
	½ tsp. pepper
1 c. chopped celery	½ tsp. vegetable salt
1 medium onion, chopped	1 tbsp. chopped parsley

Cook tomatoes, celery and onion in water until celery is tender; add salt, pepper, vegetable salt. Put through strainer and return to low heat, not allowing to come to boil. Add parsley. Serves 4.

Variations—Add 2 tsp. powdered vegetable broth, or ½ c. finely chopped cabbage, or ½ c. green beans, French-cut.

■   **CALIFORNIA MINESTRONE**

1 c. dried beans	1 tsp. salt
6 c. cold water	¼ tsp. pepper
¼ c. salad oil	1 c. tomato sauce
1 tbsp. onion, minced	2 c. rich meat stock or 1 pt. bouillon
1 clove garlic, minced	
2 tbsp. parsley, minced	1 c. raw cabbage, coarsely chopped
2 tbsp. celery, minced	
Parmesan cheese	½ c. macaroni (may be soy or whole-wheat)
¼ tsp. oregano	

Soak beans in cold water overnight. Cover and bring to boil in same water in which they were soaked. Simmer until tender.

Lightly brown onion, garlic and celery in oil. Add with remaining ingredients to beans. Simmer 30 minutes. Serve topped with grated Parmesan cheese. Serves 6.

■ SOUP STOCK

1 large soup bone or several small ones	⅓ c. chopped onion
1 tbsp. salt	4 c. cold water
⅓ c. chopped celery leaves and stems	⅓ c. chopped parsley
⅓ c. diced carrots	1 bay leaf
	1 pinch oregano
	1 pinch basil

Ask butcher to split bone. Cut meat from bones; brown if brown stock is desired. Cover meat and bones with water. Add remaining ingredients, cover, and simmer 3½ hours, adding more water as needed. If a clear stock is desired, strain, chill, remove fat and strain again.

For *Vegetable Soup,* do not strain, but add any vegetables desired in amounts you like, cut as you please. Also ¾ c. pearl barley or brown rice may be added; simmer 1 hour more.

■ PHILADELPHIA PEPPER POT

4 slices bacon, diced	½ tsp. pepper
1 onion, diced	3 potatoes, diced
1 green pepper, diced	2 tbsp. flour
2 qts. soup stock or canned bouillon	2 tbsp. drippings
1 lb. honeycomb tripe	½ c. milk
	1 tsp. salt

Brown bacon, add onion and green pepper. Cook slowly 5 minutes. Add stock or stock and tripe which has been washed and shredded. Season. Simmer 2 hours. Add potatoes and cook 30 minutes. Mix flour and drippings; stir in milk to smooth paste; thicken soup. Add salt. Serves 6-8.

■ SEA FOOD BISQUE

1 can tomato soup	¼ c. sherry or 2 tsp, lemon juice
1 can mushroom soup	
1 can crab, shrimp or lobster	

Dilute soups with milk, in quantity denoted on can. Blend and cook over very low heat, stirring until smooth and creamy. Add sea food and wine or lemon juice and simmer about 5 minutes. Serves 6-8.

■ **FISH CHOWDER**

1 lb. lean fish	12 peppercorns
4 c. cold water	½ bay leaf
1 stalk celery	6 tbsp. millet meal or flour
3 sprigs chopped parsley	1 c. green peas
1 sliced onion	2 c. carrots, diced
1 diced carrot	3 tbsp. butter
2 tsp. salt	2 c. hot milk

Cut fish into small pieces and place in saucepan. Add salt, peppercorns, celery, parsley, onion, carrot and bay leaf. Cover with water. Bring mixture to boil, then simmer 40 minutes. Strain. Add water to make 1 qt. Melt butter and stir in millet meal to make smooth paste; add to stock and bring to boil. Add peas and diced carrots. Cook until vegetables are done. Add milk; reheat. Serves 6.

■ **VEGETABLE SOUP SUPREME**

2 lbs. soup meat, cut in 1-inch pieces	1 large onion, diced
	½ green pepper, diced
1 c. brown rice, pearl barley or millet	½ c. carrots, diced
	¼ c. turnips, diced
6 qts. water	2 tsp. salt
1 can tomato purée	1 tsp. pepper

Add meat and rice, barley or millet to water; bring to boil and then cook over low heat about 2 hours. For last 30 minutes of cooking, add vegetables and seasonings. Serves 8-10.

■ **SPLIT PEA SOUP**

¼ lb. salt pork or bone from baked ham	2 tsp. salt
	1 tsp. thyme
2 c. dried split peas	½ tsp. pepper
½ c. celery, chopped	¼ tsp. oregano
3 qts. water	

Cook salt pork or ham bone in water with peas and celery, over very low heat about 2 hours, until peas are tender. Remove bone or pieces of salt pork, strain. Add seasonings and stir until smooth. Serve hot, adding bits of crisp bacon or chopped frankfurter, if desired. May serve with 1 tbsp. whipped or sour cream topping each portion, if desired. May also be topped with chopped parsley and served with buttered croutons. Serves 6-8.

■ JELLIED TOMATO SOUP

2 c. chopped fresh or canned
   tomatoes
¼ c. diced carrots
¼ c. diced onion
¼ c. diced celery
1 c. water
1 tsp. salt
½ tsp. pepper

3 cloves
1 small bay leaf
¼ tsp. thyme or 2 sprigs fresh
   thyme
1 tbsp. unflavored gelatin
¼ c. water
½ c. minced parsley

Combine tomatoes, carrots, onion, celery and seasonings in water; bring to boil, then simmer, covered, about 30 minutes. Strain. There should be 2 c. liquid; if more, cook over low heat, uncovered, until 2 c. remains; if less, add water to make 2 c. Soften gelatin in cold water and stir into hot soup until dissolved; pour into shallow pan and chill until firm. Cut in sparkling cubes and pile in bouillon cups; top with minced parsley. Garnish with lemon wedges, chopped parsley or water cress or chopped olives. Serve with crisp whole-wheat, soy or cheese crackers. Serves 4.

■ JELLIED MEAT SOUP

1 qt. clear chicken or beef consommé

½ c. cold water
2 tbsp. gelatin

Soften gelatin in cold water, add to boiling bouillon, stir well and chill. Break up in glistening pieces; serve in bouillon cups with a sprinkling of minced parsley, or lemon section. A small can of chicken, or left-over minced chicken may be added to soup before it starts to set. Serve with toasted mixed nuts. Serves 4-6.

■ FRUIT SOUP

2 c. unsweetened orange or
   pineapple juice
2 tsp. cornstarch

3 tbsp. cold water
Honey to sweeten

Place fruit juice in saucepan. When hot, add cornstarch mixed smooth with cold water. Cook slowly, stirring constantly until clear. Add honey to taste. Serve ice-cold in frosted glass sherbet cups or in well-chilled bouillon cups or soup bowls. To frost glass cups, place in freezing part of the refrigerator until ready to use. Serves 2-3.

■ **VICHYSOISSE**

6 chopped green onions or leeks	½ tsp. salt
2 tbsp. butter or oil	1 c. milk
4 small potatoes, peeled and sliced thin	2 c. half-and-half or light cream
1 carrot, scraped and sliced thin	¼ tsp. nutmeg
	1 tsp. salt
3 c. chicken broth	½ tsp. pepper
	6 tsp. chopped chives

Lightly sauté onions or leeks, being careful to cook until tender without browning. Stir in potatoes, carrots and salt. Cook in large kettle, in chicken broth, over very low heat, about 35 minutes, until vegetables are tender. Press through fine sieve or put through food mill. Add milk, half-and-half or cream, nutmeg, additional salt, and pepper. Heat to just below boiling point and strain again. Chill thoroughly. Serve very cold in bouillon cups, topped with cream and chopped chives. Serves 6.

■ **BRAN BROTH**

1 c. red-wheat bran	2 c. cold water

Soak bran in water overnight. Pour into strainer and allow to drain. Pour 1 c. hot water through bran, stirring and rinsing as thoroughly as possible. Strained bran broth is reputedly a good blood tonic. Serves 3.

■ **VEGETABLE BROTH**

6 carrots	1 small bunch celery
1 bunch parsley	½ lb. spinach
3 comfrey leaves	1 tsp. salt

Slice carrots and celery very thin. Chop parsley, comfrey and spinach. Cook carrots and celery over medium heat 30 minutes in 1 qt. water. After 20 minutes cooking, add parsley, comfrey, spinach mixture and salt. May be garnished with lemon slices. Serves 4.

■ **VEGETABLE SOUPS—MEATLESS**

1. Peel 4 tomatoes, cook 10 minutes over low heat in 1 c. water with 1 bay leaf, 1 leaf basil, 1 tsp. salt. Strain; add 3 more c. water, reheat. Serves 4.
2. Put through food chopper 3 large carrots, 1 bunch beets, 1 large celery root, 6 small onions. Cook together in 6 c. water over low heat, 10 minutes, strain if desired. Add 1 tsp. salt, ½ tsp. black pepper. Serves 4-6.

3. Skin and cut up 3 large tomatoes. Chop 3 stalks celery, leaves and all. Add 2 chopped onions, 2 c. carrot juice, 1 tsp. minced parsley, 1 tsp. salt. Bring to boiling point and serve. Serves 2.

4. Chop 6 carrots, 4 stalks celery, 1 lb. green beans, 4 tomatoes (or 1 large can tomatoes), 3 onions, ½ clove garlic. Add 2 tbsp. soy or other seed oil, ½ c. chopped parsley, ¼ tsp. thyme, marjoram or basil, 1 tsp. salt or substitute. Mix with 1 c. ground oats, rice or whole barley and cook slowly in 4 qts. water, 1½ hours. Serves 8.

5. Chop 10 small beets, 2 medium onions. Add 2 tsp. soy or other seed oil, 1 tsp. salt. Cook slowly in 2½ qts. water, 1 hour. Top each serving with sour cream or yogurt if desired. Serves 8.

6. Cut kernels off 6 ears fresh corn. Cook 1 head chopped lettuce in 2½ qts. water, until tender; add corn. Add 1 qt. green peas, 1 small chopped onion, 3 tbsp. soy or other seed oil. Cook slowly 1 hour. Season with 1 tsp. salt, ¼ tsp. black pepper. Serves 6.

■ SOUP ACCESSORIES

1. *Croutons:* spread fairly stale bread slices with creamed butter. Remove crusts and cut in ½-inch or ¼-inch cubes. Toast in hot oven until brown and crisp, or sauté in a little oil. Croutons may be added to soup before serving or passed in separate bowl.

2. *Cheese Croutons:* Cream equal amounts of butter and Cheddar cheese as spread and proceed as above.

3. *Popcorn,* buttered and served crisp and hot, can be a fun-accessory for soups as a change from croutons or crackers.

4. *Garlic Croutons* are made by blending ¼ tsp. finely minced garlic with each tbsp. butter.

5. *Whipped Cream,* slightly salted, or sour cream may be spooned on individual servings of such soups as tomato broth, borsch, etc.

6. *Grated Cheese,* usually Swiss or Cheddar, is an excellent topping for certain soups, such as vegetable, onion, etc.

7. *Crisp Bacon,* crumbled, adds a flavor-lift to many soups, including bean, pea and vegetable.

8. *Nuts,* finely chopped or grated, are a piquant accompaniment to many bland cream soups. Almonds, cashews and walnuts are particularly good.

9. *Orange or Lemon Rind,* finely grated, add delicacy to certain cream soups, as well as to cold summer soups.

10. *Curry Balls* are wonderful with most meat or chicken soups. A good basic recipe is 1 c. soft bread crumbs, mixed with 1 grated hard-cooked egg, 2 tbsp. melted butter, ½ tsp. curry powder and 1 egg yolk; form into tiny balls and add to soup about 5 minutes before serving.

11. *Tiny Meat Balls:* to 1 c. chopped cooked beef, veal or lamb, add 1 tbsp. flour, 1 tbsp. melted butter, 2 drops lemon juice, ½ tsp. thyme, 1 tsp. minced parsley, ¼ tsp. salt, ⅛ tsp. pepper, 1 egg yolk. Shape into small balls, roll in flour, brown in hot fat. Pop into vegetable soup at last minute. May also be served alone as hot hors d'oeuvres.

CHAPTER **17**

Vegetables

WHERE have they gone . . . those tender young ears of corn whisked from the stalk and shucked on the back porch, then with the milk almost bursting from the white or golden kernels, popped into boiling water for only minutes and brought to table with plenty of fresh country butter? Where are the spring peas, the kind Thomas Jefferson swore were the finest possible eating when taken straight from the vine to the pot and cooked lightly with sprigs of mint, and butter added?

Many of us have childhood memories of such lovely eating from country gardens. And, in the realm of vegetables, this is actually what we try for when we talk about eating natural foods. We are not talking about some clinical dream of a dietician. We are only going back, as best we can, to the vegetables grown in rich, unpoisoned earth, nurtured by rain and sun, with all of nature's goodness stored in them. We are trying to recapture those flavors as well as those wonderful nutrients.

True, a lot of us do not have our own gardens and so the best we can do is attempt to find sources of organically grown vegetables and whenever possible, to avoid those doused with poison sprays and those denuded of food value by having been grown on soil deficient in elements important to our health.

Man has been careless in his use of the soil from which he gets the plants he needs for survival. We still do not know the full extent of the harm done to eroded and depleted soil, but there is plenty of evidence that such soil cannot produce and maintain healthy human beings.

There is only one basic food factory; it is in the leaves and other green parts of plants. The true fertility of our soil depends upon the priceless trace minerals, which are made up of some 32 elements, such as iron, cobalt, magnesium and zinc. Many farmers and food processors do not yet realize the danger of producing foods with a growing deficiency of these vital trace elements. Fortunately there are some farmers and processors who are concerned, and who are making a concerted effort to return to the soil the trace minerals and organic matter that has been removed.

It is important to obtain fruits and vegetables which have ripened on the plant or tree, rather than those which have been picked green. The development of vitamins and proteins depends upon natural ripening. After crops are harvested, the method of handling determines to a large extent the amount of loss of nutrients. To insure high quality and food value, crops should be shipped immediately in refrigerated cars or trucks, rushed to market and then purchased as soon as possible after they reach the store.

The very *best* vegetables are those from organic gardens, either your own or a commercial grower's. Whenever possible, vegetables should be gathered just before they are to be eaten, in order to retain a maximum quantity of nutrients.

If you are buying market vegetables, try to get those which have not been soaked in spray, and are as fresh as possible. Except for a few vegetables such as potatoes, dry onions and corn on the cob, vegetables should be washed and dried immediately, then stored in a cool, dark place to stop enzyme action. When left at room temperatures and in the light, much folic acid, vitamin B_2 and half the vitamin C is lost in a few hours. When good, fresh vegetables are not obtainable, buy frozen ones, since there is a relatively short time between harvest and package, and the blanching period is not long enough to completely destroy the nutrients. Frozen vegetables, then dried vegetables are the next best buy, and canned vegetables are last on the list.

■ MEMOS ON VEGETABLE COOKERY

1. Do not soak vegetables in water before cooking, and do not allow them to stand in water after cooking. Minerals, flavor, oils and sugar are soluble and therefore lost in too much water saturation.
2. Peel vegetables only when skin is tough, bitter or too uneven to be thoroughly cleansed. If it is necessary to prepare vegetables some time before cooking, do keep them refrigerated. If prepared some time before serving, also keep carefully in refrigerator.
3. Cook vegetables in shortest time possible. Initial heating should be rapid, in order to destroy enzymes quickly and prevent loss of vitamins. Contact with oxygen should be avoided as much as possible to prevent loss of B vitamins. That is why it it best not to peel and to cook by steam when possible.

4. Try the Chinese method of cooking vegetables. Add no water, but do add a small amount of vegetable oil. The heat under the utensil must be constant and high. Oil reaches a higher temperature than water, so the foods cook very quickly. The Chinese also cut foods into small diagonal pieces. This shortens the cooking time and allows the oil to touch all parts of the vegetable. The hot oil seals the juices of the food inside, thus retaining the nutrients. Serve promptly.

5. Some vegetables may be broiled. Brush them with butter or oil and season. Place on the pan in the broiler compartment, three inches from direct heat. Cook until tender. Broil such vegetables as sliced eggplant, raw or cooked mushrooms, precooked asparagus, raw sliced potatoes, precooked potatoes and precooked squash.

6. Some vegetable acids escape in steam and the rest dissolve in liquids. Therefore green vegetables, which are most affected by acid and will quickly turn a sad olive-color, should be cooked uncovered for at least half the required time, since most of the acid escapes in steam during the first few minutes of cooking.

7. If you live where the water is hard, you will notice that green vegetables cooked in that water tend to retain their greenness. This is because the alkaline salts in the water react with the vegetable acids and neutralize them. Dried vegetables, such as beans, on the other hand, are difficult to soften in such water because the calcium has a firming effect on plant tissue. White vegetables, such as onions, potatoes and cauliflower, tend to darken when cooked in hard water. Adding a pinch of cream of tartar during the last few minutes of cooking will help whiten them.

8. Hard water, with its alkaline content, makes some red vegetables lose color. Try adding a little lemon juice or vinegar after they are cooked tender.

9. Yellow vegetables will keep their color, when cooked in hard water. But do avoid high temperatures, as their sugar changes to caramel and gives the cooked product an unpleasant flavor.

10. Sulphur is to blame for the strong flavor of vegetables such as cabbage, turnips, Brussels sprouts, cauliflower, onions and garlic. Do not overcook any of these.

11. Do not use soda in cooking water to bring out green color, since soda destroys the soluble vitamins and softens the plant tissue.

Steam or cook vegetables in a small amount of water until barely tender. Add 1½ tbsp. butter for each 1½ c. vegetables. As vegetables are low in fat it is customary to season them with butter or oil. Add sea-salt or herbs just before serving.

Combinations of different-colored vegetables make attractive plates. For example, baked yams, buttered green beans and shredded beets with lemon juice and butter are a decorative trio.

Almost any vegetable is delicious raw, if purchased while tender and fresh. Grating or shredding is the best method of preparing nearly all raw vegetables. This should be done immediately before serving to prevent as much oxidation as possible.

You can introduce many raw vegetables to your family, if you first combine them with any of the following: mashed avocado, sour cream, whipped cottage cheese, finely-chopped tomatoes, minced onion, grated raw apple, chopped celery, chopped parsley, sliced Jerusalem artichokes, lemon juice, apple cider vinegar, dribble of honey, melted butter.

Try using a mild-flavored salad oil, such as safflower oil, minced onion and a bit of garlic with your raw vegetables.

Finely ground nuts mix well with sour cream or cottage cheese and raw vegetables. Use the many delightful herbs and spices available as seasoning.

On cold days, warm some of the raw vegetables in the upper part of a double boiler or place in custard cups and warm in hot water in the oven. Turn out on lettuce leaves.

When serving a meal of raw vegetables, several kinds may be chosen, and they should vary in color, texture and flavor. Use your imagination to make attractive arrangements on the plate.

Good combinations:

1. On torn pieces of lettuce place grated raw peeled beets (if very young you need not peel), half of an avocado, parsley sprouts and cashew nuts. Pour over all a tart French dressing.

2. On Romaine lettuce place some finely-cut green pepper strips, quartered tomatoes, cauliflower flowerettes, and yellow turnip, thinly sliced and spread with peanut butter. Use a whipped cottage cheese or yogurt dressing.

3. On water cress arrange radish, then carrots and raw apple (grated) which have been mixed with mayonnaise and pressed in an oiled custard cup. Sprinkle raisins over the apple and carrot mold. Tender young peas and slivered almonds in cucumber boats can be added to this combination plate. Use French dressing.

Artichoke

Purchase 1 per serving. Select tightly closed leaves. Artichoke must appear fresh. Cut off stem and remove small dried leaves. Use kitchen scissors to clip off tips of leaves.

Cook in boiling water, salted, until leaf can be pulled easily from artichoke and stem center can be pierced easily with a fork; about 40 minutes. Place upright on individual plate with a small paper cup of melted butter or mayonnaise. Discard center leaves and cut heart in pieces. Dip in sauce.

Asparagus

Purchase 2 lbs. for 4 servings. Stalks should be green the entire length without dried, wilted tops. Break off each stalk as far down as it breaks easily. Cook stalks whole, tied together, or break in pieces.

Steam tied stalks standing in deep covered kettle with water ¼ way up stalks, until tender; about 20 minutes; or break in pieces and cook, covered, in enough boiling water to barely cover for 10 minutes. Remove carefully and serve with melted butter or cheese sauce. Young spears may be marinated raw and used in salads.

Lima Beans

Purchase beans in the pod. Allow 3 lbs. for 4 servings. Pods should be green, crisp and well-filled. It helps to shell beans if you cut off outer edge with scissors.

Cook in covered saucepan in enough water to cover; add ½ tsp. oil to keep beans from boiling over. When tender there should be no water to pour off. Season with butter and salt to taste. Cream may be added.

Green or Wax Beans

Buy 2 lbs. for 4-6 servings, firm, crisp and free from blemishes. Wash, nip off ends. May be cut or not, cut lengthwise, diagonally, or in 1-inch lengths.

Cook covered in ½-inch boiling water until tender. Season with butter and salt; add bits of cooked bacon and a small amount of chopped onion, slivered almonds and butter, mushroom soup, ham or bacon drippings. Tender young beans may be served raw in salads.

How to Buy and Prepare

How to Serve

Beets

If beets are small, purchase 2 bunches for 4 servings. Tops should be crisp and green. Beets should be smooth and firm. Cut off leaves 1 inch from beet and save. Wash beets and leaves.

Cook whole beets in boiling, salted water until tender. Cook peeled, grated beets in a few tablespoons of water about 5 minutes. Rub off skins of whole beets; serve small ones whole. Cube or slice large beets. Season with butter, salt and pepper. A little lemon juice or vinegar may be added. Beets may be shredded raw and added to salads.

Broccoli

Buy 2 lbs. for 4 servings. Should be tender, fresh, green, with compact green buds. Wash carefully, checking for insects. Peel back outside thin layer of stem. If stems are very thick, slash lengthwise so stems will cook in same time as buds.

Cook covered, in a very small amount of boiling water or steam, until tender. Serve with butter, salt or cheese or easy Hollandaise sauce. The flowerlets may be broken up to serve raw in salads.

Brussel Sprouts

Buy 1½ lbs. for 4 servings. Should be crisp, firm, compact and green. Remove loose leaves, cut off stem and wash thoroughly in cold water.

Cook covered in 1 inch of boiling, salted water until tender. Serve with melted butter or easy Hollandaise sauce.

Cabbage

Buy a head of size according to your use. Heads should be solid, hard, heavy and fresh green color. Cut in wedges or shred and remove hard core.

Cook covered in a few tablespoons of water until tender, or serve raw, shredded. Season cooked cabbage with butter and small pieces of ham or ¼ tsp. nutmeg. A little lemon juice may be added to water in which red cabbage is cooked to retain the color. Raw cabbage is good in green salads.

How to Buy and Prepare   *How to Serve*

Carrots

Buy only firm, clean, fresh, smooth, deep orange color, with fresh green tops. Do not buy loose carrots with wilted ends. Remove tops, scrub well or remove thin outer layer, if necessary. Leave whole, slice, dice, shred or cut in strips.

Cook in very little water or steam until tender. Season with butter or herbs. Preferably, serve raw. Unless carrot tops are very young and fresh, do not save. If young, add to tossed green salad.

Cauliflower

Buy size head depending upon servings required. Head should be compact with white flowerlets and fresh green jacket of outer leaves. Wash, cut off green part and separate flowerlets or leave head whole.

Cook in a few tablespoons of boiling water in tightly covered pan until barely tender, 5-8 minutes. A whole head will need ½ c. water and will cook 20-30 minutes. Serve with melted butter, cheese sauce or herb butter. Raw flowerlets are fine in salads and to dip in "dunks."

Celery

Buy green, unbleached stalks when available; this is the Pascal variety. Scrub each part of stalk to remove dirt and possible poison spray. Remove leaves only when chopped, firm pieces are desired. Save leaves and dry or use in salads.

Celery may be cut in pieces and cooked, covered, in a small amount of boiling salted water. Serve with melted butter, salt and pepper. Celery is best served raw. (See also chapter on salads, and foods for special occasions.

Celery Root (Celeriac)

Select large firm root. Cut off top, but do not peel until cooked.

Cook covered in boiling salted water until tender. Peel cooked root and cut in cubes or slice. Serve with melted butter, salt, pepper, or easy Hollandaise sauce. It may also be peeled raw and grated or sliced thinly and added to salads or served as a relish.

How to Buy and Prepare | *How to Serve*

Corn

Allow 1-2 ears per person. Should be well-filled-out with firm, milky kernels. Husks should be fresh and green. Remove husks, silks, and cut off any bad places.

Cook covered in small amount of boiling water 3-5 minutes. Serve on cob. If cut from cob, scrape to get all of kernel, and cook, covered, in a few tbsp. water about 3 minutes. Serve with butter and salt. Young, tender, fresh corn is good cut from cob and used raw in a salad.

Eggplant

Buy 1 medium heavy, firm, glossy purple eggplant for 4 people. Peel or not. Slice or cut in cubes. Do not soak in salt water.

To fry: Slice into ½-inch pieces. Dip in beaten egg to which 2 tbsp. water or milk is added. Then roll in whole-wheat bread crumbs or wheat germ. Season and fry in small amount of fat until brown on both sides. Slices may be brushed with butter and broiled.

Greens

Beet Tops, Collards, Kale, Mustard Greens, Spinach, Swiss Chard:
Chard: Buy 2 lbs. for 4 servings. Select greens which are fresh and have good color. Cut off bruised leaves and thick stems. Wash several times.

Steam or cook in only the water that clings to leaves. Swiss chard, kale and mustard greens will cook in 20-25 minutes, while the others will cook in 5-10 minutes. Serve with butter or cook with small bits of bacon. Season to taste.

Kohlrabi (resembles turnips)

Purchase 1 medium-size Kohlrabi for 4 servings. Be sure it has young tender root and leaves. Remove leaves, peel and cut in slices.

Cook covered in small amount of boiling salted water until tender. Season with butter, salt and pepper.

Mushrooms

Buy 1 lb. for 4 servings. Be sure they are commercially grown. They should be clean, firm, moist and white. Wash; do not peel young mushrooms. Leave whole or remove stems.

Cook in covered pan in butter, 10 minutes. Season with salt and pepper. Serve alone or with other vegetables.

How to Buy and Prepare	*How to Serve*

Okra

Buy 1 lb. for 4 servings. Select young, tender, brittle pods with soft seeds. Wash well and cut off stems. Leave small pods whole and slice large pods.

Cook by boiling or steaming until tender. Season with salt, pepper and butter.

Onions; Green

Young green onions, scallions and chives are marketed in bunches. Look for crisp, green tops.

These should be used raw as finger salads or in salads.

Onions

Buy 1½ lbs. for 4 servings. Select dry, hard and well-shaped onions. Red are often strong flavored. Peel under running water or pour boiling water over onions, then cool and slip off skins. Leave whole for boiling. Place cut onion on saucer, cut side down, in vegetable refrigerator bag.

Place peeled onions in several inches of boiling water. Cook, covered, 15-20 minutes for small onions and 30 minutes for large. Drain. Season with butter, salt and pepper or cream sauce. Dry onions may be served raw, chopped or minced.

Parsnips

Buy 2 small or 1 medium size per person. Select straight, smooth firm parsnips. Scrub with a stiff brush or peel. Leave whole or slice.

Cook in a small amount of boiling salted water until tender. Fry cooked slices in small amount of butter until brown on each side. May be served with butter, salt and pepper.

Parsley

Buy 1 bunch at a time and select bright green, crisp, fresh-looking parsley.

Hold under running water, shake off excess water and store in glass jar or cellophane bag in refrigerator, for garnishes and seasoning.

Peas

Purchase 3 lbs. fresh or 1 pkg. frozen peas for 4 servings. Select brittle, green, well-filled pods. Shell and wash just before cooking.

Cook covered in a few tablespoons of water 6-10 minutes. A few pods or lettuce leaves may be placed in bottom of pan before adding peas. Remove when seasoning peas. Season with butter and salt to taste. Young, tender peas may be served raw in salads.

How to Buy and Prepare   *How to Serve*

Peppers, Red or Green; Sweet or Hot

Hot peppers are not as thick fleshed. Select green or red sweet peppers. Allow 1 pepper per serving. They must be firm, well-shaped, shiny. Wash, remove stem and seeds. Cut in slices or rings. Leave whole to stuff and bake.

Steam, or cook in small amount of water; or fry slices in butter until tender. Serve raw in salads to conserve vitamins.

Potatoes; White; Sweet

Well-shaped, firm, unbruised, no green spots. Use will determine kind to buy.

Boil or bake. Baked potatoes are best to conserve vitamins. New potatoes are best when boiled in their jackets; serve with fresh-ground black pepper, butter and chopped parsley.

Squash; Summer, Patty Pan, Crookneck, Zucchini

Purchase 2 lbs. for 4 servings. Best when very small, tender, heavy for size. Wash, do not peel. Remove stem and blossom ends. Cut in slices or cubes.

Cook, covered, in small amount of boiling water or steam until tender. Serve hot, seasoned with butter and salt to taste, or fry zucchini or crookneck slices in butter until brown, or mash with butter and seasonings. Raw, tender young squash may be grated or cut in thin slices for salads.

Squash; Winter, Banana, Hubbard, Acorn

Banana and Hubbard squash may be bought in pieces or whole. The meat should be thick and all squashes must be heavy for size, with hard rind. Cut squash in pieces, remove seeds. Acorn squash is often just cut in half.

Place pieces upside down in small amount of salted water in shallow baking pan. Bake in 400° oven until tender. Turn over and place bit of butter on each. Season with salt and pepper, or a few grains of nutmeg and a little brown sugar. Serve in shell. Squash may be peeled, cooked in small amount of boiling water, mashed and seasoned. Try thinly-sliced young squash or zucchini in tossed green salad.

How to Buy and Prepare   *How to Serve*
Tomatoes; Red or Yellow

Flesh should be firm and not too ripe. Peel or not, depending on use. To peel, plunge into boiling water and remove at once, or hold on fork over flame until skin blisters.

Cook covered without water over low heat for about 5 minutes. Tomatoes are best served raw, but may also be sliced and fried; dipped in egg and bread crumbs and browned in butter; stuffed with seasoned, buttered bread crumbs, and baked.

Turnips and Rutabagas

Both should be firm, smooth, with few rootlets. Turnips will have crisp, green tops. Both will be heavy for size.

Peel carefully. Cut in slices or dice. Cook, covered, in small amount of water until tender. Season with salt and pepper or mash and season. Use thin slices of raw turnips in salads.

■ **OTHER SEASONINGS FOR VEGETABLES**

Asparagus: Lemon juice, paprika, sesame seeds, sweet or sour cream cheese.

Beans, Green String: Garlic powder, onion, bay leaf, bacon, fresh dill, basil, nutmeg.

Beans, Lima: Onion, parsley, Tabasco, sour cream, savory, basil.

Beets: Dill, vinaigrette, thyme, caraway seeds, sour cream.

Broccoli: Lemon butter, easy Hollandaise sauce, cheese sauce.

Brussels Sprouts: Sour cream, paprika, mushrooms, soy, cheese sauce.

Cabbage: Celery seed, caraway seed, yogurt, sour cream, lemon juice, curry.

Carrots: Parsley, mint, onion, salt, ginger, tomato sauce, thyme, lemon balm.

Cauliflower: Cheese sauce, butter, nutmeg, poppy and celery seeds.

Celery: Tomato sauce, chervil, green pepper, horseradish.

Swiss Chard: Onion, tomatoes, chili powder, celery soup, chives.

Corn: Tomatoes, peppers, paprika, parsley.

Eggplant: Tomatoes, onion, marjoram, garlic, mushroom soup, sage.

Onions: Beef consommé, dry mustard, celery seed.

Parsnips: Cheese sauce, marjoram, bay leaf, parsley, paprika, caraway.

Peas: Parsley, lettuce, marjoram, onion rings, rosemary, tarragon, mint.

Potatoes, Sweet: Nutmeg, brown sugar, apples, fennel, mace.

Potatoes, White: Cheese sauce, onion (young, green), chives, parsley, basil, dill, paprika.

Spinach: Bacon, marjoram, onion, cheese, hard-cooked eggs, soy, thyme.

Squash: Nutmeg, cinnamon, cheese, tomatoes, bacon, marjoram.

Tomatoes: Basil, onion, garlic, chili powder, cheese, celery, chives, parsley.

Turnips: Parsley, chives, sesame seeds, caraway seeds, paprika.

Zucchini: Onions, tomatoes, curry, marjoram, cheese, mushroom sauce.

■ GOLDEN BROCCOLI

1 pkg. frozen or 1 lb. fresh broccoli	1 tbsp. lemon juice
¼ c. water	1 can cream-of-chicken soup
½ tsp. salt	¼ c. grated Swiss or Cheddar cheese
¼ tsp. pepper	

Cook fresh broccoli in ¼ c. water; follow package directions for frozen. Cook until just tender, drain, season and place on pie plate. Sprinkle with lemon juice. Cover with soup, top with cheese and place in preheated broiler, 5 inches from low flame. Broil about 10 minutes. If preferred, bake 15-20 minutes in 400° oven. Serves 4.

■ STUFFED PEPPERS

Slice off tops of green peppers or cut in half lengthwise and remove inside seeds and fibers. Drop into boiling water, remove from fire and let stand 10-15 minutes; then drain. Prepare 1 pepper for each person. Any of the following stuffing mixtures may be used:

1. 1 c. left-over cooked beef, lamb, ham or veal mixed with 1¼ c. moistened bread crumbs, 1 tbsp. minced onion, salt and pepper to taste.
2. 1 c. cooked chopped beef mixed with ½ c. cooked tomatoes, or 2 fresh tomatoes peeled and cut up; 1 c. cooked brown rice and 1 tbsp. minced onion. Salt and pepper to taste. May add ⅔ c. sunflower seeds.
3. 1 c. cooked lima beans, chopped green beans, chopped celery, corn, diced carrots, or diced green squash mixed with ½ c. moistened bread crumbs and ½ c. grated Cheddar cheese, a little onion and salt and pepper to taste.
4. 1 c. chopped cooked sweetbreads mixed with ½ c. moistened bread crumbs, ½ c. mushrooms, stems and pieces, 1 tbsp. chopped parsley, 1 beaten egg, salt, pepper and paprika.

Fill peppers with any of these mixtures, cover with buttered crumbs or grated cheese. Set them in a shallow pan ½ filled with water. Bake in moderate oven 350°-375°, 30 minutes.

■ RAW SAUERKRAUT

Shred 3-lb. head cabbage into gallon crock. Add 1 tsp. salt to every 1-inch layer. Repeat layers until crock is filled. Add 1 stale slice of rye bread and cover with plate. Stir cabbage each day. 1 tbsp. caraway seeds may be added; onions if desired. At the end of 3-4 days, foam or bubbling will stop. Remove to cool place or refrigerate. May be stored in covered jars.

■   **SAVORY CARROTS**

Try grating crisp, fresh carrots and cooking 5 minutes in very little water, then serving with any of the following: sautéed onions or green pepper strips; chopped chives and butter; sour cream; tomato sauce; butter and a sprinkle of nutmeg; yogurt; mushroom or green pea soup.

■   **CARROTS AND PARSNIPS**

Cook sliced carrots and parsnips in separate kettles. Combine and top with grated American or Jack cheese and salt and pepper to taste. This combination may also be sautéed in butter and served with chili sauce.

■   **SUCCOTASH**

Lima beans are best seasoned with butter, salt and pepper. Succotash is a nice combination of fresh steamed lima beans and fresh corn cut and scraped from the cob. Simmer together about 5 minutes. Season with butter (or oil), salt and pepper.

■   **MINTED PEAS**

Peas should be cooked in a very small amount of water over a low fire until just tender. Season with butter, salt and pepper and snipped fresh mint. May combine with chopped cooked carrots.

■   **NEW POTATOES**

New potatoes are best cooked scrubbed, with or without a narrow strip cut off around the middle, in a small amount of water, covered, 30-40 minutes. Delicious when cooked with 6-8 sprigs fresh mint. Season with butter, chopped parsley, salt and pepper, or cream sauce, cheese sauce, yogurt, and chopped chives.

■   **SCALLOPED POTATOES**

¼ c. butter	1 qt. cooked, sliced potatoes
1 c. milk	2 tbsp. chopped chives and
¾ c. Cheddar or Tillamook cheese	parsley
¼ c. unbleached or whole-wheat pastry flour	

Pour cream sauce made of butter, flour and milk, over cooked sliced potatoes in greased casserole. Raw potatoes may be used, but slice thin. Cover with cheese, chives and parsley. Bake 50 minutes at 350°. Uncover last 30 minutes. Add more milk if potatoes become dry. Serves 4.

■ STUFFED WHITE POTATOES

2 large baked potatoes, cut in half lengthwise; scoop out pulp. Mash and mix with:

½ c. shredded yellow cheese	4 tbsp. top milk
½ tsp. salt	

Pack mixture into skins lightly. Sprinkle with paprika and put in hot oven at 400°, 10 minutes.

■ GLAZED SWEET POTATOES OR YAMS

Bake or steam unpeeled sweet potatoes or yams until nearly tender; cut in half or slice lengthwise; place in flat baking dish; dot with butter or sprinkle with ¼ c. oil. Cover lightly with brown or raw sugar, or honey. Bake until glazed and tender in moderate oven, 375°.

■ SWEET POTATOES IN ORANGE CUPS

Cook sweet potatoes or yams in their jackets until tender in boiling salted water. Peel, mash; add 1 tbsp. butter for each potato, ¼ tsp. salt and 1 tbsp. top milk. Beat well.

Cut off top of orange, scrape out center and save for fruit cup or salad. Cut edges in saw tooth manner. Fill orange cups lightly, place chopped pecans on top. Place in 400° oven to heat through and brown.

■ STUFFED ZUCCHINI

¾ c. whole-wheat bread crumbs	¼ tsp. oregano
2 tbsp. Parmesan cheese	¼ tsp. sage
⅛ tsp. rosemary	Dash of paprika
⅛ tsp. marjoram	¾ c. scooped out zucchini

Scoop out centers of partly-cooked zucchini to make ¾ c. Stuff zucchini shells with the above mixture. Bake 10 minutes in 350° oven. Sprinkle with grated Parmesan cheese. This will fill 4 medium-sized shells.

■ **ZUCCHINI CREOLE**

Wash and cut 4 zucchini in lengthwise pieces. Place in saucepan with 1 c. canned tomatoes, ¼ c. chopped onions, small clove of garlic, minced; salt and pepper to taste. Add 2 tbsp. butter or oil. Cover tightly, bring to a boil, turn fire to simmer, cook 15 minutes. Serve with grated cheddar cheese. Serves 4.

■ **BANANA SQUASH**

Cut in serving-size pieces. Place bottom side up in shallow baking pan. Fill pan with water to come up about ¼ way on squash. Add 1 tsp. salt; bake about 40 minutes at 350°. Turn squash over, slash squash several times so seasoning will not run off. Add one of the following and bake until brown:

1. Dot with butter and pour a little honey on each piece. Sprinkle sliced walnuts over top.
2. Dot pieces with butter, add dash of nutmeg and small amount of brown sugar. Bake 20 minutes more.

■ **YELLOW CROOKED-NECK SQUASH**

Wash squash, cut off stem end. Slice in ½-inch pieces. Put on to cook with 2 tbsp. water, butter, salt, and a dash of nutmeg. Cover tightly; when steam begins to escape, turn fire to lowest point and simmer 5 minutes. Add chopped parsley and serve.

■ **MASHED CROOKED-NECK SQUASH**

Cut off stem and flower ends. Cut squash in small pieces. Cook in boiling, salted water, until tender and water has cooked away. Mash with fork and season with butter and nutmeg. Cream may be added if desired.

■ **STRING BEANS WITH BACON AND HERBS**

Cook 4 slices bacon slowly until crisp. Remove and break in bits. Add 1 small onion thinly sliced to bacon drippings, sauté gently 5 minutes. Add 2½ c. cooked string beans, 2 tbsp. chopped parsley, 1 tbsp. chopped fresh oregano or ⅛ tsp. dry oregano, a pinch of rosemary, salt and pepper to taste. Simmer 5 minutes and sprinkle bacon bits over top before serving. Serves 4.

■ **MOLASSES ACORN SQUASH**

Halve 1 large acorn squash; remove seeds. Place in baking pan. Fill each half with 2 tbsp. unsulphured molasses, 1 tbsp. butter or oil, and a dash of salt and cinnamon. Cover bottom of baking pan with a small amount of hot water; bake in a moderate oven, 350°, 1 hour, or until tender. Serves 2.

■ **TENDER SOYBEANS**

Add 1 c. dried soybeans to 3 c. boiling water and soak overnight.

Add: Small ham hock or 1 tbsp. oil; then 1 small diced onion, ¼ c. diced celery, 2 bay leaves.

If necessary add water to cover. Bring to a boil, lower heat and simmer 3 hours or until tender. Salt to taste during last few minutes of cooking. Serves 4.

■ **BAKED SOYBEANS**

Follow above recipe, only add ¼ c. molasses, 1 tbsp. dry mustard and 2 tbsp. brown sugar to the beans after they have cooked 2 hours. Pour into bean pot or baking pan. Cover and bake 2 hours at 325°.

■ **BAKED TOMATOES ESPAGNOLE**

Cut thin slice from stem ends of 4 firm, large tomatoes. Scoop out pulp, being careful not to break shells. Fill with Spanish Filling.

Spanish Filling: Melt 1 tbsp. butter or heat 1 tbsp. oil in frying pan; brown ½ lb. ground beef; add 1 c. cooked rice, 1 small onion, chopped; ¼ c. catsup, 1 tsp. chili powder, 1 tsp. salt, ¼ tsp. garlic powder. Mince scooped-out tomato pulp and add to mixture. Stuff tomatoes, place in shallow baking pan and bake at 375°, 20 minutes. Serves 4.

Variations—For *Mexican Filling,* mix scooped-out tomato pulp with 1 c. canned or fresh-cooked chili con carne and beans.

For *New England Filling,* mix scooped-out tomato pulp with ¼ c. chopped onion and 1 c. corned beef hash.

For *Cheese Filling,* mix scooped-out tomato pulp with 1 c. browned whole-wheat bread crumbs, ½ c. grated Cheddar cheese and ¼ c. chopped parsley.

For *Garden Filling,* mix scooped-out tomato pulp with ¼ c. chopped green onion, 1 c. canned or cooked fresh corn, 1 tbsp. chopped olives or crumbled crisp bacon.

■ **GREEN BEANS ALMONDINE**

Cook 1 pkg. frozen French-cut green beans until not quite tender, or substitute 1 lb. French-cut fresh green beans. Drain; sauté gently in butter. Season with salt and pepper and top with ¼ c. slivered almonds. Serves 4.

■ **SHREDDED VEGETABLES**

Shredded vegetables are quick, easy and nutritious. They may come to table with only salt, pepper and butter as seasonings, or with an extra touch of chopped fresh herbs, a sprinkle of oregano, basil, nutmeg and the like. Some vegetables good for shredding are:

1. Grate scrubbed carrots and cook in just enough water to come up about ½-inch in pan. Cook 5-10 minutes, depending on tenderness of carrots.
2. Combine grated celery hearts and summer squash. Cook as for carrots.
3. Combine young beets and turnips, peeled and grated. Cook as for carrots.

■ **CREAMED VEGETABLES ON TOAST SHELLS**

2 c. cooked mixed vegetables   1 c. medium white sauce

Add vegetables to white sauce. Heat over very low flame. Serve in toast shells. Use 6 slices of bread; remove crusts; turn oven to 375°. Brush 1 side of each slice with melted butter. Place bread slices, buttered side down, in muffin pans and press to form a patty shell. Bake 20 minutes or until insides are a delicate brown. Fill with vegetable mixture. Serves 6.

■ **BAKED EGGPLANT WITH CHEESE**

2 tbsp. butter   **1 large eggplant, peeled,**
2 tbsp. whole-wheat flour   **sliced ½-inch thick**
1 c. milk
½ c. sharp Cheddar cheese,
grated

Make white sauce of butter, flour and milk; stir until smooth. Add cheese, stir until melted. Put slices of egg plant in shallow pan, cover with cheese sauce. Bake in moderate oven about 45 minutes. Liquid will be absorbed, leaving slices crisp and brown. Serves 6.

■ SWEET AND SOUR BEETS

2 c. canned or cooked beets	2 tbsp. cider vinegar
1 tbsp. cornstarch	4 tbsp. honey
¼ tsp. salt	1 tbsp. butter or oil
2 tbsp. juice from beets or water	

Slice beets thinly, or dice, as desired. Blend cornstarch and salt with beet juice or water. Stir in vinegar, honey, butter or oil. Cook over low heat until mixture thickens. Pour over beets and let stand several hours for the sauce to penetrate. Heat before serving. Serves 4-6.

■ SCALLOPED TOMATOES

4 large fresh tomatoes or 1 qt. cooked tomatoes	½ c. grated Parmesan cheese
1 tsp. salt	1 c. whole-wheat crumbs
½ tsp. pepper	2 tbsp. butter

Peel and slice fresh tomatoes; if canned are used, drain off juice. Place layer of tomato in greased baking dish; season with salt and pepper, then add layer of cheese and crumbs and dot with butter. Repeat until all ingredients are used. Bake at 350°, 30 minutes. Serves 6.

■ BROILED TOMATOES PARMESAN

6 large green or red tomatoes	¼ tsp. thyme
1 c. whole-wheat bread crumbs	½ tsp. salt
3 tbsp. chopped chives	¼ tsp. black pepper
¼ tsp. basil	2 tbsp. oil or butter
	½ c. grated Parmesan cheese

Cut tomatoes in ¾-inch slices, peeled or unpeeled. Blend crumbs with chives, basil, thyme, salt and pepper. Dip tomato slices in crumb mixture, coating well. Pour oil in shallow baking pan and add tomato slices. Place in preheated broiler, 4-inches from flame for green tomatoes, cooking 3 minutes on each side; 2-inches from flame for red tomatoes, cooking 2 minutes on each side. When nearly done, sprinkle cheese over slices and broil a very short time, to melt cheese. Serves 6.

■ **FRIED TOMATOES**

4 large green or very firm red tomatoes	1 c. whole-wheat crumbs or wheat germ
1 egg, beaten	Salt and pepper to taste
1 tbsp. water	

Slice tomatoes about ¾-inch thick. Combine beaten egg and water. Dip tomato slices first in egg, then in crumbs. Fry slowly in butter or oil, turning carefully to brown on both sides. Season with salt and pepper. Serve with topping of crumbled crisp bacon or minced parsley, if desired. Serves 4.

■ **CROUTON TOMATOES**

2 c. canned or cooked fresh tomatoes	¼ tsp. basil
2 tbsp. minced parsley	½ tsp. garlic salt or powder
1 tsp. salt	4 tbsp. oil
½ tsp. black pepper	1 c. soft whole-wheat bread cubes

Combine tomatoes with seasonings and heat over low flame. Brown bread crumbs in oil until crisp and golden. Serve on hot, cooked tomatoes.

■ **MUSHROOMS**

Unless you are a mushroom expert, don't try to pick them in the wild. Excellent fresh and canned ones are readily available.

Tender young mushrooms need only to be washed lightly. To keep them from darkening, drop caps, slices or pieces into cool water to which you have added 1 tbsp. cider vinegar. Older mushrooms must have stems removed and caps peeled. Discarded peelings and cut-off stems may be simmered with a little salt to make an excellent stock for adding to soups, sauces and gravies.

1 lb. fresh mushrooms will serve 6, as a separate course. Mushrooms toughen with overcooking. Fresh ones need only 5-6 minutes, while canned ones need only heating.

■ **MUSHROOM BROIL**

Brush mushroom caps with oil; place cap side down on broiling rack and place a bit of butter in center of each. Sprinkle with salt and pepper. Place in preheated broiler, about 4 inches below flame. Broil until golden brown, about 4-5 minutes for young mushrooms, 8-10 minutes for larger old ones. Excellent with mixed grill of broiled tomatoes, lamb chop or chopped meat.

■ SAUTÉED MUSHROOMS

Both mushroom caps and sliced stems may be used, if desired. Allow 2 tbsp. butter for each pound mushrooms. Sauté over low heat, turning frequently, 6-10 minutes. Top with minced parsley.

The versatile mushroom compliments almost every vegetable and nearly all the varieties of meats and poultry. You can scarcely think of a casserole dish that won't be more glamorous with the addition of a few mushrooms, canned or fresh. They're elegant for Sunday breakfast, too, when sautéed and served with scrambled eggs, or added to cream sauce and poured over hot toast.

■ STUFFED MUSHROOMS

Wash 10-12 large mushrooms, peel if necessary. Remove stems and drop caps into water-vinegar mixture. Chop stems finely and mix with 1 tsp. finely chopped onion and 1 tsp. parsley. Cook a few minutes in 2 tbsp. butter or oil. Stir in 2 tbsp. fine bread crumbs, ¼ tsp. salt, 1 egg yolk and cream to moisten. Fill caps, rounding well over the top. Sprinkle grated Parmesan cheese over the top. Place in a shallow baking pan, pour top milk or tomato sauce around caps and bake 15 minutes in hot oven, at 425°.

■ BAKED EGGPLANT WITH BROWN RICE

1 eggplant, peeled and sliced	1 green pepper, sliced (optional)
1 c. brown rice, cooked	
1 onion, sliced	

Prepare rice by bringing to a boil in 2½ c. water; then let stand with lid on tight for 40 minutes. Oil baking dish. Make layers of onion, eggplant, peppers, and rice. Bake 30 minutes. Serves 4-6.

■ SPINACH AND MUSHROOMS

12 medium mushrooms, raw	1 tbsp. arrowroot
3 tbsp. soy sauce	1 tbsp. water
1 c. water	2 bunches fresh young spinach

Separate mushroom stems and caps, using both if mushrooms are young and tender. Sauté in soy sauce, add water and simmer until tender. Blend arrowroot and water and thicken mushroom mixture. Wash spinach, shake off water and cook over low heat, turning several times to avoid scorching, until spinach is hot to your touch. Pour mushroom mixture over spinach and serve at once. Serves 4.

■ **BAKED MUSHROOMS**

Prepare as for broiling; place in shallow baking dish and pour over bouillon to come up about ¼ inch in pan. Bake at 425°, about 8 minutes. Light cream may be substituted for bouillon; bake in slower oven, 325°

■ **BUFFET VEGETABLE PLATTER**

1. To serve 4:—Rub 4 *baking potatoes* with oil and salt and bake as usual. When done, cut across the top of each. Squeeze to pop open, insert piece of butter and sprinkle with paprika. Serve with a bowl of thick sour cream, bowl of thinly sliced green onions and tops, and shakers of salt and pepper.
2. *Asparagus* with lemon almond butter. Cook 1 bunch asparagus in boiling salted water, until just crisp-tender. Drain and arrange on serving plate. Pour over sauce made by combining ½ c. melted butter, 2 tsp. lemon juice, and ¼ c. slivered blanched almonds.
3. *Tomatoes* are the most colorful part of this platter. Cut 4 firm ripe tomatoes into thick slices. Place in shallow baking pan, sprinkle with salt, pepper. Dot with butter and top each slice with mushroom cap. Put under broiler until just tender.

Sprouts

Why Use Sprouts? Sprouted seeds, grains, beans and peas of various kinds have long served mankind as a valuable food, because of the important nutrients they contribute to the diet. Explorers, soldiers, travellers, and others who had to live where it was not possible to obtain fresh vegetables and fruits, carried seeds with them to sprout as needed. The Chinese and some Europeans have used sprouts and have devised many ways of preparing them. To-day the problem of obtaining fruits and vegetables produced without the use of poisonous sprays, has increased the demand for good seeds and practical ways of sprouting and serving them.

What Sprouts Contribute: The value of the sprout is dependent upon the kind of seed and the soil in which it is grown. Since each seed is the plant's storehouse of minerals, vitamins, vitamin precursors, enzymes and protein for the growth of the next generation, these important factors are available in complete and organic form. Sprouting activates the vitamin precursors so that, in addition to the vitamins already present (B and E), vitamin C and some A are included.

Seeds to Use: Seeds for sprouting should be viable (capable of sprouting); free from chemical treatment (frequently true of crop seed); high in protein content, and not processed to preserve.

Garden seeds in the average grocery store are usually not intended for human consumption before planting.

The following seeds are particularly recommended for the home because they are easily sprouted, have a delightful flavor and do not need to be cooked. Here is a list:

1. *Alfalfa*—particularly good for introduction to sprouts since everyone enjoys them.
2. *Mung Beans*—the familiar bean sprouts used in many Chinese dishes.
3. *Lentils*—remembered for their use in soups, have a surprisingly sweet flavor.
4. *Wheat Sprouts*—look quite different from other sprouts, as they are fine and fuzzy.
5. *Rye*—makes an interesting change to provide variety.
6. *Sunflower Seed*—(hulled) are exceptionally tasty, but should be sprouted only a short time compared to other seeds.
7. *Soybeans*—can be used, but are not recommended because of flavor unless cooked; can be used as vegetable by cooking in heavy pan very few minutes, low heat.
8. *Radish, Parsley, Mustard*—and many others may be sprouted to add zest to salads.

■ **DIRECTIONS FOR SPROUTING**

Pick out broken seeds, as these do not sprout and may ferment.

Cover seeds with water and soak small seed as alfalfa, radish, etc., 1-3 hours.

Grains should be soaked 3 hours or more; beans, 8 hours or more because of hard shells. After soaking, drain off water and rinse.

Air and moisture are important in sprouting and the customary room temperature is adequate.

Cold temperature will slow sprouting and heat may dry out the seeds and cause fermentation.

Place soaked seeds in a glass jar, or glass pie plate. Cover and dampen frequently.

Small seeds will sprout in 3-5 days; sunflower seeds in 36 hours; grains 3-4 days; beans 3-6 days. Refrigerate sprouts as soon as they have reached desired growth in covered glass jars.

Serve sprouts raw in any tossed green salad. Also, they make delicious sandwich fillers. Spread whole-grain bread with butter, salad dressing, nut butter or cream cheese. Cover with a thick layer of alfalfa sprouts.

Wheat and rye sprouts may be ground and served with cream as a cereal (very sweet, no sugar needed).

Sprouts may be chopped fine and used in bread dough.

Use bean sprouts in your favorite Chinese recipes, or add to vegetables or stews a few minutes before removing from the fire.

Cooked sprouts must be crisp, so be careful not to overcook.

CHAPTER 18

Foods for Special Occasions

WHAT shall we have to eat?

I've been asked that question literally hundreds of times by women who want their special-occasion food to be exciting as well as nutritious. For far too many years the menus for their club meetings, P.T.A. sessions, Scout get-to-gethers and sundry other parties have been loaded with processed cheese, fizzy drinks, refined sugar and bleached white flour.

My advice is always to "take it easy" . . . plan everything with tact and care so that those who are new to nutrition will not be scared off. Set the stage psychologically for the new taste sensations you are offering; play up the eye-appeal of your buffet or tea table with imaginative color combinations and attractive appointments.

Location of the serving table is important. If you have to contend with a school cafeteria for a P.T.A. meeting, try to borrow a few bright screens to close off drinking fountains or other unattractive areas. Keep the serving table well away from the other tables in the room, yet close enough to the kitchen to provide easy access. The food table may be set off dramatically by placing card tables on either end or in back, and arranging big bouquets of flowers or leafy branches on them. This has the effect of a stage set and takes away the onus of an otherwise bare, institutional room.

Your table cloth and decorations will vary with the nature of the function, but do give a lot of thought to making it attractive. For a tea, P.T.A. or club meeting borrow someone's lace or pretty cloth, if the organization does not own one. In order to best display the food on the table make an arrangement, not too high, of any of the following: flowers, greens, candlesticks, driftwood or dried weeds and grasses.

Flowers are always lovely and may be arranged in glass pie plates or baking dishes if proper flower vases are not available. There are frogs and florist's clay to use as holders. Fruits and vegetables are colorful, too. In the fall for instance, a paper horn-of-plenty spilling over with red apples, grapes, leaves, pumpkins and nuts makes a stunning centerpiece.

A charming arrangement which can be used all year round is a piece of driftwood or other dried, weathered branch to which cut-outs or other articles have been tied. For example, at Christmas, plastic stars can be hung over the branches; in January, cotton balls dipped in "glitter" to resemble snow balls; in February, cut-out hearts of varying sizes; in March, paper shamrocks, hats or pipes; in April, if the Easter month, you might have decorated eggs. To prepare the eggs pierce one end of the egg with a hat pin and make a hole the size of a small dot at the other end; then blow the egg out into a bowl. Dry and paint with faces; make gay Easter bonnets for their "heads" and then hang on the tree with thread.

Green or dried weeds and grasses make exotic arrangements. There are plenty of flowering weeds or graceful wild grasses available to make bouquets that will bring "oh's" and "ah's" from the guests. Sprays of fruit tree blossoms or ferns are also attractive.

Candles may be used in the right kind of holders, appropriate for the occasion, as glass or silver for a tea; pottery, copper or wood for a barbecue or informal meal.

If paper napkins are used, select them to match the color scheme, and arrange attractively on the table.

The individual tables in the room should also have some small arrangement to carry out the theme of the occasion.

The next hurdle is the taste and appearance of the food itself. You have set the stage; now serve delicious, nutritious food.

If the meeting time is scheduled so that dessert is to be served, any of the following might be used. You will find recipes in this book for all of them.

Suggested Desserts:

1. Gingerbread and whipped cream or whipped skim milk or cottage cheese.
2. Cheese cake.
3. Pumpkin pie, crust or crustless, with sharp Cheddar cheese.
4. Cream puffs with fresh fruit filling.
5. Baked apples, date crystal stuffed, and cream.
6. Frozen fruit salad, cheese straws.
7. Lemon sherbet and carob brownies.
8. Fresh fruit, yogurt dressing, nut crackers.
9. Gelatin desserts with yogurt topping.
10. Assorted salted nuts and dried fruits.
11. Chilled custard, whole-wheat sunshine cake.
12. Whole-wheat fruit cake.
13. Date spice cake.
14. Pineapple upside-down cake.
15. Persimmon pudding.
16. Meringue shells filled with fresh or cooked fruit, topped with yogurt or whipped cream.
17. Fruit plate and cream or cottage cheese.
18. Lemon cream pie, coconut crust.
19. Strawberry or other fruit shortcake.

For a luncheon meeting in the spring or summer, I suggest a "Salad Bar" with hot rolls and coffee, tea, or herb tea. If it is a fall or winter meeting, a casserole should be the center of interest with salad, rolls and a light dessert.

There should be a wide selection of salads at a "Salad Bar" luncheon, some quite hearty.

Suggested Salads:

1. Shrimp.
2. Tuna.
3. Salmon.
4. Crab.
5. Lobster.
6. Chicken.
7. Pressed veal.
8. Stuffed egg.
9. Cottage cheese mixtures.
10. Cream cheese and fruit or vegetables.
11. Gelatin, fruit or vegetable salads.
12. Fresh fruit salad.
13. Fresh vegetable salad.
14. Tossed green salad.
15. Caesar salad.
16. Finger salads.
17. Waldorf salad.
18. Potato salad.

Suggested Casserole Dishes:

1. Tuna-noodle potato chip casserole.
2. Wild rice and meat casserole.
3. Tomato-cheese-meat combination.
4. Spaghetti and meat balls.
5. Tamale pie in casserole.
6. Pork sausage-rice casserole.
7. Parsley-rice casserole.
8. Eggplant caserole.
9. Brown rice and meat casserole.
10. Beef and mushroom casserole.
11. Scalloped oysters.
12. Crab fondue.
13. Cabbage and hamburger with yogurt.
14. Macaroni custard.

Other Suggestions for Special-Occasion Foods:

1. Assorted sweet, quick-bread sandwiches.
2. Fancy sandwiches open, brick or rolled.
3. Miniature cream puffs, with fruit-cream filling.
4. Cookies or carob brownies.
5. Lemon-filled cupcakes.
6. Cranberry-raisin tarts.
7. Iced fresh pineapple or unsweetened pineapple chunks, and natural coconut. Orange and dates may be added, also yogurt-honey dressing.
8. Apple crumble, with honey-oats topping and whipped cream.
9. Delicious apple dessert.
10. Sunshine whole-wheat cake, mocha filling.

Beverages may be tea, coffee, herb tea or fruit punch.

For evening club or P.T.A. meetings, when the men are present and you wish to serve a little something afterward, any of these foods are suitable:

1. Gingerbread, cream cheese roses.
2. Cheese cake.
3. Pumpkin pie.
4. Fish, cheese or egg open sandwiches.
5. Apple cobbler and cheese.
6. Individual chicken pies.
7. Fresh fruit on nut tasties, cream cheese or yogurt.
8. Yogurt-pineapple sherbet, carob brownies.
9. Lemon pie.
10. Cantaloupe and ice cream, or sliced cantaloupe filled with fruit and cream cheese balls.

Coffee is preferred by most men, but hot herb tea is delicious. For a change, serve spiced apple cider, hot or cold.

What to serve at *children's parties* that is nutritionally good and yet make the occasion festive?

In my experience as a homemaking teacher in charge of parties for children of all ages, I find the idea that they all want candy, rich cake and sugar-loaded ice cream, is principally in the minds of the adults. Little children do not demand these rich foods, while adolescents often find them too sweet, and most teen-agers are thinking of their figures and complexions.

The traditional birthday cake need not be relegated to the past, but it *can* be made of ingredients that are acceptable and delicious.

Let's face it: your children will be attending parties at other homes and often eating food we do not approve of. Therefore it is a challenge to you to serve such delicious "good" food that the guests will ask their mothers to have that kind of food at their homes. It takes gentle guidance to form a new pattern of eating, but I see evidence on every hand that it *is* taking place.

Children's parties for the 3-6-year-old group should include fruit juice, such as a combination of lemon, orange and pineapple juice, and whole-grain flour cookies. If the cookies are the rolled kind and animal cutters are used, the small guests will have fun talking about the "animals" they are eating and not be so interested in the fact that the cookies are also good for them! Try cookie lollipops—large cookies baked on a skewer with currant faces. Frozen fruit juice lollipops are popular, too. We have found that no other food was necessary in order to insure a happy time for everyone.

The 7-12 age group likes doughnuts, cookies, red apples, popcorn, peanuts or cupcakes with their party drinks. They have graduated to the more complex punch. This punch should have a greater variety of fruit juices, with a garnish of sliced banana, cherries, or strawberries. They also like apple cider and milk shakes.

■ **SPECIAL PARTY CAKE**

When making the Basic Whole-Wheat Bread recipe (in Bread section), try using half the dough for a "bread cake." Add to it ¼ tsp. parsley flakes, ½ tsp. instant minced onion flakes, ¼ tsp. oregano.

Divide and place in 2 round 8-inch greased cake pans. Let rise as for bread. Bake 30 minutes at 375°. Remove from pans, cool and split each loaf into 2 layers.

Spread with egg salad filling or chicken and avocado filling or any of your family favorites. "Frost" top and sides with cream cheese. Decorate, if desired, with orange gelatin cut into stars or animals.

Young-girl organizations like to serve easy-to-eat, rather hearty foods. They are at the growing period when their bodies demand a lot to eat. Some suggestions are:

1. Molasses cookies, blender milk shakes.
2. Waffles, honey-butter or maple syrup spread.
3. Grilled cheese sandwiches, lemonade.
4. Apple and banana witches, milk.
5. Doughnuts and cider.
6. Carob or chocolate milk shakes.
7. Oatmeal cookies, lemon or banana nog.
8. Watermelon.
9. Hamburgers or "tasti" pie burgers.
10. Hot dogs, pears and apples.
11. Baby Pizzas.

As boys this age are growing fast too, they have a terrific need for protein. Young-boy organizations also like hearty food at their meetings and they love "cooking out" as often as possible. Some suggestions are:

1. Chili bean, brown bread sandwich; milk.
2. Cheese stuffed "burgers," lemonade.
3. Grilled hot dogs, whole-wheat-buns, milk.
4. Doughnuts, popcorn, cider.
5. Watermelon.
6. Ham sandwiches, milk shakes.
7. Meat, cheese stacks; cookies or apples.
8. Fresh coconut to crack and eat, bananas filled with peanut butter.

The problem of what to serve at teen-age parties is often a puzzling one. The food must not be too radically different from the traditional "poor" food usually consumed or the children will complain that it looks "queer." Teen-agers are not yet philosophical enough to want to be different from the crowd, so you will have to invent clever disguises for the delicious nutritional food which children actually love if it is presented acceptably.

Again, decorations can set the stage and they should be quite elaborate for a school party. Intriguing party themes will determine the decor—South Sea Islands, Gay 90's, Come As You Are, Western, Masquerade, Sock Hop, Starlight Roof, etc.

The most important food at any party is the liquid refreshment. There must be plenty of it, constantly available. A colorful "juice bar" may be set up with small glasses or paper cups; or you may rent the customary soda fountain metal cups with paper fills. A student to serve behind the bar is more acceptable than an adult. If the punch is on a table, then trays of clean cups should be close by so that the young people can help themselves.

At a very informal dance, potato chips, corn chips, popcorn or cheese crackers are often served. Cookies or doughnuts, and plenty of them, are popular at any party. Dips are another favorite, with plenty of raw vegetable pieces; also pizzas.

When the party is a home one, the food picture changes. There is the same demand for plenty to drink, but you may include any of the following: milk shakes, malts, lemon nog, fruit punch, or cider. Hamburgers and hot dogs are preferred, with potato chips, pickles, relishes, salted nuts and cookies. Apples and bananas are popular to munch on.

Teen-agers like to barbecue their own hamburgers or hot dogs. They also like to have the "fixins" put out for them to make their own "Dagwood" sandwiches. There should be slices of freshly baked whole-grain bread, stacks of cold meats, slices of Cheddar or Swiss cheese, sliced tomatoes, onions, pickles, lettuce and lots of relishes, catsup, prepared mustard, chili sauce, chili beans, and green pepper rings. Peanut butter, cream cheese spread, chopped olives and deviled eggs may be added to this glorious array!

Teen-agers actually prefer to eat their fill of the above foods instead of a lot of sweets. However, there is always some demand for wholesome cookies, and bowls of fresh fruit should be available.

All children have need of snacks to meet the demands of their rapidly growing bodies. If snacks are nutritionally acceptable, you need not worry if the children do not want a large evening meal. They are better off with a good snack late in the afternoon, and then a light supper. In the morning, parents as well as children will then be more ready for the large breakfast we all should eat.

The mid-morning snack for small children should be milk and any of the following: whole-wheat crackers, orange juice, apple, banana, or other fruit in season, and dried fruits. Frozen fruit-juice lollipops are always a success.

In most junior high schools the child does not have any morning time for snacks, so it is imperative to give them a good breakfast in order to have the mental and physical energy to carry them through to lunch.

The list of snacks that follows is principally for after-school eating, but may also be put in lunch boxes, served at supper time, or whenever that little "extra" food is needed.

Snack Suggestions:

1. Milk and cheese foods—
    Milk, with orange-juice lollipops.
    Blender milk shakes.
    Cheese chunks.
    Carob malts.
    Date crystal shakes.
    Banana frosties.
2. Sandwiches and crackers—
    Banana and peanut butter.
    Apple slices and minced ham.
    Apple slices with Cheddar cheese.
    Leftover meat and cheese.
    Cold cuts and cheese.
    Peanut butter and raisins.
    Cold waffles with honey-butter spread.
    Grilled cheese sandwich.
    Cheese straws or crackers.
    Whole-wheat crackers (salted).
    Chili bean sandwiches.
3. Fruits and juices—
    Dried fruits:

Prunes.	Raisins.
Peaches.	Currants.
Figs.	Dates.
Apricots.	

    Fresh fruit or berries in season.
    Fruit juices.
    Fruit-nut candy.
4. Nuts and seeds—
    Peanuts, salted or in shells.
    Soy nuts.
    Parched corn.
    Pine nuts.
    Sunflower seeds, shelled or toasted.
    Coconut in shell.
    Toasted coconut chips.
    Popcorn, plain or with variations.
    Assorted nuts.

5. Miscellaneous—
    Nutritional food wafers.
    Molasses cookies.
    Celery stuffed with chive
       cheese, cream cheese
       or cottage cheese.
    Dill pickle.
    Hard-cooked eggs.
    Stuffed eggs.
    Watermelon or other
       melon.
    Dried beef and Cheddar
       cheese roll-ups.
    Left-over hotcakes.
    Gingerbread or ginger
       cookies.
    Whole-grain cookies.
    Home-stuffed olives.
    Pumpkin seed chews.
    Seed and nut mix.

Some other Fun-ideas:—

1. *Frozen Bananas:* Peel bananas and place in glass jar, or stand in freezer container. Do not allow to remain at room temperature even a few minutes. Bananas become sweeter after freezing. They freeze with a smooth creamy texture.

2. *Banana Lollipops:* Peel ripe bananas, cut off small piece of one end and spear with flat wooden sticks, place in deep freeze at once.

Peanut Butter-Banana Suckers:—4 frozen bananas; ¼ c. nutty non-homogenized peanut butter, ¼ c. powdered milk, 1 tbsp. honey, ⅓ c. top milk or canned milk, ⅓ c. chopped peanuts. Place all ingredients except chopped peanuts and bananas in blender, or deep bowl. Blend 1 minute, or beat with egg beater until smooth. Roll the frozen bananas in the peanut butter mixture. You may need to spread it on the bananas. Sprinkle with chopped peanuts. Immediately return to deep freeze. Frozen bananas may also be dipped in orange juice and then rolled in ground nuts, or nut meal.

Carob Banana Suckers: ¼ c. carob powder, ¼ c. powdered milk, ⅓ c. canned milk (or top milk), 1 tbsp. honey, ½ tsp. vanilla. Place all ingredients in blender and blend about 30 seconds. More milk may be needed if mixture is too stiff. This carob mixture may also be beaten in a very deep bowl with an egg beater. Spoon carob mixture over frozen bananas; sprinkle finely chopped walnuts over bananas and return to deep freeze. They may be rolled in parchment or cellophane papers; or stand in freezer container. Covers 3 good-sized bananas.

Pineapple Suckers: Cut fresh pineapple into spears or use canned pineapple spears. Spear with flat or round wooden sticks. Roll in finely crushed macaroon coconut. Place in deep freeze. They may be rolled in parchment or cellophane paper; or stand up in freezer containers.

Persimmon Suckers: Place soft persimmons in small unwaxed paper cups, or muffin pan molds. Spear with flat wooden sticks. Place in deep freeze. After they are frozen, place pans in warm water, only long enough to be able to remove; then return to freezer. They can easily be stacked in a freezer container after being frozen.

■ SWEDISH SMORGASBORD

The Swedish smorgasbord takes the place of our buffet lunch or supper. It is especially adaptable for a large crowd, when the exact number to come is not known.

A smorgasbord table should be very colorful, with a large variety of foods and special attention given to garnishes. These garnishes may be combinations of hard-cooked eggs, olives, pickles, parsley, water cress, pimiento, tomatoes, turnips, beets, radishes, celery, green peppers, carrots, cucumbers, oranges, lemons, dried fruits, seeds such as sesame or sunflower; several kinds of nuts and cheese.

A number of trips to the smorgasbord table are expected, so do not load your plate the first time. The following are only suggestive; you will find more ideas in a good delicatessen. The number of dishes depends upon the approximate number to be served.

Desserts may be placed on a separate table and they should be simple, as fruit and cheese, apples, lingonberry or raspberry dessert, cookies or spice cake.

Smorgasbord Suggestions:

1. Swedish meat balls.
2. Marinated cucumbers.
3. Tomato aspic.
4. Salmon in cold court bouillon.
5. Jellied veal loaf.
6. Sea food salad.
7. Liver pâte mold.
8. Baked beans.
9. Cooked vegetable salad, pickled beets.
10. Assorted cheese, as goat, caraway, etc.
11. Baked ham, hard salami.
12. Finger salads.
13. Scrambled eggs with him or sausage.
14. Roasted turkey.
15. Cold roast beef.
16. Smoked fish.
17. Stuffed eggs.
18. Potato salad.
19. Celery stuffed with cheese.
20. Waldorf salad.
21. Assorted pickled fish.
22. Assorted breads.
23. Cookies.
24. Apple dessert with custard sauce.
25. Spice cake.
26. Cranberry raisin pie.
27. Fruit.

Recipes for the above will be found under their proper headings in this book.

■ **APPETIZERS AND SPREADS**

There is an endless variety of appetizers, limited only by your imagination. They come in many sizes, shapes, colors and textures; their piquant flavors are appetite stimulants. But they should always be served in small portions, preferably on a tray so that guests may help themselves.

Appetizers may be divided into three groups—canapés, hors d'oeuvres and spreads.

Canapés are made from any type of non-sweet day-old bread you desire. Their chief characteristic is their shape, and the fact that they are "open" with an intriguing covering. The bread is cut into ¼-inch thick slices, then cut into circles, crescents, diamonds, triangles or other fancy shapes. These pieces of bread are frequently sautéed lightly in a little fat or toasted on one side under the broiler to a delicate brown. The filling is spread on the buttered, toasted side and may be any of the following:

1. *Cream cheese* mixed with cream or top milk to a consistency to spread; on this base may be placed:
   A. finely chopped hard-cooked white of egg mixed with a little mayonnaise and a sprig of parsley in the center;
   B. egg yolk pressed throuth a sieve over cheese and chopped egg white, outlining the bread; thin slice of stuffed olive in the center;
   C. ripe pitted olives cut in eighths and laid in petal-shape on cheese; caper or bit of egg yolk as center;
   D. finely chopped dried beef, with thin slice of ripe olive in center;
   E. anchovy center, sides of bread spread with cheese and rolled in finely chopped parsley;
   F. narrow pimiento strip, fashioned into a bow-knot, chopped parsley outlining bread;
   G. Christmas wreath, made of parsley outline, with bits of pimiento to represent holly berries, and a pimiento bow;
   H. cream cheese mixed with finely chopped parsley and forced through pastry tube; chopped ripe olives outline bread.
2. *Canapés* may also be covered with mayonnaise, anchovy butter, sardine butter, water cress or parsley butter. For the fish butters, blend 1 tsp. anchovy paste, or sardine paste with 1 tsp. lemon juice and ⅓ c. softened butter. Finely chopped parsley of water cress is blended with softened butter.

Suggested mixtures to place on top:

A. Chopped lobster, crab meat mixed with sardines, cream cheese or cream, lemon juice, salt and pepper. Frozen flaked lobster and crab may be substituted when the fresh is not available. Canned may also be used.
B. Thinly sliced smoked fish, with minced parsley edging the bread.
C. Meat spreads, such as liver, ham or tongue paste, smoked tongue. Tiny pieces of any cold meats may be combined with mayonnaise, and the buttered sides of canapé dipped in chopped parsley, with a tiny pearl onion in the center.
D. Cheese spreads.

Hors d'oeuvres are small, dainty foods of various kinds. A variety of them will make a colorful, attractive platter. Here are some suggestions:

1. *Stuffed celery ring:* 1 medium bunch celery; cut off tops, wash and dry each stalk well with a cloth. Fill smallest stalk with cheese filling, then the next smallest stalk, and press firmly into the first one. Continue until all the celery is formed into a bunch. Tie with string, wrap in oiled paper; chill. Slice crosswise with very sharp knife into ½-inch slices. Favorite cheese fillings include:
   A. Mix 1 part chopped shrimp with 2 parts cream cheese.
   B. Mix 1 part minced ham with 2 parts cream cheese.
   C. Combine 2 parts cream cheese and 1 part chopped olives.
2. Stuffed carrots: Cooked or raw carrots, hollowed out with an apple corer and centers filled with mixture of cream cheese and nuts. Chill and slice just before serving.
3. Small yellow and red tomatoes with stems, or leaf section to hold by; dip in cheese or onion soup dip.
4. Miniature cream puffs filled with chicken or fish salad, as crab or shrimp. Serve hot or cold.
5. Small Mexican tamales cut in 1-inch pieces. May be wrapped in bacon. Place on toothpicks to serve. Broil and serve hot.
6. Cheese pecan or walnut balls: Mix cream cheese with ground sunflower seeds and minced ham. Make balls and place 2 walnut halves on sides.
7. Carrot curls and celery fans are made by shaving slices from carrots; curl up, fasten with toothpick and place in ice water. Celery is cut in 3-inch pieces and narrow strips are cut at each end, almost to the center. Place in ice water to crisp.
8. Mix peanut butter, dates and coconut butter, roll between two pieces of oiled paper, slice and serve.

9. Radish roses and accordions are made by cutting off roots and tops. Roses are made by cuts on 4 sides of the top; accordions are slashed all the way crosswise, almost through.
10. Marinate the following cooked vegetables in your favorite salad dressing: cauliflower flowerets, artichoke bottoms, tiny beets, mushrooms, tiny onion.
11. All sorts of delicious raw foods may be added to the tray: cauliflower flowerets, sliced cucumbers, avocado chunks dipped in lemon juice and rolled in crushed whole-wheat crackers, melon strips, fresh pineapple chunks or strips, olives of all kinds; tiny tomatoes, red and yellow.
12. Horns-of-plenty: bologna slices filled with chive cottage cheese or strips or Cheddar cheese.
13. Olives wrapped with bacon, grilled under broiler.
14. Stuffed hard-cooked eggs.
15. Cheese of all kinds, in chunks, strips or balls.
16. Small sausages stuffed at either end with almonds.
17. Cooked artichoke hearts marinated in French dressing, stuffed with pitted black olives.

■ CHEESE HORS D'OEUVRES

Make whole-wheat crust for pie shell; line shallow 9-inch pan.

2 slices lean bacon, chopped	½ tsp. salt
½ medium onion, minced	¼ tsp. pepper
½ small garlic, minced	½ tsp. caraway seed or ground
¾ c. grated Swiss cheese	caraway
3 eggs, well beaten	½ c. chopped parsley
¼ c. sour cream	

Lightly brown bacon, add onions and cook over low heat until cooked through. Add garlic. Remove from fire; add cheese, eggs and sour cream, salt, pepper, caraway seed and half of parsley.

Pour cheese mixture into crust, sprinkle with remaining parsley. Bake in moderate 375° oven, 30 minutes. Cut into thin strips or wedges. Serve hot.

■ EGG SNACKS

Mash 4 hard-cooked eggs, add 1 tsp. salt. ¼ tsp. pepper, ⅓ c. minced parsley and 1 well beaten egg. Shape into small balls, roll in flour, fry until brown in melted butter or oil. Stick tooth-picks into each to serve.

■   **HOME-STUFFED OLIVES**

Split green ripe olives; pit. Put back together with Neufchatel cheese softened with a little cream.

■   **DRIED BEEF-CHEESE ROLL UPS**

1. Place a ¼-inch stick of Cheddar cheese in center of a thin slice of dried beef. Add a little chili sauce and roll up.
2. Place a teaspoonful of chive cheese in center of a slice of dried beef and roll up.

■   **VEGETABLE ROLL UPS**

Thin slices of raw turnips, carrots, or zuchinni may be spread with seasoned cream cheese. Cucumber slices may be spread with chive cheese, but do not roll unless first made limp by placing a few minutes in French dressing.

■   **CHEESE-MEAT BALLS**

Mix cream cheese with minced ham, grated Cheddar cheese or minced onion. Roll in balls, and roll balls in chopped chipped beef, or minced parsley. Place on toothpicks or pretzel sticks.

■   **BACON ROLL UPS**

10 slices bacon	1 c. grated Cheddar cheese
20 strips whole-wheat bread, cut 1¼ inches by 3 inches	

Cut bacon slices in half; place bread strips on bacon and cover with cheese. Roll up loosely and fasten with toothpicks. Place on broiler rack so that the top of the rolls are 3-4 inches from broiler unit. Broil 2-3 minutes on each side. Makes 20 rolls.

■   **TEEN SNACKS**

½ c. salad dressing	1 tsp. chutney
1 tbsp. lemon juice	¼ tsp. salt
1 tbsp. minced onion	3 tbsp. chopped parsley
⅛ tsp. curry powder	

Mix first 6 ingredients with 2 tbsp. parsley. Use 1 tbsp. parsley to garnish the dip. Serve with chilled, cooked shrimps. Also serve potato chips or crackers and let each one prepare his own snack.

■ PINEAPPLE BOWL

Cut crown from pineapple about 2 inches down from top. (You can follow scallops of the shell.) Remove core and hollow out fruit with a sharp knife. Soften ¼ lb. Bleu cheese with 1 8-oz. pkg. cream cheese. Fold in chopped pineapple, return to shell and refrigerate overnight. Serve with crackers. This same pineapple bowl can be filled with fresh cut-up fruits added to the pineapple, and a little ginger ale mixed with the fruit at the last minute, then brought to the table and spooned into cocktail glasses for a delicious appetizer.

■ AEGEAN OLIVES

Make a small incision with a knife in each olive; put them in layers in a jar with pieces of cut garlic, 3 stalks thyme, small piece of chili pepper. Fill the jars with olive oil and cover them. They will be well-flavored in a couple of days and can be stored for many months.

■ DILL PICKLE SLICES

Top pickle slices with cottage cheese mixed with garlic powder. Surround dish with tidbits of Camembert cheese.

■ PICKLED BEETS

Juice of 1 lemon	1 tbsp. honey
2 tsp. sesame oil	⅛ tsp. powdered cloves
1 can beets or 1 c. self-cooked beets	⅛ tsp. tarragon
	⅛ tsp. allspice

Marinate beets in this dressing overnight, or several days if kept cold.

■ POPCORN PARMESAN

Toss 3 c. popcorn with ¼ c. melted butter, ¼ c. grated Parmesan cheese, ⅛ tsp. garlic powder.

■ PUMPKIN SEED CHEWS

Cook 1 c. shelled pumpkin seeds in 2 qts. water for 15 minutes with ½ c. salt substitute. Drain, but do not rinse. Dry slowly in warm oven.

■   **OLIVE STUFFED CELERY**

Cut ripe or stuffed olives in small pieces to measure ½ c. Mix 1 3-oz. pkg. cream cheese with 2 tbsp. mayonnaise or sour cream. Add 1 tbsp. finely chopped onion, chives or parsley. Season with salt. Fill celery stalks. Chill and serve.

■   **NUT NIBBLERS**

½ c. shelled sunflower seeds or	½ c. peanuts or cashews
squash seeds	½ c. pecans or walnuts
½ c. pignolia nuts or soy nuts	

Sauté seeds and nuts in 3 tbsp. butter in sauce pan. Add 2 tsp. Worcestershire sauce, ½ tsp. garlic salt, ½ tsp. salt, dash of Tabasco. Place in shallow baking pan. Bake in 325° oven, 20 minutes. Stir occasionally. Serve warm or cold. Makes 2-3 c.

■   **PIZZA ON WHOLE-WHEAT CRACKERS**

Combine ¼ c. tomato paste, undiluted, with 1 minced garlic clove, ¼ tsp. oregano. Add ¾ lb. bulk sausage which has been browned and fat drained off. Season to taste. Top each cracker with tomato mixture and thin slice of sharp Cheddar cheese. Bake in 450° oven, 3-5 minutes.

■   **SURPRISE "BURGERS"**

8 whole-wheat hamburger	1 lb. hamburger
rolls	1 tbsp. chopped onion
½ c. chopped green pepper	½ c. tomato sauce

Cut a side off the rolls. Take out some of the bread. Mix hamburger, pepper, onion, tomato sauce, egg, and 1 c. of bread crumbs from inside the rolls. Pack mixture into rolls, being sure to fill to the crust rim. Bake 20 minutes at 350° for medium well-cooked. Small French rolls may also be used.

■   **SALTED SOYBEANS**

1½ c. soybeans (dried)	2 tbsp. melted butter or oil

Soak beans over night and cook 1 hour next day. Drain. Spread beans on cookie sheet. Pour over melted butter or oil and mix well. Sprinkle with salt. Bake at 350°, 1½-2 hours, stirring beans frequently.

Spreads and dips are very popular. Potato chips are favorite carriers for the spreads, but the following also are good: raw vegetables, such as carrot strips, celery strips, cauliflower, sweet turnip slices, cucumber strips, corn chips, waffle sections; cheese, soy or wheat crackers.

■ SOUR CREAM OR YOGURT DIP FOR VEGETABLES

Mix 2 c. sour cream or 1 container of yogurt with 1 tbsp. lemon juice, 1 tsp. salt, 1 tsp. grated onion, ½ tsp. garlic salt, Worcestershire sauce to taste.

■ CLAM DIP

Mix ½ c. drained minced clams, ¼ c. clam broth with 1 8-oz. pkg. cream cheese or 1 pt. farmer-style cottage cheese. Add 1 tsp. lemon juice, ½ tsp. garlic powder and ½ tsp. salt.

■ AVOCADO DIP

1 c. mashed avocado	½ tsp. salt
1½ tsp. minced onion	Dash of pepper
1 tsp. lemon or lime juice	½ tsp. Worcestershire sauce

■ CHIVE-CHEESE DIP

1 pkg. chive cottage cheese	1½ tsp. finely grated onion
½ tsp. salt	1 tbsp. mayonnaise

■ ONION SOUP DIP

Mix 1 pkg. dry onion soup with 1 container of Yogurt, ½ c. chopped parsley or 1 8-oz. pkg. of cream cheese thinned with cream.

■ CHIVE-YOGURT EGG DIP

1 6-oz. pkg. soft chive cream cheese	1 tsp. prepared mustard
1 container yogurt	2 tbsp. mayonnaise
3 hard-cooked eggs, chopped	½ tsp. Worcestershire sauce
Freshly ground pepper to taste	¼ tsp. salt

■ BEAN SOUP-CREAM CHEESE DIP

Blend 1 can black bean soup or bacon bean soup with 2 3-oz. pkg. cream cheese, ½ tsp. Worcestershire sauce, 2 tbsp. minced onion, 3 tbsp. minced parsley, ¼ c. yogurt or 2 tbsp. mayonnaise, salt and pepper to taste. Add a dash of Tabasco if hot dip is desired.

■ YOGURT DIP

Mix 1 c. cottage cheese and 1 c. yogurt to the consistency of thick mayonnaise. Add 1 tbsp. finely chopped parsley, 1 tbsp. finely chopped onions and tops; add ½ tsp. salt, ½ tsp. pepper. Mix well and serve with celery sticks, cauliflower buds, tender carrots, cucumber slices, green and red pepper slices, small red and yellow tomatoes.

■ COTTAGE CHEESE DIP

2 c. cottage cheese	1 tsp. celery salt
2 tbsp. minced green pepper	1 tbsp. finely chopped sweet
2 tbsp. minced chives	pickles
2 tsp. celery seed	2 tbsp. chopped pimiento

Cream the cheese until smooth, adding a little sour cream or yogurt if necessary. Add other ingredients and blend well. Chill for several hours, then serve. Use as salad, sandwich spread, or vegetable dip.

■ SHRIMP DIP

Cut 1 c. cooked shrimp into tiny pieces. Cream together ½ lb. cream cheese, 1 tbsp. curry powder, ¼ tsp. garlic powder, ¼ c. chutney cut into small pieces. Add shrimp, ½ c. commercial sour cream and 2 tbsp. milk. Stir thoroughly and store in refrigerator. Serve as dip for walnuts or Brazil nuts, pumpernickle crackers, carrot chips, celery sticks, raw cauliflower, etc.

■ EXOTIC OLIVE DIP

2 3-oz. pkgs. cream cheese	½ c. chopped ripe olives
1 can black bean soup	

Soften cheese with undiluted soup. Stir in olives. Serve as dip for potato chips or wheat crackers.

■ WALNUT CHEESE SPREAD

4 3-oz. pkgs. cream cheese	2 drops Tabasco
½ c. finely cut or ground walnuts	5 tbsp. lemon juice
	2 tbsp. Worcestershire sauce

Beat all ingredients except walnuts until smooth. Blend in walnuts. Crisp bacon may be substituted for walnuts.

■ GUACAMOLE SPREAD

1 large avocado, peeled and mashed	Small clove garlic, minced
	1 tbsp. lemon juice
4 green onions, chopped, (tops and all)	1 tsp. olive oil
	10 drops Tabasco
1 tsp. Worcestershire sauce	½ tsp. salt
1 tsp. mayonnaise	½ tsp. pepper
½ small tomato, diced fine	

Mix together. Chill for 1 hour. Serve with potato chips.

■ SARDINE SPREAD

Drain sardines from 3½-oz. flat can; mash, add 3 oz. cream cheese, ¼ tsp. salt, 1 tsp. lemon juice, ½ tsp. Worcestershire sauce.

■ ANCHOVY SPREAD

½ tube anchovy paste mixed with 1 8-oz. pkg. cream cheese, 1 tsp. minced onion or onion powder, 1 tsp. Worcestershire sauce.

■ BLEU CHEESE SPREAD

1 8-oz. pkg. cream cheese blended with 1 wedge Bleu cheese, ⅓ c. finely minced parsley, 1 tsp. onion powder or juice, cream to moisten, add salt and pepper to taste. Dash of Tabasco is good.

■ CAMEMBERT SPREAD

Soft Camembert cheese mixed with a little chopped dill pickle. Have some unmixed Camembert on the tray as well. Serve with small squares of rye or pumpernickle bread.

■ GARLIC CHEESE SPREAD

1 c. Cheddar cheese, grated; add 1 c. sour cream; ¼ c. sweet cream, 1 tsp. garlic powder and 4 tbsp. minced onion.

■ CHEESE ROLL SPREAD

5 oz. Roquefort cheese	Juice of 1 onion
2 3-oz. pkgs. cream cheese	1 tsp. Worcestershire sauce
5 oz. soft Cheddar cheese	½ lb. pecans, crushed

Mix with electric beater all except pecans. Add half pecans cut fine. Place in bowl lined with wax paper. Let stand in refrigerator overnight. Remove 1½ hours before serving. Roll in mixture of remaining crushed pecans and 2 tbsp. chopped parsley.

■ LET'S HAVE A PICNIC

Picnics are a part of our American heritage. We all have memories of delightful places where we went for a picnic; under the pines close to a tumbling mountain stream, beside a sunlit lake, on a river bank or beside the sea. Maybe the picnic you remember with the most nostalgia was one you had in a city park, or in your own back yard. Wherever it was, it was out of doors—which is the chief requisite to make any meal a picnic.

For the classic picnic, as differing from a barbecue, the food is usually cooked ahead of time. This does not mean you can't roast hot dogs, and corn, or cook hamburgers, but usually the foods are taken to the picnic all ready prepared.

Do you remember the crisp, golden fried chicken, delicious potato salad, deviled eggs, homemade ice cream and watermelon of yesteryear? And don't you sometimes think, "Oh! I wish I knew something different to take this time."? Well, here are lots of picnic ideas for you. Some are the old traditional ones and some may be new to you, but all can be prepared ahead of time, so all you have to do is spread the cloth, set out the paper plates, cups, wooden or plastic spoons and forks, and then put on the food.

There are a few important things to remember in planning a picnic: the food must be easy to eat sitting on the ground, or at makeshift tables; foods that should be served cold must *be* cold, not lukewarm, and the hot foods should retain as much heat as possible. This can be accomplished by packing the salads in a covered receptacle surrounded by ice; the hot foods containers can be wrapped in an old piece of blanket or in newspapers. The drinks should be in a thermos jug, but a glass bottle may also be packed in a bucket of ice, or chilled and wrapped in newspapers. When you pack your cold picnic foods, arrange them to take advantage of the coolness of the ice you have packed around the salad.

A good plan is to have several small cartons or baskets. This breaks up the load so several can help in carrying, and it also makes possible the placing of cloth, napkins, plates, cups, etc. in the box you plan to open first. The main dish is in another, and the salad in still another. I pack my fruit desserts in the box with the cold salad. Odds and ends can be tucked into the empty spaces in all 3 cartons.

Recipes for all the picnic foods are in this book under their proper headings.

Sandwiches are traditional and if they are to be the main dish they should be hearty. If you plan to travel several hours before the meal it is best not to include the lettuce or thinly sliced vegetables in the sandwich, but pack lettuce in a plastic bag with a few ice cubes around it and the moist sliced vegetables in separate covered containers. Wilted lettuce and droopy tomatoes do not make an appetizing sandwich. Cut sandwiches in sections that are easy to hold and bite into, place each in a sandwich bag, or wrap individually in waxed paper. Put an identification tag on the top of each stack of sandwiches, so you will not have to open the bags and peek inside to see what kind it is. Use different breads and fillings, but be sure to have protein the main ingredient of the fillings. If you wish to eliminate bread, place 2 slices of meat with a filler of cheese, or 2 slices of cheese with a filler of sliced radishes, cucumbers or tomatoes.

Instead of regulation sandwiches, try making Cornish pasties —1 for each person. These pasties may be varied by using ½ c. grated cheddar cheese and 1 tsp. caraway seeds in the pastry and using cooked seasoned hamburger meat for the filling. Serve both with chili sauce and relish.

Stuffed rolls make an interesting change, as do squares of cornbread filled with an egg, cheese or vegetable mixture.

Meats or casseroles may be your main picnic course, such as: meat loaf, sliced cold meats, left over roast, fried chicken, rabbit, pork chops, barbecued chicken or spareribs. They should be served warm, if possible, with plenty of paper napkins for gooey fingers. A casserole dish, such as meat pie or vegetable nut loaf, should be kept warm. Baked beans with sliced baked ham are good picnic fare, hot or cold.

To accompany the main dish there should be a salad, as: finger salads, raw vegetables, in pieces suitable to eat with the fingers; tossed green salads; cooked vegetable salads; raw vegetable salads; potato salad; vegetable and fruit kabobs.

There are scores of accompanying picnic foods. A few are:

Hard-cooked eggs.

Pickled eggs.

Pickles.

Potato chips.

Smoked fish or oysters.

Stuffed eggs.

Pickled beets.

Olives, plain or stuffed.

Slices or chunks of unprocessed cheese.

Stuffed celery.

Hot or cold soups packed in thermos bottles or jugs.

Picnic desserts, include melons, fresh fruit, fruit cut up and served in paper sauce dishes, cookies, Banbury tarts or cake. You may prefer dates, or other dried fruits, nuts, or seeds such as sunflower or pumpkin seeds, or pieces of fresh coconut.

Water may not be available, so be sure to take plenty to drink; cold milk, fruit juice, herb tea, or some of each.

Have fun! Don't mind the flies, ants, yellow jackets or blowing sand; it's all part of a picnic.

■ PICNIC KABOBS

Kabobs are very satisfactory for picnics because they are in small pieces and come strung on meat or wooden skewers, or short plastic colored knitting needles. They may be a combination of protein foods, fruits and vegetables or variations such as:

1. Chunks of ham, pineapple and green pepper.
2. Chunks of ham, apple, and cooked yams.
3. Chunks of beef, cucumbers, cheese.
4. Chunks of lamb; cooked; marinated zucchini; softened dried apricots.
5. Chunks of lamb, dates, pickled whole beets.
6. Chunks of dried fish, tomatoes, cheese.
7. Chunks of cucumbers, crook-neck squash, baby beets.
8. Small whole tomatoes, half of artichoke heart, marinated.
9. Thick disk of cooked carrot, small patty pan squash, marinated.
10. Cooked cauliflower, marinated; wedge of tomato, chunks of cheese.
11. Pitted olives, radishes, cooked baby carrots, chunks of cheese.

Wrap 2 kabobs in freezer paper for each person.

■ COOKING FOR A CROWD

Planning meals for a large number of persons may seem overwhelming, but with suggestions for planning, proportions needed to feed them well, and proven recipes to go by, you can achieve success. The secret in planning meals for a large number of persons is to select plain recipes that are easy to enlarge, such as:

1. Fruit cocktail.
2. Waldorf salad.
3. Tossed green salad.
4. Italian meat balls and spaghetti.
5. Veal scallopini.
6. Meat loaf.
7. Baked beans.
8. Apple pudding.
9. Tomato aspic.
10. Cole slaw.
11. Tamale pie.
12. Stuffed baked pork chops.
13. Barbecued spareribs.
14. Meat pie with brown biscuits.
15. Chicken pie.
16. Apple crispy.

These are only a few of the dishes suitable for easy enlarging. But I must caution you *not* to triple a quick-bread or cake recipe. It is better to make 2 or 3 single recipes, as the figuring becomes so involved that desirable results may not be forthcoming.

Delicious, nutritious meals for a crowd must be planned carefully for flavor and variety, and budgeted for cost. This requires intelligent organization, planning and buying.

If the meal is for a church, club, family reunion, or P.T.A., a capable chairman must be chosen and hard-working committees assigned to plan, market, prepare the food, take charge of the dining room and clean up. Before you begin to plan the meal you must know what cooking facilities are available. If it is a meal where there is a charge, you must figure in advance how much you can charge, about how many people to expect and whether the food will be donated, purchased, or both. It is vital, also, to have an accurate count of the number and ability of the workers.

Some planning suggestions:

1. Plan a simple menu, with foods easy to prepare.
2. Plan a meal in which part of the preparation can be completed ahead of time without affecting the quality of the food.
3. Choose foods with "keeping" qualities to take care of late comers.
4. Have one very popular dish, usually a main dish or dessert.
5. Do not waste money on expensive vegetables or fruits.
6. Cut down on courses; make one do double duty, . . . For example, serve fruit salad as a first course instead of fruit cocktail, and skip the salad course. Serve tomato juice and substitute a less expensive vegetable with the main course.
7. Little touches, such as relishes, pickles, orange slices, parsley will add interest to the meal but will increase cost, so must be considered both ways.
8. Feature foods for which your town or home is particularly famous, such as homemade rolls, baked beans, fried chicken, blueberry pie.

Getting the food:

1. Purchase foods in as large units as practical and buy the grades best suited to your budget.
2. If food is to be donated, ask for specific contributions.
3. When foods are to be prepared in the home, distribute recipes to each cook, so the dishes will be as nearly alike as possible. Avoid creamed dishes that spoil quickly.
4. Check delivery of all items purchased and return all unused bottles, crates and returnable goods, as canned foods.

Preparation and Serving:

1. Do as much of the work as possible the day before.
2. Work-schedules, menus, working area and recipes should be posted in the kitchen.
3. Each group should be responsible for washing pots and pans they have used, leaving work area clean.
4. Taste all foods before serving, with special attention to good, definitive seasoning.
5. Serve the plates assembly-line style. If possible, use standard serving equipment, such as ice cream scoops to measure servings.

Dining Room Committee:

1. Decorates the dining room, sets the tables, serves the meals and clears the tables after the meal is over.
2. Depending upon the facilities, space for serving, desire for formal or informal service, number of workers, the service may be family style, buffet, cafeteria, or table service. Family service is informal, provides a home-like atmosphere; table service is suitable for banquets; buffet service provides an informal atmosphere and is used when only a few guests are served; cafeteria may be modified between buffet and table service.
3. Allow 24 inches of table space per guest.
4. If waitresses are necessary, plan on 1 waitress for each 10 guests, with an extra waitress for 20 guests, to serve the beverage.
5. Locate serving stations in the dining room, where trays can be placed, extra silver, water, butter or coffee can be placed.

Clean-Up Committee:

1. This group should be a fresh one as they will attack the problem with more enthusiasm.
2. The committee is responsible for scraping, separating the glasses, silver, dishes, and pans. Wash in the above order, in hot sudsy water, changing water as soon as it cools or gets greasy.
3. Rinse in very hot water.
4. Trash and rubbish cans removed.
5. Kitchen left immaculate.

Some Tips for Quantity Meals:

1. 3 lbs. of potato chips serve 50 people.
2. 2 lbs. of coffee will make 90 cups.
3. 3 pts. of light cream for coffee for 50 people.
4. 2 10-lb. boneless, skinned ready-to-eat ham for 50 people.
5. 6 lbs. of chicken makes 3 qts. of salad combined with fresh green vege-tables and hard-cooked eggs; will serve 40.

6. 10 lbs. of potatoes will serve 25.
7. Plan on ¼-lb. steak, roast or ground meat per person.
8. 1 lb. of ground meat in meat loaf will serve 6.
9. You can get 32 pats of butter from 1 lb.
10. 7 lbs. of cabbage feeds 50.
11. 10 lbs. of hamburger serves 50, with 2 each.
12. 6 cans of cream style corn makes enough corn pudding to serve 35.
13. 4 qts. of ice cream will serve 24.
14. ¾-lb. tea equals 30 cups.
15. 2 25-lb. turkeys will serve 50.
16. Allow 4 buns per person when serving hamburgers to teen-agers.
17. 9 qts. of thinly sliced potatoes will make scalloped potatoes for 50.

You may send to the following companies for free booklets:

1. *Feeding 50 or More:* Hotel and Institution Dept., Armour and Company, Union Stock Yards, Chicago 9, Illinois.
2. *Hostess Recipes for 50, or 25, or More:* Home Economics Division, Research Laboratories, Swift and Company, Chicago 9, Illinois.
3. *Feeding a Crowd:* General Food Kitchens, White Plains, New York.

■ AMOUNTS TO SERVE 80, 100 OR 300

25 lbs. hamburger for patties (80)
10 cans hot sauce mixed with 5 cans water (80)
25 lbs. potatoes for scalloped potatoes (80)
1 gal. milk; ½ lb. butter, for scalloped potatoes (80)
8 doz. rolls (80)
3 lbs. butter (80)
20 lbs. potatoes for mashed potatoes (80)
20 c. flour, 20 tsp. baking powder, 2 c. oil, 4 tsp. salt for biscuits (80)
40 lbs. pot roast of beef (100) Thicken gravy with 5 c. flour
12 doz. rolls (100)
4 lbs. butter (100)
2 25-lb. turkeys (100)
8 large loaves bread for dressing
6 c. flour for thickening turkey gravy
35 lbs. potatoes, mashed (100)
10 bunches celery (100)
20 bunches radishes (100)
1 gal. olives (100)
4 lbs. cranberries (100)
3 lbs. coffee, 8 gal. water (100)
12 heads lettuce (100)
14 lbs. cabbage; 2 No. 2½ cans broken pineapple pieces, for slaw (100)
22 picnic hams (300) Boil until nearly done, then bake.

■ **MEAT LOAF FOR 75**

18 lbs. hamburger	*Sauce:*
9 c. rolled oats	12 c. catsup
7 large cans milk	6 c. water
2 c. chopped onion	4 c. chopped onions
1 c. salt	1 bottle Worcestershire Sauce
3 tsp. pepper	

Mix meat, oats, milk, onion, salt and pepper into loaves. Make sauce and pour over meat, before baking. Bake 1½ hours at 350°.

■ **SWEDISH MEAT BALLS FOR 50**

10 lbs. hamburger	2 tbsp. salt
20 slices bread	1 tsp. pepper
2½ c. milk	10 medium onions, grated
10 eggs	5 qts. canned tomatoes
10 medium-sized potatoes, grated	

Beat eggs slightly and add to milk. Soak bread in milk and egg, 10-15 minutes. Mix thoroughly all ingredients except onion and tomato and form into balls (2 balls per serving). Roll the balls in flour, brown in oil and arrange in large baking pans. Place onions over balls and pour tomatoes over them. Cover and simmer 1 hour.

■ **RICE AND MEAT BALLS FOR 50**

12 lbs. ground beef	¼ tsp. pepper
3 c. raw brown rice	5 qts. tomato puree
4 tbsp. salt	5 qts. water

Mix rice, meat and seasonings. Shape into balls the size of large walnuts and place in greased baking pan. Cover meat balls with liquid and bake in moderate oven, 350°, 1½ hours. Add water, if sauce cooks dry.

■ **PHILIPPA'S MAP CAKE**

4 lbs. raw cashew nuts, ground	1 tsp. cinnamon
4 lbs. sun-dried dates, seeded	1 tsp. nutmeg
4 lbs. black figs	½ tsp. powdered cloves
4 lbs. sun-dried raisins	¼ lb. powdered coconut, un-
3 ¼-lb. bars sweet butter	sweetened
1-lb. can whole powdered milk	¼ lb. dried skim milk

Put each of the fruits through food grinder separately. Use 3 separate bowls for the mixtures. In first bowl, place ground dates and blend with 1 bar butter and 2 lbs. of the ground cashews. Add nutmeg. To ground figs, add remaining cashews and ½ powdered skim milk. Blend in 1 bar butter, add cinnamon. To ground raisins, add ½ the powdered coconut, blend in 1 bar butter, add remaining powdered whole milk and cloves. Knead as for bread dough, adding more of dry ingredient if necessary. Mold into layers, one on top of other. Place waxed paper on any traced map, of the United States or any country desired; mold layers to fit map contours. Top with remaining coconut and dried skim milk. Chill in refrigerator. Peel off wax paper. May use small candles to denote major cities, and in topping, may trace with toothpick the courses of major rivers. A marvelous fun cake for a children's party, as it teaches a little about geography and provides a cake brimful of vitamins . . . and minus both salt and sugar! This cake was invented by the mother of Philippa Schuyler, concert pianist and writer, who molded it into a map of Africa on the occasion of a party marking publication of a new book by Philippa, on the Congo. Cut in fairly small slices, as cake is rich. Serves 20-25.

CHAPTER 19

Outdoor Cooking

*B*ARBECUE comes from the Spanish and originally referred to the rude wooden frame above the ground, where fish and meats were roasted . . . and where, occasionally, people slept!

When the United States first adopted the barbecue, it became a big outdoor get-together, often paid for by politicians and adorned with brass bands and speeches.

Then, almost overnight, the cook-out swept the nation and men by the thousands donned oversized aprons and chef's caps and presided over elaborate outdoor equipment in their backyards and patios. Giving a barbecue no longer means roasting whole pigs or steers and inviting a hundred-odd guests. A barbecue in its modern version can be anything from chops broiled over coals in the kitchen to cook-outs featuring steaks and hamburgers.

When you give a barbecue you can choose from a number of intriguing methods:

1. *The Outdoor Grill*—Usually made of rods, bars or pipes placed 2-3 inches apart and 6-12 inches above the coals.
2. *The Portable Barbecue*—Available in sizes to serve small groups; usually uses briquettes of charcoal. Popular because it can be used anywhere.
3. *The Hubachi*—These brazier and bucket type barbecues came from Japan, but are being manufactured here and are popular for outdoor cooking for 4-6 people. Briquettes are usually the fuel used.
4. *The Luau*—The West Coast has adopted the favorite outdoor feast of our 50th state. The Hawaiians use a deep pit in which coals or rocks are heated. A whole pig is the classic feature of a luau.

It is not possible to give the exact time of cooking in barbecues; one must experiment and test for doneness; and it is better to serve the food underdone than burned to a crisp: one can always return the food for further cooking if underdone.

It is suggested that many meats may be cooked without any sauce at all as the unadorned flavor of the meat is excellent.

Portable, small barbecues are becoming most popular as they can be used anywhere, give a lot of heat with a small amount of fuel. These are not practical for cooking for large groups unless several barbecues are available. Brazier and bucket-types are made in America; iron and pottery ones called hibachis come from Japan.

Outdoor broiling or grill cooking is the most fun. Grills are usually made of rods, bars or pipes placed 2-3 inches apart over hot coals. The distance from grill to coals may be between 6-12 inches. Rub the grill with salad oil to prevent meat sticking to the bars. The excess fat you trim off the meat may be used to grease the bars. (The fat is trimmed off to prevent flames.) Turn the meat frequently. Have a sprinkling can or bottle of water handy to douse meat or coals if they flame.

Broiling can be done over charcoal, over wood, or in your broiler-rotisserie in your own kitchen.

The steaks to buy for broiling should be at least 1 inch thick and allow from ½-1 lb. per serving. Slash fat edges to prevent curling of steaks and chops. Whether it is a rib, T-bone, tenderloin, sirloin, rump, sirloin tip, cube, minute or London broil, marinate 15-30 minutes in a barbecue sauce, or a marinade of ½ c. salad oil, ¼ c. cider or wine vinegar, ¼ c. chopped onion, 1 tsp. salt, freshly-ground pepper, 1 or 2 crushed cloves of garlic and 2 tsp. Worcestershire sauce.

Place steaks on hot grill and use long tongs for turning. Season with butter, salt and pepper when done.

Suggested timing: 1-inch steak, medium done; 8 to 10 minutes on each side; 1-inch steak, rare: 5 minutes on each side; 1-inch steak, well done: 10 minutes on each side.

Doneness can be tested by making a small gash in center of steak and looking at the color. Minute steaks can be cooked only 1 minute on each side. London broil means a flank steak, scored on both sides. It should marinate 8 to 10 hours, turning occasionally. Grill about 6 to 8 minutes on each side. Cut into thin slantwise slices.

Hamburgers should be cooked in a folding wire broiler about 3 to 5 inches from the hot coals. Grill over hot coals 4 to 5 minutes on each side. When served, place thin slice of cheese on meat and place between buttered, toasted bun. Any desired relish, onion slices, chili sauce, lettuce, sliced tomato or salad dressing may be spread on bun.

■   **BARBECUED CHICKEN AND TURKEY**

Cut young fryers about 1½ to 2½ lbs. in halves or quarters. Let stand in any barbecue sauce several hours. Grill over hot coals slowly about 50 to 60 minutes. Baste often. Young 3 to 6 lb. turkey broilers are cooked the same as chicken, broil 1½ to 2 hours.

Chicken or turkey may be broiled without first placing in marinade. Fowl is brushed with melted butter or oil; season with salt and pepper; brown on all sides; brush with barbecue sauce or melted butter and lemon juice or garlic.

■   **GRILLED LAMB CHOPS**

Select chops or lamb steaks 1 to 2 inches thick. Marinate in any barbecue sauce 30 to 40 minutes. Cook the same as steak, brushing with sauce as they cook. 1-inch chops, medium-well done will take about 10 to 15 minutes on each side.

■   **BARBECUED SPARERIBS**

Cut spareribs into 3 to 4-rib portions. They may be cooked first until almost tender, about 1 hour, or after marinating in barbecue sauce with a little tenderizer added, for 1 or 2 hours. They may be broiled over an open fire. The uncooked ribs will need to broil 1½ to 2 hours or until no sign of pink in meat next to the bones. Brush ribs while grilling with barbecue sauce.

■   **BARBECUED FRANKFURTERS**

Cut frankfurters lengthwise, almost through but not quite, and spread cut sides with mustard or thick barbecue sauce. Arrange on grill cut side down, turn to brown evenly. Cook 5 to 10 minutes.

■   **SHISH KABOBS**

Individual skewers may be used to make shish kabobs. These are a combination of meat, fruit or vegetables. After threading food on skewers, marinate in a good sauce for 30 minutes to 1 hour and brush with the sauce while cooking.

Some combinations are:

1. Mushroom caps, lamb chunks, quarter of tomato and piece of onion.
2. Lamb cubes, tomato quarters, slice of bacon, green pepper.
3. Beef cubes, mushrooms and onions.
4. Frankfurters cut in 1-inch pieces, pineapple chunks and slices of bacon.
5. Chicken or calves liver cut into 1-inch cubes, mushrooms and slice of bacon.
6. Cooked ham cubes and pineapple chunks.

When fruits and vegetables are cooked on skewers they must be watched carefully or they will fall off. Fruits are in chunks and dipped in butter first. Most vegetables need to be parboiled about 10 minutes unless very young and tender. Possible vegetables to use are onions, mushrooms, sweet potatoes, yams, zucchini, green peppers, summer squash, eggplant or young, small potatoes, quarters of red or green tomatoes. When grilling vegetables, it is best to put them in a hinged grill which will hold the tender pieces and make the basting with butter easy.

Marinate in French dressing for 1 hour before grilling red or green tomato wedges, rounds of parboiled carrots, artichoke hearts, zucchini rounds, unpeeled eggplant wedges. Corn may be grilled. Husk the ear and butter, wrap in bacon; or pit cook after removing silks and fold again in husks; tie with strings and roast in hot ashes. The husked ear of corn may be wrapped in foil after the first wrapping in parchment paper or other heavy paper.

Red or green tomatoes, yams, sweet potatoes are cut in thick slices brushed with butter, salt and pepper and broiled first, cut side down.

Bananas are a favorite broiled. Peel, brush with melted butter or wrap in bacon strips. They may be wrapped unpeeled in foil and roasted in ashes. Apples also are good roasted. They are peeled (unless not sprayed), cored and cavities filled with cream cheese, dates, currants or raisins, then wrapped in heavy paper and foil. Dried fruits such as dates, prunes and apricots are good broiled. Soak first to get soft, 1 or 2 hours, then stuff with cheese, cream or nut butter.

■ MIXED GRILL

4 lamb chops	2 medium tomatoes, halved
4 slices pineapple	2 cooked sweet potatoes
8 strips bacon	4 lamb kidneys or 2 small beef
2 tsp. Kitchen Bouquet	kidneys

Wash kidneys; remove any fat and split in half. Soak in cold water 15 minutes, pat dry. Brush lamb chops and kidneys with Kitchen Bouquet. Arrange on broiler and broil 4 inches from moderate heat for 15 minutes. Remove from broiler and turn; place halved strips of bacon on each piece of meat. Arrange tomatoes, cut side up. Cut sweet potatoes in half, place on rack with sliced pineapple. Place piece of butter on tomatoes and brush sweet potatoes with fat. Sprinkle with salt and pepper. Continue broiling until chops are done, about 10 minutes.

■ BARBECUED FLANK STEAK

For 6 persons buy 2 flank steaks. Lay flat and score 1 side, or ask butcher to do it. Dice 1 c. onions and mix with ½ c. minced parsley. Sprinkle liberally over steaks. Roll each piece tightly; tie rolls with twine; and slip on spit. Cook 1½ hours over medium fire. Serve by cutting as for jelly roll.

■ BARBECUED BEEF HEART

Ask butcher to cut a beef heart so it lies flat. Remove fat and hard tissue. Interlace on spit as you would for spare ribs. Brush lightly with oil. Cook 1¼ hours over medium heat and heart will be tender and juicy.

■ CHICKEN GRILLED WITH SOY SAUCE

Have 2 frying chickens split in half; sprinkle each half liberally with soy sauce and marinate in the soy sauce 1 hour. Work excess sauce into chicken by rubbing. Place on grill, skin side down, over medium heat for 20 minutes. Turn and, if possible, cover with large pan. Cook 20 minutes; remove pan; turn chicken again and cook 15 more minutes.

If using whole chickens on spit, rub soy sauce into bird, sprinkle cavity and cook as usual. Do not use salt or pepper in either method.

■ BARBECUED BEEF KABOBS

1½ lbs. beef, cut 1½ inches thick (chuck, sirloin, or round)	½ tsp. rosemary, crushed
	½ c. wine vinegar
	1 tbsp. Worcestershire sauce
1 clove garlic, minced	1 tbsp. meat sauce
3 tbsp. salad oil	¼ c. catsup
¼ tsp. dry mustard	Onions, green peppers, toma-
1½ tbsp. soy sauce	toes or mushrooms

Cut meat into 1-inch squares and place in shallow dish. Sprinkle meat with monosodium glutanate if desired. Sauté garlic in oil. Blend in mustard, soy sauce, rosemary and wine vinegar. Pour mixture over cut meat. Place in refrigerator to marinate and chill for 24 hours. Turn meat occasionally. Arrange chunks of meat on skewers alternately with pieces of onion, green pepper and tomato. Place filled skewers on cold broiler grid. To remaining marinade, add the rest of ingredients and brush meat and vegetables on skewers generously with this sauce. Place broiler pan with kabobs in broiler compartment, with top of meat and vegetables 3 inches from tip of broiler flame. Broil kabobs 5 to 8 minutes. Turn. Brush again with sauce. Broil for 5 to 8 minutes on second side. Broiling time depends on thickness of meat, amount of browning desired and degree of doneness preferred.

■ BASIC BARBECUE SAUCE

¼ c. olive or salad oil	½ c. cider vinegar
1 tsp. garlic salt or 2 cloves of garlic chipped fine	¾ c. chopped onion
	½ c. catsup
2 tbsp. Worcestershire sauce	½ c. chili sauce
2 tbsp. honey or brown sugar	1 tbsp. dry mustard
1 tsp. oregano	1 tsp. salt
1 tsp. black pepper	

Heat oil, add onion and garlic; cook until tender; add remaining ingredients and cook on simmer about ½ hour. Add water if sauce gets too thick. This sauce may be poured into sterilized jars and stored in the refrigerator.

■ SMOKE FLAVORED SAUCE

1 tsp. salt	1 tsp. dry mustard
½ tsp. pepper	1 medium onion, finely chopped
2 tbsp. soy sauce	
⅔ c. catsup	2 tbsp. liquid smoke
⅓ c. water	¼ tsp. cayenne pepper
1 tsp. brown sugar or honey	4 tsp. Worcestershire sauce

Simmer all ingredients 30 to 40 minutes.

■ BARBECUE SAUCE FOR CHICKEN OR DUCK

Melt 2 tbsp. butter, add ¼ c. chopped onion and ½ clove garlic, minced. Add 2 tbsp. lemon juice, 1 tsp. salt, ½ tsp. brown sugar, 1 tsp. prepared mustard, ⅛ tsp. Tabasco, 1 tsp. Worcestershire sauce or Kitchen Bouquet, ½ c. tomato catsup, and ¼ c. water. Bring to a boil and cook 5 minutes.

■ BARBECUE SAUCE FOR TURKEY

Brown ¼ lb. sausage, add ½ c. finely-chopped onion, 1 garlic clove, minced, 1 tsp. Kitchen Bouquet or Worcestershire sauce, 1 c. tomato sauce, 1 tsp. salt, 1 tsp. dry mustard, ¼ c. vinegar, 1 tbsp. brown sugar, and ⅓ c. water. Bring to a boil and remove from fire.

■ **LEMON BARBECUE SAUCE**

Good for chicken or veal: ½ tsp. black pepper
1 small clove garlic   ¼ c. salad oil
½ tsp. salt   ½ c. lemon juice
2 tbsp. grated onion   ½ tsp. dried thyme

Mash garlic with salt in a bowl; stir in remaining ingredients. Allow 1 hour to blend flavors.

■ **SOY BASTING SAUCE FOR PORK PRODUCTS**

¼ c. soy sauce   1 small clove garlic, crushed
1 c. chicken consommé   1 tsp. dry mustard
¼ c. honey or 2 tbsp. brown   2 tbsp. tomato catsup
  sugar (optional)

Combine all ingredients and cook over low heat, 10 or 15 minutes.

■ **HOT BARBECUE SAUCE**

2 small onions, finely chopped   1 tbsp. brown sugar (optional)
1 clove garlic, chopped   1 tsp. salt
½ c. catsup   1 tsp. dry mustard
½ tsp. Tabasco   ¼ c. water
¼ c. vinegar

Combine ingredients and cook 5 minutes.

CHAPTER 20

Freezing Foods

---

*F*ROZEN foods retain most of the qualities of fresh foods, such as nutritive value, color, and flavor. Freezing is the easiest method of food preservation. It prevents foods from spoiling by slowing down the development of spoilage agents; a few are killed, while the others remain dormant at temperatures from zero to $-10°$. One can freeze foods in the freezer part of your refrigerator, but unless that temperature is zero or below, it is not so desirable, as ice crystals formed in the foods during this slow freezing are large and will break the cell walls when the food is thawed, so that it will be soft, limp or mushy. Also, if the temperature control in the freezing part of your refrigerator is not separate from the rest of the box, the food elsewhere will freeze if the common control is set for zero. The ice-cube section can be used to hold frozen food for a limited time.

If large amounts of food are placed in a freezer at one time the temperature is raised before the food is frozen and spoilage will occur. It is better not to add more than 2 lbs. of food per cubic foot of freezer space, at any single time.

In the event of power failure dry ice, which has a temperature of $-110°$, will keep the food from spoiling, or if dry ice (solid carbon dioxide) is not available, a heavy blanket wrapped around the box will act as insulation for 2 days.

The reason that thawed foods are not advised to be refrozen is that bacterial spoilage may have occurred during the thawing period; also, there may be a change in texture. The need for thawing before use varies with the food and uses. Fruit is best served only partially thawed. Unless otherwise directed, foods should be thawed in their original sealed packages.

Rules to follow in packaging, selection and preparing foods for freezing:

Packaging:

Good packaging materials and correct methods of packaging are as important as selecting good quality in the foods you freeze. Here is a list of basic packaging materials to have on hand:

1. Parchment paper to wrap around all foods that are to be wrapped in aluminum foil, such as meat, poultry, fish and irregular shaped fresh or cooked foods.
2. Cellophane bags of assorted sizes. Cellophane bags with code numbers MSAT83, MSAT87, and JSB83 are made from wood pulp, not a coal tar product.
3. Freezer jars of glass resistant to sudden temperature changes. If plastic or waxed cartons are used be sure and place a cellophane liner in first.
4. Locker and tape and/or you can use the low setting on your hand iron. Do not use Scotch tape.
5. Laminated papers with cellophane laminated to a good quality paper. Household wax paper is not recommended, nor locker paper with a heavy wax coating; neither hold up for any length of time.
6. Coffee cans or other cans may be used if their interior coatings are not damaged for soups or non-acid foods. They must be scalded, dried and tape sealed.
7. Stockinette—a protective overwrap. Each end should be slit and tied to make easy access. It cannot be used by itself as it is porous and not air tight. Label carefully all packages.
8. The "Drugstore-Wrap": This is the standard freezer wrapping method. It gives the most ideal protection with the least material. It is one of the easiest, most efficient methods. To drugstore-wrap irregularly shaped foods, place food in center of wrapping material to be used, allowing enough to cover the food plus an overlap of 3 to 4 inches. Bring longest edges together over the food and fold over about 1 inch. Fold over until edges are flat and tight against package. Eliminate air pockets. Fold edges and tuck ends under package to make secure and tight. Heat sealing on cellophane and pliofilm gives best results, but is not necessary.

Selection of Foods:

Nearly all meats, fruits, melons, berries, vegetables, and poultry will freeze successfully. Select fruits that are at their best for table use, neither over-ripe nor under-ripe, firm, fresh and in perfect condition. Taste to be sure of high flavor. Vegetables that are cooked before eating freeze very satisfactorily. Vegetables that are usually eaten raw and the kind that are used in salads because of crispness, are usually not desirable for freezing. Freeze fruits and vegetables as soon as possible after picking as they deteriorate quickly after harvesting. If delay is unavoidable keep refrigerated.

Choose meats of top quality for freezing. A bit of fat prevents drying of the lean part during storage. Meats of poorer quality, and less tender cuts, should be made into ground meat, or wrapped, for cooking by moist heat methods.

Fish should be frozen as soon as possible after catching. If you cannot freeze the fish soon after catching, clean and prepare them as you would for eating, and then refrigerate or place on ice. Dry ice can be used to keep fish until arrival at home.

Select eggs that are from chickens on the ground with a rooster. These eggs must be clean and fresh with no cracks or abrasions on the shells. A fresh egg has a slightly rough surface with an easily visible "bloom" and a dull look on the shell. Egg whites freeze easily without treatment, but whole eggs and egg yolks must be treated to prevent coagulation of the yolk.

To freeze whole eggs break into a bowl, add 1 tsp. salt to 1 c. eggs, beat with fork just enough to mix. Package in liquid-tight container, label with the number of eggs and the date. This may be done for large or small quantities. 2 tbsp. honey may be added if the eggs are to be used for baking. Frozen unbeaten whites of eggs are satisfactory for baking. Package, label and freeze promptly. Freezing causes yolks to become gummy. 1 c. egg yolks may be mixed with 2 tbsp. honey or 1 tsp. salt. Do not over-stir; package and freeze quickly. Whole eggs may be frozen for scrambling, poaching or frying by breaking them carefully and dropping them into muffin tins lined with paper muffin cups. Freeze, remove from muffin tins, pack in cartons and seal. Salt or sugar does not need to be added as the change in the yolks is not noticeable when cooking them by either method.

Butter may be frozen by wrapping in packaging material. If you make your own butter, chill it fresh, unsalted in pound sizes or ¼-pound cubes. Wrap in moisture-vapor proof paper, seal and freeze promptly.

Cream of high butter fat content, 40% or more, can be placed in liquid-tight containers, allowing room for expansion. Ice cream must be placed in liquid-tight containers. Frequent opening of a large container shortens the storage life of ice cream, so it is better to store it in small quantities.

Cheddar cheese cut in small pieces about 1-inch thick will freeze satisfactorily. Place in freezer paper and freeze rapidly. Use a day or two after thawing. Soft cheeses do not freeze well.

Preparation:

In preparing fruits for freezing work with small quantities. Little handling, quick washing and cooking prevents bruising and loss of nutrients from water soaking. Wash the fruit in cold water to keep fruit firm and it will freeze faster. Juicy sweet fruits may be mixed with sugar to the proportions of 6 parts fruit to 1 part sugar. Fruits may be frozen without sugar or sugar syrup. Fruits without sugar store better if slightly crushed so that the spaces are filled with juice. Light colored fruits, such as apples, apricots, peaches, plums, pears and sweet cherries will discolor when exposed to air after slicing or peeling. It is necessary to use ascorbic acid (vitamin C) to prevent discoloration. Buy pure ascorbic acid. Use ½ tsp. ascorbic acid for each quart of syrup or dissolve 10 200-miligram pure ascorbic acid tablets in ½ c. hot water for each quart of syrup. Pour over fruit at once and package quickly. The dissolved ascorbic acid may be sprinkled over the unsweetened fruit. Turn the fruit carefully to cover all pieces. Bananas can be frozen; see chapter on Children's Foods. Prepare fruits for freezing as you would for table use. Allow space for fruit to expand. Honey may be used instead of sugar.

Vegetables contain certain substances known as enzymes which cause deterioration. These must be inactivated in most vegetables to insure proper preservation. This is accomplished by blanching, or scalding in hot water or steam. To blanch with water place washed, prepared vegetables in a wire basket or colander and immerse in rapidly boiling water, moving basket up and down slowly; when water boils, no longer than 2 to 4 minutes should be required. Remove then, as over-scalding can result in loss of flavor, color and nutrients. Work with small quantities. Young vegetables require less time than older ones. Place under running cold water to cool and package promptly. Freeze at once. Allow some space for expansion in the container.

It is best to write to the U.S. Department of Agriculture or your local extension office for the most recent methods of freezing meat, poultry, and fish. There is considerable detailed information that must be considered.

If you wish to go ahead on your own, clean and cut these foods as for meal preparation, keeping all as cold as possible during the preparation. Never let these protein foods stand at room temperature before freezing.

Cooked and baked foods may be frozen successfully. When you are planning to bake, prepare soups, casserole dishes, or stews, make an extra quantity to freeze. It is smart to bake extra loaves of bread and place in moisture-proof materials, then freeze for a later day.

Pies, cakes and cookies freeze well. Use unbaked cookie dough within 6 months. Date or nut muffins will keep to about 6 months. Baked apples and baked pears should be used within 3 months. Soups keep up to 2 months.

Beat and freeze dabs of whipping cream for future desserts. Add 1 tbsp. melted gelatin to each pint of cream before shipping. Cream will hold consistency and flavor better. It will keep up to 2 months.

Beat and freeze dabs of whipping cream for future desserts. Add 1 tbsp. melted gelatin to each pint of cream before shipping. Cream will hold consistency and flavor better. It will keep up to 2 months.

You can freeze left-overs, such as left-over beef roasts, baked hams, chili beans, baked beans, etc. Plan to use left-over foods within 2 or 3 weeks.

Freeze slices of bread instead of a whole loaf. They are easy to break apart and spread, and will thaw out in lunch box in time to eat.

■ **FREEZE OR CAN THE EASY, MODERN WAY**

Fruit frozen in all-honey syrup does not require the use of vitamin C powder, tablets or ascorbic acid to prevent browning or darkening of fruit. Use top quality and fully ripened fruit. Freezing or canning does not improve flavor or quality of fruit, so start with the best. Honey syrup may be prepared in quantity and stored in refrigerator ready for use.

■ **FOR FREEZING PEACHES**

Set up 6 quart-size freezer containers in assembly-line fashion. Pour ¾ cup cold honey syrup into each container. Wash peaches quickly in cold water. Peel 1 peach at a time and slice directly into prepared syrup. Work quickly until fruit and syrup are within 1 inch of top of container. Be sure syrup is blended with fruit. Cover top with piece of crumpled freezer foil to keep fruit under syrup while freezing. Seal tightly with cover and freeze. To keep color of peaches just right, always defrost fruit in sealed freezer containers. Serve very cold.

CHAPTER 21

P.S. - In Case You Didn't Know

1. Be sure to use a standard measuring cup, with ¼ measurements marked off, as well as a set of 4 measuring spoons divided into 1 tbsp., 1 tsp., ½ tsp. and ¼ tsp.
2. When measuring dry ingredients into cup or spoon, heap ingredients and then level off with a knife.
3. To measure butter, first have it at room temperature, then put compensating amount of water in measuring cup and add butter until cup is filled; drain off water; e.g., when ⅔ c. butter is called for, fill measuring c. with ⅓ c. water, then add butter until liquid reaches top; pour off liquid.
4. Recipes in standard cookbooks may be adapted to good nutrition in many cases: Some examples . . .
   A. In quick bread recipes, use ½ c. of the flour called for and for the remaining quantity, substitute whole-wheat pastry flour; or use 1 c. of the flour called for and substitute for the remaining quantity, ¼ c. soy, rice flour or cornmeal and the rest whole-wheat pastry flour.
   B. For pie crusts, cookies and cakes, substitute for regular flour same amount of unbleached white flour, or use ½ whole-wheat pastry flour and ½ rice flour.
   C. For yeast bread, substitute for regular flour called for, whole-wheat flour plus ¼ c. wheat germ.
   D. Add 1 tsp. powdered brewer's yeast and ½ c. wheat germ to standard recipes for yeast breads and quick breads.
   E. In standard recipes calling for 1 c. sugar, you may substitute ¾ c. honey and reduce liquid to ¼ c.
   F. For each square of chocolate called for in standard recipes, you may substitute 3 tbsp. carob powder and 2 tbsp. milk or water.

EQUIVALENTS

⅓ c. = 5 tbsp. & 1 tsp.	½ c. = 8 tbsp.
⅜ c. = ¼ cup & 2 tbsp.	⅔ c. = 10 tbsp. & 2 tsp.
⅝ c. = ½ cup & 2 tbsp.	¾ c. = 12 tbsp.
⅞ c. = ¾ cup & 2 tbsp.	¼ c. = 4 tbsp.

1 lb. whole dates = 2½ c. or 2 c. pitted, or 1-¾ c. cut up
1 lb. figs = 2-¾ c. or 2-⅔ cut up
1 lb. Cheddar cheese = 4 c. grated
1 pt. heavy cream = 4 c. whipped
1 lb. almonds in shell = 1 to 1-¾ c. nutmeats
1 lb. walnuts in shell = 1-⅔ c. nutmeats
1 lb. almonds shelled = 3½ c. nutmeats
1 lb. walnuts shelled = 4 c.
2 medium eggs = ⅓ c.
2 large eggs = ½ c.
3 medium eggs = ½ c.
3 large eggs = ⅔ c.
5 large eggs = 1 c.
3 tsp. = 1 tbsp.
2 tbsp. = ⅛ c.
4 tbsp. = ¼ c.
6 tbsp. = ½ c.
12 tbsp. = ¾ c.

16 tbsp. = 1 c.
60 drops = 1 tsp.
16 fluid ounces = 2 c.
2 tbsp. = 1 fluid oz.
28 grams = 1 oz.
16 ounces = 1 lb.
5 grams = 1 tsp.
Pinch or dash = less than ⅛ tsp.
4 cups flour = 1 lb.
2-¾ c. brown sugar = 1 lb.
2-¾ c. raw sugar = 1 lb.
1 c. honey = ¾ lb.
1 pt. = 2 c.
2 pts. = 1 qt.
1 lge. lemon = ¼ c. juice
1 medium orange = ½ c. juice
12-16 egg yolks = 1 c.
8-10 egg whites = 1 c.
2 c. butter = 1 lb.
1 c. solid shortening = ⅔ c. salad oil
1 c. shortening = ½ lb.
1 c. raw rice = 2 c. cooked

MODIFICATIONS OF RECIPES

Recipe calls for:	*Same results with:*
1 tbsp. flour	½ tbsp. cornstarch
1-⅓ c. brown or raw sugar	1 c. white sugar
⅔ c. chicken fat	1 c. butter
⅞ c. lard or oil	1 c. butter
½ c. suet	1 c. butter
1 c. enriched white flour	⅞ c. whole-wheat pastry flour
1 c. whole-wheat pastry flour	⅞ c. unbleached white flour
1 c. honey	¾ c. sugar plus ¼ c. liquid

1 c. molasses	½ c. sugar plus ¼ c. liquid
1 oz. chocolate	(3 tbsp. cocoa plus ½ tbsp. fat *or*
	(4 tbsp. carob powder plus 1 tbsp. fat
1 egg	½ tsp. baking powder 2 tbsp. flour
	& ½ tbsp. fat
1 c. shortening	⅔ c. salad oil

ADJUSTMENTS FOR HIGH ALTITUDE BAKING

	3,000 Ft.	5,000 Ft.	7,000 Ft.
Reduce baking powder			
For each teaspoon, decrease	⅛ tsp.	⅛-¼ tsp.	¼-½ tsp.
Reduce shortening			
For each cup, decrease	1-2 tbsp.	2 tbsp.	2-3 tbsp.
Increase liquid			
For each cup, add	1-2 tbsp.	2-3 tbsp.	3-4 tbsp.
Increase baking temperature	6-10° F	10-15° F	15-25° F

Decrease baking time 5-10 minutes when recipes have been tested at sea level.

NOTE: When 2 amounts are given, try the smaller amount first; then if cake still needs improvement, use the larger amount the next time you make the cake.

A FEW MORE IDEAS

1. Have lemons at room temperature or warmed before squeezing; you will get a lot more juice.
2. To keep bread or cake moist, place a small piece of apple in the box.
3. Add pinch of salt to egg whites or cream before whipping.
4. When measuring honey or molasses, use cup previously used for measuring fat or oil.
5. If you wish to make your own baking powder, mix ¼ tsp. soda with ½ tsp. cream of tartar—equal to 1 tsp. baking powder.
6. Plump seedless raisins by washing and spreading them out in a pie pan. Cover and heat slowly at 350° until they puff up.
7. Use kitchen scissors to cut dates, nuts, ham into small pieces; also to cut edges of chops, steaks or bacon.
8. Try baking meat loaf in muffin tins, for a change.
9. When stewing dried fruits, the addition of a small amount of lemon juice and a bit of lemon rind will give a better flavor.

10. To keep that dark green line from appearing around the yolk of hard-cooked eggs, watch the cooking time and plunge eggs immediately into cold water.

11. To avoid lumps and curdling when using eggs in any mixture in a double boiler, be sure water in lower part does not touch upper pan.

12. Include chopped almonds, cashews or peanuts in creamed chicken mixtures.

13. Add pistachio nuts to curried rice.

14. Put chopped walnuts in meat loaf or stuffing for pork chops or fowl.

15. Vary your scalloped or creamed potato casseroles by adding canned shrimp.

16. Use dried powdered saffron by adding to the milk in bread or coffee cake recipes. Add just enough to give the lovely yellow color; flavor is bitter if too much is used.

17. For a between-meal snack, try 2-3 tsp. powdered whey. There are some delicious kinds on the market. Use powdered whey over tart fresh or frozen fruit. The natural milk sugar present is a sufficient sweetener.

18. Use saltless, organic seasonings on hamburger or other meat, or cooked vegetables.

19. Put 1 tbsp. vinegar in bottom of double boiler to prevent mineral deposit.

20. To chop celery, carrots, peppers, cucumbers in a hurry, lay stalks or strips on cutting board and with a sharp knife slash though several at a time. To chop an onion, cut it in half lengthwise; lay flat side down on board; slice with sharp knife, then chop.

21. Use dried pears, peaches and apples in cookies; as dessert; on cereals. Try to find lightly sulphured, fruit, or not sulphured at all, which is best.

22. Use your kitchen shears for dicing and cutting in strips fruits, vegetables and meats.

Index